PRAISE FOR
ENTER THE BABYLON SYSTEM

"A passionate and illuminating discussion of the links (or lack thereof) between hip-hop music and gun culture. . . . Bascuñán and Pearce, adamant believers in hip-hop's positive 'political and cultural voice,' are also honest and sincere reporters."   —Macleans.ca

"A well researched, easily navigated tome."   —*Toronto Star*

"Bascuñán and Pearce have used their industry credentials to gain access to some of the major players in the multi-billion dollar hip-hop industry and the multi-billion dollar gun industry. Their thoroughly researched book looks at gun culture from all angles: economic, cultural and political."   —*The Gazette* (Montreal)

"*Enter the Babylon System* is engaging and straightforward, written in a fast-paced, journalistic style. . . . The book is well researched, with enough sources and statistics to make a point without bogging the reader down. Best of all, Bascuñán and Pearce seem to really have the inside story on gun culture, particularly in hip-hop."
—*Quill & Quire*

"*Enter the Babylon System* navigates the small-arms industry's twisting corridors, delving into gun design, manufacturing, marketing, lobbying and legislation along the way."   —CBC.ca

UNPACKING GUN CULTURE
FROM SAMUEL COLT TO 50 CENT

ENTER THE BABYLON SYSTEM

**RODRIGO BASCUÑÁN
& CHRISTIAN PEARCE**

VINTAGE CANADA

VINTAGE CANADA EDITION, 2008

Copyright © 2007 Rodrigo Bascuñán and Christian Pearce

Published in Canada by Vintage Canada, a division of Random House of Canada
Limited, Toronto, in 2008. Originally published in hardcover in Canada by Random
House Canada, a division of Random House of Canada Limited, Toronto, in 2007.
Distributed by Random House of Canada Limited, Toronto.

Vintage Canada and colophon are registered trademarks of
Random House of Canada Limited.

www.randomhouse.ca

Library and Archives Canada Cataloguing in Publication

Bascuñán, Rodrigo
Enter the Babylon system : unpacking gun culture from Samuel
Colt to 50 Cent / Rodrigo Bascuñán & Christian Pearce.

Includes index.
ISBN 978-0-679-31389-2

1. Firearms–Social aspects–United States. 2. Firearms–Social
aspects–Canada. 3. Violence in popular culture. 4. Hip-hop.
I. Pearce, Christian II. Title.

HV7435.B38 2008   303.6   C2007-903613-9

Illustrations appear throughout from the following artists: Case (1, 83, 225), Shingo
Shimizu (3, 31, 42, 50, 62, 64, 66, 74, 99, 118, 133, 142, 162, 169, 175, 182, 186-7, 203,
261, 279), Steve Jenkinson (19), EGR (110), Jacqui Oakley (144), Roxanne Musterer
(149), Mirak Jamal (199), Elicser (218), Berzerker (293), Patrick Martinez (311).

Text design: Kelly Hill

Printed and bound in the United States of America

2 4 6 8 9 7 5 3 1

To our families

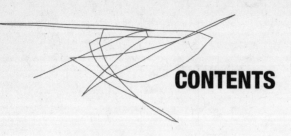

CONTENTS

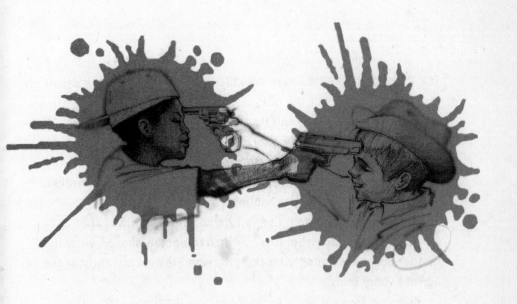

WALK THROUGH THE VALLEY
OF THE BABYLON SYSTEM

THE COPS DON'T KNOW where the killer came from, or where it's gone since. Maybe it sits at the bottom of some river running beneath a bridge, or perhaps police will find it only after it has killed again. All we know is that it found its way into the hands of a young man with a calloused heart and a fragile ego, that in one moment, a flash really, that young man used it to take from this world forever a son, a brother, a mentor and a best friend. A soulmate.

On December 13, 2003, Clayton Kempton Howard was shot once in the head outside the Toronto apartment he shared with his mother, Joan, and younger brother, Kareem. He died instantly, at the age of twenty-four.

Kempton Howard was a lover of hip-hop. For those within the culture, hip-hop is much more than just music. It is a way of life, the practice of being yourself. And in so many ways, Kempton's self projected greatness. Taiwo Bah can tell you. He is that soulmate. "I've never known anyone that's into music as much as he was," Tai said. "For him, it's a life, it's a whole culture to it. He embodied hip-hop."

When we first met Taiwo face to face in the summer of 2004, it was at Joan Howard's new house. The city had assisted in an expeditious move to a nice townhouse at the end of a tree-lined street. We got the feeling that Joan and Kareem weren't yet at home there. Taiwo had been staying with them to ease the transition. As we sat at the kitchen table, sunlight pouring in around still-drawn blinds, Kempton's blank dog-tags dangled from Taiwo's neck. It was a late mid-week morning, and Joan and Kareem were resting upstairs. Sleep hadn't come easily to them of late.

Taiwo had already been approached by a slew of reporters seeking quotes for stories on Kempton's killing. Our conversation was different. As he said, we're his people. You'd never know it from the stories that followed his death, but Kempton's life exemplified our culture. "I mean, deejaying, emceeing, breakdancing and graffiti—he had it all," Taiwo said. "He was hip-hop. He was loyal to the music from day one." Another point that Taiwo emphasized: Kempton's homeboys call him *Kemp'n.*

They also both worked with children in their community. "He's like the MVP of the Boys and Girls Club staff," explained Taiwo. "'Cause he's worked at three different Boys and Girls Clubs in this city." In 2001 Kempton started the Torch Club, a group for nine- to thirteen-year-olds at Eastview Community Centre, in his and Taiwo's Blake-Boultbee neighbourhood in Toronto's east end. The program revolved around a handful of core principles: leadership development, education and career exploration, volunteering in the community, social recreation, lifestyle and fitness. In practice it meant fundraising, braving the winter cold to break ice off the community centre's stairs, learning about hygiene, and summer games of football wherever an open field could be found. "Most times his team would beat my team," said Tai. "It was fun, man!"

"Kemp'n"

Contrary to some people's preconceptions about a young black man rocking a black do-rag with an Atlanta Falcons jersey, Kempton Howard just tried to do the right thing. As a result, his murder drew significant attention from the city's major media and, by extension, politicians. A lengthy piece in the *Toronto Star*, a moment of silence at City Hall and mention of his name in the House of Commons—his killing didn't pass as "Homicide 61/2003," just another number in police records. But it all still fell short of doing Kempton's life justice.

"If there's a story in it then they'll talk about it," said Taiwo. "So branding him as a community leader—and I guess he is—but branding him as a community leader makes the story more poignant, and I guess it helps to form an idea of who he was, and an image and stuff like that. He was a lot more than that to me." The media's response also made clear how much less the city's other victims of gun violence meant. "His death would not normally have earned more than a day's worth of media coverage," said CBC's *News Online* on January 28, 2004, with surprising candour. "After all, he was a young black man living in a low-income neighbourhood. On Toronto's 2003 homicide roster, that description hardly made him stand out."

Most on that sad list would be publicly characterized more like O'Neil Ricardo Greenland, a.k.a. Heavy D, written up by the *Toronto Sun*'s Ian Robertson on February 8, 2004, as just "one more in a long line of black street thugs slain in Toronto." Police know where the gun that Heavy D used to kill ended up. They found it on the ground beside him after he was shot several times in a Scarborough strip-mall parking lot, dead at twenty-two in what the cops told Robertson was a case of "simple retribution and revenge." Two weeks earlier Heavy D had used his 9mm Bryco pistol to kill two people and wound another outside a storefront nightclub. "That was just one helluva night," recalled Robertson, referring to late 2002's "bloody Sunday"— so named by Toronto police for four murders committed within just eighty minutes. "Then [Heavy D] thirteen days later buying it in the way he knew he'd buy it."

Beneath his newspaper's sensational headlines, which on the last day of 2003 labelled Toronto "Gun City," Robertson used police sources to trace Heavy D's gun from southern California's "Ring of Fire"—

where cheap, easily concealable Saturday-night-special handguns such as Greenland's 9mm were once made—through a Florida pawnshop and across the forty-ninth parallel into Heavy D's hands. When forensic scientists finally raised the gun's serial numbers, they discovered the digits 1460666, which, wrote Robertson, "branded it as the Devil's gun." He told us, "Heavy D knew he'd die. There's no way he couldn't have. And he was just a starter. There are other killers in this city who've killed a lot more people than he did."

> Recollect your thoughts, don't get caught up in the mix
> 'Cause the media is full of dirty tricks
> —2Pac, "Only God Can Judge Me," off *All Eyez on Me* (1996)

Linda Diebel covered Kempton Howard's murder for the *Toronto Star*. An award-winning journalist, Diebel has reported from Colombia, Haiti and others among the world's poorest and most violent places. For the kids who suffered what she saw as the "mistrust, suspicion and pain" in the Blake-Boultbee community following Kempton's killing, Diebel wrote, "the danger is everywhere." Taiwo's was a prominent voice in her article, but he believes Diebel's take was twisted. "We're a community!" Tai said. "Most people interact with people when they see you in the street. So it's more of a friendly type of neighbourhood. And we have Eastview Neighbourhood Community Centre, which is one of the greatest places on earth."

Diebel described Kempton Howard's body as it was prepared for burial—"cold, so cold"—and the violence and fear that had supposedly shaken and cowed a community. "I don't feel that way," said Taiwo, now twenty-six, "and my brother didn't feel that way either."

In May 2005 we ate lunch with Taiwo and his brother. Also a close friend of Kempton's, Taiwo's twin, Kehinde (pronounced *Kaneday*) Bah, is one of the city's most respected youth activists and a member of Toronto mayor David Miller's Community Safety Advisory Committee. Over Greek food on nearby Danforth Avenue—Kempton and Tai's favourite place to grab grub—we talked about Kehinde's recent trip to Nigeria, the brothers' country of origin; hip-hop; a couple of recent shootings in the neighbourhood around the

Eastview Community Centre and their effect on the Torch Club kids; and Diebel's story. Kehinde said he wanted to use the opportunity that Diebel's article offered to suggest solutions to the problem of gun violence among youth in our city.

"I was still pretty fucked up about what happened," Kehinde remembered of his meeting with Diebel. "But here's this woman, just like, 'I don't want to talk about solutions. No, don't worry—I been to Compton, I been to South Central, I've done stories from there. Can you take me to Regent Park [a troubled neighbourhood in a different part of town] and walk me around and get me interviews with some guys? We'll give you seventy-five bucks a day.' I'm like, 'Who is this woman, yo? What da heck? Who are you?' Like, I just want to talk about solutions." Kehinde never appears in Diebel's 2,700-word story.

Asked to comment on Kehinde's version of her visit, Diebel would say only, "Was Kehinde Bah supposed to be mentioned in my story about Kempton? His twin, Taiwo, was part of the narrative, as you saw, because he dressed Kempton [at the funeral], etc. I don't think I can help you further because writing this story as well as follow when suspects were arrested and charged with Kempton's murder was all I did." The *Toronto Star*'s approach isn't that surprising. In so many ways, the voice of youth, their own perspective on the problems they deal with, goes ignored. "How the media frames it," said Kehinde, "is young people are [committing] crimes. These people are really wild and really just uncontrollable. They ain't like a regular breed of normal kids."

The media's casting of youth as a social threat is by no means unique to Toronto. John Dilulio, then a professor of politics and public affairs at Princeton University, wrote a November 27, 1995, cover story for *Weekly Standard* magazine titled "The Coming of the Super-Predators." Dilulio's article warned of the emergence of "ever growing numbers of hardened, remorseless juvenile criminals [who] are creating a group of 'super-predators' that has not yet begun to crest. Americans are sitting atop a demographic time bomb of youth offenders who maim or kill on impulse, without any intelligible motive for rehabilitation."

"And it's funny," Kehinde continued, "because most of the time the violence occurs between youth. Yet they find some way to put it on the news, on mainstream news, and cover it like it's affecting everybody, when everybody don't really care." In November 2003 then police chief Julian Fantino added his own take on the situation in Toronto, telling CBC News, "These gun-toting gangsters we have here now have absolutely no fear of the system, no fear of the law." It would be a familiar refrain during Fantino's five-year tenure as the city's top cop. Before he "hung up his guns," as the *National Post* put it, on March 26, 2005 (the city opted not to renew his contract), Fantino in a February 14, 2005, CTV News report again warned of the many "hard-core gun-crazed gangsters" running Toronto's streets. The *Toronto Sun* called them the "gang time bomb." Fantino warned the public of another potential threat.

> I ain't a Blood or a Crip, I'm doin' my own thang
> G-Unit! Shit, I done started my own gang
> I don't do that funny dance, I don't throw gang signs
> But I'm gangsta to the core, so I stay with a 9
> — 50 Cent, "Bump That," off *50 Cent Is the Future* (2002)

In April 2004, at a church in Toronto's long-troubled Jane-Finch community, Chief Fantino joined a "town hall" meeting convened to discuss local gun violence. The chief was asked by a woman in the audience whether the sale of toy guns might somehow be prevented. Choosing to dismiss her concern, saying, "We can't police everything," Fantino instead attacked the influence of a menace much nearer to his heart—rap music.

A small media scrum followed, during which a forthright radio reporter and black activist, Denise Burnett, contended that she and her friends "had grown up with music videos and rap and hadn't been 'influenced' to pick up a gun." Fantino clarified that he was "talking about how people are influenced by the negatives that do happen to be out there. If you're influenced positively by 50 Cent, who talks about killing people and raping women and killing cops, then God bless you."

8

During the exchange the chief twice labelled rapper 50 Cent a criminal. He also shot back that he had written more than once to then minister of immigration Denis Coderre to prevent the New York City native from entering Canada to perform in Toronto. Fantino cited a murder that took place in the summer of 2003 after a Toronto concert featuring 50 Cent and fellow rapper Jay-Z. As crowds departing the concert and a fireworks display on the nearby lakeshore converged, twenty-four-year-old Msemaji Granger was gunned down in a homicide that remains unsolved.

MuchMusic, Canada's music television station, asked us, as co-creators of Canada's foremost hip-hop magazine, to respond to Fantino's town hall comments. Nearly an hour of interviews with us produced only a few ten-second sound bites, including something like "Fantino doesn't know hip-hop, he doesn't know 50 Cent and he should shut his mouth." Our thoughts on the roots of gun violence, the need to address context and the lack of opportunity were mostly lost to the station's archives; our efforts to speak seriously were reduced to a few confrontational clips.

Taiwo remembers the first time he heard 50 Cent. While he was working in downtown Toronto, a bootlegger put a mix-tape into his hands: "I'm like, 'What da? What is this?' I tried to listen to it and it's just all killin' and da, da, da. 'Yo, I can't listen to this. This is a joke! Ain't this the guy that got dissed by Jay-Z? Forget this, man! 50 Cent?!' He's holdin' a gun with a cross hangin' from the barrel—this guy's goin' to hell too!"

As Taiwo often did, he passed the mix-tape on to Kempton. "He was in love with Fifty! He was like, 'Yo, when Fifty blows!' And then 50 Cent got signed to Shady [Eminem's record label]. Uh-oh. And then 50 Cent blew up, and Kemp'n was just on board from day one. The first mix-tape, he was on board. It was crazy—crazy how he called that. He does that frequently."

When you think about it, Julian Fantino and 50 Cent aren't that different. In February 2004 the *Toronto Star* described the chief as "always controversial, never shy, often embroiled in controversy." The description would work equally well for Fifty. "If all that controversy wasn't making money, he wouldn't do it," Taiwo said. "Fantino's helping him. That's buyin' into the persona."

When Rodrigo sat down to interview him in San Francisco in February 2005, 50 Cent admitted as much. Buns told Fiddy he was from Toronto. "I think you know our police chief, Julian Fantino."

"Yeah," Fiddy answered, "he don't really like me."

"He called you a criminal," Rodrigo said. "He wrote a letter to Immigration, and he didn't want you to get through. What do you think about that?"

"Well, you know, you have people that go on your past. My past is my shadow. I was active illegally. I had the opportunity to make music. I understand where he is making his assumption, so I'm not upset with him. I just think he needs to broaden his thinking."

"Actually," Fifty added later, "what he does by saying that—'cause he's not that bright—is he turns kids on to us more. When you tell a kid they can't do something, they wanna know why. 'I can't listen to this 'cause you said so? Now I wanna hear it even more.'" *The New York Times* reported on December 26, 2004, that Fifty had made roughly $50 million that year. Condemnations such as Fantino's have evidently profited both 50 Cent and the corporations he works for.

A continent away, the offensive against "gangsta rap" had taken on a British accent. As a New Year's Day party in Birmingham, England, crept into the early hours of January 2, 2003, two innocent women, eighteen-year-old Charlene Ellis and Letisha Shakespeare, who was just seventeen, were killed by submachine-gun fire in a drive-by shooting. The tragedy provided, in the words of Shakespeare's aunt, a "wake-up call" for a community while drawing the attention of a nation. BBC News declared the shooting "revenge" and a "botched gang attack." Not a week later on January 6, 2003, the BBC also reported that Britain's home secretary David Blunkett had "launched an attack on violent gangster rap music, condemning it as 'appalling.'" Appearing on BBC Radio 2, Blunkett pointed to a connection between rap, drugs and gun violence.

"I am not going to get into the issue of censoring," Blunkett said— stopping short of measures taken in the Democratic Republic of

Congo, where authorities banned foreign rap music in June 2004—
"but I am concerned that we need to talk to the record producers, to
the distributors, to those who are actually engaged in the music business about what is and isn't acceptable." Blunkett reportedly made
his statements after listening to Jay-Z's song "U Don't Know Me."

If Blunkett were a tad more tuned in, he would have realized that
he'd missed rap's prime target. On April 18, 2005, *Business Week*'s
David Kiley reported that 50 Cent's "Reebok line, I am told, is outselling Jay-Z's Reeboks, which were already outselling basketball
star Allen Iverson's." Anti-gun activists in the U.K. were more on the
mark when they denounced a commercial from Reebok's "I Am What
I Am" campaign. In the ad 50 Cent counts from one to nine, indicating the number of times he was shot in a now infamous drug-related
incident in Queens, New York. When asked by the commercial's dis-
embodied interviewer, "Tell me, who do you plan to massacre next?"
Fifty can only laugh—his recently released album was titled *The
Massacre*. Responding to over fifty viewer complaints, the U.K.'s
Advertising Standards Authority (ASA) said it had been persuaded
that "the advertisement endorsed [Fifty's] type of lifestyle and disre-
garded the unsavoury and perilous aspects of it by implying it was
possible to survive being shot nine times." Reebok soon pulled the
plug; their spokesperson said the ad was "intended to be a positive
and empowering celebration of this right of freedom of self-expression, individuality and authenticity." The commitment of footwear
companies to individual self-expression is also evident along so
many Third World assembly lines.

Although the anti-gun advocates succeeded in pushing the ASA to
remove the ad from British airwaves, they did little to discourage
those who helped make 2004 one of the most financially successful
years in Reebok's history. And the media had helped by pouring out
free publicity. John Rosenthal, of the New England–based anti-gun
group Stop Handgun Violence, joined the fray, calling the advertisement "unconscionable." "If Reebok doesn't take the ad off the air in
the US, it should be ashamed of itself," the *Boston Globe* further
quoted Rosenthal. "To glorify the fact that 50 Cent has been shot
nine times, and to use him as a role model for inner-city kids to sell

your product is a dangerous thing." Except a lot of inner-city kids can't afford a new pair of Reeboks.

"Maybe he is a negative influence," Taiwo clarified, "but I don't think it's on the 'hood so much as it's on the suburbs. They're the ones that buy most hip-hop, right? Seventy percent. If you go to a concert, what colour you gonna see in the crowd? You gonna see all white folks. Ain't nothin' wrong with that, but these artists, they know that. They know that it's kind of an inside-out mentality that people have—where they're outside, but they hear about and they see in movies and they have their perception of how it is in the 'hood. So there's this whole kinda fascination with that whole culture and that whole way of life. That's why I think it's so popular. These guys are just sayin' how it is and how they livin', and people are like, 'Wow!' They're just kinda peekin' over the fence."

In the early nineties, as she pursued a PhD in criminology, Deanna Wilkinson employed peer mentors to interview some four hundred young men in New York about their experiences with violence in the inner city. "The thing that kept hitting me in the head," she said, "was the fact that none of the people who were supposedly trying to solve the problem had *any idea* what was going on with youth. So my thought was, well, if we really want to understand community dynamics we need to hear from the youth and find out what they're struggling with."

The study culminated in her book *Guns, Violence and Identity among African-American and Latino Youth.* Through vivid personal accounts, Dr. Wilkinson's research provides an insightful look into the causes of urban violence among young minority males. Nowhere in her book is "gangster rap" mentioned. We asked Dr. Wilkinson, now a professor of criminal justice at Ohio State University, whether rap music came up in the many lengthy interviews that were conducted for her study. "Many of them saw being performers in the music industry or trying to cut an album as a rapper as a way of social mobility," she answered. "And in terms of that influencing their violent event, or the context of more and more violence in the neighbourhood, I don't think they made any connection whatsoever to that. I don't think it had any real causal link. It was more like look-ing at a mirror, instead of looking at an open door."

Brooklyn, New York, rap artist Shyne knows how to distinguish reality from fiction. He's already been involved in more than one vio-lent event in his short life. At fifteen Shyne almost lost an arm to a shotgun blast. At twenty-two he was sentenced to ten years in prison for his role in a December 1999 nightclub shootout in New York City. Shyne contends that he was defending not just himself, but also those he was partying with, including rapper P. Diddy and his then girl-friend, Jennifer Lopez.

"Somebody pulled out a gun and shot!" Shyne, locked up in New York State's Clinton Correctional Facility said emphatically of the confrontation at Club New York. "That's how I pulled my ratchet out. That whole situation was serious. Once again—*real* killas. It wasn't no punks, it wasn't no rappers that talk in the studio. These were some real killas. That's what they do: they shoot people for fun, ya understand? So I knew when they pulled that thing out, this wasn't no rap video; this is for real. Somebody was gonna die. It wasn't gonna be me."

Shyne explained why he thinks hip-hop is so often named as the source of the gun problem: "It's a scapegoat theory. It's easy to just point to the disenfranchised, 'cause we're not Rupert Murdoch—we don't own the media channels that's gonna get our point across. So it's easy to just say anything about us and there won't be any counter-balance to it, ya dig?"

The vast majority of fans don't take to rap music as gospel, but hip-hop lyrics do provide some balance against the demonization of young black men apparent in mainstream media. Lyrics can illumi-nate how youth see their world and how they feel the need, right or wrong, to survive it. The bible of firearms research, *Small Arms Survey*, reveals in its 2006 edition that young men between the ages of 15 and 29 account for half of all gun murders annually, amounting to as many as 100,000 homicides worldwide each year. Most often produced by the same demographic, hip-hop can provide an inside perspective from those who are both the most vulnerable to victim-ization by guns and the most likely to perpetrate gun crime. Hate it or love it, 50 Cent's music represents an attitude that already exists among many young men. But young men aren't the only ones with an affinity for firearms.

While a younger generation of males destroys itself in the poor communities of the West, there is an older, deeper and richer side to gun culture that goes on without sparking the horrendous headlines. As guns are bought, bodied, tossed and replaced, as blood flows in the streets, the profits trickle straight to the top.

Man, I ain't dense, I know what you represent
Guns or tobacco, the richest one per cent
— Mighty Casey, "Down with Bush," off *Original Rudebwoy* (2004)

In June 2006, the *Smoking Gun* posted a catalogue of gifts given to U.S. government officials in 2004. Among the presents accepted by President George W. Bush were a Dakota Arms sniper rifle valued at $10,000 and ten vintage firearms worth another $12,000. All came from Jordan's King Abdullah, including a circa-1884 Colt revolver.

CNN separately reported that in 2004 the most expensive Christmas gift the President received was a shotgun valued at $14,153. The shotgun was a gift from Ed Weatherby, the son of Roy Weatherby, a legend in gun design and manufacturing. The younger Weatherby had previously presented George Bush Sr. with, according to Weatherby's website, the "first U.S.-produced Custom Mark V rifle."

We're not sure whether the president keeps any of the aforementioned guns in the White House. But they'd complement rather nicely another piece that George Jr. keeps on display for his guests. On June 7, 2004, *Time* magazine reported that troops involved in pulling ousted Iraqi dictator Saddam Hussein from his hole had presented the president with the handgun that Hussein was clutching when he was captured. Presumably because the twin AK-47s Hussein also had with him would have been a bit overstated, the mounted pistol now sits at 1600 Pennsylvania Avenue. "He really liked showing it off," *Time* quoted a visitor who had seen it. "He was really proud of it."

14

Another son of a gun-loving dad, Trigger Tha Gambler learned at a tender age from his "straight gangster" father how to use firearms. Talking to us from a friend's balcony overlooking the projects where he grew up, the Brownsville, New York, rap artist remembered the first time he and his brother, Smoothe Da Hustler, were exposed to guns. "My father was kinda like the first one that showed us how to really shoot a weapon, took us on the roof and showed us, and that was at the age of four and five," Trig explained. "Because it's the same thing that's going on in a lot of other countries, where they raisin' they kids and showin' 'em how to shoot off those weapons. That's protection. Guns is power."

Maybe it was the blunt he was smoking, but Trigger got open when we asked about gun violence in New York City. "It got more violent, honestly," he said. "People think it slowed down because the World Trade Center went down and terrorists, so they took all of the attention off what's really happening in the communities, but a lot of things are still going on out here. My friend runs King's County Morgue that's out here. And we'll go by the morgue to pick him up and see him, and he's in there with over forty young men that's in the age range of I'd say from seventeen to twenty-seven, that's dead, all from a bullet shot—*one* bullet shot. I saw that one day—I walked in the morgue and there were so many guys laid in there, and every one had one bullet shot: one to the head, one to the neck, one in the chest, one here, one there—and I'm looking at this and I'm like, 'Well, damn! I doubt if half of these fuckin' people will ever be talked about.' The news need to come out and really show what's going on out here in the communities, and not just the shit they want to *hand-pick* to talk about."

When youth have had their voices stripped away through obvious and insidious means, it's easy to blame them for the gun problem, to frame the issue as one of evil kids from scary neighbourhoods pushed to pull triggers by similarly wicked rappers. The stereotypes are already there for politicians and the media to build on.

Few would deny that rap music plays a role in the problem with guns—especially not us. We took on this subject partly because of how irresponsible gun-talk had become in the music we love. And what hip-hop says can make a lot of difference. "Hip-Hop has to bear some of the responsibility," said Boston's Ed O.G., a gang member turned positive rap artist. "I don't think we should take the full blame for half of the shit that's goin' on out here, but we do talk about it and we do promote it, *all* the time."

Rap music may have picked up the torch of gun glorification in America, but that flame has been burning since before William F. Cody began mythologizing frontier life in his travelling show, "Buffalo Bill's Wild West," which he created in 1882. Pimping gun culture, rappers join an elite class. Whatever blame is due some emcees for gun violence, at least as much is due outside of hip-hop: on the factories where firearms are manufactured, on the halls of government where laws take shape, on the offices of corporate media where decisions are made to take financial advantage of a profound fascination with the image of guns. In *Enter the Babylon System* we look closer at this broader culture of firearms, its many contributing factors and faces and, finally, at its impact on our society. By the end of this book we hope it's clear that when it comes to guns, to borrow the immortal words of dead prez, the problem is "bigger than hip-hop"—much bigger.

Like Kempton and Taiwo, countless kids before us and millions since, we became friends through hip-hop, the music providing the sound-track to our lives and the backbone of our friendship.

In 1997 we travelled together to Havana, Cuba, for the World Festival of Youth and Students, taking sacks of cassettes with us but only Walkmans to play them on. We soon realized the error of our self-centred North American ways and bought a boom box at a local American-style, no-Cubans-allowed department store. We jammed some batteries in the back, popped in EPMD's *Business as Usual* and travelled the city with the volume on ten and a satchel full of backup batteries, the boom box quickly becoming our calling card. At the conference's American pavilion (as in *nuestra America*) we sat on the huge concrete dock, boom box booming, rapping to the music. Everyone stopped to chat, but the hip-hoppers—Colombian, Mexican, Cuban and American—stayed to chill. We traded tapes, trivia and stories with our new friends, just as the two of us had done years earlier.

The following spring we began work on the second stage of our hip-hop lives—we became contributors to the culture. In May 1998 *Pound* magazine was born. We sought to capture the essence of the culture in print, but also, and more important, to represent the philosophies and ideas that had birthed it, from Martin and Malcolm to Kool Herc and Bambaataa.

Our third issue, in May 2000, gave rise to what would eventually lead to this book: the "Babylon System" column. The name came from reggae music, where the ancient name "Babylon" refers to oppressive colonial and imperial powers. In our hands, Babylon came to mean a broader view of injustice—injustice so ingrained as to have become, we believed, as much systemic and self-perpetuating as it was the result of individual agendas. The column's first instalment featured a snippet about the LAPD's Rampart Division CRASH program (Community Resources Against Street Hoodlums), an anti-gang squad of elite officers who were eventually implicated in drug trafficking, robbery and even attempted murder. The other item in that first column outlined an in-studio stabbing incident between Ja-Rule's crew and a then little-known rapper—50 Cent.

What began as a small idea soon evolved into our most popular section. Our February 2002 issue featured a "Babylon System" column about the "war on drugs." The columns mixed hip-hop lyrics with commentary from world-renowned academics and hip-hop artists, thus creating an intersection between the hip-hop generation and the rest of the world. Those early pieces would define the style of our political coverage and proved to be the platform we had always wanted to create: a socio-political voice for our culture that would also reach the community at large.

In November 2003 we published a five-thousand-word examination of gun culture and gun violence. One rapper after another described the violence they had seen in their communities; all had lost friends, and many had been shot at or wounded. While the stories of carnage surprised us, the rappers recounted in a non-sensational, almost mundane fashion.

When we met 50 Cent in 2005, his G-Unit crew had five members, and four of them had been shot. Asked if this experience had created a special bond between them, Fifty responded in the same laid-back monotone with which he answers all questions: "No, I think when you come from that actual environment you're subjected to those things. That just goes to show you how common that is for something like that to happen where we come from. [Getting] shot is not even a big deal. It's like, 'What? Where you got shot at?' 'At the club.'"

There is outrage in the communities affected by gun violence; organizations and activists work tirelessly to lower the body count and increase the peace. But within the hip-hop community there is also a disturbing sense of resignation and acceptance.

In February 2006 we bumped into Canada's most critically acclaimed, commercially successful hip-hop artist, k-os. Kevin Brereton knew that we were writing a book and asked for an on-the-spot synopsis. "It's about gun culture and gun violence," Rodrigo told him, "from a hip-hop perspective." Kevin grimaced. "Great," he said. "Like the world needs another reason to put hip-hop and guns together." It stung to hear those words from an artist and friend, but maybe Kevin was right.

Hip-Hop has long been stigmatized as a violent culture, the public's perception provoked by news reports of dead rappers and the menacing swagger of artists in movies and videos. But at its best hip-hop is about knowledge and empowerment first, and here we combine the insights of lyrics with the lessons of experience and share them with the larger community. *Enter the Babylon System* is our attempt to reassert hip-hop's stature as a political and cultural voice.

The rifle as an aid to civilzation

"the **bullet** is the pioneer of civilization,
for it has gone hand in hand with the axe that
cleared the forest, and with the family Bible
and schoolbook.
...for without the rifle ball we of America
would not be to-day in the possession
of a **free and united** country,
and mighty in our strength."
-The Hon. W. F. Cody

FIRST CHAMBER
THE TRADE OF THE TOOLS

IN TRYING TO UNDERSTAND the presence of guns and the culture that surrounds them, it made sense to start at the beginning, with those who make the guns. It made sense too to start with the sources closest to home, the small handful of very successful firearms manufacturers in our own country. Savage Arms, headquartered in Massachusetts, turns out old-school sporting rifles at their factory in Lakefield, Ontario. But Statistics Canada reports that between 1974 and 2003 the percentage of rifles and shotguns used in homicides in Canada decreased from 64 percent to just 20 percent. American statistics reflect a similar trend, as does popular culture. On the other hand, the number of handguns used in Canadian homicides increased from 27 percent in 1974 to 68 percent in 2003. It's the little gats that get us.

Of the weapons industry, British journalist Gideon Burrows has written in his *No-Nonsense Guide to the Arms Trade*, "The arms business in today's world has a friendly, respectable face, but it is as murky, secretive and amoral as it has always been." It isn't all so secretive. Most of the gun manufacturers we approached responded to our polite inquiries in kind, and we successfully solicited the thoughts of numerous industry leaders. When it came to Canada's only handgun maker, however, we weren't quite as successful.

PARA-NOID

The first time we heard of Canada's only maker of handguns, it was in an interview with Matthew Behrens of Homes Not Bombs (HNB), a Toronto-based coalition of activists who oppose the weapons industry and the Canadian government's financial support of arms manufacturers, arguing that those dollars would be better spent housing the homeless. Behrens can talk for hours about SNC TEC of Le Gardeur,

Quebec, a member of a multinational consortium of weapons manufacturers organized to help the U.S. Department of Defense meet its "emergency" demand for small-arms ammunition in Iraq. He also knows
plenty about a company in Kitchener, Ontario, previously known as
Diemaco, Canada's lone manufacturer of machine guns and assault
rifles. When we spoke with him in early 2002, we asked if he knew
of any other gun makers in Canada.

"There's one in Scarborough called something-Ordnance,"
Behrens answered, at first uncertain. "Para-Ordnance! That's what
they're called." The name was all Matt could give us. It was the first
time we had heard of the company. Since that conversation with
Matt, we've spoken with others involved in researching the weapons
business who knew surprisingly little about this obscure gun maker
in the Toronto suburbs.

Project Ploughshares is a non-governmental organization (NGO)
based in Kitchener, Ontario, that conducts peace-seeking research
on the arms industry in Canada and abroad. In the summer of 2004
we sat down in their offices with a couple of the NGO's representatives, Lynne Griffiths-Fulton and Ken Epps. Having studied Canadian
military exports and imports for many years, weapons-wise there
isn't much Epps can't update you on. "Para-Ordnance I know virtually
nothing about," he confessed, "and I've been looking at this stuff for
a while."

> They took away my right to bear arms
> What I'm 'posed to fight with, bare palms?
> — Eminem, "We as Americans," off *Encore* (2004)

Attila "Ted" Szabo's family became refugees after the 1956 Hungarian
revolution, in which students led a movement to break the Soviet
Union's iron-fisted grip on their country. Joseph Stalin had died three
years before, and young Hungarians were ready to get free or die trying. After student marches in the streets of Budapest inspired the
masses to join them, the Hungarian police opened fire on crowds of
protestors, killing hundreds. In response, the workers at arms factories distributed guns to the people, and the rest, as they say, is history.

In the wake of the revolution, Szabo's family fled Hungary for Greece, where, as a boy, he met Thanos Polyzos. Eventually both Szabo and Polyzos settled in Canada, where Szabo asked his old friend, a lawyer, to become his partner at Para-Ordnance in the mid-1980s. In the years since, *Guns & Ammo* magazine has declared, the "T&T team has proved to be a fruitful and dynamic partnership."

In one of several "president's letters" posted on his company's website, Szabo shares his views on individual liberty. "There are elitists that believe they know what is best for others," he writes. "We must constantly be on guard against those who would limit our personal freedoms for their agendas of how they think the average man should spend his life. The American Bill of Rights is an important guarantee of personal freedoms. You have to live without such freedoms as the right to speak your mind, to worship as you choose, and to protect yourself and your family to really appreciate them. I know firsthand the tyranny of oppression, because as a boy my family followed that beacon of freedom to North America from behind the Iron Curtain."

Szabo's is a fascinating story and, wanting to learn more, we contacted his company for an interview and tour of their factory. Obviously we didn't expect Para-Ordnance to be so terribly "on guard." The company's first reply thanked us for our interest, but declined our request as a matter of policy. When we pressed, Para were quick to remind us that we were playing with the big guns now:

> Dear Sir:
>
> It has been the long standing policy of this company not to grant tours or interviews. Whether it be for security reasons that we wish not to do so, or otherwise, we believe that we live in a country that grants us that choice....
>
> Given the fact that your magazine appears to have no connection to the business world or our specific industry, and also given the times we live in, we feel it prudent to turn this matter over to the authorities who are better equipped to investigate the motives behind your inexorable interest in our company. We will also be handing this matter over to

legal counsel for any civil action that we may be advised
to pursue against you and your employers.

Govern yourselves accordingly.

In the same president's letter, Szabo further expands upon his perspective on freedom: "Everyone involved in our industry should be thankful for the Second Amendment in the Constitution of the United States of America. The spirit of freedom and responsibility espoused in the Second Amendment is the guarantor of all personal freedoms. It continues to be a guiding light wherever terrorists and tyrants try to hobble the rights of the people. Remember that gun control is really about people control. Wherever people are not able to protect themselves, there will be those that will foster slavery, or worse, upon them."

Canada has nothing in its constitution like the Second Amendment, which reads, "A well regulated militia, being necessary to the security of a free State, the right of the People to keep and bear arms, shall not be infringed." Instead, nearly two hundred years later, Canada instituted the Charter of Rights and Freedoms, which seems to work relatively well as a guarantor of individual liberty against abuses by the state and its agents. As a marketing tool for selling guns, it's much less useful.

A man with more demands on his time than Eminem, MIT linguistics professor and author Noam Chomsky told journalist David Barsamian in 1994, "After decades of intensive business propaganda, people feel that the government is some kind of enemy and that they have to defend themselves from it." A decade later, when we told him about Szabo's position, his attitude hadn't changed. "It is utterly fanciful," Chomsky maintained. "I presume many of those who invoke a dubious interpretation of the Second Amendment are quite serious about defending freedom, more's the pity. It's a real pathology, and is surely being exploited very cynically."

The industry, stay in the dirt, play in the dirt
Test the wrong one in the industry and you will get hurt
I'm not an industry artist; I'm an artist in the industry
— DMX, "The Industry," off *Year of the Dog Again* (2006)

Ted Szabo sees himself as an artist. In another president's letter he reveals, "For me, the art of handgun design has been my lifelong passion and my sculptures come from the molds we make here at Para. Just as artists from one generation look to the genius of the previous generation, I have been inspired by John Moses Browning. Browning created a beautiful work of art when he designed the 1911 pistol. For some people it is the ultimate example of form and function. As great as Browning's 1911 was, I dreamed of making it even better by giving it more capacity."

Although John Browning's name would never become a famous brand, the Colts and Winchesters of the world owe much of their fame to his genius. Browning was, in the words of military weapons historian and author Robert Slayton, "simply the greatest inventor in the history of firearms." Born in 1855 and raised as a Mormon in Ogden, Utah, Browning designed his first gun at the age of ten. By the time John was twenty, his father, also a gun designer, proclaimed that his son's designs were the best he had seen. Browning would soon sell his first patent for a legendary lever-action rifle, later labelled the Winchester 1885. But it would be his handgun patent purchased by the Colt Firearms company that really established Browning's reputation.

As the nineteenth century was drawing to an end, Browning engineered among the world's most famous handguns. Known as the Model 1911 or, more commonly, the Colt .45, Browning's original creation would be hailed by many as the perfect pistol. His sidearm would go on to serve the American military, among others, for the next seventy years.

John Browning was hard at work on what would become another classic design when he died in 1926. His protegé, Dieudonné Saive, completed the project, a 9mm semi-automatic handgun that featured the first high-capacity double-column magazine. Eventually manufactured by Belgium's Fabrique Nationale, or FN Herstal, the Model 1935 Grand Puissance held thirteen rounds. This final contribution from the man the History Channel called "the Einstein of gun design" would become popularly known as the Browning Hi-Power. (He couldn't say with certainty, because the gun had yet to be recovered, but when we asked about the handgun used to kill Kempton Howard, Toronto homicide detective Randy Carter said, "I believe the gun was a Browning 9mm semi-automatic.")

Ted Szabo's claim to fame is his engineering of a 1911 that holds double the seven rounds handled by Browning's original design. For those below the border with a penchant for carrying concealed weapons, Para-Ordnance has also added an "abbreviated" version of the 1911. The Para-Carry holds seven rounds and features a tidy three-inch barrel. For its accomplishments in firearms design Para-Ordnance won three consecutive awards from *Guns & Ammo* magazine, culminating in the 2001 Innovation of the Year editors' award for the Para-Carry.

According to Industry Canada, Para-Ordnance now exports between $500,000 and $1 million worth of product annually, although a 2006 report by Ken Epps—he'd evidently brushed up on Para since we first met—believes "this volume range may be understated." The company has shipped to several countries, including Brazil, South Africa, the Philippines and Algeria, as well as just about every U.S. state. In a relatively short time—around two decades—Para-Ordnance has made a mark on the firearms business comparable to companies ten times its age.

BLOWING SMOKE

In May 2005 we got the chance to visit Inner City Visions in Toronto's Lakeshore area. It's a community group established to, among other things, help young musicians develop their careers, providing free studio time and other services. We'd been invited by Mayhem Morearty, a member of Hu$tlemann, a rap group that includes several members from Toronto's Jane-Finch community. Upon arrival, Mayhem introduced us to his homeboys Jet Black and C-4. In a boardroom above the I. C. Visions studio, we sat down with the three young artists to get their take on the gun situation in Toronto.

Jet Black, now in his mid-twenties, drew attention to generational differences. "Before was like you get a gun when you're like eighteen, or like twenty. Now it's like fifteen, sixteen—ten!" he exclaimed. "I don't wanna blame music, 'cause it's not really music or hip-hop or none of that, so dead all that."

"So you don't think hip-hop has an influence?"

"I'd be lying if I said it wasn't a factor," Mayhem answered.

"'Cause that's where you mostly hear about the guns," Black admitted. "The new kind of gun, then you're like, 'Yooooo!' And then you go, you'll kill yourself to look for it, to buy it."

Then Mayhem surprised us. "A lot of people don't know," he said, "Canada is one of the biggest manufacturers for guns, youknowhat-Imean?"

"For everything!" Jet Black interjected.

"It's just that our legislation most of the time prohibits the carrying, the possession of firearms," Mayhem continued. "But Canada actually manufactures the majority of the guns on the market." We knew it's nowhere close to the majority, but we let it slide, too interested in what Mayhem, who has himself been arrested on gun charges until cleared based on an illegal search, might know about the handgun maker that had proven so elusive. "Yeah, like Para-Ordnance," Chris said. "What about those? Can you get those on the streets?"

"Oh, yeah, man. Para-Ordnance got that new joint with thirty in the clip," Mayhem laughed. "It's like an Uzi, but it's not, youknowhat-Imean? It's crazy! Big shout-outs to Para-Ordnance, man! Y'all need to sponsor me."

I'm'a ride in the stolen Grand Am
Me and Mayhem, with big burners in both hands
Hop out the whip and your folks ran
So much guns, we could be the *Shooting Guide* spokesman
Big MACs, P89s, .357 Mags or the Glock 9 do me just fine
— Jet Black, off Hu$tlemann's "Guns Are For" 12-inch (2005)

As far as we know, Para-Ordnance has yet to produce a thirty-round fully automatic handgun. Glock has engineered such a pistol, and various Browning handguns, including the Hi-Power, can reportedly be illegally modified to fire in full-auto mode. While rappers can tell you a lot about firearms and, often from painful life experience, about an aspect of gun culture the industry would rather not discuss, they remain entertainers, and often entertain as much in interviews as on stage.

In 1997 researchers in Washington, D.C., attempted to evaluate knowledge of firearms brands and manufacturers among 135 young inmates. The juvenile detainees were each shown pictures of nine different guns and asked to match each gun with its name and manufacturer on their own. Among fifteen- to nineteen-year-old prisoners in the District of Columbia, 96 percent successfully matched the guns with their correct names. Like the youth in the D.C. study, most rappers are familiar with the gun industry's established manufacturers—and they let listeners know it.

Based in San Francisco, California, American Brandstand tracks the appearance of brand names in lyrics of songs that appear in the *Billboard* Top 20 singles chart. Included in their 2004 report is a detailed discussion of hip-hop's commercial influence that calls the culture a "great barometer of consumer aspiration." Brandstand's Lucian James writes further, "Many brands do not appreciate the full power of hip-hop culture. . . . It is the defining youth movement of our era—and it's global." Compared with other genres such as pop and rock, which deal with "eternal themes" like love, James argues, "hip-hop tells us about now."

In the past, most brands that rappers referred to in the Top 20 *Billboard* singles represented car, clothing and alcohol companies. But Brandstand recently identified an increasingly prevalent force in the *Billboard* brand mix. According to their report, "Another unexpected trend in 2004 was the rise in weaponry. The weapon count jumped from 11 mentions in 2003 to 53 in 2004." The weapons brands in question were, of course, all the products of gun manufacturers.

In August 2005 we contacted Lucian James for an update. Even more so than in '04, hip-hop had the *Billboard* charts poppin'. "Until this year," James said, "there have been surprisingly few weapons brands in the chart, but the 'thug' culture of G-Unit and others have created a market for lyrical violence, and weapons brands have begun to soar." Among the gun brand name-droppers James cited were The Game, Trick Daddy, Snoop Dogg and Pharrell Williams.

28

"I don't think it is any accident that this is happening," said Tom Diaz, author of *Making a Killing*, an account of the gun business in America. "When you have an industry that just pours this pollution into our culture, it's going to start showing up in lots of different ways, and [rap music] is just one of them. The problem really is that these [gun brands] become icons that young people look up to or think that—an old guy like me would say—[they're] 'cool' to have."

Gun companies are getting for free what McDonald's has already offered to pay for. According to the marketing monitor *Advertising Age*, Mickey Dee's was willing to pay between $1 and $5 every time a rap song with a reference to their signature sandwich, the notorious Big Mac, reached the radio waves. "If 50 Cent says so, they're gonna buy so many Big Macs," the *New York Daily News* quoted one young resident of the Bronx as saying. But what happens if 50 Cent says "Beretta"?

American Brandstand believes hip-hop has the power to "make or break a brand." In their report Lucian James cites the case of Tommy Hilfiger, who was at first opposed to any association between his clothing lines and hip-hop. "[Tommy] didn't have a clue as to the power rappers had until I did that," Brand Nubian's Grand Puba told the *Village Voice* of wearing the Hilfiger logo. In time, however, Hilfiger recognized a connection between hip-hop and his bottom line, eventually sending rappers down the runway in his fashion shows. But in hip-hop's cutthroat race for style, fashion trends can go over the rail faster than Indy cars. According to James, when hip-hop's image leaders grew tired of Hilfiger's all too familiar logo, his "brand suffered a steep decline."

When we interviewed Reginald C. Dennis, co-founder of *XXL* magazine, hip-hop's most commercially successful cultural monthly, he went to great lengths imagining the marketing possibilities for firearms manufacturers in hip-hop. "Who's gonna be the first company," he mused lightheartedly, "to come up with a brand new gun and say, 'You know what, I want the G-Unit to promote this gun. They're gonna have an ad.' Why not? Why aren't they doing this? This is the elephant in the room that no one's talking about. This must be done!"

"The line doesn't need to be crossed, because the damage is already done," Dennis added more seriously, pointing to the example of St. Ides' forty-ounce beers. "If you can use rappers to promote malt liquor and get kids to drink malt liquor at a young age, why not have the G-Unit promote your gun? I know the sales would go up."

While virtually every other industry manoeuvres to exploit hip-hop's commercial influence, gun manufacturers have been saved the work. Guns are a big part of life, death and status in the same neighbourhoods that hip-hop grew up in. It only makes sense that firearms brands would come to pervade rap music. The author of the definitive history of hip-hop, Jeff Chang, writes in *Can't Stop Won't Stop*, "The tension between culture and commerce would become one of the main storylines of the hip-hop generation." With the remainder of this first chamber, we look more closely at a most extreme manifestation of that tension, examining a few firearms that have become the object of many a young man's fascination.

ORIGINAL BLAST MASTERS

Gunpowder is one of the world's oldest technologies, and a few firearms makers have been investing in their brands for centuries. Over 350 years before Germany's Karl Benz patented the first car in 1886, Mastro Bartolomeo Beretta was making gun barrels in the Italian village of Gardone Val Trompia. By the time Henry Ford began making Benz's idea roll in America, Samuel Colt, Oliver Winchester, Horace Smith and Daniel Wesson were already established names.

Bringing the heat for more than 150 years, the Springfield, Massachusetts, firm of Smith & Wesson has a lengthy history of its own. The storied manufacturer has made some crucial contributions to the evolution of handguns—revolvers in particular—and developed the rim-fire cartridge, one of the earliest self-contained cartridges, which did away with the need to load powder, primer and bullets separately. The modern Smith & Wesson Holding Corporation manufactures high-quality handguns, from small yet powerful "super snubbies" up to the monster of all big-bore revolvers, the Model 500. Unveiled in January 2003, Smith & Wesson's polished steel .50 calibre Magnum revolver has, applauded *Guns & Ammo*, "delighted power enthusiasts, killed elephants, provoked controversy and intimidated at least one gunwriter."

GUN SLANGIN'

Possibly taken from the Norse woman's name Gunnildr, the word *gun* emerged in
Europe around the mid-1300s. In hip-hop, however, calling things by their correct name
is considered lacking in imagination, and therefore lame. Back in Humphrey Bogart's day,
actors playing hard-boiled detectives or lowlife criminals popularized the term *gat* (from
Gatling gun). But in the years since its birth, hip-hop has introduced listeners to innumerable other slang names for the gun. In order to help our readers through some of the
street talk that comes up in this book, we've prepared a little multiple-choice quiz. Time
to learn some slanguage!

1. Which of the following terms means to carry a gun?	**2. Which of the following terms means to shoot someone?**	**3. Which of the following is a term for a gun?**
a) packin'	a) wet	a) pound
b) totin'	b) cap	b) heater
c) strapped	c) clap	c) ratchet
d) holdin'	d) blast	d) twister
e) all of the above	e) buck	e) whistle
	f) pop	f) banger
	g) murk	g) burner
	h) spray	h) toaster
	i) let off	i) oven
	j) all of the above	j) steel
		k) paddle
		l) pump
		m) hammer
		n) oowop
		o) thang
		p) blinker
		q) jammy
		r) iron
		s) shotty
		t) tool
		u) chrome
		v) flamer
		w) biscuit
		x) piece
		y) blix
		z) all of the above

Answers: 1. (e); 2. (j); 3. (z).

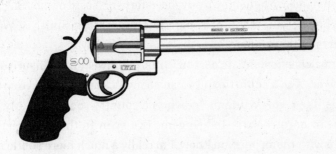

S&W Model 500

Every day in his home office in the Berkshire Hills, Massachusetts, Roy Jinks, Smith & Wesson's in-house historian since joining the company in 1962, basks in the aura of the manufacturer's history. According to the *Boston Globe* on January 6, 2005, before the old S&W factory was levelled in 1971, the City of Springfield gave Jinks a week to search for and collect anything he thought had value. Jinks took the original chestnut panelling from Daniel Wesson's office and installed it in his own house. He also has "every firearms patent issued in the United States from June 29, 1832, to May 17, 1921." In addition to the patents, which were originally collected by D. B. Wesson himself, Jinks has collected a museum's worth of invoices, advertisements, catalogues and correspondence.

Jinks explained how Smith & Wesson has historically marketed its products. "Well, certainly word of mouth," he said, "[and] a tremendous amount of magazine advertising have been the most successful. They advertised in almost every major magazine, when you could do that." Back in the day, gun ads weren't confined to the likes of *Guns & Ammo*. According to Jinks, up until the 1970s manufacturers advertised in such mainstream magazines as the *Saturday Evening Post* and *Collier's*. But, lamented Jinks, the "anti-gun movement" put an end to that. "Magazines got very politically conscious and became very anti-gun."

In recent years a number of hip-hop artists have helped compensate for the mainstream's political consciousness, endorsing the Smith & Wesson name with their own advanced form of "word of mouth."

"What do you think of rap artists promoting Smith & Wesson products in their music?"

"I'm a classical music person," Jinks said, seeming unsure of how to answer. "I'm a country-and-western music fan. And I have so many friends like Hank Williams Jr., who's a country rock [star]. My other friend, in hard rock, is Ted Nugent. I've been to their concerts and worked with them, but, you know, I'm really a much more subtle music person."

"And do those guys mention Smith & Wesson in their music?"

"Not that I know of. Hank has done a lot with mentioning our guns in different interviews, but I don't think he's ever done it in songs that I know of."

Roy Jinks has been missing out. Hank Williams Jr. not only mentions Jinks's company in song, but actually casts a Smith & Wesson revolver as the light of justice in an otherwise dark world. "I've Got Rights," off 1979's *Family Tradition* album, is about a gross failure of the legal system, about the need to take the law into one's own hands, along with a .44 Magnum. If Hank Williams ever wanted to collaborate with rappers on a cut much iller than that Nelly and Tim McGraw track, "Over And Over," at least one group would work perfectly.

> Your family cries as your body lies in its casket
> I keep a black Smith & Wesson in my Polo jacket
> Sixteen shots, for all ya hardrocks
> —Steele, "Black Smif-N-Wessun," off Black Moon's *Enta da Stage* (1992)

Recognized as one of the great underground groups in rap history, Steele and his partner in crime (PNC) Tek would together identify themselves as Smif-N-Wessun—that is, until Smith & Wesson got word of the unauthorized use of its name. Dru Ha was head of the Duck Down collective of artists, which included Tek and Steele, when Smif-N-Wessun released their first full-length record; *Dah Shinin'* was originally distributed by Nervous Records in 1995. A young Jewish brother who rolls with a bunch of mostly short, dreadlocked dudes, Dru is a down-to-earth straight shooter. We tracked him down at his office in New York.

"They were clear in their cease-and-desist letter," Dru explained, "that the group wasn't an official sponsor of what they represent." S&W's attorneys had Nervous absolutely petrified, and the label agreed to stop printing copies of *Dah Shinin'* with the Smif-N-Wessun name. In addition, Tek and Steele changed the name of their group to the Cocoa Brovaz. "The argument was that we were infringing on their trademark," Dru said. "But there's no way we were, because no one would ever confuse music with guns."

Roy Jinks confirmed that Smith & Wesson is indeed more protective of its trademark than other companies "because it's such an important and such a well-recognized trademark, which has been in existence since 1878. And we have vigorously protected it. We don't want to lose it to public domain."

Smith & Wesson is the brand I'm strapped with
More than the name of the band I rap with
—Tek, "War," off *Smif-N-Wessun: Reloaded* (2005)

In August 2005, as Tek and Steele prepared to release their fourth album, we interviewed Tek. Despite S&W's warnings, the Duck Down duo had recommitted themselves to their original moniker. "Under heel and boot," Tek declared, "we're gonna be Smif-N-Wessun 'til the day we die." Asked what he thought of Smith & Wesson's original opposition to his group's use of its name, Tek said, "That just let you know that, even in this day and time, or that day and time, hip-hop's still not appreciated in some places."

"Do you think they were worried about being associated with crime?"

"They're sellin' fuckin' guns!" Tek blasted us. "If anything, they should have supported us, as many guns as they got floatin' in the hood or they sellin' to us. If anything, they should have been our number-one sponsor. You know what that could have done for their sales?"

The American Bureau of Alcohol, Tobacco and Firearms (ATF) compiles data on the guns most often recovered at crime scenes in the United States, broken down by manufacturer and type of firearm. In 1990 Smith & Wesson had three models among the top ten firearms most frequently confiscated in the course of criminal investigations, including S&W .38 calibre revolvers, .357 revolvers and 9mm semi-automatic pistols. According to the ATF's figures, 2000 saw Smith & Wesson once again take three of the top ten spots: their .38 revolvers led the nation that year, while their .357 revolvers and 9mm pistols also made the list.

"It's so two-sided," Dru Ha remarked. "They make it, but they promote it in a different light. They don't want to be affiliated with the violence and, of course, the robberies and the crime that the rappers sometimes put the name in."

STOCK UP

When he died in 2002 at the age of eighty-six, Bill Ruger had lived long enough to see his partner's investment of $50,000 in 1949 evolve into a company worth hundreds of millions of dollars. Ruger's partner, Alex Sturm, died just a few years after the business was created, never to see Sturm, Ruger and Company, Inc. grow into America's largest and most successful firearms manufacturer. "We have a little moneymaking machine here," Ruger told *Forbes* he had realized back in 1959. "All we have to do is keep introducing the correct new products." With Ruger's prolific gift for gun design, engineering enough products to satisfy the civilian market proved no problem.

William B. Ruger was among the last of a dying breed. He made efforts to promote gun safety, and voluntarily recalled some products because of safety concerns. Once upon a time Ruger also decided to limit the magazine capacity of his company's firearms—a decision that would eventually be overruled by market forces. A November 2002 memorial piece in *Shooting Times* quoted an old interview in which Ruger even complained of the trend towards ever larger calibres (a measurement of a bullet's diameter in inches or millimetres). "I must say," he commented, "that I'm a little bit offended by these firearms that have exaggerated performance. You know, why stop at the 10mm, why not go on and make the thing a .45. I mean it gets to be kinda to the point of bearing on the absurd, and

HI, MY NAME IS . . .

Nicknames serve the same purpose for hip-hoppers as they do for superheroes: they define your skills and persona while obscuring your "government" identity. From the martial arts–inspired Grandmasters (Flash, Caz) to the Wu's Mafia-influenced Gambino monikers (Maximillion, Noodles), hip-hoppers, like superheroes, gravitate towards handles that project strength. As Dru Ha, manager of Smif-N-Wessun, the Originoo Gunn Clappaz and Buckshot, explained, "They choose gun names because of what the gun represents: power." We asked some of hip-hop's Bruce Waynes why they'd rather be Gatman than Batman.

M-1 of dead prez (Brooklyn, NY)

Firstly, my name is Mutulu. And the M1—as a gun, a rifle, a .22 calibre rifle—it's like a symbol, an old symbol of kinda resistance struggles. It's the hood weapon. It's the resources that we have handed down. I mean, of course, nowadays you're looking at very high-tech, and brothers got that high-tech—that's good. But the M1 is like old, tried-tested-and-true, gonna be there. It's the piece that the old dread pull out the back of the closet that Grandma might have.

Tech N9ne (Kansas City, MO)

I didn't have no name. It was just my middle name, Dontez, and that was wack as a motherfucker. But in '88 I got with this cat named Black Walt [and he's like,] "You need a name, dog." So I'm like, "I don't got a name." And he had already a nigga named Mac-10 in the group. In '88 he was going through a *Guns & Ammo* book, flippin' through it, like, "Mac-11?" I'm like, "Hell, nah." He's like, "Uzi?" I'm like, "No." "Twelve-gauge!?" I'm like, "Nooooo!" And he turned the book over, and on the back there was a picture of a Tec-9. He said "Tec-9?" I'm like, "Yeah, that's cool." And he said, "That's gonna be your name 'til we find something else." So I been stuck with it ever since then. Ha ha ha.

Trigger Tha Gambler (Brownsville, NY)

The gun itself don't work without the trigger. So me, basically, I just put it together like—Okay, I could be as powerful as a gun, but what releases that gun? It's the trigger. And at the same time, just me being out there and always carrying weapons and movin' around. I was a weapon carrier, so a lot of guys that knew me used to say, "Okay, you know what? That's Trigger right there." And when I heard someone call me that name—an O.G. [original gangster]—I was like, "Whoa, I like that name!" So ever since then a lot of people that knew me basically shouted out that name, 'cause they know if you can't hold that name down, somebody woulda took it from you.

> **Klashnekoff (London, England)**
>
> It's good to be peaceful, man. It's all about that, that's the centre of me. That's the centre of Klashnekoff, even though I've used a gun as my name. To me that doesn't mean nothin', because there's a guy called Tony Blair, and there's a guy called George Bush, and they've killed thousands of people, and they've got very nice names and they wear suits. In my opinion, they're responsible for killing thousands and thousands of people. That's my point. I call myself Klashnekoff and I want to provoke a response. You want to cuss me and judge me because I've called myself Klashnekoff, but a rose by any other name is just the same.
>
> Here's a list of fifty emcees named after guns and ammo. Believe it or not, there are others.

6 Shot	Thugs)	Peter Gunz
9 Glock	Gloc 9	Pistol
12 Gauge	Glokk	Pistol Maine
.38 (PSK-13)	GUN	Pistol Pete
40 Cal	Gunshot	Pistoleros
Ak-9ine	Hollow Point	Shotti & Dead
AK-47	Hollow Tip	Slug
AK the Teflon Don	Kach .22	Tec-9
AP-9	Lil' A-K	Texas Tech9
AR-15	Lil Glock	Three Glock
Beretta 9 (Killarmy)	Mac 10	Timmy Two-Gats
BR Gunna	Mack 10	Tommy Gun
Buckshot	Mausberg	Tre-8
Bukshot	Mr. 45	The Uzi Bros.
Chris Calico	Nine	Young Gunz
Colt MPC	Oaktown 357	Young Uzi
G.A.T. (Gangstas and	Originoo Gunn Clappaz	Yungun

the 10mm is just about there." With his relatively unusual views on firearms design as its guiding force, Ruger's company had manufactured over twenty million guns by 2002, including such classic models as the .357 Blackhawk revolver and the Mini-14 rifle.

When compared favourably to John Browning and Samuel Colt, Ruger responded modestly. Where he considered the other men to be inventors, he called himself a simple designer. Of Browning, Ruger said his "ideas were so sound, so numerous that there was never any room for anybody to be as good as he was." Colt inspired Ruger in another way: "Colt's business and inventive characteristics are something that I'd have to say I've always wanted to emulate. Not Sam Colt alone." By most accounts, not too many people would want to be like "Sam Colt alone."

Born in 1814, Samuel Colt is said to have designed his revolver at the age of sixteen during an ocean voyage to India. Li'l Sam became frustrated because he was unable to fire his gun more than once at a time at passing porpoises and whales. Colt noticed how the helmsman's wheel aligned with a clutch, and immediately whittled a wooden model of his revolver. Although revolvers had been around since the 1600s, Colt was the first to patent a cylinder that locked with the barrel. In his spectacular book *Gunpowder*, historian Jack Kelly describes Colt as "typically American: abrasive, self-made, persistent, eminently practical in his thinking, as imaginative as he was mercenary, an opportunist, a liar, a genius." It's unclear which of those characteristics, if any, influenced Ruger, but he too was mercenary, refusing to sell his guns to wholesalers who also carried the products of Smith & Wesson, which he called his main competitor. Whatever he had learned from his predecessors, it worked.

Like Smith & Wesson, Sturm, Ruger is a publicly traded company. But while S&W limits itself to handguns, Ruger produces thirty-four models of firearms across the four main categories: rifles, shotguns, pistols and revolvers. For the year ending in August 2005, sales of Ruger's firearms and other products (including titanium golf clubs) earned the company a net income of $149.7 million. At the same time, while profits for the four previous quarters totalled just $4.11 million, *Forbes* reported that shares in RGR looked "locked and loaded," ready to shoot up. Ruger's plan to make guns for the average man—"shooter, hunter and collector"—has apparently paid off.

We doubt that rappers would fit into Ruger's idea of the average man, but they too have bought into the power of his brand. When Rodrigo phoned Young Chris of Philadelphia's Young Gunz, Chris was playing with his killer toys. "I'm in my old crib," he said. "I was just upstairs counting a box—bunch of shells, all that. For all types of shit: 9s, four-pounds, all that shit."

"What's the piece of choice these days?" Buns asked.

"Right now I'm sitting with a four-pound. A .45—all hollow-nose. And a big-ass .357 Ruger. No lie."

"How'd you get those?"

"What you mean, 'How'd you get those?'—I bought 'em."

My rhymes get Ruger endorsements
My song boost Intratec sales through the ceilin'
Let's talk with guns, convo 'til the police come
Give you a red shirt with a wet hat to match
— Prodigy, "Tres Leches," off Big Punisher's *Capital Punishment* (1998)

Where bloodlusty lyrics are concerned, Prodigy is a certified freak. One half of the Queensbridge duo Mobb Deep, the P offers perhaps hip-hop's most vividly alluring rhymes about homicide. On the phone with Prodigy and his partner Havoc, Chris asked P what inspired his references to Ruger.

"Just a name," he said, his answer less riveting than his rhymes. "Just a name of a gun."

"Nothing special about Rugers?"

"They definitely make a good handgun."

Prodigy's thoughtless response was frustrating. We should have clued in when he earlier offered the conventional hip-hop cop-out for his violent lyrics: "The entire CD is entertainment." A Ruger spokesman commented more extensively on rap music featuring his company's name. Formerly director of marketing and communication with Smith & Wesson, Ken Jorgensen sent us some Ruger promotional materials arguing that solving the problem of gun violence involves "rethinking what we accept as 'entertainment.'" It continues, "The saturation of youth with gory violence in the name of 'entertainment' has a desensitizing effect upon their willingness to take up arms against each other. Let's not pretend otherwise." Jorgensen also wrote us a two-page letter that expanded on Ruger's corporate perspective.

As an initial matter, I must confess that I am not familiar with the artists or lyrics you mentioned, so it is difficult for me to respond to specific references.

I thought perhaps a little background on Sturm, Ruger might be helpful in understanding my comments. Our motto, "Arms Makers For Responsible Citizens" is not just a catchy phrase; it is a corporate philosophy that permeates everything we do. . . .

Sturm, Ruger was the first company to run full-page firearms safety ads, televise public service announcements, and imprint our firearms with a safety message. We are supporters of the International Hunter Education Association, the efforts of the National Shooting Sports Foundation and the training and safety programs of the National Rifle Association. We publish a variety of materials promoting safe and responsible firearms ownership. . . . Where possible, we have tried to correct misrepresentations or misconceptions related to our products propagated by the media. For example, we worked to have the Ruger name removed from a violent video game. When we become aware our products are misrepresented in entertainment media (TV and movies, for example) we do our best to correct it. . . .

Given these efforts to promote safe and responsible firearms ownership and usage, you will understand why we are strongly opposed to lyrics, films or other media that promote or glorify the criminal use of firearms. Any suggestion that we seek to profit from such messages is simply ludicrous. . . .

On the other hand, "it's a free country," as they say. The simple fact is that we cannot control how actors, musicians, and the printed media represent or misrepresent our products. We value and recognize free speech as a fundamental precept of our society. However, supporting the rights of others to make the statement does not mean that we condone or approve of the message.

.... The entertainment industry must bear a serious responsibility in shaping the public's perception of what constitutes normal and correct use of firearms.

For the most part, popular entertainment tends to portray firearms solely as instruments of mayhem, which is simply wrong. Hunters and sportsmen alike use firearms safely and effectively. (Indeed, despite a many-fold increase in the number of guns and gun owners, firearms accidents have been steadily declining for decades. Right now they are at an all time low.) This is the reality of how the vast, vast majority of firearms are used and it stands in stark contrast to the manner in which firearms are portrayed in the popular media and by certain factions in our government. Unfortunately, I doubt this is something we will ever hear about in rap lyrics. . . .

"I think that is a pretty lukewarm answer," Tom Diaz scoffed at Jorgensen's reply. "Because what does that mean actually? When you break it down, what does it mean to say 'Well, our products are misrepresented'? Here's a company that makes these guns that are used to kill real people by other real people, and that's their purpose. And then they say, 'Well, we don't like it when somebody in the entertainment world makes reference to what our guns do.'"

In 2000 Ruger 9mm pistols were second only to Smith & Wesson .38 calibre revolvers on the list of the top ten crime guns traced by the ATF. In an interview with the *New Hampshire Business Review*, published July 22, 1994, Bill Ruger commented on his role in the arming of criminals. "It's not my fault," he said. "It really isn't."

PLASTIC HAMMERS

In the broad daylight of June 27, 1999, Austrian pistol maker Gaston Glock accompanied his business associate of fifteen years, Charles Ewert, to a parking garage in Luxembourg. Ewert said there was a hot set of wheels inside the lot that the seventy-year-old Glock just had to see. According to *Forbes* magazine on March 31, 2003, when Glock leaned over to check out the car, a "massive, masked man leaped from behind and smashed a rubber mallet into Glock's skull." Ewert ran. As an assassination attempt it was as ironic as it was irrational. The powerful Glock fought for his life and knocked out several of his attacker's teeth before the hammer-wielding hitman collapsed unconscious on top of his target.

An employee in the United States had warned Glock that Ewert might be fraudulently diverting company funds, and the chief was beginning to ask questions. Glock's growing awareness of the skullduggery meant it was time for the old man to go. Absurdly, the middle-aged Ewert chose a sixty-seven-year-old ex-mercenary and former wrestler, Jacques "Spartacus" Pêcheur, to help him execute his plan. The attempt on Glock's life earned Ewert and Pêcheur a total of thirty-seven years behind bars. "The attack was the best thing that happened to me," Glock told *Forbes.* "Otherwise, I would have gone on trusting Ewert."

Gaston Glock founded his company in Deutsch-Wagram, a small town near Vienna, in 1963. It produced curtain rings and plastic grenade shells before someone dared Glock to make a handgun for the Austrian army. Constructed of steel and polymers (a fancy term for plastic), Glock's design would hold the most rounds of any available handgun. By 1983 Glock had received an order for twenty-five thousand of his guns from the Austrian armed forces. In about two decades the business spread beyond Europe into South America, Asia, Australia and, of course, North America, developing thirty-seven pistol models in eight different calibres. Glock has now sold an estimated three million handguns in a hundred countries.

In the words of Ruger's booklets, we represent the "technically unsophisticated media." Having a technical expert such as Whit Collins to talk to has proven critical. Acknowledged as the original designer of the 10mm (.40 calibre) round for the Browning Hi-Power, he is also a former *Guns & Ammo* editor and an outspoken critic of Glock's products. Glock produces guns with inexpensive materials so that, he said, "All the money can be put into the things that make it attractive, like very powerful calibres."

"What you have," Collins continued, "is somebody who is making more money per unit sometimes than somebody who is selling a very much better-made gun of an arguably higher level of design, a gun with a lot of safety features." Unlike Browning, Colt and even Ruger, "Gaston Glock is not a great firearms designer," Collins concluded.

Quality aside, the success of Glock's product speaks for itself. His company's pistols are considered lightweight, reliable, easy to maintain and even easier to use, and the company brings in an estimated $100 million in annual sales, two-thirds of which comes from the United States. In 1985, Glock set up shop in Smyrna, Georgia, assembling pistol parts imported from Austria. Much like southward-gazing Para-Ordnance, Glock since pledged allegiance to the home of the green. Magazines such as *Combat Handguns* have run advertisements for the Austrian-based company with an American flag waving proudly in the background. In front of the flag stand three of Glock's "champion" shooters, their pistols pressed against their hearts in a show of pure patriotism.

Whit Collins

Glock is also down with the boys in blue. The weapons of choice for more than seven thousand American law enforcement agencies, including about 65 percent of all U.S. officers, Glock's guns ended the reigns of Beretta and Smith & Wesson in the holsters of most North American police. In 1999 Gaston Glock presented the two-millionth pistol produced by his company, autographed and engraved, to the International Association of Chiefs of Police (IACP).

The pistol was a symbol of recognition, says the company's website, that a "large part of [Glock's] success was due to the overwhelming acceptance by the law enforcement market."

"It was a conscious decision to go after the law enforcement market first," Gaston Glock told *Advertising Age* in June 1995. "In marketing terms, we assumed that, by pursuing the law enforcement market, we would then receive the benefit of 'after sales' in the commercial market." With Miami cops in '86 becoming the first of many police departments to adopt the Glock 9mm, the old-timer's savvy strategy was dead-on.

> Keep my shit cocked, 'cause the cops got a Glock too
> What the fuck would you do, drop them or let 'em drop you?
> I chose droppin' the cop, I got me a Glock
> And a Glock for the niggas on my block
> — 2Pac, "Soulja's Story," off *2Pacalypse Now* (1991)

Ill Bill is a Jewish rap artist from Brooklyn's Glenwood projects and a member of the underground group Non-Phixion. "Glock's a real good gun," he said, while maintaining that gun ownership is, to him, strictly a matter of self-defence. "You got a lot of rounds—but there's no safety. Part of the reason why they made it with no safety is so that when you gotta get poppin', you get poppin'. You don't have to worry about nothin'. That second that you have to take the gun off safety, you could get your head popped off."

In addition to the absence of a safety on many of its guns, Glocks are known for having an extremely light trigger pull. One ballistics expert quoted in the *Detroit News* on December 15, 2003, described Glock pistols as "almost too eager to fire."

In April 2004 a classroom full of children in Orlando, Florida, learned just how eager. "This is a Glock .40," Drug Enforcement Administration (DEA) Special Agent Lee Paige told them during a gun safety talk. "50 Cent, Too Short, all of 'em talk about Glock .40s, okay? I'm the only one in this room professional enough that I know of to carry this Glock .40." A split-second later, as Paige holstered his pistol, the weapon went off, shooting him in the thigh. While the agent courageously carried on, the lesson in the dangers of guns—more specifically, Glocks—was complete.

Glock also manufactures what it calls a "subcompact submachine gun . . . designed for use by special forces." With one pull of the pistol's trigger, the fully automatic Glock 18 can empty a 30-round magazine in less than two seconds (as opposed to a semi-automatic pistol, which requires a pull of the trigger for every single shot). *Guns & Weapons for Law Enforcement*, published by Harris Publications, the same company that produces *XXL* magazine, recommends carrying a "hand cannon" like the Glock 18 in a "bag of McDonald's Freedom Fries," hiding "deadly force behind a smiling Ronald McDonald."

Although the Glock 18 is available only to elite law enforcement units, Glock's other pistols allegedly have yet another frightening feature: they can be converted to fire as a full-auto weapon. While Whit Collins is restricted from demonstrating such a conversion because he lacks a machine-gun manufacturing licence, this issue concerns him greatly. "The industry guys," he said, "especially Glock's attorneys, always say that if I haven't done it, I shouldn't be allowed to say it. And they act [as if] the Internet, the publishers and the notifications to lab workers in the firearms examination industry don't count."

Paladin Press, of Boulder, Colorado, is one source of instruction for Glock conversions. In addition to titles such as *Ultimate Sniper*, *Drug Smuggling: The Forbidden Book* and *The Ancient Art of Strangulation*, Paladin sells a book to the general public called *Glock Exotic Weapons System*, which explains how, "with a few scraps of metal and some simple hand tools, any Glock can be converted to full automatic."

Although the manufacturer has worked to disable some websites that illustrate such conversions, Glock does not deny that they are possible. "It makes the pistol illegal," Glock's current counsel, Carlos Guevara, told us in August 2006, "and exposes the person to additional danger." When a mid-priced pistol can so easily be turned into what essentially amounts to a special-forces weapon, the danger to the shooter would seem to be the least of society's worries.

If he try to pull a move we can take him to the lot
Trunk pop, stash-box, pull the automatic Glock
— Paul Wall, "Play Dirty," off *Get Ya Mind Correct* (2002)

In May 2005 we visited the University of Southern California to inter-view Dr. Todd Boyd, an author who has written extensively about hip-hop and its transformative effect on American culture. Labelled the "hip-hop professor" by CNN, Boyd lounges in his office in the latest high-end hip-hop fashions. "Hip-Hop is a name-brand culture," he clarified. "So the same way you want somebody to know that Versace did your shirt, you want 'em to know you got a Glock."

"It's funny though," Boyd said later, "'cause most people think of Glock as like—not as a brand name, but like the actual name of a gun. Like the way people use Xerox to stand in for copying, like 'Make me a Xerox.' Well, Xerox is a *brand*, but that brand has become so identified with what it does—make copies—that you have the same thing in terms of Glock: it gets used so much you think Glock is another way of saying a gun." The Glock brand name becoming another term for a pistol represents a nightmare for the company. During his tenure, Paul Jannuzzo, the company's former senior attorney, confronted twelve record labels to protest the use of the Glock name in rap tracks. According to *Forbes,* the pistol maker acted "mainly out of fear that Glock's name will become a generic term for handgun."

Rappers and Glocks go back like babies and pacifiers. In 2004 Glock hit number 18 on the American Brandstand list of brands most often mentioned in the *Billboard* Top 20 singles. With twenty mentions over twelve months, Glock squeezed in between Dom Perignon Champagne and Victoria's Secret lingerie. Jannuzzo's suc-cessor, Charles Grosse, since replaced by Guevara, told us what Gaston Glock's company thought of the trend.

"We are not in favour of our name, trademark, trade-dress [the look of a product]," he said in lawyerly fashion, "being used in any type of music or—let's just call it in general—entertainment. The reason being, we're very careful about protecting our intellectual property. And the trade name Glock, as well as the trade-dress of the

THE GLOCK 17

You don't wanna mess with that Glock, boy
Test me with that Glock, you get popped, boy
— C-Murder, "Y'all Heard of Me," off *The TRUest Shit I Ever Said* (2005)

Convicted in September 2003, rapper C-Murder was serving a life sentence in the New Orleans nightclub shooting death of a sixteen-year-old when we got him on the phone. Maintaining his innocence, C-Murder says his songs, fame, wealth and name have hurt him hugely. Still, we wanted to know whether any facts backed up C-Murder's mean raps, quizzing him on lyrics off an album he recorded and released while imprisoned: *The TRUest Shit I Ever Said.* "You say your 'waist stays Glocked.' Are you a fan of Glocks?"

"Oh, off top, dog!" he answered excitedly. "Especially that nice .45, the all-black one with the 'TRU' on it. You gotta see that one, the Kevlar material. The semi, that got 'T-R-U' on there in green. TRU shit, ya *hearrrrd* me?" Tru-Dot sights for Glock pistols allow for "improved rapid instinctive aiming" and are available on eBay. TRU is also the name of a rap group from New Orleans made up of C-Murder and two of his brothers, Silkk the Shocker and Master P.

Here are seventeen songs that also reference Gaston Glock's black pistols.

Three 6 Mafia	"Mask and da Glock" (1991)
Cypress Hill	"Hand on the Glock" (1993)
TRU	"Ain't No Glock" (1995)
Smoothe Da Hustler	"Glocks on Cock" (1996)
Mac Dre	"Maggots on My Glock" (1996)
Heather B.	"All Glocks Down" (1996)
Bone Thugs-N-Harmony	"Shots 2 da Double Glock" (1998)
Terror Squad	"Pass the Glock" (1999)
T.I.	"2 Glock 9s" (2000)
Wu-Tang Clan	"The Glock" (2001)
The RZA	"Glocko Pop" (2001)
2Pac	"2 Glocks" (2003)
Cee-Lo	"Glockapella" (2004)
Los Tres Mosqueteros	"Con Mi Glock-Glock" (2004)
Juelz Santana	"Glock Pop!" (2005)
Papoose	"2 Glocks" (2005)
Lloyd Banks	"Without My Glock" (2006)

pistol itself—the design, what makes that pistol a Glock pistol—is very, very valuable, and very important for us to protect. So any time that there is an unauthorized, unlicensed use of either of those things, we tend to take action about it. And I know that's an issue with the entertainment industry. . . . As you can imagine, in some of the songs that are in those top twenty-five hip-hop songs—"

"Those are the top twenty songs overall in America," Chris corrected him.

"Yeah, overall in America," Grosse continued, "there are some negative references for use of our product in crime. That's very concerning to us. The vast majority of our sales efforts are towards the law enforcement market. And that's really counterproductive to those sales efforts."

But Glock's potential in rhyme—*drop*, *pop*, *lock* and, of course, *cock*—make it an obvious choice. Paris, a revolutionary rap artist from Oakland, California, denounces the attraction: "I think the trend right now is to promote anything name-brand by name. Most people who talk about a Glock, they can't tell you a model number or how many shots it holds. They've never fired it, they've never felt spent shells hit them and burn their forearm, they've never done any of that shit. So you ask most people about this, a lot of rappers are emulating what they heard in somebody else's record, or speaking on some stats that they read in *Guns & Ammo*. It's all bullshit, the vast majority of it. Most people whose knuckles are draggin' in the streets aren't making records."

BIG BIRD

Although it doesn't have as long a history in hip-hop as Glock, another brand of handgun has increasingly landed in rap lyrics. "The new thing is the Desert Eagle," Trigger Tha Gambler declared. "It gives you the feel of having a handgun, but it gives you the authority like a big gun, like if you was walking around with an M1 or an SK."

Manufactured by Minneapolis, Minnesota's Magnum Research Inc., the Desert Eagle is bulky and frighteningly beautiful. Patented in 1980, it first arrived on the market in '83, and is the calibre-king of the pistol world, challenged only by handguns like Smith & Wesson's

48

similarly beastly Model 500 revolver. More like the pterodactyl of pistols, the most recent evolution of the Desert Eagle, the Mark XIX, is capable of chambering a round "once considered impossible to build," the company boasts—the .50 calibre Action Express (AE). And while the Desert Eagle ain't cheap, its price tag didn't dissuade rapper Capone. "Hey, that's my best friend," he exclaimed. "I sleep with the bird."

"Desert Eagle is a hot little biscuit," Ill Bill confirmed. Having heard the rave reviews from rappers, we had to find out how Magnum Research felt about hip-hop mouth-feeding its most famous firearm's popularity. We also wanted to know what Magnum thought about rap music's contribution to the company's brand recognition. We e-mailed a few examples, including the following:

> The most beautifullest thing in the world is a fo'-fo' Desert Eagle
> Nigga, that shit is DIESEL!!!
> Lethal hollow point slugs bust through any object
> Squeeze it at rapid fire, clear the whole projects
> — Billy Danze, "Stick to Ya Gunz," off M.O.P.'s *Firing Squad* (1996)

The response from Magnum Research was so brief that, until we learned more about the company's distinctly matter-of-fact perspective, we assumed some anonymous cog was committing corporate suicide. It read simply: "Advertising is always good!" Blown away, we wrote back. We explained more about *Enter the Babylon System* and asked Magnum to expand upon its previous reply. "Our Chairman will be contacting you directly," came the response.

Chris was so excited he had to piss, and in the process he missed the call from Magnum Research's CEO. "Chris, John Risdall," his voice message began, "and I'm the chairman of the board of Magnum Research, and I'm the one responsible for several websites, including MagnumFilms and Magnumresearch.com." The friendly and youthful-sounding voice spoke briefly to our concerns: "There's a concept called—in marketing and in society—social acceptance, which means that as your product or your brand generally [develops] to a point where if somebody mentions [the] Desert Eagle pistol, they know what it is. And that's what we attempt to do with the Desert Eagle pistol—is just get it to the point where people know what it is, what it can do, understand it. And so early on we worked with [the] print medium, we worked with most of the prop masters, weapons masters in the country, and the rest is history. The pistol just works its own magic, because it's just such a cool-looking piece of goods."

> I was made to kill, that's why they keep me concealed
> Under car seats, they sneak me in clubs
> Been in the hands of mad thugs
> They feed me when they load me wit' mad slugs
> Seventeen precisely, one in my head
> They call me Desert Eagle, semi-auto with lead
> — Nas, "I Gave You Power," off *It Was Written* (1996)

Other rappers have taken a gun's point of view in their poetry, but none has done it better than Queensbridge's Nas. From a top-drawer meeting with a defaced Tec-9 to jamming in a life-or-death shoot-out against another, newer Desert Eagle, the song tells a story of firearms that's more familiar to many urbanites than the industry's usual sporting pastorals and nightmarish self-defence scenarios. There are just a couple of small but instructive inaccuracies in "I Gave You Power."

First, while a few competing pistols hold seventeen rounds, that's not Magnum Research's market niche. The Desert Eagle XIX, for example, holds nine rounds of .357 Magnum, eight rounds of .44 Magnum and just seven rounds of .50 calibre AE ammunition. Second, its use in crime is relatively rare. The Desert Eagle is largely a status symbol. It's pretty, expensive and tough to conceal.

A specialist with the Forensic Firearms Unit of the Vancouver Police Department, Robert Caunt examines guns retrieved from local crime scenes. Caunt told us that the only time he'll see a Desert Eagle is when cops confiscate a husband's guns after a domestic disturbance call. As John Risdall explained when Chris returned his call, "If somebody's got one, they're not selling it. It's in their collection. They're keeping it. That's the cool part: we don't get footballed around."

For Nas, the brand name of Risdall's pistol just sounded hot. And it wasn't the first instance of the name working well on wax. "The first time we knew Desert Eagle was in a song," Risdall said, "was Sammy Paul and 'Desert Eagle Talk' about fifteen years ago. You into that one?"

"That one I don't know so well. I gotta look it up." It was actually reggae artist Frankie Paul who released the track in 1991 on *Should I*, one of over a hundred albums he recorded.

John Risdall

"I scanned the [Magnum Research] site," Chris said to Risdall, "and you include all the stuff on movies and video games. I was more curious about your attitude towards Magnum products appearing in hip-hop music."

"Music is music," he answered. "What's the point?"

"So it doesn't matter if it comes up in a criminal context?"

"I don't think so. That's gonna happen. What can I do about it? I mean, it's just how it is. I think art doesn't try and pervert reality; art tries to sort of reflect reality. So in the *National Treasure* movie,

Baby Eagles were in the hands of the bad guys. That doesn't bother me a bit. I'd hate to see, heaven forbid, a Desert Eagle shooting the Pope or something like that, 'cause I'd prefer people not to even think of my product in those terms—and yet that could happen. So I would much rather it be a picture of God and he had one in two holsters."

John Risdall's company made the Desert Eagle, but it took Andre 3000 of Atlanta's OutKast to make it pink. Wearing white pearls and a sash and hat to match, Dre grips the smoking engraved pink pistol on the cover of OutKast's 2003 double disc *Speakerboxxx/The Love Below*, which went diamond (over 10 million sold) and won a Grammy for album of the year. "I suspect that Andre 3000 pistol would be a smash," said Jeton Ademaj, a member of the New York City chapter of the Pink Pistols, a gay pro-gun group, "if it were widely marketing at a competitive price!"

Unlike other gun manufacturers, who were clueless to all things hip-hop, John Risdall was at least a little familiar with the famous ATLiens and Dre's use of his product. "Is that [customization] something you guys do internally," Chris asked, "or did he do that privately?"

"That's a . . . uhh, what the heck is that? Oh God . . . Oh boy," John answered eagerly. "I can tell you the finish, but what he's done on top of one of our standard finishes is he's also done some engraving on that gun, and so that is *special*. That could've either been done by a real gun engraver or it could've obviously been done in Photoshop too, so who's to say?"

Risdall added, "I love that album too."

"You're one of the few industry people who actually knows any-thing about hip-hop."

"Well, how can you miss OutKast, though? It's like, for a year there, did they get any airtime? From the NBA All-Star game to every-thing," he said, laughing.

Risdall encouraged Chris to try shooting a Desert Eagle for him-self, except Vancouver ranges don't rent guns. "So go to Toronto," Risdall advised. "I got a great friend in Toronto, runs the big gun company up there—Para-Ordnance."

"Those guys were a little more reluctant to talk."

"They're brilliant guys. A guy named Thanos Polyzos runs Para."

"He's a lawyer by training, isn't he?"

"Yeah, he's really sharp. Sweetheart of a guy."

"I imagine. Their products have kinda come out of nowhere to make an impact, haven't they?"

"He does a really nice job. He's a very sharp guy; runs a great company, and a very responsible company."

TOP GUNS

Niggas pullin' guns on me damn near drove me crazy
— Lil Scrappy, "Be Real," off *Lil Scrappy* (2004)

In April 2006, we asked twenty-three-year-old Lil Scrappy, the G-Unit's Georgian affiliate, about the guns he's seeing used in crime in his city.

"AKs, pumps and Desert Eagles—the new shit."

"Do you see Desert Eagles in the streets?"

"I don't see 'em *in* the streets," the young crunk king corrected us. "I see 'em *on* the street. Seein' 'em in the streets is like seein' 'em in a store or whatever. Seein' 'em on the streets is like actually when you see a nigga wit' it. They get in the club with that mutherfucker." But while Lil Scrappy claims illegal Eagles are preying on his native Atlanta, the bird doesn't register in the metropolis that most of his G-Unit brethren call home. Here's a list of the crime guns most frequently recovered by the law in NYC in 2005, according to the ATF.

1. Smith & Wesson .38	236
2. Hi-Point 9mm	199
3. Smith & Wesson 9mm	134
4. Raven MP25	123
5. Bryco 9mm	122
6. Bryco .380	121
7. Lorcin .380	119
8. Ruger 9mm	114
9. Glock 9mm	109
10. Mossberg 12-gauge	96
11. Davis .380	95
12. Hi-Point .380	94
13. Smith & Wesson .357	89

JUNK IN THE TRUNK

In the seventies, car developer Lee Iacocca set out to build a car that met two criteria: it had to cost less than $2,000 and weigh less than two thousand pounds. This recipe for lemonade created the Ford Pinto, a car with major design flaws. "Pintos leave you with that warm feeling," ad copy said. When struck from behind at high speed, Pintos folded up like accordions, trapping everyone inside and oozing gas everywhere. One spark and you were lemon pie. Ford identified the problem before the lemon hit the stands and estimated that it would cost just a few dollars to sweeten the mix and fix it, but winced and let their sour creation hit the market as it was. "People who work for corporations often must develop a split personality," University of British Columbia law professor and author of *The Corporation* Joel Bakan said of a similar situation involving General Motors. "One, their human, normal, moral sensibility; and the other their amoral corporate persona. It's almost like they check their morality at the door when they go to work."

So if the Desert Eagle is the Hummer of guns—oversized, flamboyant and hard to handle in street situations (i.e., mostly meant to stunt)—what is the Pinto of the gun world? Actually, the right question is, What *are* the Pintos of the gun world?

Hip-Hop music is not the place to learn about Pintos; it's often an aspirational art form. Everybody's seen hoopties—that's real life. They want to hear about Cadillac Escalades equipped with twenty-four-inch rims and Lamborghini doors—that's rap life. So while rap lyrics are riddled with references to more prestigious handgun makers such as Glock and Ruger, you'll very rarely hear mentions of Bryco, Jennings, Phoenix, Raven, Hi-Point or Lorcin, even though millions of these guns are in circulation. In a culture that espouses reality, it's a glaring contradiction.

Truth is, just as your first ride probably won't be a mayonnaise-coloured Mercedes, the average youth's first firearm probably won't be a gold-plated Desert Eagle. As Whit Collins said of the drug trade, "The entry-level tool is still a cheap pistol." Starting at under $100, these junk guns—more popularly called Saturday night specials—are very cheap commodities, so much so that they tend to get passed around quickly and frequently, trickling down to the poorest and youngest members of society. The ATF's 2000 crime-gun trace reports show that for juveniles (seventeen years old and younger), six of the ten most frequently traced crime guns are Saturday night specials. In contrast, traces for adults twenty-five years and older showed that these guns comprised only two of the top ten.

Motown's Royce Da 5'9", promoting his newest album over a cell-phone from a Burger King in Jersey, explained how he purchased his first junk gun. "I was sixteen when I had my first gun," he said. "It was a .38 and I bought it from one of my friends. If it's a crew that's gettin' money, they carry designer guns. They carry Smith & Wessons, Rugers, Glocks, shit like that. Regular niggas that's not getting money like that, they just carry, like, old things—old .357s, scuffed-up guns, guns that look like somebody tossed them and then they got 'em."

"How'd your friend get it?" Rodrigo asked, referring to Royce's first gun.

After pausing for a second, he answered, "I have no idea."

Sunny southern California served as ground zero for the major junk-gun makers in the 1990s. These manufacturers, collectively dubbed the Ring of Fire, took pride in serving everyman and promoted their companies as equal-opportunity armourers. Bruce Jennings founded Bryco, a Ring of Fire company that produced 251,163 of these cheap handguns in 1993 alone. In a June 1997 episode, Jennings told PBS's *Frontline*, "Our main contribution has been that we have supplied millions of firearms legitimately to the vast population of the lower-income groups."

Jim Waldorf, Jennings's high-school friend and founder of another Ring of Fire company, Lorcin, took the argument one step further on the same *Frontline* program, "Hot Guns": "When you start looking at prohibiting ownership of a firearm based on the price of a firearm, you've just told a very large segment of society that because they don't belong to an elitist class, they have no right to defend their family." Waldorf would later add that taking away Lorcin's right to produce guns for the low-income market is "as discriminatory as slavery."

While the fraternity of fire liked to portray themselves as egalitarian defenders of the Second Amendment, the affordability of their products also meant that purchasers paid a steep price in quality. Most quality handguns are made from a combination of steel and wood, and increasingly from polymers. But cheap guns are often made of zinc, a relatively soft metal, which allows the manufacturers to use inferior machining techniques. This in turn creates less precise guns. Some manufacturers also cut costs by eliminating life-saving features like safeties, which prevent accidental firing. As a result, junk guns jam frequently, shoot inaccurately, are less durable and can be more dangerous to users than to their intended targets.

> Got the Raven two-five inside of my denim
> Some said I was the child with the devil in him
> — Prince Markie Dee, "Ghetto Bound," off *Free* (1992)

In 1968 the U.S. Congress passed new gun control laws that imposed standards of size, quality and performance on imported handguns. The new restrictions effectively ended importation of European-manufactured Saturday night specials, which up until then had dominated the American market. Recognizing the opportunity for domestic manufacturers, George Jennings, Bruce's father, transformed his airplane parts factory into the first of the Ring of Fire companies, Raven Arms, and began production in 1970. Raven manufactured just one gun, the MP25, a .25 calibre semi-automatic handgun that would sell over three million units in twenty years.

Raven Arms and later the rest of the RoF companies produced guns that were more easily concealed and had greater capacity and larger calibres than those made in Europe. Consequently, legislation that was meant to protect citizens from cheap handguns ultimately resulted in the streets being flooded with even more lethal weaponry—at the same price point, no less—but with a nice big "Made in America" stamp. The Ring of Fire's success translated into havoc on the streets. From 1989 to 1996 two Ring guns, Raven's MP25 and Lorcin's L380, monopolized the top spot for the ATF's most frequently traced crime guns. During those years, which saw the homicide rate in the United States rise from 7.9 per 100,000 citizens in 1984 to 9.5 per 100,000 citizens in 1994—an increase of nearly six thousand deaths—Ring of Fire brands would figure in 60 percent of all ATF crime-gun traces.

The release of the ATF's findings would spur numerous criticisms of the Ring of Fire companies. Bryco's Bruce Jennings responded on *Frontline*: "The concept that our guns would be used more in crime is incorrect. Our products are used the same as anybody else's products." Waldorf's retort on the same program followed similar logic. "Let me ask you this question," he said. "Are there more Chevrolets in accidents than there are Mercedes? I would just assume that there probably are. And it doesn't mean that Chevrolet contributes to motor vehicle accidents. It just means that there are more Chevys out there than there are Mercedes."

The "old line," as Tom Diaz calls the established American handgun manufacturers—Colt, Smith & Wesson and Ruger—eagerly distinguish between their products and junk guns, portraying themselves as honourable artisans and junk-gun makers as irresponsible miscreants. Ruger's motto, "Arms makers for responsible citizens," elevates its customers and denigrates the competition. Smith & Wesson's "Trust. Quality. Innovation" recalls the company's storied history and sets the stage for the future. On the other hand, Lorcin's motto—"The world's most affordable handguns"—did not exactly win friends in an industry that places a premium on quality and tradition. But in the end the dollars were too hard to ignore. As sales rose for the Ring of Fire, the old line fell in line and began to produce lower-priced guns.

In 1997, after eight years of Ring of Fire domination of the ATF's crime-gun list, Smith & Wesson's .38 Special revolver, a handgun that costs about three times as much as most RoF firearms, took the top slot. In fact, the old line had wholly re-emerged, claiming six of the ten spots. Increasingly criminals were interested in using quality handguns—the same marketing techniques used to sway the general public had worked on them as well.

In the end, negative media attention and, more significantly, lawsuits, ended the Ring of Fire's reign. But their demise was not the end of the downscale market. Companies such as Hi-Point and Cobra Enterprises have picked up the torch of low-priced power.

Hi-Point, which produces several semi-automatics for just over $100, as well as an eight-round .380 that can be purchased for $80, has emerged as the new down-market leader. Hi-Point's output doesn't approach that of the Ring of Fire companies in the nineties, in part because of competition from the old line, but in 2003 Hi-Point still sold 81,150 pistols, up from 66,994 in 2002. Sales continue to rise because of Hi-Point's no-hassle lifetime guarantee and improved product reliability—relative to the Ring of Fire, that is.

Hi-Point also operates Haskell Manufacturing and Iberia Firearms. The three companies produced 101,670 handguns in 2004. The head of the operation, Charlie Brown, defends his handguns with the same logic as his low-price predecessors, telling *Shooting Times* in an October 6, 2005, article, "[Our guns] are used for the exact same things that all the other gunmakers' guns are used for! They offer a man/woman who may not have an extra $300 to $700 for a gun, a gun that's reliable and affordable."

We spoke to Charlie Brown himself in March 2006, when Rodrigo accidentally called him directly while looking for a contact at his company (every other number he'd found was out of service). After Rodrigo explained that we were working on a book about "gun culture," Brown forcefully asked, "What exactly is 'gun culture'?"

Rodrigo tried to clarify. "I'd rather not talk to you," came the response, which was followed by the slamming down of his receiver.

A few minutes later Rodrigo called Brown again. "Let me explain myself—" he started.

Instead, Brown interrupted, "You saying to a gun manufacturer that you're working on a book about gun culture is like calling a police officer and saying you're working on a book about pigs." Mr. Brown wouldn't answer any questions that day, but did say, "I'm just bombarded by the media, when I'm just a professional in a business making a product."

THE FREAKS COME OUT AT NIGHT

Newark, New Jersey, rapper Joe Budden was minding his own business doing what rappers do—in this case, playing with the new TVs in his ride—when a man rolled up on a bicycle and pulled a gun on Budden and crew. He pointed the weapon at Joe and pulled the trigger; it clicked, but didn't bang. Foiled, the two-wheeled would-be assassin sheepishly pleaded, "My bad, I was playin'," and sped away. A chase ensued, ending with the attacker's arrest. Asked what the piece looked like, Budden, well acquainted with most weapons but baffled by his assailant's unidentified armament, said, "It looked like some shit from out *The Jetsons*." The following pieces ain't from *The Jetsons*, but are otherworldly in their own way.

The Liberator

The junkiest of all junk guns, the Liberator was a single-shot "assassin" pistol produced by General Motors during the Second World War. At a cost of $2.10 a piece, a million were produced in eleven weeks, each made in less than seven seconds. Allied planes dropped them in plastic bags all over Europe, along with graphic instructions (no text), ten rounds of .45 calibre ACP and a little wooden stick to eject the cartridge after firing.

The Apache

If the Apache were marketed today, its motto might be "the only weapon that meets the demands of today's global thug." *Apache* was actually a Parisian term for thug, and this abomination of weapons was popular in early-1900s Europe. The compact Belgian-made weapon featured brass knuckles attached to a six-shot revolver and a folding knife.

The Kolibri

The Kolibri, German for "hummingbird," is the smallest functioning semi-automatic gun in history. Introduced in 1914 by designer Franz Pfannl, the Kolibri used a 2.7 mm cartridge, had a 1⅜-inch (3.5 cm) barrel and weighed eight ounces (220 g) fully loaded. It produced so little energy the "Hummingbird" could barely hurt a fly.

The Cell-Phone Gun

The cell-phone gun looks just like a regular black cellular, but when you press 5, 6, 7 or 8 it fires .22 calibre bullets through the antenna. The maker of the four-shot celly is unknown, but after numerous seizures in Eastern Europe they are believed to be coming from Yugoslavia. Finally, the cell-phone feature every terrorist has been waiting for!

CRIME SPRAYS

Stepping off the glass elevator onto the top floor of the Pan Pacific Hotel in San Francisco, Rodrigo was confronted by two members of 50 Cent's brolic bodyguard corps. The first one moved towards him and pushed his palm in the direction of Buns's chest. "You got any guns on you?" he asked aggressively.

Rodrigo looked at him incredulously. Standing nearby was Olivia, 50 Cent's petite R&B protegé. Buns quickly glanced at her, searching for an ally. She dropped her head slightly and smiled sweetly at him.

"I left them in my hotel room today." The gatekeepers laughed large and let him by. "Be good today," the other one said, slapping him on the back, still laughing. Rodrigo turned towards Olivia and smiled back.

Interscope, the company that distributes Fifty's records, had rented out the entire floor of the hotel for this particular press day. A few journalists were hanging around in post-interview ecstasy. Fifty, wearing clothes from his own $100-million-a-year brand, was holding court at a patio table outdoors. The publicist led Rodrigo to the table and Fifty stood up to greet him. He looked heavier than the first time we saw him backstage in Toronto, but calmer and more focused.

They sat down for some small talk before starting the interview. Fifty leaned forward. "What's your name?" he asked quietly.

"Rodrigo." He mimicked Fifty's movements, their faces inches apart.

"Where you from, Rodrigo?"

"Toronto," he said. Fifty smiled, a distinct dimple forming on his left cheek that was both interrupted and enhanced by a bullet wound.

Fiddy was in San Fran to kick off the radio promo tour for his record *The Massacre*. Rodrigo asked Fifty, who pleaded guilty to heroin trafficking in 1994, what the relationship is between trafficking and guns. "You need guns if you hustlin'," he said. "You need them to keep niggas off you. 'Cause as soon as you start gettin' money, you got those problems, you got jealousy issues. They'll eat you up. They'll run up in your house. They do what they gotta do to get the bread."

The title of 50 Cent's *The Massacre* was originally intended to be *The St. Valentine's Day Massacre,* a reference to the bloody 1929 shooting that left six members of George "Bugs" Moran's gang dead in a Chicago garage, but the album title was changed when the release date was pushed from February to March. Like the perpetrators of the original massacre, Fifty has a "get rich or die tryin'" attitude. It's a sentiment espoused by gangsters of all eras. Whether hawking heroin in South Jamaica, Queens, in the nineties or running rum across the Windsor Bridge in the twenties, if you make your living outside the law, you need to defend yourself without the law—and that generally means being armed with guns.

The St. Valentine's Day Massacre thugs chose the "Chicago typewriter"—better known as the Tommy gun—for their slaughter, because it was the most powerful firearm available at the time. Prohibition-era gangsters probably weren't in the habit of reading *Scientific American*, but that magazine proclaimed the Tommy gun "the most efficient mankiller of any firearm yet produced." Although the media dubbed it the Tommy gun and inventor General John Taliaferro Thompson eventually trademarked that nickname, its official name was the Thompson submachine gun. General Thompson had intended to create a weapon suitable for close combat in the First World War. His early designs incorporated larger rifle ammunition, but the Tommy gun used pistol ammunition, which allowed him to make a smaller, lighter weapon. That switch marked the invention of the submachine gun, distinguishing such firearms from assault rifles, which use rifle ammunition.

Unfortunately for Thompson, he didn't finalize his design until after the war ended. Having invested many years of his life creating the Tommy gun, Thompson and his design partners at Auto-Ordnance Inc. needed to recoup their investment, and were forced to seek non-military markets. Thompson's team originally targeted police departments, but the gun was too expensive for most forces. A single Tommy gun cost as much as eleven standard police pistols. Stymied, but too far in debt to turn back, Auto-Ordnance's owners directed their energy towards the civilian market, promoting their 725-round-per-minute creation as "the ideal weapon for protection." The underworld got the message. Colt would manufacture the first fifteen thousand Tommy guns.

The exploits of "Pretty Boy" Floyd, "Baby Face" Nelson, "Machine Gun" Kelly, Bonnie and Clyde, and John Dillinger would pound the Tommy into public consciousness. Thompson tried to control his creation's image, stating in advertisements that the gun was meant for "responsible parties," but it was too little, too late. Eighty years later, the Tommy gun is still synonymous with the mob era, the phrase "the gun that made the twenties roar" forever attached to its notorious silhouette.

Comin' up, I was taught never back down
That's why I act the way I act now, hold the MAC down
32 shots, squeeze 'til there ain't a shell left
Come with my gun smokin', you can smell death
— 50 Cent, "Fuck You," off *Guess Who's Back?* (2002)

In the July 1998 issue of *Shotgun News*, gun manufacturer Cobray ran an advertisement with the tagline "the gun that made the eighties roar." The allusion was obvious: Cobray's product, the MAC-11, was being positioned as the Tommy's heir to the crime-gun throne.

In the September 2006 issue of *XXL*, Fifty recalls a moment of clarity experienced years ago while carrying a MAC into a meeting full of his adversaries in the drug trade: "I had a MAC, 32 shot clip. I came to the building, and didn't go in. 'Cause my brain tells me— when I use it . . . you kill someone in that building, then you're done."

Fifty's MAC descended from its fully automatic predecessor the M-10, a gun designed by Gordon Ingram in 1964. When Ingram sold the rights to the Military Armament Corporation (MAC), the gun became the MAC-10. Ingram's goal had been to create an inexpensive, compact submachine gun. Capable of unloading its entire thirty-shot magazine in about two seconds, the MAC-10, with its utilitarian, blocky design, is a fearsome firearm. University of Toronto professor Mark Kingwell, an expert on the meaning of style and form, described the gun nicely. "MAC-10s have a kind of negative aesthetic," he told us. "They're chunky and kind of gangsterish."

Like the Tommy gun, the MAC-10 and its variants quickly became popular with the underground set. It sprays bullets in extremely rapid fire—ideal for unskilled criminals in tight situations. Detroit's Royce

MAC-10

Da 5'9" admitted that he had a MAC-11 in his personal arsenal. When asked why he would ever need such a weapon, he said, "I'm not that good of an aimer. I've got bad vision. If I ever have any problems, I ain't gonna aim, I'm just gonna start dumpin'."

Royce's admission underlines a problem both inherent in and intensified by small submachine guns like the MAC. The MAC's design does not facilitate control of the weapon, since holding it with two hands would require gripping the hot barrel. Additionally, its rapid firing exacerbates the problem by creating intense recoil, making controlling it even more difficult—it's a gun of the "spray and pray" variety.

As if it weren't enough that the MAC is a gun with little sporting purpose, it was also widely distributed and very affordable. In the twenties a Tommy gun sold for as much as $2,000 on the black market, a huge sum in those days. But the MAC-10, because of its simple design, was available in the eighties for less than $300. To compound matters, the many makers of the MAC line designed options and accessories that suited criminal needs: a suitcase that hid the gun, silencers, and semi-automatic versions that could be converted to full-auto in less than a minute.

Nigga respect mine or anger the Tec-9
Chi-chick-pow! Move from the gate now
— Raekwon, "C.R.E.A.M," off *Enter the Wu-Tang: 36 Chambers* (1993)

Perhaps the only challenger to the MAC-10's title as the most fear-some-looking firearm is Intratec's Tec-9. Although most people out-side of hip-hop culture have never heard of a Tec, they'd probably rec-ognize its frightening profile. Like the MAC-10, the Tec has been featured in countless movies and video games, from 1986's *Big Trouble in Little China* to 2005's *Crime Life: Gang Wars.* In hip-hop its status is legendary. Its extensive lyrical rap sheet, however, is dwarfed by its criminal rap sheet. While the Ring of Fire's total sales were in the millions, Tec-9's all-time sales were about two hundred thousand. Nonetheless, the gun continually found its way onto the ATF's top crime-guns list in the eighties and nineties.

It is the Tec's look that continues to appeal to many people. As Kansas City veteran emcee Tech N9ne told us, "When you look it up in one of the *Guns & Ammo* books, it'll tell you that it's known for its menacing look. And I think motherfuckers love the barrel on it, and I think it's a beautiful gun. It looks and it *spits* like a motherfucker."

The Tec-9, originally called the KG-9, was created in Sweden by Interdynamics. Defined aesthetically by its shrouded barrel, the compact submachine gun could "spit" out a thirty-two-round maga-zine in about 2.5 seconds. Realizing that the Swedes weren't inter-ested in such a gun, Interdynamics opened up shop in Miami, a more receptive market. The KG-9, which was easily converted to full-auto, would join the MAC guns as a favourite of drug dealers and gang-sters—an unsurprising result, since, like the MAC, the Tec-9 was too inaccurate to be a sporting gun and too big to be used for personal protection. But it was cheap, retailing for about $250 in the late eighties. And it looked mean.

Interdynamics, which was renamed Intratec in the mid-eighties, would not ignore their marginal market. Their advertising read "tougher than your toughest customer" and promoted their gun as "resistant to fingerprints." When their advertising drew controversy, Intratec pleaded innocent. They claimed the ads referred to the gun's resistance to fingerprint oils, which cause guns to rust. Their dubious intentions became more transparent when Intratec produced barrel screw-ons that looked like silencers but had no actual function—except to make an already intimidating gun look even deadlier.

Tec-9

When the federal assault-weapons ban came into effect in 1994, it outlawed the Tec-9's threaded barrel and thirty-two-round magazine from future production. To undermine the spirit of the law, Intratec changed the name of the Tec-9 to AB-10 (AB is rumoured to stand for "after ban"), removed the threaded barrel and included pre-ban thirty-two-round magazines (still legal because they were produced before the ban started) with each purchase of an AB-10.

Despite Intratec's efforts, production of their guns dropped from 75,102 in 1994 to 5,820 in 1996, according to ATF data, and they were forced to close up shop in 2001. Tec-9s have not been produced for eleven years, but they continue to show up on both real rap sheets and rappers' rap sheets. On his 2005 *Billboard* hit single "Bring 'Em Out," young Atlanta rapper T.I. shouts out the submachine gun: "Work well wit' 9s, AKs and Tecs." The infamous barrel shroud still holds its powers of seduction, proving that its menacing look and fearsome legacy in the street will not soon be forgotten.

FROM RUSSIA WITH SLUGS

"It's not the designer's fault or the weapon's fault when terrible things happen—it's the politicians'," Mikhail Kalashnikov told the Knight-Ridder online news service. It's a defence the legendary eighty-seven-year-old repeats like a mantra, insisting he actually "sleeps quite soundly."

According to the 2001 *Small Arms Survey*, approximately 347 million small arms were produced worldwide between 1945 and 2000. Of those, seventy to a hundred million were AK-47s, making Kalashnikov's AK the most manufactured firearm in history. In the nineties alone the AK-47 is credited with causing the majority of the three hundred thousand deaths that occurred annually in armed conflicts worldwide. It would seem like an incredible burden for anyone to carry, and Kalashnikov has had to answer for his gun more than any other weapons designer in history. This is due in part to the fact that he makes himself so available to the press. As Rebecca Peters, director of the International Action Network of Small Arms (IANSA), said from her office in London, "I think he likes to be in the limelight."

> Here's a murder rap to keep ya dancin'
> With a crime record like Charles Manson
> AK-47 is the tool
> Don't make me act a motherfuckin' fool
> — Ice Cube, "Straight Outta Compton," off N.W.A's
> *Straight Outta Compton* (1988)

Kalashnikov created his assault rifle for a simple reason. "I did it to protect the motherland," he said in the German documentary *Avtomat Kalashnikow*. But, like many of the facts surrounding the invention of the AK-47, this rationale has been doubted. Depending on whom you believe, Kalashnikov is either a visionary designer, a lucky beneficiary of the work of others or, even more disparagingly, a copycat.

Some details regarding Kalashnikov are clearer. Mikhail Timofeyvich Kalashnikov was born on November 10, 1919, two years after the October Revolution that created the communist Soviet

66

state. His large peasant family was exiled to Siberia, forced to eke out a gruelling and isolated existence as farmers. Kalashnikov joined the army, rising to become a tank sergeant in the Soviet fight against the Nazis in the Second World War. In a battle in Brjansk he was badly wounded and sent to a military hospital to recover. During his stay, Kalashnikov, who had no experience as a gun designer, became restless and began to think about designing firearms.

Upon his release from the hospital, Kalashnikov began submitting gun designs to various Soviet agencies. His abilities were soon recognized and he rose through the military hierarchy, quickly finding himself in the company of Russia's greatest gun designers. Kalashnikov's timing was perfect. The Russians were very interested in equalizing the balance of firepower after the Germans had equipped their soldiers with the infamous MP44. The MP44 combined the size and speed of a submachine gun with the power of a rifle, and it proved ideal for modern warfare. Hitler called the firearm *Sturmgewehr*—literally, "storm rifle"—a name that would be commonly translated as "assault rifle" and would come to define a whole class of guns.

AK-47

A surface examination of the AK-47 reveals an obvious similarity to the MP44. According to Whit Collins, "the Kalashnikov and its cartridge are copies of the German *Sturmgewehr*." Less cynically, many accept that Kalashnikov submitted his MP44-influenced design when the Soviets held a competition after the war to create a comparable assault rifle. Upon approval of his first design, Kalashnikov put together a team of specialists who could focus on specific aspects of the weapon in order to meet the state-imposed deadline. Finally, after many prototypes, the Avtomat Kalashnikova Model 47 won, and was put into production by the Soviet military in 1949.

Today the term *AK* is used to describe a whole family of guns that differ incrementally, as improvements were made over the years. The most common of these are the AK-47, the AKM and the AK-74. Despite differences in cartridges, barrel length and other features, the defining characteristics of all AKs are robustness, simplicity, low maintenance requirements and ease of duplication. These qualities have made the AK an ideal weapon for modern warfare, enabling it to become the world's most popular firearm. "The weapons have become so widely used," Kalashnikov, by now a lieutenant-general, told us, "thanks to the perfect construction and high exploitation and fighting qualities."

I got that AK with me
Don't play with me
Because I'm spittin' non-stop
Anything within my target—chop, chop
— B.G., "Represent," off *Chopper City* (1997)

The man who coined the term *bling-bling* also conceived a more sinister phrase. Original Cash Money Millionaire member B.G.—which stands for Baby Gangster—explained why he named New Orleans "Chopper City." "We call AKs choppers in New Orleans," he said. "At one point in time in New Orleans, like '94, '95, '96, that's all motherfuckers was usin'. That's all niggas was sprayin' in the corners, was AKs. So I nicknamed New Orleans Chopper City way back when." When Tupac was killed in '96, his killer used an AK-47.

"I am always very sorry and very much distressed," Kalashnikov commented, "when the guns bearing my name are used by criminal units and terrorists." Despite the distress on the general's conscience, Kalashnikovs have become known as "bin-Ladens" on U.S. streets since 9/11.

Queens rapper Tragedy Khadafi, who rapped under the name Intelligent Hoodlum when he first emerged in the late eighties, described the rifle this way: "The AK-47 is a motherfuckin' street-sweeper. That shit lays shit down." As a result of that now notorious power, the AK-47 was 2005's most frequently mentioned weapon in *Billboard*'s Top 20 singles, according to American Brandstand, getting thirty-three shout-outs—good for tenth place overall, but still behind luxury-item brands Cristal and Louis Vuitton.

In September 2002 MTV reported that Atlanta's Killer Mike had wanted to call a track off his debut album "AK-47," in honour of the famous assault rifle. But his friend and industry mentor, OutKast's Big Boi, convinced Killer to call the cut "AKshon (Yeah!)," in order to make the song more radio-friendly. "It was supposed to be called 'AK-47,' because that's the revolution's gun," Killer Mike told us of the track. "People throughout Third World countries that are fighting against oppressive regimes, imperialism, things of that nature, that's the gun of choice, the Russian-made AK-47. So it was just symbolic of me saying I was goin' against the grain of what's on the radio." The AK gets a lot of press in North America, but its presence is felt more significantly elsewhere.

"I've seen pictures of ten-year-old boys holdin' the Kalashnikov," said U.K. rapper Klashnekoff, a.k.a. the Black Russian, illuminating the more prevalent use of his namesake. "When I looked at it, it was like, these people don't have anything. Voting doesn't work for them, and tryin' to talk to the politicians don't work for them. So they have to go for their Kalashnikovs to liberate themselves."

As director of IANSA, Rebecca Peters confronts the deadly effects of the AK on a daily basis. Nevertheless, she maintains her sense of humour regarding Kalashnikov and his gun. "There seems to be every now and then," she said, "a film or an article about General Kalashnikov celebrating the something-millionth gun, or some anniversary of the most successful killing machine. I guess it's the most widely replicated gun. I read somewhere that he said that he would rather have invented a lawnmower that sold millions and millions of copies around the world. I wish he'd invented the lawnmower too."

When Kalashnikov designed the AK sixty years ago, he was not granted any patents on the gun—only the Soviet equivalent, an "author's certificate." As part of the proletariat workforce, as Kalashnikov explained to the *Moscow Times*, he "didn't get a single kopek." He did receive a lump sum of 150,000 rubles, enough to buy him ten cars at the time. But considering the success of his weapon, by capitalist standards his lifestyle today is far from opulent. After witnessing the 2002 legal battle between several Russian arms makers for the rights to the AK, which was eventually won by Russia's Izhmash, Kalashnikov elaborated: "I didn't have a patent. This is not fair. I was in America and know how other designers live, but I am a child of that time and had to live [with] the laws. I didn't make anything."

During the height of the Cold War, the Soviets put millions of AK-47s into circulation, giving them away to countries and armed forces they believed could advance communist ideology world-wide. According to the 2004 *Small Arms Survey*, AKs now serve the militaries of seventy-eight different countries. At least nine-teen countries produce the AK on a large scale, and a handful more manufacture smaller quantities. A few are even being made by hand in Pakistani households.

The modern-day Russian attitude towards the AK is informed more by dollars than by doctrine. As Rebecca Peters said, "The Russians in the U.N. conference [on illicit small arms in 2005] were complaining that Chinese copies of the AK-47, cheap copies, have flooded into Sudan and they're not marked. They look like Kalashnikovs, they look like the Russian gun, and so Russia is complaining that they're getting bad press from being the suppliers of guns in Sudan." She added later, with a laugh, "They're probably just cranky 'cause they missed out on the contract."

The Russians have their work cut out for them. Not only is the gun made illegally in small underground factories worldwide, it is also blatantly imitated. "If we make pirated CDs, it is considered a crime," Pyotr Litavrin, deputy head of security and disarmament at the Russian foreign ministry, complained in the *Moscow Times*. "But when it comes to weapons, which is more serious, they turn a blind eye to it."

As a result, Russia has moved to have the AK's intellectual property rights recognized by the U.N. And while Russia battles the world for rights to the AK-47, the world continues to battle, for right or wrong, with the AK-47. These millions of guns create an ever-mounting death toll that the World Policy Institute's William Hartung told us grows incrementally, but unceasingly. "If you have fifty, a hundred people armed with those," he said of AKs, "they go into a village and they're intent on doing mayhem, they can slaughter a couple of hundred people in short order. If that is repeated day after day and month after month in a civil war, pretty soon you can tear apart the fabric of a whole society."

KALASHING IN

When British entrepreneur John Florey finally caught up with General Kalashnikov after two years of searching, the two men sat down for, as Florey described it, "a very, very long lunch and a lot of vodka." Somewhere between shots of the transparent liquor, Florey charmed the general: "You have one of the strongest brands to ever come out of Russia." Kalashnikov, still active in his eighties, looked at Florey and said, "I know." Sensing an opening, the Brit made his pitch: "Do you think we can have a discussion on how we can extend that?" "Absolutely," Kalashnikov answered, hoping some of these products might take a little of the sting off his name and legacy—and maybe add a little bling to his personal life.

Kalashnikov Vodka
Who: Kalashnikov Joint Stock Vodka Company
Where: United Kingdom
What: A £19 "premium" vodka that features Kalashnikov's face on the inside of the bottle. Promoted in British clubs by a team of pseudo-military but genuinely scantily clad "Nikita" girls.
Kalashing in? The general gets a percentage and is honorary chairman of the company.

Vodka Kalashnikov
Who: LVZ Glazov
Where: Russia
What: Made from sugar, glycerin, salt and vanilla, this vodka apparently wasn't much liked by Mikhail himself. Comes in a glass bottle shaped like the rifle, with individually numbered dog-tags included.
Kalashing in? What's a ruble worth, anyway?

Kalashnikov Umbrellas

Who: MMI Company

Where: Germany

What: The general's grandson Igor Krasnovski struck a deal with MMI to put Kalashnikov's name on a whole range of products, including pens, energy drinks, umbrellas and snowboards.

Kalashing in? Kalashnikov owns 30 percent of the company, but hasn't seen a dime from the Germans.

Kalashnikov Lamp

Who: Philippe Starck

Where: France

What: Renowned designer Starck introduced a line of lamps that feature guns as their shafts. Explaining his creation to *Metropolis* magazine, he said, "The first thing for us to remember is that creativity has a duty of political action. [Our governments] create dictators, we sell them weapons, they kill people of their country, and we try to kill them when we cannot use them any more."

Kalashing in? Hell no!

AK MP3 Jukebox

Who: Audiobooksforfree.com

Where: United Kingdom

What: An MP3 player built into the magazine of the rifle. The creators hope their 20 GB MP3 player will ensure that "many militants and terrorists will use their AK-47s to listen to music and audiobooks. They need to chill out and take it easy."

Kalashing in? Nobody makes money on the Internet.

Kalashnikov Guitars

Who: César Lopez

Where: Columbia

What: Called *escopetarras*, a combination of the Spanish words *escopeta* (shotgun) and *guitarra* (guitar), designer and street musician César López told the *Miami Herald*, "We found the worst human invention, which is the gun, and the most beautiful, which could be a guitar, and in the end . . . the gun dies and the guitar is born."

Kalashing in? "We're not trying to sell them," López said. "We're just trying to get the word out."

BLACK RIFLES

While Major-General Kalashnikov lives out his retirement in relative poverty, his American counterpart, Eugene Stoner, died a rich and rather less recognizable figure. A U.S. marine who fought in the Second World War, Stoner was chief engineer with ArmaLite, then a division of the Fairchild Engine and Airplane Corporation, from the mid- to late 1950s. During that time Stoner was a central contributor to the development of a rifle known nearly as well around the world as the AK-47.

The fifteenth in a series of ArmaLite designs, the AR-15 featured a unique gas-operated firing mechanism in a polymer-and-metal rifle. Stoner's innovation allowed for a lighter, more accurate weapon. Always quick to capitalize on the genius of firearms engineers outside the company, Colt licensed the military rights to the rifle in 1959. Although Armalite retains limited rights to produce and sell their AR-15, Stoner left the company the next year to act as consultant to Colt.

Updated to fire selectively in semi- or fully automatic modes, the Colt-manufactured AR-15 was adopted as the standard rifle of the U.S. Army on February 28, 1967, and designated the M-16. In the decades since, ArmaLite has watched its most famous firearm become a critical money-maker for Connecticut-based Colt. Colt's website provides a complete list of countries that "have bought Colt weapon systems [primarily the M-16]," including Haiti, Indonesia, Liberia and Iran.

In April 2003 we spoke with the current president of ArmaLite, Mark Westrom. Like Stoner a firearms engineer and veteran of the U.S. military, he compared the M-16 with the AK-47. "They're based for two different armies," Westrom explained. "They're both very good rifles. The AK-47 is not made to be very accurate. It's made for close-in, fast battle, very rugged, something that can be handled by relatively less experienced soldiers. The AR-15 suits American military doctrine, which calls for more accurate shooting. And that's what allows the rifle to be so flexible for other uses like hunting and target shooting and such."

There aren't too many rappers we can be sure know much about either AK-47s or AR-15s. There is at least one rap artist, however, about whose expertise we have no doubt.

Losin' my patience, maybe I been here too long

But y'all is fittin' to pay me back for those soldiers not goin' home
Seen too many of us wounded, I won't be the next one
So the only Arabic I'm speakin' is gettin' spoke through this gun
— Big Neal, "I Ride," off 4th25's *Live from Iraq* (2005)

When we spoke to twenty-nine-year-old Sergeant Neal Saunders, a.k.a Big Neal, he'd already made it safely back to the U.S. Army's Fort Hood in Killeen, Texas. Unlike a couple of thousand others who never saw their families and friends again, Big Neal returned from his tour of duty in Iraq in one piece. He brought with him what he called "the realest album ever produced. The only album that was ever produced in theatre about conflict, about war." Big Neal used his free time in Iraq to build a makeshift studio and form a group with other soldiers they named 4th25 (pronounced "fourth quarter"). Neal himself handled most of the rapping and production on *Live from Iraq*'s fifteen songs. In June 2005 *Newsweek* reported, "Rap is becoming the pulse of the Iraq war, as the sounds of Jimi Hendrix and Jim Morrison were for Vietnam."

"What did you use over there—M-16?" Chris asked Big Neal.

"Well, M-16, M-4—same thing. The M-4 is just a shorter, lighter version of the M-16."

Associated Press reported in August 2003 that, contrary to army policy, U.S. troops were using AK-47s confiscated from Iraqis—in part because of a shortage of rifles and also for the "psychological effect on the enemy when you fire back on them with their own weapons." On his website, Neal posted images of a silver AK-47 with bayonet, taken from the cache of a local bomb maker, and photographed on the keyboard of 4th25's Iraq studio.

"I mean, you'll see pictures of soldiers with them and you'll shoot 'em," Neal admitted. "But the thing is, we don't carry that ammunition, so all that shit we just kinda stockpile and keep, and save it for the Iraqi police or bodyguards."

Initially criticized by U.S. troops in Vietnam for the small bullet it fired and problems with jamming, the M-16 has developed to a point where at least a few soldiers are satisfied with its performance in the

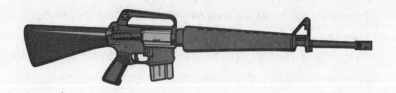

M-16

field. "Well, me, shit, an AK-47 is fully auto, so you just wastin' ammunition," Neal pointed out. "Then, the rounds are big. That kinda shit gets heavy, you luggin' that around all day. You can carry more ammunition with the shit that we use, and it's smaller, more accurate. It's just what I'm used to shootin', so I'll take my M-4 over a AK." Beyond Big Neal, the many references in rap music to the AR-15 and M-16 become substantially less credible.

"Honestly, none of these guys are riding around with an AR-15 in their car," Trigger Tha Gambler joked. "Because you can't toss it if you gettin' chased by some damn police." But Mississippi's gold-selling rap king David Banner owns a couple. "I have two AR-15s," he said eagerly. "I have an AR-15, the assault sniper rifle, but then I also have the AR-15 pistol. The AR-15 short pistol is my favourite gun."

Mark Westrom spoke to us about his company's consumer base among the rap ranks: "I think a lot of it is history, because ArmaLite is where [the M-16] started. And the other [reason] is [that] a lot of the entertainers have pretty good income, and they can go out and afford to frankly buy a little bit higher-quality piece of gear."

"I just hope that their appreciation doesn't show up in their music," Westrom qualified. "Rap music is like any music: there are positive messages and negative ones. And we sure hope to stay out of the negative ones."

Ride on the record labels! Chump your A&R's!
Fuck the contract! Grease the AR!
— dead prez, "Fuck the Law," *off Get Free or Die Tryin'* (2003)

dead prez's music grows from the seeds of revolutionary consciousness planted by the Black Panther Party. As with the Panthers, dp's
stic.man and M-1 are committed to self-defence by any means necessary. In other words, they aren't afraid to hit the range. We asked stic
and M-1 about their references to the AR-15.

"The AR-15?" stic.man said, somewhat surprised. "Ask Bush. All
his troops got 'em."

"They use it in the army," M-1 clarified.

"It go through all kind of shit, dog," stic came back. "It go
through concrete, it go through police vest, it go through all that. So
the AR-15, man, I ain't make one, I ain't create it—ask Oliver North
and them about slangin' 'em."

"Yeah, assault rifles," M-1 added. "That's what they're made to do:
assault a motherfucker."

"Somehow we ended up with 'em in our hood," stic said. "I don't
know how, but they around."

"You can find ARs that easily?"

"I ain't lookin for 'em," stic answered. "They already there. They
found us." It's no shock that ARs have ended up in stic.man and M-1's
'hood. According to Colt, of the estimated eight million M-16s it has
manufactured, "more than 90 percent remain in service." At the
same time, another dozen-odd American companies produce AR-15
clones, mostly for civilian consumers, adding to the millions that
have already been produced.

> For God so loved the world, every man packs an M-16
> — Wyclef Jean, "John 3:16," off *DJ Muggs*
> *Presents the Soul Assassins* (1997)

In August 1999 *Salon* reported that Richard Dyke, the owner of
Bushmaster, had resigned three weeks earlier as George W. Bush's
chief campaign fundraiser in the state of Maine. Dyke had personally
given to Bush's campaign the maximum individual contribution
allowed by law, and had raised "tens of thousands" more to help then
Governor Bush take over the White House. The resignation came
after a reporter called the campaign office to inquire about Bush's

connection to Dyke. Evidently having an assault rifle maker as one of your leading fundraisers was just too much PR to manage. As it turned out, Dyke withdrew at just the right time.

On August 10, 1999, a mentally ill white supremacist, Buford Furrow, walked into a Jewish community centre in a Los Angeles suburb and let loose seventy bullets, wounding five people, including three small children. An hour later Furrow murdered a Philippines-born postal worker, Joseph Ileto, with a Glock Model 26. Hours after these hate crimes were committed, President Bill Clinton told reporters, "Once again our nation has been shaken and our hearts torn by an act of gun violence." For his assault on the community centre, Furrow had selected a relatively inexpensive but powerful rifle: the Bushmaster AR-15.

In 2001, citing data collected by the ATF, the company crowed on its website, "Bushmaster is #1 again." Compared with the higher-priced Colt and ArmaLite, which produced 29,950 and 8,475 AR-15s in 2000, respectively, Bushmaster turned out a whopping 39,932 AR-15s during the same period. Bushmaster's success that year helped keep more than one politician indebted to Richard Dyke.

On March 20, 2000, *The New York Times* reported: "Hillary Rodham Clinton's spokesman yesterday accused Mayor Rudolph W. Giuliani of using what appeared to be a typographical error to mask the identity of a donor." That same day, *The Washington Post* waxed pun-etic on 2000's New York Senate race, writing that Giuliani's campaign finance report was "missing a little ire." The report had listed a contribution from Richard Dyke as a donation from the chairman of "Bushmaster Farms."

According to its website, "Bushmaster has always tried to be open and honest with the press in an effort to help them see the other side and to educate them on the real issues." They did not respond to our repeated requests for an interview. Instead, we asked ArmaLite's Mark Westrom about the use of AR-15s in crime. "The misuse of rifles of all sorts, and especially rifles like ours, is very, very rare," he said. "Mostly it's shotguns, cheap handguns or stolen handguns, and very inexpensive rifles." On its website Bushmaster also champions the appropriateness of their AR-15 for the civilian market, maintaining, "Our rifle is a smaller caliber than most hunting rifles on the market."

"That's not the point," Tom Diaz said, rebutting the argument. "The point is the design features of these guns. The ability to accept high-capacity magazines—you know, 20, 40, 100, 120 rounds of ammunition in one loading, the way they are designed to be fired in a sort of spray fashion." Mark Westrom's answer did avoid a major issue: assault rifles' devastating potential to kill when they *are* used.

We first heard assault rifles referred to as "weapons of mass destruction" during an online radio interview with William Hartung. Since then it's become a politically trendy way to refer to small arms. We put the designation to Big Neal. "It sounds good to me," he said, "and I'll tell you what, you put somebody behind a 240 machine gun or an RPK [a light machine-gun version of the AK-47] or any kind of machine gun—I don't give a fuck what kind of machine gun it is—yeah, if he knows what he's doing, he's got a weapon of mass destruction, 'cause he can fuck some shit up."

HOW THE PYRAMID WAS BUILT

"Tomorrow's wars will be fought in the unmapped streets and alleys of the Third World's sprawling slums," predicted a September 1998 story in *Popular Mechanics* on the Pentagon's OICW (objective individual combat weapon). In addition to a primary barrel designed to fire .223 calibre rifle rounds, a second barrel on the impractical monstrosity shoots "high explosive air-bursting fragmentation" ammunition, which can be programmed to detonate after penetrating a wall of sheet metal—a feature, said the magazine, that "could be especially useful in Third World shantytowns, where abandoned or pirated cargo containers are popular building materials." Here are a few more creations representing the system's core values.

Bertha
Creator: Metal Storm
Capacity: Partly financed by the Pentagon's highly secret, taxpayer-funded DARPA (Defense Advanced Research Projects Agency), the Guinness-record-holding Bertha is an electronic gun designed in Australia by physicist Mike O'Dwyer. Functioning like an inkjet printer, with electric impulses cuing the release of rounds from stacked barrels at "infinitely tailorable rates and sequences," in the words of *Guns* magazine, Bertha, a thirty-six-barrel

9mm prototype, successfully fired 180 bullets in about 0.01 of a second, a rate of more than one million rounds per minute. CNN reported that the world's most advanced ballistic weapon can "shred a target in a blink of an eye, or throw up a defensive wall against an incoming missile."

Active Denial System (ADS)
Creator: Raytheon, CPI, Malibu Research
Capacity: Classed as "less lethal" by the Pentagon, an ADS ray gun hits targets with a microwave beam travelling at light speed, heating the skin to an excruciating 130° Fahrenheit (54° C) in two seconds, forcing retreat. Mounted on vehicles and scheduled for use in riot control by the U.S. military and police forces, ADS technology makes an enemy's firearms too hot to hold.

Project Babylon
Creator: Gerald Bull
Capacity: Dr. Gerald Bull had a dream. A University of Toronto engineering science graduate originally from North Bay, Ontario, Bull imagined a gun so large and powerful it could fire into space. He persuaded Saddam Hussein of his gun's potential merits, and spent the 1980s working for the dictatorship in Iraq. With a barrel 150 metres long and a one-metre bore, "Big Babylon," as Bull labelled the plan for his giant gat, would be able to launch both satellites and nukes. Although he successfully fired a forty-metre prototype named "Baby Babylon," Bull was shot five times and killed outside his Belgium apartment in March 1990.

READY TO DIEMACO

An hour and a half from Toronto's near-daily shootings, the twin city of Kitchener-Waterloo rests in one of those quaint regions in which the stores, houses and factories blend into a quiet, monotonous sprawl. That may be why people choose to make guns there—nobody notices. In a remote corner of Kitchener, around the corner and across a bridge from the local Toys "R" Us, Diemaco's ninety-odd employees are free, for the most part, to manufacture their assault rifles, machine guns and grenade launchers in peace. Diemaco welcomed our request for an interview and tour of the company's facility.

In April 2003 Chris travelled to Kitchener, where Diemaco's director of sales and marketing, Francis Bleeker, buzzed him through the doors of the factory. Its weather-worn and duly unremarkable concrete exterior provides appropriate camouflage among the other build-ings on the block. Diemaco has supplied the Canadian military with rifles since 1984, and hails itself as "Canada's assured source of small arms."

Diemaco is a beneficiary of the Munitions Supply Program (MSP), which ensures the Canadian government a reliable source of assorted military hardware, from ammunition to aircraft. Diemaco's primary contribution to the program is its C-7 rifle and C-8 carbine, the Canadian versions of the M-16 and M-4, manufactured under licence from Colt. And because the Canadian government doesn't want its supply to dry up, it keeps Diemaco financially afloat when contracts stop flowing. "It's like having your dad pulling out his wal-let if you screw up," Bleeker explained. "So they will keep an eye on us, but we are supposed to look after ourselves." Unlike American manufacturers, who can aggressively market their rifles to the pub-lic, Bleeker said, "You have a product that you can't sell on the streets. You can't push it as if it were a car or a lawnmower." Diemaco sells exclusively to militaries and tactical law enforcement units.

Outside of Canada, Diemaco sells to a "very limited" number of western European countries as permitted by Colt's licence. "The Netherlands, Denmark and Norway are our exclusive markets, so Colt is not *that* generous," Bleeker grumbled. "They have the rest of the world. They can export to Asia, Latin America, the Mideast." Diemaco was also awarded a prestigious contract to supply the British Special Forces with assault rifles. Among the guns made in the plant is the SFW (special forces weapon), the "ultimate in reli-able, accurate firepower."

Bleeker escorted Chris out onto Diemaco's factory floor, where the workday had mostly ended. On the surface, it's hard to discern exactly what this place makes—the massive machines and unprocessed piles of metal pipes revealed little about the products that leave the factory. On the other hand, a box of cylinders that looked like the beginnings of M203 grenade launchers provided a hint. A few dedicated craftsmen remained late, focusing on their work with the intimate attention of watchmakers. Bleeker intro-duced a Diemaco employee of sixteen years, the man's diminutive stature accentuated by Bleeker's six-foot-plus frame. After he detailed how the inside of a barrel is rifled—a procedure that gives a bullet its rotation and accuracy—Chris asked the smocked machinist about Diemaco's maximum monthly output of rifles.

"Twenty-five hundred," he said, smiling proudly at Bleeker from behind protective glasses. "And we're depending on this guy to get us there." Bleeker looked uncomfortably between his co-worker and visitor.

At the time, the most recent war on Iraq had only just begun. By that point many Canadians had considered the possibility that the war might not be about terrorism or liberation. "We haven't really been exchanging views on Iraq very much," Bleeker said. "I mean, we know it's going on. Nobody likes war, so we think just like the average Canadian thinks."

"Has the rate of sales gone up because of Iraq? The answer is no," Bleeker spelled it out. "It's not something that you can say, 'Oh shit, we're going out for a fight today. Let's buy a few extra rifles.' It's a long-term investment. On our part, it takes years to fulfill, and these countries will have these weapons for years." Consequently, Diemaco depends on a few large contracts that come up every couple of decades. During our talk with Bleeker, Diemaco was in competition with several European manufacturers, including FN Herstal and Heckler & Koch, for an order of thirty thousand new rifles from the Norwegian armed forces. "It would take us a couple of years to fulfill that order," Bleeker said. "So it really is a question of survival to get an order like that."

By the time we spoke with Bleeker, Diemaco's weapons had already made it to Afghanistan and, to a lesser extent, Iraq. "Obviously, if we see anything in the media," he said proudly, "whenever there was a firefight: 'Well, they were using *our* products.'"

If the media is gonna be here, let 'em see the truth
Don't ask soldiers to pose, and pretend war is cute
And fuck 'em if they don't understand the job we are here to do
This is war and people will die, innocent ones too
— Big Neal, "Behind the Screens," off 4th25's *Live from Iraq* (2005)

Whether or not the gun industry closes its eyes to the consequences of its creations, the cost of small arms in human terms is very real and very substantial. In June 2006 Reuters reported on statistics compiled by the International Action Network on Small Arms (IANSA), which put the daily death toll from firearms at 1,000 people globally. Of these deaths, 560 are criminal murders, 250 are casualties of war, 140 are suicides and 50 are due to accidents or undetermined causes. For every gun death, three more people are injured. But from the perspective of the gun maker, it's all someone else's fault, somebody else's problem.

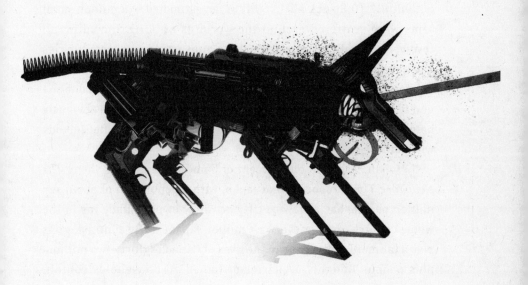

SECOND CHAMBER
LOOSE CANNONS

ACCORDING TO SMALL ARMS SURVEY, an estimated 638 million small arms were scattered around the world as of 2002, including all revolvers, pistols, rifles, submachine guns, carbines, assault rifles and light machine guns. Civilians owned at least 378 million of these, or about 60 percent. Although the global total amounts to about one gun for every ten people on the planet, some countries are obviously home to more guns than others, as are some individual households within those countries.

In Japan, less than one percent of homes have guns in them. *The New York Times* reported that Japan, with a population of about 125 million people, has as few as fifty privately owned handguns in the whole country—one for every 2.5 million Japanese. By contrast, guns play a far more central role in the lives of Canada's thirty-two-million-plus people. Roughly a quarter of Canadian households contain firearms, amounting to about seven million guns owned by three million people. Canucks have registered about half a million handguns.

On the other side of the world's longest undefended border, Americans own between 238 million and 276 million guns, more than 70 percent of which are in civilian hands. America's roughly three hundred million people are nearing the statistical landmark of one gun for every citizen. But just over 40 percent of U.S. households have firearms in them, while only one in four American adults owns a gun. Americans own a mind-blowing sixty-five million handguns.

The problem with small arms, however, has less to do with their numbers than it does with who owns them and how they're used. Of course, the more guns there are, the harder it is to prevent them from falling into the wrong hands. *Foreign Policy* magazine called the proliferation of illegal small arms one of the "wars of globalization"—a war, said *FP* in January 2003, "we're losing."

"It's crazy for them to be as readily available as they are," said Queens, New York's Pharoahe Monch, one of many hip-hop artists who have lived on the frontlines of that war. "It goes back to something that we talk about when we talk about government: really, why are and how do the shits become so readily available like that?"

> Tons o' guns, real easy to get
> Tons o' guns, bringin' nothin' but death
> Tons o' guns, but I don't glorify
> 'Cause more guns will come and much more will die
> — Guru, "Tonz o' Gunz," off GangStarr's *Hard to Earn* (1994)

While criminals, terrorists and drug dealers can buy a wide range of firearms as easily on the street as in some gun stores, more disturbing is the availability of guns to children. "The urban environments are oversaturated with guns," GangStarr's Guru, a Boston-born hip-hop legend who grew up in New York, said. "And nobody is claiming any responsibility for how they got there. And so at a younger and younger age, kids are having to deal with the presence of weapons. Back in the day when there was a confrontation or a problem or a conflict, and things were settled by fists, as we used to call a 'fair one'–that doesn't exist anymore."

Professor Noam Chomsky also remembers such a time, long past, when kids were free to fight as kids do, without fearing the introduction of firearms. "Back in the days, when I was a kid growing up in urban communities, there was violence, like race riots and stuff like that," he reflected, "but you didn't blow somebody's head off with a gun. As soon as you can turn to guns, it just escalates the terror and violence enormously, and it's having a horrendous effect on inner cities."

Mayhem Morearty has seen the same thing in his own Toronto neighbourhood, Lawrence Heights, nicknamed "the Jungle" by young residents. On his track "Guns Are For," Mayhem raps that he's "from where the Just Desserts murderers from"–citing an infamous Toronto shooting in '94. He seethed when asked about the availability of guns in the T-Dot's poorest communities. "We happen to have all the access to that, just for some reason," Mayhem said, his tone faintly sarcastic. "The guns are easily accessible to the people that don't have no other resource to refer to."

Those with the most profound attachment to firearms embrace the cliché "If you outlaw guns, only outlaws will have guns." But in this Second Chamber we examine how the legal trade in small arms leaves outlaws every opening they need to get all the guns their cold hearts desire.

HIT FACTORIES

It was a chilly and overcast May morning in Toronto, and Chris was waiting outside a Second Cup coffee shop. We're not sure we'd say we're down with OPP, but Ontario Provincial Police officer Stephen Clegg seemed pretty cool, offering to drive the forty-five minutes from headquarters in Oshawa to meet. Clegg is unit commander with the organized crime division of the OPP's Provincial Weapons Enforcement Unit (PWEU).

A man sporting a long coat and a head of light hair buzzed close to the scalp approached. His friendly posture was at odds with the image of cops cultivated in our heads by rap music and reality. "Christian?" Clegg said, with a smile.

The PWEU was formed in July 1994 after the shooting of twenty-three-year-old Georgina Leimonis in April of the same year. Leimonis was hit by over two hundred pellets from a sawed-off shotgun when four men attempted to hold up a Just Desserts café in the popular Annex area of Toronto's downtown. Leimonis's tragic murder became known as the "Just Desserts shooting," and motivated Ontario's government to create the PWEU to stem the illegal flow of firearms into and around the province.

They sat down in the back of the coffee shop to chat. Clegg wanted to know more about the book, and Chris tried to break it down for him. In the process, he happened to mention Para-Ordnance. Clegg, his fingers clasped below his chin, smiled slyly. He looked like a chess player two moves ahead of his opponent. "They've been the victim of one of our investigations," he said. But we knew that already; it was a big part of why we wanted to meet with Clegg.

There are reasons why firearms manufacturers keep a low pro-file. Most people don't want a gun factory in their neighbourhood. Some factories lose product to what small-arms analysts call "diversion"—the process by which legally owned, sold or manufac-tured firearms move from the porous legal sphere into the black market. In a factory, diversion involves employees stealing the guns and gun parts they manufacture in order to sell illegal heat on the streets.

A few months after Para-Ordnance issued their legal warning, we phoned again, hoping our time-out might have left them in a better mood to talk. A representative told us that Para still wasn't inter-ested in an interview. "It's a high-security building right here," she said. However, in November 2001, agents of the PWEU and the ATF wrapped up Project TUG (Trace Unserialized Guns), a year-long inter-national probe into arms trafficking in the Greater Toronto Area, with seven arrests. They seized ninety-five handguns, fourteen long-barrelled guns, hundreds of magazines and more than five hundred thousand rounds of ammunition. It was the biggest seizure of illegal guns in Canada in a decade.

At the centre of the Project TUG investigation was a native of Hungary who had settled in Mississauga, Zoltan Balatoni. In his late forties, Balatoni was a gunsmith who took a salary from Para-Ordnance for his day job, and supplies from their factory for his evening pursuits. Smuggling gun parts out of the Scarborough plant with the help of two other Para employees, including forty-nine-year-old Jozsef Gyimothy (who was charged with a lesser offence), Balatoni was assembling weapons at home in his basement, and had amassed one of Canada's biggest stockpiles of handguns. Balatoni and his trafficking team had been selling the handguns for between $500 and $1,200 on the streets for an unknown number of years—that is, until they sold more than forty guns to assorted informants, and then to Project TUG's undercover officers.

The high-quality 9mm, .40 calibre and .45 calibre semi-automatic pistols had a priceless feature: the smugglers had nabbed the frames from Para before they'd been stamped with serial numbers, render-ing the guns untraceable. During Balatoni's trial in early 2004 (he received a seven-year prison sentence), a PWEU detective, Mark Johnstone, testified that 224 Para-Ordnance handguns had been found at crime scenes in Ontario since 1992, of which 130 were missing serial numbers. "Para-Ordnance we're still finding," Detective Clegg said. "We still find them associated to crime scenes, criminal activities, throughout southern Ontario—actually, throughout the province. They seem to trickle all over, move themselves around. Yeah, we're still finding them."

Canada's reigning rap king, Kardinal Offishall, is a resident of Toronto's Vaughan-Oakwood community. Kardi wasn't surprised when we mentioned the trafficking ring. "That stuff has a direct correlation in what happens in my neighbourhood," he said, "and other neighbourhoods around the city. We know when those gun places get raided, we know when they misplace guns, we know when things go missing and whatever, 'cause it ends up right around the corner from my house, and all my people that I know, right around the corner from their house."

While some manufacturers, like Smith & Wesson, lock down their stock like Fort Knox, Kahr Arms, based in Worcester, Massachusetts, has faced similar problems with theft in the past. Kahr Arms' principal owner and lead designer is Kook Jin (Justin) Moon, son of the Reverend Sun Myung Moon, the Korean-born creator of the Unification Church who is considered the Messiah by his followers. On March 21, 1999, the *Boston Globe* titled a story "His Father Preaches Peace, and He Makes Guns." Justin Moon founded Kahr Arms in the mid-1990s with a $5-million investment from his father. Justin's business has since carved out an industry niche for itself with tiny concealed-carry pistols in 9mm, .40 calibre and .45 calibre. The younger Moon boasted to the *Globe*, "I am proud of Kahr Arms, our employees, and our product."

On Christmas Eve 1999, just nine months later, twenty-six-year-old Danny Guzman, an innocent bystander, was shot with a 9mm handgun outside a Worcester nightclub. Guzman died at the scene, leaving behind a wife and two infant daughters. Within the week, a four-year-old child picked up a loaded Kahr Arms pistol abandoned outside an apartment building near where Guzman was killed.

Although the gun was missing a serial number, ballistics tests conducted by police revealed that it was the weapon that had ended Guzman's life.

In March 2000 local police and agents of the ATF raided the Kahr Arms factory, arresting two employees on charges of theft, including Mark Cronin, who would later plead guilty to stealing guns from the factory. Like Balatoni, Cronin had been smuggling pistols out of his workplace before they were stamped with serial numbers. In July 2005 the Republican senator from Ohio, Mike DeWine, explained in a speech before President Bush that Cronin "bragged, in fact, that it was so easy to remove guns that he 'does it all the time,' and that he can just walk out with them." The Kahr manufacturing facility lacked effective security measures—metal detectors, for example—to prevent employee theft. Justin Moon's company had also failed to do background screening of employees such as Cronin, a crack addict with a criminal record that included violent offences. Police determined that Cronin had been exchanging the Kahr pistols for drugs and money. The Kahr Arms 9mm used to kill Danny Guzman was one of those weapons.

ROBBIN' STEEL

When Rodrigo interviewed 50 Cent in San Fran, they exchanged a few words about the first gun Fifty owned. "What was your first experience with guns?" Buns asked.

"Man, c'mon. I came in contact with pistols early, real early. I think I was like thirteen."

"Do you remember the circumstances?"

"I bought one."

"How much did you pay for it?"

"Three hundred."

"For what?"

"Three eighty."

"It was clean?"

"Yeah, it was a new pistol. Somebody had bought it. It was probably just stolen."

Fifty's guess was a good one. Every day—from factories, gun shops, homes, even police and military stockpiles—guns go missing.

The 2004 edition of *Small Arms Survey* called the "casual loss" of firearms "the tyranny of small actions." When taken together, these many small acts of theft and disappearance constitute an enormous problem: wherever they're found, guns get lost.

Many pawn shops and gun retailers adopt few measures to secure their stock, usually because of the costs of doing so. Consequently, thieves pry open doors, cut locks and crash cars through storefronts, helping themselves to as many guns as they can carry. Thieves target handguns because of their liquidity on the streets, as was the case in September 2002, when several robbers burst into Ontario Sporting Supplies in a brazen robbery in Vaughan, Ontario. The masked men made off with more than seventy-five handguns, but not before shooting forty-year-old store clerk John Fullerton, who died a day later.

Early in 2005 thieves robbed four Bay Area gun stores over just five weeks. They took 128 guns, more than half of them handguns, and at least three of those were .50 calibre. The *San Jose Mercury News* reported, "Officials worry that those 128 stolen guns will end up in the hands of criminals." Actually, the moment display cases are smashed and guns looted, they're already in the hands of criminals. The U.S. Department of Justice (DoJ) is clear: "By definition, stolen guns are available to criminals." As such, stolen firearms have among the highest probability of being used in violent crimes, particularly armed robbery.

Joseph Vince is a former head of the ATF's crime-gun analysis branch, and now a partner in Crime Gun Solutions, a Maryland-based agency that consults on firearms issues. "The damage that can be caused is huge," he told us of robberies from gun shops. "We've got to do a better job of making sure that people not only are looking at theft from inside, but also burglaries and so forth, and I think that's where the government has to step in."

While retailers' security measures are often limited, many private gun owners have virtually no protection from theft beyond a locked front door. Ironically, the same firearms frequently touted as tools of home defence can make a house a more tempting target for thieves. Small-scale burglary from private homes produces the majority of stolen guns. In Canada, for example, around five thousand privately owned guns were stolen annually between 1997 and 2001.

Near the beginning of 2004, sixty-eight-year-old Mike Hargreaves became another victim of gun theft. On January 7, 2006, the *Toronto Star* reported that while Hargreaves was in Florida, thieves broke into his seventeenth-floor Toronto apartment, stealing upwards of thirty guns worth an estimated forty grand, including pistols, assault rifles and machine guns. Hargreaves had been a close friend of John Fullerton and was the man who successfully lobbied T-Dot cops to adopt the Glock in the early nineties. It took the thieves two days, a sledgehammer and a blowtorch to crack Hargreaves' 770-kilogram safe—a far more costly anti-theft measure than most collectors are willing to invest in for their hobby. Nonetheless, police charged Hargreaves with improper storage of his weapons. "The residential stuff," said the OPP's Clegg, "sometimes it's word-of-mouth that an individual has a cache of firearms. Word gets on the street, and then they become victims for the break-and-enters. We've got organized criminal gangs that are actually focusing on gun collectors."

Although theft from private collectors in Canada is a significant problem, in that area, *Small Arms Survey* finds, "the most incisive lessons come from the United States." In 1997 an American criminologist, Gary Kleck, used the U.S. National Crime Victimization Survey to determine that between 570,000 and 1,820,000 guns are stolen each year in the United States. Although Kleck's conclusions have been challenged, even the most conservative estimates set the number of guns stolen annually in the U.S. at a staggering five hundred thousand firearms. To protect against such losses, the National Rifle Association's platinum edition Visa card offers $1,000 in insurance against the theft or loss of a firearm purchased with said piece of plastic.

Despite the scale of the problem, some gun owners do nothing to secure their firearms against theft. In March 2005, teenagers in Alden Bridge, Texas, stole thirty-three firearms and silencers from a Hummer parked outside the owner's house. According to Montgomery County's *Courier* newspaper, the stealthy gun nut had left his SUV unlocked.

Shit gets deep as we creep up the block by the kids slangin' rocks
And holdin' Glocks stolen from the cops to get props
— Kool G. Rap, "Ghetto Knows," off *4,5,6* (1995)

The FBI's National Crime Information Center (NCIC) tracks data on
guns stolen across the United States. As of March 1995, the NCIC contained over two million reports of firearms stolen from private owners, about 60 percent of which were handguns. But theft from factories, retailers and gun owners' homes doesn't account for all the
stolen firearms. In mid-2001, after a DoJ audit, the FBI was ready to
expand the NCIC stolen-gun file with a few hundred reports from its
own armouries. According to *The Washington Post* in July 2001, the
audit revealed that the FBI had lost almost 450 firearms over the previous decade. "That was a point in time," Whit Collins observed, "just
like now, where the main issue [law-enforcement] handgun was either
a 9mm or a .40-calibre Glock. So anytime the police forces themselves—who have brought their own supply of Glocks into many communities—lose one, or two, or four hundred, those are potential submachine guns on the street. And many, many perpetrators know how
to make that conversion."

While it's not known whether any of the Glock pistols were actually converted to fully automatic, the BBC reported in August 2002
that two of the FBI's lost guns had surfaced in armed robberies, and
another was used in a New Orleans homicide after it was stolen
from the home of a local FBI agent. Such incidents, Collins said, are
"part of the attrition rate in small arms—police and military both,
they get lost." As another example, on July 7, 2006, CTV News
reported that after seizing some hundred-odd small arms in a trafficking bust, police in Vancouver traced a quantity of the guns back
to the Canadian military.

"My big brother had a bunch of guns back in the day when I was a
little kid—rifles," the Bronx's Fat Joe told us. "His man was in the
army and stole a bunch of rifles and brung it back. And I remember
lookin' at it, touchin' it, pullin' the shit back. That's the first time I
ever really seen a gun."

GOT UR SELF A GUN

It's simple arithmetic really. There are thirty million teenagers in America. Gender ratios dictate that fifteen million of them are boys. There are two things that these fifteen million teenage boys want to shoot badly: their guns, and their "guns." But gender ratios also determine that there are only fifteen million teenage girls—and they think teenage boys are gross. Hold on, though; before you all get depressed and decide to go home and "clean your barrel," let's add in a new factor: America also has over two hundred million guns that don't think anything. In sum, which guns do you think are gonna get unloaded first? These emcees were kind enough to tell their stories of the magical moment they first popped their pistols.

Beretta 9 of Killarmy (Steubenville, OH)

I actually had a Dillinger, the two-shot Dillinger. It was just a hand-me-down from one of my mentors in the street. I always had it in one of the fingers of my glove, so you couldn't tell. I used to ride my bicycle, and niggas said, "Yo, your finger's always straight." But they couldn't tell I had a Dillinger in my joint. [Rappers sometimes confuse the name of the 1930s gangster with super-compact derringer handguns.]

Necro (New York, NY)

Maybe eighteen I had my first gat. I was always thugged out, fuckin' with weapons, and always walkin' around with knives and all that. But probably I couldn't afford guns really, up until I was eighteen. That's when I started makin' money probably, be able to go buy 'em. Uncle Howie sold gats in the projects, but he would've never given me anything at such a young age. He only gave me other weapons, like blowguns and fuckin' Cobracons [a type of knife].

Tech N9ne (Kansas City, MO)

I got one for my twenty-second birthday; my auntie bought me one. Can you fuckin' believe that?! I used to live with her and she was a real hard-core gangsta, my auntie was. She bought me a goddamn Tec-9 gun for my twenty-second birthday, dog! Ha ha ha! It was semi-automatic, it wasn't fully automatic, but it was as loud as a motherfucker! Pow! Pow! Pow! I had to give it away a couple of years later, because I was doing real bad. I was bummed out. All I had was my talent, and I started getting bad ideas to run up somewhere, and that ain't even in my heart to do that, so I sold it for like ninety bucks, to get it out of my hands.

RA the Rugged Man (New York, NY)

My father was a hero, a war hero. He was a Green Beret. He had like nine pistols in the house. Now I can't say what they was, because I'm like four years old. But he had a lot of different weapons, and he used to take me in the backyard and set the shit up, and let me fire the guns into the targets. And I couldn't even do that right, ha ha ha!

Bun B (Houston, TX)

First one I bought was off a road manager. I gave him $150 for a nine. And then some cat I knew got into it with some people, and I gave my strap to him and that was the last time I saw my strap. '97—that was my first handgun. We always had gauges. Niggas' daddies always gave them guns. I remember sittin' in my homeboy's bedroom, sawing off my uncle's Winchester barrel, making a sawed-off and shit. We cut the butt off, put duct tape around the butt—havin' no idea that that shit is like a federal case.

Ill Bill of Non-Phixion (New York, NY)

My boy had guns; his father was a gun collector. He had all kinds of shit. I'm not even just talkin' about easy shit like rifles. I'm talkin' about he had Tecs. When I was able to actually see the threaded barrel of a Tec-9 in front of my face [at 14 years old], I couldn't believe it. Yo, I was open, I'm not gonna front—to actually hold a biscuit, and just see all that shit. We used to take his shit out the house and his father had so many guns that it didn't even matter, he didn't even know shit was missing. The only way he found out eventually is because my boy ended up getting arrested with one of the biscuits. And I would tell you right now, man, to me, it's almost like as a country, as a nation, we're doin' it to ourselves.

SHOP 'TIL THEY DROP

I keep my hip on pound 'cause shit gets hectic in my town
— Lloyd Banks, "Die One Day," off *The Hunger for More* (2004)

The G-Unit's youngest member, Lloyd Banks is a pretty stoic cat. His disposition isn't that surprising when you consider how much bloodshed he has witnessed in his life, most of it involving guns. "I've seen my first murder when I was ten years old," Banks said. "I seen a man get shot three times in the head in front of me. So I was exposed to a lot of things as a young 'un that kind of made me grow up a little bit faster."

At nineteen Banks was himself a victim of gun violence. As he stood outside a nightclub in Queens, he and several other bystanders were hit by random gunfire. "It was anywhere from twenty to thirty guns in that club," Banks explained. "It was to the point where everybody was standing outside, and it was over ten guns going off at the same time. So it doesn't necessarily mean that it was meant for me, but that's what happens when you're standing outside of a club—people get shot. And about five, six people got shot that night."

Hit in the liver, Banks ran, dizzy and bleeding, to the nearest hospital. He awoke in the trauma unit the next morning—September 11, 2001. As staff scurried around frantically in response to the morning's unfathomable tragedy, Banks thought it best to get up, get out and get somewhere else. Since then Lloyd Banks has watched his star rise, achieving platinum status (over a million sold) for the G-Unit LP as well as his own debut disc. But, to borrow the words of De La Soul, "It ain't all good." "Just recently, we left to come overseas," Banks said over the phone while on tour in Europe. "And it's crazy, because I lost two of my closest friends. One of my friends got shot to death a couple of days before we left, so I missed the funeral. I was in, I think, Germany. And a week later I lost my closest friend. He got stabbed."

"How easy is it to get a gun in New York?"

"You could buy a gun like how you can buy a brownie. I think right now it's probably easier than it's ever been. It's very easy. My little brother could go get a gun," he explained. "My little brother's only fifteen years old, but he knows people. He got friends that got older brothers, and if he wanted to, he could get one of his own. And I wouldn't be surprised if he did get one of his own, because in my environment that's kind of like a necessity."

If the older brother of a friend bought Banks's fifteen-year-old brother a gun from a licensed gun store, the sale would be what's known as a straw purchase. Like buying liquor for a minor, a straw purchase is an illegal transaction in which an individual buys a gun for somebody who can't legally buy one for himself. Straw purchases from gun shops are responsible for the majority of firearms that end up in the hands of juveniles and criminals. In April 2003 PBS's *NOW with Bill Moyers* aired footage of a March '99 sting operation by cops near Detroit, during which a straw purchase was caught on tape. With one officer posing as a felon and another as a friend trying to buy him a handgun, the undercover agents had no trouble convincing a gun-store clerk to make the sale. "When the manager comes over to check this, it's your gun," the salesman stresses, referring to the felon's friend. "You're not purchasing it for him. It's *your* gun."

"Oh," says one of the cops, acting clueless, "because the manager has to—"

"This is called a straw purchase," clarifies the clerk. "It's *highly* illegal." Nonetheless, the salesman exchanges the gun for cash, wishing the undercover officers well. "There you go, guys," he says. "Enjoy it."

According to a study released in September 2003 by researchers from UCLA, a survey of salesmen at gun shops across the United States found that 52.5 percent were willing to sell a handgun in a "situation like a 'straw purchase.'" The study also determined that gun stores in the northeastern states were less likely to make such a sale than were dealers in the midwestern, western and southern U.S.

Bonecrusher, Georgia's friendly giant of rap, talked about the availability of guns in his neck of the woods. "It's easy to get a gun," he lamented. "That's the bad thing, is that it's so easy to get. You can get any kind of gun you want to: automatic, semi-automatic, whatever, shotgun. It's easy, especially down south. You can get a shotgun in a Wal-Mart, with no permit." Not every Wal-Mart store in Georgia sells shotguns—but the Wal-Mart Supercenter on Dogwood Drive in Conyers does, including shotties by Beretta, Ruger and Remington. We called the Conyers store. "Sporting goods," answered an unenthusiastic male voice.

"Hey, you guys sell shotguns?"

"Yes," the clerk said, subtly suspicious (perhaps he detected the foreign accent).

"What do I need to get one?"

"Driver's licence and, depending on what kind it is, eighteen or twenty-one [years old]."

"No permit or anything like that?"

"You have to do an FBI [instant] background check," he said, uncertain whether Chris was a cop or an idiot. "If the federal government tells me it's all right [we can sell it]," the clerk stated, making clear that, even if you don't need a permit, it ain't *that* easy.

Unfortunately, the retail leviathan's employees haven't always been so diligent. In January 2005 the BBC reported that the Wal-Mart Corporation had agreed to pay $14.5 million to settle a lawsuit launched by the State of California. Between 2000 and 2003 California's department of justice documented 2,891 gun-sales violations at Wal-Mart stores in the state. Among the violations were thirty-six straw purchases for people prohibited by law from owning firearms.

Still, when compared with some gun retailers, the Wal-Marts of the world don't seem so bad. Because of legislative reforms that were enacted in the mid-1990s, the number of federally licensed firearms dealers in the United States has dropped by 78 percent since 1994. At the time there were more legal gun sellers stateside than gas stations. The decline correlates with a decrease in the number of federally licensed "kitchen-table" dealers, who conduct business without a traditional storefront, and those who used their licences to buy guns for themselves at wholesale. Despite this dramatic drop, a few crooked licensees have managed to hang around. "When we look at the information," Joseph Vince said, "we see really high-volume places, like Wal-Marts or K-Marts or even wholesalers, who don't get as many crime guns traced back to them as some dealers. That tells you either that there's some corruption going on or [the dealers] have very poor business practices." There's another factor: Wal-Mart hasn't sold handguns since '93.

.357s and .44s, bought inside corner stores
Provide sparks for wars
— Inspectah Deck, "Cold World," off GZA's *Liquid Swords* (1995)

For years, for the price of $50, the Bureau of Alcohol, Tobacco and Firearms released information to the public under the Freedom of Information Act on the retail origins of guns found at crime scenes across the United States. But between 2003 and 2006 a Republican congressman and National Rifle Association ally from Kansas, Todd Tiahrt, added a series of amendments to ATF funding legislation that prevented the agency from continuing this practice, effectively classifying the information. Before Tiahrt's amendments, fifty bucks could tell you a lot about a big source of crime guns.

In February 2000 the ATF revealed in its *Commerce in Firearms in the United States* that just 1.2 percent of licensed gun dealers—1,020 stores—accounted for 57 percent of all crime-gun traces in 1998. Furthermore, 132 then active dealers had fifty or more crime guns traced back to them in the same year. Making up just 0.2 percent of active dealers, these 132 stores accounted for 27 percent of all 1998 crime-gun traces. The figures reflected an ongoing trend.

Titled "The Ten Worst 'Bad Apple' Gun Dealers in America," a July 2003 report by the Brady Campaign to Prevent Gun Violence drew further attention to ATF numbers. Leading the list, Badger Outdoors Inc. of West Milwaukee, Wisconsin, moved 554 firearms across its counter that were traced to crimes between 1989 and 1996. In May 2006 ATF figures—released as the result of a federal lawsuit by a California gun store suing to keep its licence—revealed that Badger Outdoors had once again led licensed dealers in number of crime guns traced back to its operation during the previous year, with 537 traces in 2005 alone. "You could knock me over with a feather," store owner and NRA member Mick Beatovic said in the *Milwaukee Journal Sentinel*, "because I didn't think we had that many traces."

Shyne, imprisoned in New York's Clinton Correctional for criminal possession of a weapon following the '99 nightclub incident, shed light on the environment that bad-apple dealers contribute to. "I [grew up] in the 'hood, the ghetto—I wasn't in the suburbs, I wasn't in a middle-class neighbourhood—and that's where all the guns and all the crack is at. I been exposed to that since I was like eight years old. You know, my brother [friend] got shot, got his brains blown out, when I was like eleven. I got shot when I was fifteen, and was totin' ratchets since then." The Brooklyn, New York, native made clear that weapons such as MAC-10s, Tec-9s, AK-47s and AR-15s were accessible to youth in NYC's inner city. "Yeah, anything is available on the street, blood," he said, amused by our naive questions.

"What do you think is responsible for the problem?"

"I mean, we not the gun manufacturers. So I'd be real curious to know how those guns get into our 'hood."

The gun manufacturers know. They had access to the ATF's information, just like everyone else. A former gun industry lobbyist who began his career in 1981 as legal counsel to the NRA, Robert Ricker has testified to as much. Before he was pressured out of his position as executive director of the American Sports Shooting Council (ASSC) in 1999, Ricker toed the industry line in award-winning fashion. As recently as February '99, the Citizens Committee for the Right to Keep and Bear Arms (CCRKBA) named Ricker Gun Rights Defender of the Month. But behind the closed doors of what he called gun industry "lawyers' meetings," Ricker voiced more radical ideas.

Robert Ricker

Beginning in the 1980s and continuing throughout the nineties, gun manufacturers and dealers had been subjected to a series of civil liability lawsuits. As with earlier suits against the tobacco industry, many were an attempt to bleed the gun business to death. While most of the lawsuits failed miserably in court, by the turn of the millennium the industry's legal fees were taking an enormous financial toll. To avoid a potentially monumental legal loss, Ricker advocated a "proactive approach" to the industry's problem: make its products safer and address dirty dealers.

After the Columbine massacre in April 1999, Ricker became more vocal, working closely with President Clinton on several safety initiatives. In response, at least one trade association executive made an effort to have him gagged. In June '99, Robert Delfay, then CEO of both the NSSF (National Shooting Sports Foundation) and SAAMI (Sporting Arms and Ammunition Manufacturers' Institute), circulated a memo to four gun industry executives entitled "Reigning [sic] in Ricker." Wrote Delfay, "Someone in a position of authority at ASSC needs to direct Mr. Ricker to become silent." Not a month later, Robert Ricker was out of a job, his ASSC merged into Delfay's NSSF. Since then Ricker has become what The New York Times called "the first case of a gun industry whistle-blower."

It's no wonder Robert Delfay wanted Ricker silenced. An affidavit filed by Ricker in February 2003 reads like a .50 calibre blast against the gun industry. According to Ricker's sworn declaration,

> The firearms industry . . . has long known that the diversion of firearms from legal channels of commerce to the illegal black market . . . occurs principally at the distributor/dealer level. Many of those firearms pass quickly from licensed dealers to juveniles and criminals through such avenues as straw sales, large-volume sales to gun traffickers and various other channels by corrupt dealers or distributors who go to great lengths to avoid detection by law enforcement authorities. Leaders in the industry have long known that greater industry action to prevent illegal transactions is possible and would curb the supply of firearms to the illegal market. However . . . leaders in the industry have consistently resisted taking constructive voluntary action to prevent firearms from ending up in the illegal gun market and have sought to silence others within the industry who have advocated reform.

In February 2005, when we got Ricker on the phone, he was busy working on a bill for the State of Virginia, legislation "dealing with bringing guns into bars and restaurants"—a controversial issue in several states. Prior to speaking with him we had scanned a July 2004 article in the *Cornell Law Review* that considered the possibility that child soldiers globally might be represented in a lawsuit against the gun industry, based in part on Ricker's insider knowledge—previously a missing link in liability suits. "Did you expect or want your statement to have the broad effect it did?"

"Well, yeah, I think I did," said Ricker, nowadays Joe Vince's partner in Crime Gun Solutions. "Because I think that someone needed to come forward in an official context and kind of set the record straight. If you talk to people like Larry Keane [VP and general counsel of the NSSF] and others, they basically throw their hands up and say, 'Well, there's nothing the industry can do.' And that's just not the case. The industry has known about rogue gun dealers, bad apple gun dealers, people who operate outside the law—I mean, they've known about it for years and years."

> Guns are bein' bought over the counter like candy
> Comin' in handy for chumps to act manly
> Once before they were only for the law
> But no more, for sure, lookin' at a L.A. gun war
> Even in Brooklyn, lives are bein' tooken
> — Big Daddy Kane, "Dance with the Devil," off *Taste of Chocolate* (1990)

With Ricker as a star witness, the National Association for the Advancement of Colored People (NAACP) filed a lawsuit in a Brooklyn, New York, court in mid-2003. The NAACP's suit named as defendants eighty manufacturers and importers of firearms and fifty gun distributors. Among the companies named in the suit were Colt, Para-Ordnance, Glock and Magnum Research, all of which were found "not liable" by a jury, as well as Smith & Wesson, Ruger, Bryco, Lorcin and Hi-Point, on whose liability the jury concluded "no verdict." After the jury returned its decisions on the case, Larry Keane said, "We have laid bare the NAACP's case. The emperor has no clothes."

Not quite. As Judge Jack Weinstein saw the NAACP's case, it was more like the emperor was dipped in fresh gear but missing the right kicks to walk into court with. Judge Weinstein decided that under applicable New York law, the "Plaintiff [had] failed to prove it suffered special damages different in kind from those of other organizations and people in New York subject to gun violence as a result of the marketing failure of defendants to prudently merchandise their products."

"Although the NAACP lost the suit," Ricker told us, "because they couldn't prove special damages to the organization itself, the findings of Judge Weinstein are devastating against the industry." Weinstein found that with the data available from the ATF, a manufacturer would "be able to know most traces related to guns sold by specific dealers and could use this information to require responsible merchandising by such retailers, thus substantially reducing the flow of guns into criminal hands." Judge Weinstein wrote that the defendants "could do, and could have done, much more in preventing their products from falling into the wrong hands."

The NAACP couldn't prove that it suffered "special harm," because gun violence has never been isolated to a single community. "All types of misuse of firearms," Weinstein declared, "fall disproportionately on the poor and overwhelmingly on males rather than females, but no group is spared. All segments of society, whether White, Occidental, African-American, Native American, Black, Hispanic, Oriental or other, suffer from handgun violence which would be reduced in New York were more prudent merchandising policies followed by defendants."

But "more prudent policies" would mean less substantial profits. A story on Ricker's testimony by *NOW with Bill Moyers* reported that as many as 25 percent of all handguns sold in the United States eventually show up in a crime. If the firearms industry were forced to limit its sales to those who plink responsibly, it might be gun businesses going under instead of Lloyd Banks's and Shyne's friends.

"One of the experts in the NAACP case estimated that approximately 20 percent of the [gun industry's] profits were a direct result of illegal gun sales," Ricker explained. "Now, if those illegal gun sales are shut down, that means the industry loses about 20 percent of its profit, and they of course don't want to do that."

Unless faced with a real threat of liability, the gun industry has little incentive to alter the way it does business. With the decision in the NAACP's most recent case, it seemed that the winds of change could have been whistling by industry ears like passing hollow-points. But, as *Small Arms Survey* noted in 2003, "the American firearms industry has friends like few others; it may still emerge from its legal conflicts relatively unscathed."

GUN FOR THE BORDER

A man who worked his way from homelessness to millions, Mississippi's flag bearer, David Banner, holds a master's degree in business from the University of Southern Mississippi. The humble and good-humoured performer talked to us about one of his favourite pastimes. "People collect coins; I collect guns," he said in a rich Southern accent. "Man, people can't believe the amount of guns I got. I love it, dog. Like, I just do. I go to the gun shop like I go grocery shoppin'—'Oh, I want that, that, and I want that, that, that, that, that, that and that. And give me a whoooooole bunch of bullets.'" Banner let out a cheerful laugh.

While Banner will take his nine *that*s—count 'em—back to the crib, adding to a home arsenal that could already equip a small guer-rilla army, many who leave gun shops after purchasing a large quan-tity of firearms will set up shop for themselves. Whereas David Banner will probably buy nine different *that*s, increasing the variety of his collection, a trafficker might buy, for example, nine Saturday night specials—not exactly the mark of a collector. West Milwaukee's Badger Outdoors, for example, sold a minimum of 1,563 handguns in multiple sales between 1989 and 1996, according to ATF figures. Gun dealers can, and often do, report suspicious purchases of multiple guns to authorities—after collecting their cash and allowing a likely trafficker to hit the road.

Most gunrunners who do business out of the backs of cars don't run far. ATF analysis shows that throughout the U.S. the majority of crime guns traced in 1999 were initially purchased from licensed dealers in the same state in which the guns were recovered. In seven-teen cities, including southern hotspots such as Miami, Atlanta,

Houston and New Orleans, 80 percent or more of crime guns were purchased from dealers in state. Up north, it's a different story.

> Everything ain't how it seems, I got bagged at 14
> On the highway, runnin' guns out of New Orleans
> — LA the Darkman, "Devil in a Blue Dress," off DJ Muggs's
> *The Soul Assassins Chapter 1* (1997)

Asked how hard it is to get hold of a gun in Louisiana, New Orleans native C-Murder said, "It's easy, man. You need a few dollars, ya heard me? Depends on what kind you want."

And if you wanted to get a big gun in the Big Easy? An AK-47, for example?

"You just let it be known you want one—you'll have about fifty people tryin' to get to you, straight up."

C-Murder's homeboy B.G. confirmed the fact. "Yeah, yeah, yeah," B. Gizzle agreed. "At eighteen you could go and buy an AK over the counter in the gun store."

The kind of accessibility C-Murder and B.G. spoke about is as strange to Americans who live in the northeastern states as it is to Canadians. When we interviewed Joe Budden of Newark, New Jersey, he told us about the regulation of firearms around his part of the country. "I can't be too mad about the policies where I'm from," Budden said. "You can't just go into the store when you want to buy one, you can't just shoot when you want to shoot, and you damn sure can't have one in plain view. So when it gets like that up here, then I might start beefin'."

Formed by Sarah Brady after her husband, James, then White House press secretary, was paralyzed during a shooting attempt on Ronald Reagan's life in March 1981, the Brady Campaign to Prevent Gun Violence annually publishes state report cards on "laws shielding families from gun violence." Grades depend on whether, for example, a state limits the sale of assault weapons such as AK-47s or requires buyer background checks at any of the more than five thousand gun shows held annually across the U.S., and whether it has one-handgun-per-month anti-trafficking laws. As opposed to

David Banner's Mississippi and C-Murder's Louisiana—states that both received an F grade in '05—Joe Budden's New Jersey earned an A-. In Mississippi and Louisiana, a visitor to a gun show can purchase a firearm from a private seller without ever undergoing the criminal background check required to buy a gun from a licensed dealer—perfect for a purchaser with a record of felonies.

As a result of New Jersey's strict policies, most of the crime guns found there come from out of state. In Budden's Brick City, 80.2 percent of crime guns recovered in 2000 came from what the ATF calls "national sources"—a collection of states with lax gun laws, including Florida (F+), Georgia (D), Indiana (D) and Pennsylvania (D+). The majority of crime guns in cities such as Boston, Detroit and New York City are also attributed to these sources. You don't need an MBA to understand that where something is harder to get, it's gonna cost more cheddar. The more restrictive gun laws become, the higher illegal gun prices rise. With the relatively heavy regulation of firearms in the state of New York (B+), where background checks at gun shows are required, guns are sold on the streets of NYC at between two and ten times their retail price down south.

Houston is hometown to the "People's Champ," Paul Wall. The ice-grilled nice guy broke down his collection of burners when Rodrigo visited, including the infamous Avtomat Kalashnikov Model 1947. "How much did you pay for the AK?" Buns asked.

"That one I think was like four hundred," Paul answered. "Guns down here are a lot cheaper than in New York and stuff. My boy was telling me, like, I got some four hundred-dollar-guns—in New York, they're like a thousand dollars." Sometimes more.

When Chris interviewed Mobb Deep's Prodigy, a Queens, New York, representative, they also talked about assault rifles. "What about the AR-15s and AK-47s that keep coming up in lyrics?" he asked. "How often is that made up?"

"Them shits is on the streets," said P.

"You can get an AR in the streets?"

"Fifteen hundred dollars."

"What about an AK?"

"Around the same price."

With the difference in the price of an AK-47 between Houston and New York City, the 1,500-mile (2,400 km) drive from Magnolia City to the Big Apple would be worth the time and trouble to many gun traffickers. South-to-north gunrunning is so common the phenomenon has become known as the iron pipeline.

> I got silencers, scopes, military-issue pistols
> Holla at me, whatever you need, homie, I can get you
> — 50 Cent, "Gunz for Sale" 12-inch (2003)

At a local video store in Vancouver, we met John. He seemed to know a lot about weapons, and after he heard about our book, John said, "You need to talk to my cousin." Catching up with John's cousin Mike during one of his shifts at the store, he recommended *Runaway Jury*, a movie loosely based on the 1993 shootings at a law firm in San Francisco, during which Gian Luigi Ferri used two Tec-9s to kill eight and wound six before killing himself—all in about four minutes. The flick was alright.

Like most true tough guys, Mike doesn't look the part. Half Asian and half Caucasian, with a round, grinning face not unlike that of the Campbell's Soup kid, Mike doesn't need a gun to defend himself. He and John used to manage a Van City strip club frequented by drunk and belligerent Asian gangsters who packed like campers. Even in such a seedy environment, Mike was rarely tested.

By his mid-teens Mike was studying martial arts in China, and since then he's read up on everything from knife fighting to assassination techniques. No one would mess with Mike at the club because, as he said, "Everyone knows I got something on me." Usually a knife, "something" he can throw accurately up to ten metres. Mike also knows a lot about guns. Growing up on Vancouver Island, he and his friends used to shoot his granddad's shotgun for fun. Now in his mid-twenties, Mike's pulled the trigger on everything from a .357 to a sawed-off to a Desert Eagle. He isn't the type who looks for trouble, but, he said, "I wouldn't say I could never shoot somebody."

John had suggested that his cousin might know some gunrunners, and we followed up. "Oh, yeah," Mike said, smiling. "Lots." He described one of his gunrunner friends as a "scrounger," a disorganized seller who hawks any gun he can get his hands on, clean or dirty. Months later, Mike updated us on that "scrounger." He'd been busted trying to cross the border with a hundred guns in his trunk—stun guns, that is. The cheapest stun guns can be bought stateside for twenty bucks and sold at five times their retail price on Canadian streets, where they're prohibited weapons. Months after the scrounger's arrest, the local media began reporting on the rise in cross-border stun-gun trafficking. Mike seemed to know what he was talking about.

Another friend of Mike's is a rather more methodical individual. Focused primarily on marijuana production, he sells guns on the side. Having recently moved from B.C. to Alberta—the province with the highest percentage of households with guns in them—his new home even has a soundproofed shooting range in the basement, allowing customers to try out their selections before buying. In his early thirties, Mike's buddy—we'll call him Ben—just seems like a guy with a brilliant mind for crime. When he and Mike were younger and Mike had just returned from China, the two friends were challenged to a fight late one night by six street thugs. "It was *so* easy," Mike smirked. After witnessing his friend's enhanced hand-to-hand combat skills, Ben tried to convince him to become the star of an underground fight club, complete with a gambling racket. Mike passed on the opportunity.

Ben would eventually get rich without his pal. With money he earned in the drug trade, he purchased property in the Vancouver area, using his real estate as temporary grow-houses before selling the homes off at a profit. Long before Matt's buddy agreed to an interview, we knew he would be guarded in what he said. Unlike many rappers, who can freely rhyme about all the drugs and guns they supposedly sell, knowing full well they aren't incriminating themselves for anything they're actually doing, Ben has made himself a millionaire by avoiding the wrong kind of attention. He has nothing to gain, and everything to lose, from fame. Although he wouldn't meet us, he agreed to the interview only because Mike's his dog—and because he thought the idea was kind of funny. We provided Mike with questions and he wrote down his old friend's answers. Ben would never, of course, allow himself to be recorded, so take the words for what they're worth.

"Which brands of guns would be available for purchase on the black market in Canada?" Mike asked.

"You can get anything you order from the likes of me. But the common [brands] floating around are Colt, Ruger, Glock, Beretta."

"Who are your clients?"

"Guys who want one. *All* types. Those who don't want to get one from a store. Hitmen. Cops who feel they are above the law."

"Will you sell to anyone who wants to buy one?"

"Sure, no questions asked. I just provide. [I] don't dictate use.... Truth is, the less you know and the less they know, the better. Know what you have to. If you know it's going to come back to bite you in the ass, then *don't do it*."

No scrounger, Ben doesn't sell guns that can be connected with crimes already committed. "There are those who will sell dirty pieces," he said, "just not me. Clean 'em and move 'em." As he explained, cleaning a gun means switching parts, filing barrels and drilling, scrubbing or using acid to obliterate serial numbers, rendering the guns untraceable. Once he's cleaned the pieces, Ben will usually mark up his source's price "50 percent, or more if you think you can get more." It all depends on how difficult it is to get the gun in question. Mike checked whether the price of guns on Canada's black market was going up or down.

"Down, unfortunately," Ben said. "[They're] easier to get. More floating around locally."

"How effective do you think the law has been in controlling the black market in guns?"

"Don't know. Haven't had to deal with it much. I know they are strict. They treat guns up here like they do pot down there. They try, I guess."

"How difficult is it to move guns across the border?"

"Easier than drugs."

"What are some of the ways that guns are transported across the border with the United States?"

"I'm not saying I do, 'cause I never stay with one source too long. But it's a long border. Some crossings are used more than others."

From most media reports, you'd assume every gun crime was connected with "gangsters." Not so. Like Mike's pal, many gunrunners prefer working mostly alone. Fewer people to depend on means less sharing of profits and, more important, less chance of betrayal.

Ben made another important point. It's already extremely difficult to stop firearms coming across at any given crossing when, as opposed to drugs, there's no cost-effective way to detect hidden guns. But with so many crossings, it becomes virtually impossible to stop the illegal flow across our border.

I got a hundred gun, two hundred clips
Goin' to New York, New York
I'm in a hotel, off 95 North
Everything's fine, and yes, me on course
— KRS-One, "100 Guns," off Boogie Down
Productions' *Edutainment* (1990)

Interstate 95 is a highway connecting the southern states with New York. Guns travel up the I-95 so frequently that the media has nicknamed it the "firearms freeway"—one of many routes in the iron pipeline. And the guns don't always stop in New York. If a trafficker is willing to drive all the way from Houston to NYC, he may not mind travelling a few hundred miles more to Montreal. On December 8, 2004, the CBC reported that a man from Texas had been arrested in Montreal with twenty-nine pistols and revolvers he'd bought at a gun show and smuggled across the border, and which he intended to sell to Lebanese organized-crime groups. According to the story, Robert Farnsworth "was never searched by Canadian border officials when he first entered the country." Gun smugglers rarely are, especially when, like Farnsworth, they're middle-aged white men who pass through isolated crossings in the dead of night.

An August 10, 2005, story by *Maclean's* reported on stats from the RCMP-directed National Weapons Enforcement Support Team, back out west, which found that 94 percent of guns recovered at

Vancouver crime scenes in 2003 originated in the U.S. "A lot of them come up the I-5," homicide detective Sean Trowski told us of Van City's crime guns. The Interstate 5 runs from the U.S. border with Mexico all the way up to the Canadian border. "You got the L.A.-to-Vancouver drugs and guns goin' back and forth along this strip," Trowski explained, listing the most popular brands as "Smith & Wesson, a lot of Glocks, a lot of Berettas."

In March 2005 the *Ottawa Sun* obtained a report by the Canada Border Services Agency showing that over a five-year stretch Canada Customs officials had intercepted 5,446 guns at the U.S.-Canada border, including 2,010 prohibited firearms (which

include short-barrelled handguns, sawed-off shotguns and auto-matic firearms). Officials also seized another 20,129 prohibited weapons, including stun guns. CTV News further reported on an estimate by the Customs Excise Union, which represents border guards, suggesting that only one in twenty smuggled guns are apprehended at the border. If that estimate is correct, then more than twenty-one thousand guns are entering Canada illegally each year from the States, about eight thousand of which are prohibited.

As a result, a significant portion of crime guns in Canada's most populous city come from the United States. The OPP's Stephen Clegg suggests that between 25 and 45 percent of Toronto's crime guns are U.S.-bought, but other estimates put the figure at about half of Toronto's total. Anecdotally, the share seems even greater. "When it comes to murders," Toronto homicide detective Randy Carter said of his own investigations, "most of the time they're guns that have been smuggled into Canada from the United States somewhere."

BEWARE OF BUYER

As the world's most common and widely circulated firearm, the AK-47 is in demand across the globe. But as the list of black-market prices below illustrates (USD), costs vary.

Afghanistan	$10
Cambodia	$40
Uganda	$86
Nicaragua	$100
Pakistan	$250
Osh, Kyrgyzstan	$250
Iraq	$300
Houston, TX	$400
Tajikistan	$400
Colombia	$800
Bishkek, Kyrgyzstan	$900
New York City, NY	$1,000
Gaza, Palestine	$1,200
Vancouver, BC	$1,500
India	$3,800

Canadians aren't alone in worrying about U.S.-bought guns coming into our country. On August 1, 2005, the U.S. government closed its consulate in Nuevo Laredo, Mexico, a virtually lawless city of 330,000 people just across the Texas border. The closure came in response to a battle between warring drug cartels involving "unusually advanced weaponry," according to Bloomberg.com. In June 2005 cartel members firing assault rifles out of Chevy Suburbans had assassinated new police chief Alejandro Dominguez just seven hours after he'd accepted the job.

In Mexico, which has introduced stringent firearms laws, approximately 95 percent of confiscated crime guns were originally bought legally in the United States, the *Miami Herald* reported on January 9, 2006. The guns are smuggled across Mexico's three-thousand-kilometre border with the U.S., sometimes one at a time—increasingly the same method being used to move guns into Canada. Mexican authorities have described this flow as the "ant trade," but "termite trade" might be more fitting: together the individual guns can eat away at the framework of a society.

"Arms flow from unregulated jurisdictions to regulated jurisdictions," said Wendy Cukier, founder of Canada's Coalition for Gun Control, during a presentation to a small-arms working group we attended in Ottawa. "And that's true whether you're talking about guns flowing out of South Africa into Botswana or Zimbabwe, or whether you're talking about guns from the United States flowing into Canada, Mexico, the Caribbean [and] Latin American countries. So it's not possible to address the illicit trafficking in small arms without addressing the licit trade."

Gun control requires cooperation between jurisdictions, as much within the United States as between the U.S. and the rest of the world. Whether it's the Great Lakes region of North America or the Great Lakes region of Africa—one of the hardest hit by the buildup of illegal guns—international harmonization of gun laws is needed to curb the flow of illegal firearms, especially between adjacent countries. Most of the world has shown a willingness to address the flow of illegal guns, but in the United States there are other factors at play, other actors at work.

CRITICAL MASS

On August 19, 1987, Michael Ryan walked down the streets of tiny Hungerford, England, armed with an AK-47, a Beretta pistol and, in his own words that afternoon, "a bad dream." By the end of the nightmare, Ryan had killed sixteen people, including his mother, wounded another fifteen and ended his own life. Ryan's arsenal was legally acquired, a fact that scandalized Britons. But the country reacted quickly, enacting legislation a year later that banned nearly all semi-automatic rifles, like Ryan's AK-47.

Unfortunately, another massacre would menace the United Kingdom nine years later, when disaffected former Boy Scout leader Thomas Hamilton entered a primary school in Dunblane, Scotland, on March 13, 1996, and killed sixteen children and a teacher with a handgun. Like Michael Ryan, Hamilton had acquired his firearm legally, and once again, the British government responded to the tragedy by stiffening firearms legislation—this time, banning all handguns.

A month and a half later and a world away, Australian Martin Bryant killed thirty-five people in Port Arthur, Tasmania, using an AR-15 with thirty-round magazines. Twelve days later, after massive public outrage, Australia enacted new gun measures banning assault weapons. Within the next year and a half, the government bought back from citizens and destroyed seven hundred thousand guns—one-fifth of all the guns in Australia. In the ten years leading up to the Port Arthur massacre, Australia had been subjected to eleven mass shootings, in which a hundred people were killed and another fifty-four wounded. In the years since Australia's assault weapons ban came into effect, there have been none.

It's like this, what's more fun than sliced wrists?
Kill that teacher that you hate and spray 25 kids
You'll be famous just like me if you did what I did
— Ill Bill, "Anatomy of a School Shooting,"
off *What's Wrong with Bill?* (2004)

When we asked New York native Ill Bill about his song "Anatomy of a School Shooting," which imagines the Columbine massacre from the perspective of gunman Eric Harris, Bill reflected on how the mas-sacre revealed America's attitude towards guns. "People couldn't really get guns as easily as you can now, twenty, thirty, forty years ago," he said. "Now it's all out of control really, you could get a gun anywhere. It's as easy as goin' into one of your parents' bedrooms and just findin' out where they hide the shits, because everybody has guns in the United States, compared to other parts of the world."

Eric Harris and Dylan Klebold's infamous spree claimed the lives of twelve students and a teacher at Columbine High School on April 20, 1999. Harris and Klebold didn't raid their parents' homes for their weapons, but still had no trouble acquiring them. The Tec-DC9 and Hi-Point 9mm carbine they used were purchased illegally from two men, Mark Manes and Philip Duran. Manes admitted sell-ing Harris and Klebold the Tec-9 for $500 three months before the attack, after being introduced to them by Duran. On a videotape found by police, Harris and Klebold thanked the two men, saying, "Mark and Phil . . . you helped us do what we needed to do. Thank you." For their service Duran and Manes would be sentenced to four and a half and six years respectively, with Manes stating before his sentencing, "I never want to see a gun for the rest of my life." Like Duran and Manes, eighteen-year-old Columbine student Robyn Anderson violated federal law when she provided Harris and Klebold with two shotguns, but avoided jail by cooperating with investigators.

Unlike larger killing sprees such as the San Ysidro, California, McDonald's massacre in 1984 and the Killeen, Texas, Luby's Restaurant massacre in 1991, which claimed twenty-one and twenty-four lives respectively, Columbine, because it was partially caught on tape and involved high-school students, received intense media cov-erage. Subsequent public outrage prompted some new legislation to further strengthen laws restricting the sale of firearms to criminals. Still, unlike in Australia or the United Kingdom, there would be no sweeping reforms in response to Columbine, or to any other gun massacre in America.

—

Before George W. Bush became commander-in-chief, he had to two-step through a sticky period in NRA–Republican relations, telling *The New York Times* while campaigning in May 2000, "I've never been a member of the NRA. Gore has been, if I'm not mistaken." While the National Rifle Association has never confirmed Gore's membership, Bush had managed to distance himself from the pro-gun faction during the intensely contested 2000 election. A leaked recording of NRA president Kayne Robinson prompted the move, one in which he states, "If we [Republicans] win we'll have a president—with at least one of the people that's running—a president where we work out of their office. Unbelievably friendly relations."

"That wasn't an empty boast," Josh Sugarmann, author of 1992's *National Rifle Association: Money, Firepower and Fear*, explained to us. "I think this [NRA] administration probably wields the greatest influence over any President we've ever seen in history."

While Bush can safely endorse pro-gun initiatives today, back in 2000 America was, in Junior's own words, "still wrestling with the lessons of Columbine." Bush's campaign team knew that aligning their candidate too closely with the powerful, but not mainstream, NRA could cost him votes in a close election. But positioning the would-be president as a moderate in the gun debate was a tall order. As governor of Texas, he had outlawed cities in the state from suing gun manufacturers, refused to make background checks mandatory at gun shows and allowed Texas to remain the only state with no minimum age for legal handgun possession.

As a coping strategy, Bush's team fabricated a safe-gun policy platform that would appeal to more voters. His election website promised "banning juveniles from possession of semi-automatic 'assault' weapons . . . [and] banning the importation of foreign made, 'high-capacity' ammunition clips." Bush's election promises were already federal law. The campaign manoeuvre appeased a major political player and gave the GOP a more mainstream facade. The Republican Party remained the party of choice for the NRA, and Bush's team would continue to accept a less controversial form of their support. From 1989 to 2004, the NRA donated $14 million to political campaigns, with over 90 percent of that money supporting

Republican candidates. The NRA spent $11 million more between 1997 and 2003 on lobbying, and another $18 million on media in support of Republicans.

But the NRA's strength does not lie in dollars alone. While they do control an annual budget exceeding $120 million, the association still donates comparatively less than other groups. In the 2002 election cycle alone, pharmaceutical and health product companies gave nearly $30 million to political campaigns, dwarfing the NRA contributions. The NRA's greater influence lies in its ability to mobilize its 4.3 million members. "Because of the NRA's heralded grassroots," Josh Sugarmann said, "and their ability to have them just follow their marching orders quite directly, it has become very important to the conservative movement."

In his autobiography, *My Life*, Bill Clinton recalls the NRA's pull in the 1994 congressional election. "The gun lobby claimed to have defeated nineteen of the twenty-four members on its hit list," wrote Clinton. "They did at least that much damage and could rightly claim to have made Gingrich the House Speaker." According to the NRA's "What Is the Gun Lobby?" fact sheet,

> in the 2004 elections, more NRA resources were better
> deployed in more critical battles than ever before. Millions of
> dollars were spent on direct campaign donations, independent
> campaign expenditures and on mobilizing the most aggressive
> grassroots operation in NRA history. There were 6.5 million
> endorsement cards and letters sent, 2.4 million endorsement
> phone calls, 1.6 million bumper stickers, nearly 50,00 [*sic*]
> television, radio and newspaper ads and 510 billboards.... In
> 2004, NRA was involved in 265 campaigns for the U.S. House
> and Senate, winning in 254 of those races. These victories
> represent the re-election of pro-gun majorities in both the
> U.S. House and Senate.

IANSA director Rebecca Peters, whom the NRA described as an "international anti-gun zealot," made it clear how the NRA motivates its members: "The NRA would have you believe that gun own-

ership is the single most important issue in the lives of Americans."
Indeed, the NRA equates gun ownership with free speech, stating
in their fact sheet "Fables, Myths and Other Tall Tales," "like the
tools of the free press, firearms are among the few products that
the Bill of Rights specifically protects the right of the people to
own, possess and use." Having focused the concerns of its membership, the NRA leadership inspires them to send letters, march on
Capitol Hill, make phone calls to local politicians and, most impor-
tantly, to vote.

The NRA positions itself as a member-focused organization, as
its website reassures prospective members, "The NRA is you—its
members." Todd Vandermyde, lobbyist for the NRA, told the *Chicago
Tribune* on May 22, 2005, "It's a natural organization. What does the
anti-gun crowd do on a weekend? Get together and talk about the gun
they didn't buy? The deer they didn't hunt?" Nonetheless, the organization's track record reveals that its membership's well-being is
hardly its greatest concern.

Tom Diaz, Josh Sugarmann's colleague at the Violence Policy
Center, offered us an example: "If [the NRA] really represented its
members, don't you think even at the very, very minimum—forget
about gun control per se—but this whole problem of firearms that
explode, that are poorly designed and poorly manufactured from
the point of view of the user—wouldn't you think that in an organization that truly represented the user, that would be the first thing
on their agenda, to have some kind of product safety regimen that
really worked?"

According to the NRA's "Fables, Myths" fact sheet, Fable XI is
"Firearms are unsafe and therefore ought to be regulated under the
consumer protection laws." While the NRA would have us believe
that exploding guns are a mere fairy tale, the association does
appear to accept some industry standards, citing uncritically those
set by the Sporting Arms and Ammunition Manufacturers Institute
(SAAMI), an organization founded in 1926 at the request of the federal government: "Today, SAAMI publishes more than 700 voluntary
standards related to firearm and ammunition quality and safety."
While the U.S. government initiated SAAMI's creation, the organi-

Tom Diaz

zation is closely linked to the firearms industry's trade organization, the National Shooting Sports Foundation—indeed, they share the same mailing address and current president, Doug Painter. Furthermore, SAAMI's standards, as they clearly state in their material, are voluntary.

For her part, Rebecca Peters feels that if the NRA didn't exist, a constructive dialogue with gun owners might occur. "We know that gun owners are not inherently paranoid," she said. "It's just the NRA." Peters's claims are strengthened by NRA executive vice-president and CEO Wayne LaPierre's own words. LaPierre, an association staff member since 1978, has authored several books, including *Guns, Bush & Kerry*: *How the Outcome of the 2004 Presidential Election Affects Your Right to Keep and Bear Arms*. A speech he gave members at the NRA's 2002 annual convention about the founding of Americans for Gun Safety by wealthy dot-commer Andrew McKelvey exemplifies his polemic style:

McKelvey's network kind of operates and sounds a lot like
Osama bin-Laden and the al-Qaeda. An extremist billionaire
with a political agenda, subverting honest diplomacy, using
personal wealth to train and deploy activists, looking for
vulnerabilities to attack, fomenting fear for political gain,
and funding an ongoing campaign to hijack your freedom
and take a box-cutter to the Constitution of the United States.
That's political terrorism. That's political terrorism, and it's a
far greater threat to your freedom than any foreign force.

These days LaPierre's speeches to his members are more upbeat.
At the 2005 annual convention, he proclaimed victory over his anti-
gun rivals: "Because you restored the Second Amendment, this freedom can be passed on to your children, and to their children, and to
their children's children." LaPierre continued,

> This most precious of birthrights can be conferred upon
> every infant whose first breath is drawn beneath our
> American skies.
>
> So let the enemies of freedom beyond these walls hear our
> solemn promise. Let arrogant billionaires buckle under the
> weight of defiant, free people. Let the U.N. schemers, and
> global plotters, and one-world planners be deafened by the
> roar of this united voice.
>
> Let the politicians who think calling us bad is good for
> their career, hear us now—or pay for it later!
>
> Assault the Second Amendment at your own political risk!
>
> Attack this association at your own political peril!
>
> After a quarter-century of climbing this mountain, we will
> not surrender one damn inch!

George W. Bush later addressed the same crowd via previously
recorded video. While he had distanced himself during the 2000
election, Bush felt free to show his true colours. "I was honoured
to have the endorsement of the National Rifle Association in last
year's election," Bush told the admiring crowd. "I am grateful for

your support and tonight I thank each of you for all of your hard work in 2004. The energy and dedication of more than four million members of the NRA is a testimony to the power and principles the NRA holds. You believe as I do that the Second Amendment gives every law-abiding American the individual right to bear arms."

After Bush's speech, a satisfied LaPierre would ask the audience, "Isn't it great to have a friend of freedom in the White House?"

BANDIED ABOUT

"You got an AK?" Rodrigo asked Paul Wall, Texas's Caucasian lone star of rap, as they stood in a driveway in downtown Houston. "Is it legal?"

"Uh, no," Paul paused. "The one I have isn't. But they just passed a law. I think that you can have those now." Paul Wall was referring to the expiration of the federal assault weapons ban, formally known as Subtitle A of Title XI of the Federal Violent Crime Control and Law Enforcement Act of 1994. The ban expired on September 13, 2004, five months before Rodrigo's conversation with Paul, and exactly ten years after the law was originally enacted. Subtitle A carried a "sunset clause" that required Congress to actively reauthorize the ban in order for it to continue. George W. Bush's Congress didn't, and the ban died a quiet death.

The sunset clause was just one of the many flaws in the assault weapons ban that resulted from the many compromises made before President Clinton could sign it into law. Some of the ban's main provisions included halting production on ammunition clips holding more than ten rounds, prohibition of pistol grips on assault-type weapons and shotguns, banning threaded muzzles and shrouded barrels and—most significant—the ban of nineteen specific weapons, including the AR-15, Tec-9, MAC-10, Uzi and AK-47. While the ban was much celebrated initially, receiving political support from Jimmy Carter, George Bush Sr. and Ronald Reagan, it was ultimately equally unpopular with both pro- and anti-gun activists.

"I'm very happy to call that assault weapons ban a total joke," Tom Diaz said. "If anything, it encouraged the domestic design and manufacture of new models of assault weapons." Indeed, manufacturers simply produced new versions of existing models with minor, non-performance-related changes. It's a rare point of agreement between Diaz and the NRA's Wayne LaPierre, who told the *Toronto Star* in 2003, "There's not a dime worth of difference in the performance characteristics between the guns on the banned list and the guns not on the banned list."

Further undermining the ban was its "grandfather clause," which allowed for any pre-existing banned guns to remain legal. The clause provided a loophole that manufacturers would exploit cleverly. For example, in the five years leading up to the ban, Intratec, the makers of the Tec-9, made an average of 33,578 guns per year. But in the final year before the ban began, in order to capitalize on the grandfather clause, Intratec ramped up production to 102,682 firearms.

While the ban was a nuisance, it had little impact on business. According to the Violence Policy Center, there were 1.5 million privately owned assault weapons before the 1994 ban. Since then, another 1.17 million assault weapons have entered the market. It's something that Rebecca Peters, who spearheaded the successful campaign to ban assault weapons in Australia, laments. "At the very least," she told us, "something that all countries should do is to ban military-styled assault weapons. But what's amazing is that [assault weapons have] been allowed to drift into civilian ownership, and therefore into the hands of all kinds of armed criminals."

The ban's effect on the criminal use of assault weapons is disputed. The most optimistic reports cite a 3 percent drop in the ATF crime-gun traces, which says nothing of the fact that, aside from the Tec-9 and MAC-10, most of the banned weapons rarely showed up in crime scenes before September 13, 1994. But the ban's aim was never to target the majority of criminal gun uses; it was to eliminate the possibility of the horrifying mass murder scenarios that these weapons have contributed to. There is also a normative effect to such legislation: the ban provided a guideline as to what weapons citizens found acceptable in their neighbourhoods. As Tom Diaz asked us to consider, "What does it mean when you're arming up entire communities with military-style weapons?"

The answer to Diaz's question would once again come from the most unlikely of sources, when a pre-presidential George Bush Jr.

told the *Houston Chronicle*, "It makes no sense for assault weapons to be around our society." Unfortunately, George let the sun set on that thought.

TERROR RISKS

In April 2005 Congressman Chris Van Hollen, a Maryland Democrat, angrily confronted the new U.S. attorney general, Alberto Gonzales. Said Van Hollen, "Does it make sense to you that we can stop a person from boarding [an] airline in order to protect the public safety, [but] that individual can turn around, get in their car, go to the local gun shop, and buy 20 semiautomatic assault weapons? Does that make sense to you, Mr. Attorney General?" Gonzales' response was atypically soft for an administration that's supposedly tough on terror. "We don't want terrorists to have firearms," he said, "but at the end of the day, we have to enforce the law. And unless they have a disability under the statute, then they're entitled to a weapon."

When Florin Krasniqi, a former gunrunner, explained in March 2005 to *60 Minutes'* Ed Bradley how he easily smuggled arms bought legally in the U.S. to Albanian combatants, he added, "I took advantage of a liberal law here in this country to help my old country. And I believe in my heart I did it for the good. But some people can do it for the bad." Indeed, Krasniqi's specialty items—.50 calibre sniper rifles—are reputedly able to pierce engine blocks from a kilometre away, sparking fears that terrorists will use them to shoot down aircraft in the United States. Krasniqi boasts of a single shipment of a hundred such guns that he sent by plane to Albania.

The *60 Minutes* report would be attacked by pro-gun elements as gun-control propaganda, but an April 2004 profile on Ronnie Barrett, the creator of the .50 calibre sniper rifle, in *American Rifleman*, an NRA publication, identifies why the .50 calibre is a unique weapon. Assistant technical editor Glenn M. Gilbert reports: "The .50 BMG round fired by a Barrett . . . has enough power to stop a truck, but is more precise than a machine gun."

Two months after the World Trade Center and Pentagon attacks, George W. Bush made a speech to the U.N. General Assembly, stating definitively, "We have a responsibility to deny weapons to terrorists and to actively prevent private citizens from providing them." But in January 2004 Bush passed the $328-billion omnibus appropriations bill that carried a clause requiring all records of arms purchases kept by the ATF to be destroyed within twenty-four hours, seriously hampering any attempt to track potential terrorist purchases of guns from American retailers. The clause, initiated by then attorney general (and NRA member) John Ashcroft, reduced the period of record-keeping down from ninety days. "We are losing a great source of intelligence information," Joseph Vince, a former ATF agent, told us. "We should have learned after 9/11. Everybody said our agencies weren't able to connect the dots. What we do now is we take the dots off the paper."

The passage of the bill seems glaringly incongruous beside the stance of an administration whose Patriot Act has proven it more than willing to impinge on the rights of its citizens in the name of fighting terror. Bush's move prompted New Jersey Democratic senator Frank R. Lautenberg to request an inquiry into the vulnerabilities created by the president's manoeuvre. The report, conducted by the Government Accountability Office and released in January 2005, reveals that in a nine-month period during 2004 there were forty-four attempts by suspected terrorists living in America to purchase guns. In thirty-five cases, they succeeded.

IF THE SUIT FITS

On October 30, 1998, New Orleans mayor Marc Morial addressed his constituents about an initiative that would intensify the battle for gun control in America for the next seven years—a lawsuit on behalf of the City of New Orleans against fifteen gun manufacturers. "We have been so focused here in New Orleans on fighting crime," Mayor Morial said, "getting guns off the street, and protecting our citizens. We have already reduced crime in New Orleans by 40 percent since 1994. This lawsuit is the next step in making New Orleans the safest city in America." In 1994 Morial's New Orleans, known to some as "Chopper City," was home to a staggering 421 murders among its 475,000 residents. To put this into perspective, if the Big Easy were the size of the Big Apple, there'd have been over seven thousand homicides that year.

It's rainin' choppers so get a bulletproof roof

— B.G., "All on U," off *Chopper City* (1997)

N'Awlins native B.G. came up in what was once America's most murderous city (before Hurricane Katrina). "In New Orleans you can get
killed just for looking at a nigga wrong," he said. B.G., like many in
his community, has felt the violence first-hand. His father was shot
and killed by robbers when the rap star was just a little boy. His
mother, left in poverty to fend for him and his brother, tried to raise
B.G. right. But as the Baby Gangsta put it, "When my daddy got
killed, that's when I jumped off the porch." As he paused to reflect on
the violence that's claimed so many in his hometown, B.G. sounded
resigned. "I don't know if it's in the water or in the air," he said. "It's
just been like that since I remember."

Morial's lawsuit on behalf of the City of New Orleans was an
attempt to curb the violence that citizens like B.G. considered
inescapable. The suit named fifteen major handgun manufacturers,
three gun industry trade organizations and several gun dealers, and
was America's first lawsuit launched by a government entity against
the gun industry. According to court documents in *Mayor Marc H.
Morial and The City of New Orleans v. Smith & Wesson Corporation,
et al.*, the New Orleans government claimed that the city had suffered harm "associated with the manufacture, marketing, promo-
tion, and sale of firearms which are unreasonably dangerous under
Louisiana law." Further, the city alleged that "actions by defendants
have caused the city to pay out large sums of money to provide services including but not limited to necessary police, medical and emergency services, health care, police pension benefits and related
expenditures, as well as to have lost substantial tax revenues due to
lost productivity."

The gun industry had anticipated lawsuits, and held meetings in
the late 1990s with mayors across America to dissuade them from
taking such actions. So when Morial made his announcement, the
industry was ready for, as the *National Review*'s Dave Kopel called it,
their "Pearl Harbor." Morial was immediately attacked as a hyp-
ocrite. *Salon* reported that his administration, through an Indiana

broker, had sold 7,300 guns seized from criminals, including 230 assault rifles, putting them back onto the streets of America—many of them lacking the same features, such as safeties, that Morial's suit alleged the gun industry was irresponsible for not including on all their firearms.

Attacks on Morial proved unnecessary. In July 1999 Louisiana governor Murphy J. Foster passed two laws excluding gun manufacturers from Louisiana's Products Liability Act, effectively ending the New Orleans lawsuit. Despite the Orleans Parish Civil District Court's ruling that the new bill was unconstitutional, the Louisiana Supreme Court upheld it by a 5-2 vote, claiming the city's lawsuit was an indirect attempt to regulate the lawful design, manufacture, marketing and sale of firearms. New Orleans failed, but the city's move inspired many other government entities to follow suit. Over the next few years, thirty-three cities and counties, including Chicago, Washington, Boston, Cleveland, Miami and New York City, launched lawsuits against gun manufacturers and organizations that support them.

According to an August 7, 2005 editorial penned for the *San Francisco Gate* by Doug Painter, president and CEO of the NSSF, "The gun industry has already spent $225 million defending itself against this legal shakedown—a massive sum for an industry that, if its individual companies were taken together, would barely make the Fortune 1000." Painter's pleas of pauperdom were superfluous—by the time he wrote his editorial, all but four of the government suits had been dismissed, closed or impeded by state legislation. Nonetheless, in the late nineties and early millennium, the industry feared that the litigious atmosphere could eventually put them out of business. As Painter put it, "While we have had some success in the courtroom, one bad decision could wipe out our industry."

During this time of anxiety in the gun industry, Smith & Wesson made a stunning move to avoid future litigation against the company. "In the nineties," S&W historian Roy Jinks explained, "[Smith & Wesson] had a president who felt that if we could do something to prevent all the foolish lawsuits, we could help the industry. His

approach was to try and cut a deal with the people in the federal government to stop some of these lawsuits, and the whole thing back-
fired because, one, they weren't interested in stopping them and,
two, it irritated the National Rifle Association and a whole bunch of
other people." Glock considered joining S&W in the settlement and
did participate in the negotiations, but ultimately did not partake.
Smith & Wesson would go it alone.

The highlights of Smith & Wesson's agreement with President
Clinton included requiring safety locking devices for all handguns
and pistols, devoting 2 percent of annual firearms revenues to the
development of "smart guns," limiting magazines to ten rounds,
restricting multiple handgun sales and establishing a commission
to oversee the agreement. S&W's move amounted to treason in the
gun community. Gun Owners of America, a powerful pro-gun lobbying group, commented on the deal in a press release on March 21,
2000: "The firearms manufacturer's lamentable decision to 'settle'
with the most anti-gun Administration in history cannot go without
a pointed response by all those who seriously cherish and believe in
the God-given right of individual self defense." The press release
added, "We are aware of the 'extortionary' pressure that Smith &
Wesson was under from the maniacal Clinton-Gore Administration,
and the costly legal struggle that [the company] faced. However, to
defeat such a vicious and cunning opponent requires courage and
perseverance, not capitulation."

Gun World editor Jan Libourel reflected on Smith & Wesson's
decision, telling us, "They brokered a very complex arrangement
with the Clinton administration regarding gun sales, which in
essence would allow them to self-police their sales, distribution and
advertising far beyond the bounds imposed by any public law." Asked
how he felt personally about the decision, Libourel said, "They sold
out. They kind of gave away the farm."

The industry's reaction went well beyond words. Discussing
S&W's "sell-out" Robert Ricker explained, "That was a huge split
within the industry and within the NRA. Smith & Wesson was the
largest handgun maker in the world and probably one of the most
well-known brand names, and when that happened, the NRA reacted

very violently against them and called for a boycott, and it almost destroyed the whole company."

When then British-owned Smith & Wesson brokered its deal with the Clinton administration, Ed Schultz, at that time the president of S&W, believed that if any company could go against the industry, it was his. It was an overestimation of his company's power, and a gross underestimation of the wrath and reach of the gun industry and community. Ricker summarized Smith & Wesson's fate: "The company was sold almost two years later [in 2001], for pennies on the dollar." Fifteen million dollars, to be exact. By contrast, in 1987 owners Tomkins of London purchased the company for US $112.5 million.

S&W's near collapse served as a lesson to other gun manufacturers: there would be no compromising and no agreements. With Bill Clinton exiting office less than a year after Smith & Wesson, the industry's fortunes changed completely. Incoming president George W. Bush, a new Congress and the Senate were all largely pro-gun, providing the perfect environment for the industry to realize its final solution: immunity.

"Should Ford or Chrysler be held responsible if a drunk or negligent driver injures someone? Sensible Americans say no, and that's what this bill reflects." That's part of a speech that Republican senator Larry Craig has delivered on countless occasions to promote a "Protection of Lawful Commerce in Arms Act." Craig's comments are unsurprisingly similar to the words of the gun industry itself. NSSF president Doug Painter's version, as printed in his August 7, 2005, *S.F. Gate* editorial, goes like this: "Blaming members of our highly regulated industry for the criminal misuses of a lawfully sold product is like saying Ford Motor Company should be held accountable for the harm caused when a drunk driver misuses one of its cars."

The similarities come as no surprise to anyone who understands Craig's allegiances. He has been on the NRA's board of directors since 2001. During the past two sessions of Congress, the Idaho senator has tried to get this immunity bill through on four different occasions. The gun industry insists that it desperately needs such a bill, but opponents like Rhode Island Democratic senator Jack Reed declare otherwise. "The gun lobby says it needs protection because it's faced with a litigation crisis," Reed told *USA Today* on July 28, 2005. "The facts tell precisely the opposite story."

Reed pointed to Securities and Exchange Commission filings by Ruger and Smith & Wesson, in which both companies reported that the foreseeable suits would be manageable. Ruger's 2004 SEC filing states: "While it is not possible to forecast the outcome of litigation or the timing of costs, in the opinion of management, after consultation with special and corporate counsel, it is not probable and is unlikely that litigation, including punitive damage claims, will have a material adverse effect on the financial position of the Company." Smith & Wesson's 2004 filing includes a similar forecast: "We do not anticipate a material adverse judgment and intend to defend ourselves vigorously. In light of our views of the merits of the underlying claims, we believe that we have provided adequate reserves and insurance with respect to such claims."

In the same SEC filing Smith & Wesson reported spending $1.5 million in defence and administrative costs relating to these lawsuits while paying out $16,039 in settlements over the fiscal year—not exactly back-breaking numbers for a company that showed revenues of $125 million in the same year, and claimed gross profits of $39.1 million. Nonetheless, the industry and its supporters knew they had the clout to pass a bill that could turn those payouts into zeroes.

The gun industry came close to immunity in 2004 when Larry Craig tried to pass S.1805, his latest version of the "Protection of Lawful Commerce in Arms Act." He appeared to have the support of influential Senate minority leader Tom Daschle, a Democrat from South Dakota, to push the bill through the Senate. While Daschle publicly backed the bill, he and other Democrats manoeuvred to include a clause in S.1805 that would extend the assault-weapons ban. Daschle's amendment proved to be a "poison pill" for the bill—an addition so unattractive to the supporters of the legislation that it effectively killed its progress.

ARMS AROUND THE WORLD

You got guns? We got guns
Yo, I got straps, we got straps
A million muthafuckers on the planet Earth
Talk that hard bullshit, 'cause it's all they worth
> —Dr. Dre, "Been There, Done That," off *The Aftermath* (1996)

It should come as no surprise that Americans own more guns than the people of any other nation, doubling second-place Yemen's per capita statistics. But who woulda thunk that the sweet Suomis in Finland would rank third? How about Gaza getting outgunned by Canada? Or Uruguay usurping Kosovo? In the wide world of gunplay, all the planet's a stage, and all the players merely targets.

Territory	Firearms (millions)	Firearms per 100 Civilians
Afghanistan	0.5–1.5	1.7–5.0
Australia	2.3	11.8
Brazil	23.5–33.5	13.1–18.8
Canada	7.0	21.9
China**	40.0	4.0
Finland*	1.8	39.0
France*	17.8	30.0
Gaza/West Bank	0.05	21.0
Germany*	24.2	30.0
Iraq	7.0–8.0	27.0–30.8
Israel	0.4	6.0
Jamaica	0.08–0.2	2.9–7.3
Mexico	4.9–17.9	4.7–17.3
Nigeria	1.0	0.9
Russia*	6.5	4.0
Serbia/Montenegro*	1.0	10.5
South Africa	4.7	11.0
Uganda	0.6–1.0	3.0–4.5
Uruguay*	1.0–1.7	26.5–49.4
Venezuela	1.6–6.4	4.7–23.3
Yemen	8.0	40.0
U.S.A.	238.0–276.0	83.0–96.0
World	639.0	10.3

* Civilian-owned   ** Unconfirmed by source

Daschle's sinking of the bill came at a price. In the 2004 election the NRA launched a massive campaign to have him defeated, and Daschle became the first Senate minority leader to lose his seat in fifty-two years. NSSF general counsel Larry Keane commented to the *Washington Post* on July 28, 2005, "We believe it cost him his Senate seat." Daschle's defeat left other Democrats cowed. With four new pro-gun senators elected in 2004, the stage was finally set for Craig to pass the latest incarnation of the immunity bill, S.397.

Several organizations, including the American Bar Association and former heads of the ATF, made last-minute pleas to Congress to halt what seemed like the imminent passage of S.397. A letter from seventy-five law professors representing some of America's most prestigious universities, led by the University of Michigan's Sherman Clark, made clear the act's true implications and offered a frightening example of the failings of the bill:

> Under this bill, a firearms dealer, distributor, or
> manufacturer could park an unguarded open pickup truck
> full of loaded assault rifles on a city street corner, leave it
> there for a week, and yet be free from any negligence liability
> if and when the guns were stolen and used to do harm. A
> firearms dealer, in most states, could sell 100 guns to the
> same individual every day, even after the dealer is informed
> that these guns are being used in crime—even, say, by the
> same violent street gang.

Proponents of the bill claimed that the act left plenty of room for negligence litigation, and on July 29, 2005, S.397 passed the Senate with a 65–31 vote, receiving support from 96 percent of Republicans and 32 percent of Democrats. Senator Craig quickly delivered a victory speech. "Today," he stated, "the Senate made a strong stand against predatory lawsuits and the practice of achieving a social agenda through the courts, rather than the legislative process. Private citizens seeking self-defense, law enforcement officers, the armed services and our national security all won today." But, as usual, the real winners were the gun manufacturers—by that after-noon the value of Smith & Wesson's shares had jumped by 46.2 percent, while stock in Ruger rose by 16.9 percent.

UNRA

Antonio Evora, the Small Arms Team leader for the United Nations Department of Disarmament Affairs (UNDDA), greeted Rodrigo at the U.N.'s visitor entrance in New York City with a handshake and a wide smile. He was neatly dressed in a solid navy blue suit and tie. The suit was snug, the pants almost floodish. His name, accent and countenance provided no hints of his origin—he could pass as a native of nearly any continent. Indeed, Evora looks like a composite of the U.N. Assembly.

"I'm sorry for making you wait, Rodrigo," Evora said, adding a slight *jh* sound to the beginning of his name. He led Rodrigo down a series of expansive hallways that alternated between long curves and ninety-degree angles, tourists passing by as they walked and gawked in designated areas.

Unlike the airiness of the lobby, UNDDA's office hallways are grey and cramped; the furniture and signage look like U.N. originals from the fifties. They headed into Evora's office—small, undecorated and dominated by paper. An incredible view of Manhattan's concrete expanse was only slightly obstructed by a small trophy—a revolver with its barrel tied in a knot—sitting on the windowsill.

Evora, a native of Cape Verde (a group of islands off the west coast of Africa), is in charge of the monumental task of reducing the trade and stockpiles of illicit small arms around the world. He leads a multicultural team of fifteen who produce reports, create legislative suggestions (or, as Evora calls them, "instruments") for the U.N. Assembly to consider, and then produce more reports, sometimes even reporting on reports. It's an endless cycle of bureaucracy and protocols that could dampen even the most ebullient soul, but Evora seems genuinely jovial. Still, a noticeable tension emerged when the subject turned to his work.

"Rodrigo, as I said before, it's not my personal views. I'll be speaking as a U.N. official."

Accepting his caveat, Rodrigo asked, "How many illicit guns are there?"

"That's a difficult question, because they are illicit," he said, laughing as he finished the sentence. "I cannot give you a number. I do not have an estimate. I would not venture to give you any." The best estimates, reported in the 2001 *Small Arms Survey*, put the illicit market's value at US$1 billion annually, or 10 to 20 percent of the total small-arms market. The illicit market includes the illegal black market—the primary source of guns for drug dealers and criminals—and the technically legal but illicit grey market, which funnels guns—often through state-sanctioned measures that exploit the incoherence of international law—to insurgents, guerrillas and proxy armies.

When it comes to the proliferation of illicit arms, Evora explained, "Africa is the continent that is most affected. In West Africa in conflict situations and in eastern Africa, you have a serious problem [that] relates to the Somalia problem—those weapons end up being used by criminals." As Evora's statement indicates, one porous border, one unstable government is all it takes for an entire region to become inundated with firearms. While Somalia plays the role in eastern Africa and Liberia and Sierra Leone do the same in the west, Africa is not alone in dealing with the problems of the illicit market.

As Evora elucidated, "In parts of Latin America like Brazil, even though they have adopted a very serious policy on small arms, they still have a problem in the urban areas. Of course, Afghanistan, Iraq—the Middle East has many areas where small arms are completely uncontrolled." Iraq, in fact, was the scene of the greatest illegal transfer of arms in the history of the world. When the American-led coalition toppled Saddam Hussein's regime, civilians raided an estimated seven to eight million small arms from military caches, the weapons so numerous in certain areas that they initially held no cash value.

To combat this worldwide problem, the U.N.'s and Evora's main instrument in reducing the illicit trade is the lengthily titled *Program of Action to Prevent, Combat and Eradicate the Illicit Trade in Small Arms and Light Weapons in All Its Aspects*, commonly referred to as the Program of Action or, even more succinctly, the PoA. It was established after a two-week meeting of the U.N. General Assembly in July 2001. Its key initiatives are to establish international norms for tracing, firearm marking and exchanging information, and to promote governmental and manufacturing transparency. It's the U.N.'s first major initiative to curb the illicit small-arms trade; consequently, the PoA has attracted plenty of criticism. One major problem is that it is not legally binding. In Evora's words, "The U.N. encourages destruction of weapons; the PoA recommends the destruction of weapons." The U.N. can encourage and recommend, but it cannot enforce.

Rebecca Peters attended the meetings at which the PoA was drafted, and explained why it lacks effectiveness: "The original PoA does not explicitly mention the regulation of civilian possession of guns or national gun-control laws, and that was because, when it was being drafted, the U.S. insisted that there could be no mention of national gun laws. And one reason for that seems to us to be the strong influence the gun lobby has with the United States government."

When asked if he had encountered opposition from America gun manufacturers, Evora answered nebulously: "No, not opposition

Rebecca Peters

really from the manufacturing companies. Maybe opposition from certain groups that perhaps don't understand what is going on or think that the U.N. should not be dealing with this issue at all. But not from manufacturing companies."

"Is that the NRA you're talking about?"

"Well, there are groups, as you know from the media, that believe that the U.N. is trying to create a ban on guns or small arms or light weapons. But that's not the reality; that's not what's going on in the United Nations." While Evora avoided naming names, the NRA's Wayne LaPierre feels no such compunction. His position is made clear in the title of his 2006 book, *The Global War on Your Guns: Inside the UN Plan to Destroy the Bill of Rights.*

The Washington Times reported that in February 2005 LaPierre addressed attendees at the Conservative Political Action Conference, the United States' largest gathering of conservatives, saying, "If you take away the right to bear arms, all other freedoms are at risk and, in time, lost. But confiscating civilian firearms worldwide is a major mission of the U.N. right now. That's why I want the U.N. out of the U.S." He continued, "The U.N. is the world's wealthiest and most organized enemy of the very freedoms our nation can offer all mankind. It's time for the freedom-haters to pack up and get the hell outta freedom's last sanctuary."

Rebecca Peters pointed to a different agenda: "I think that they see the international issue as a source for fundraising; they whip up paranoia among provincial members who are suspicious about the rest of the world and ask them for donations. I think that they see the U.N. as a bogeyman that will stir up contributions." She added, "The gun lobby has become very interested in IANSA and in me and my American colleagues because they don't have anyone to hit on in the United States [government], and it's important for them to be fighting someone in order to raise money."

In 2003, with the Brazilian Congress considering an important law that called for a national referendum on the outright ban of firearms sales to civilians, the NRA mobilized voices and bodies to stop its passing. The NRA sent lobbyist Charles Cunningham to talk strategy with Brazilian pro-gun groups at an event hosted by the

Brazilian Society for the Defence of Tradition, Family and Property. Cunningham informed the crowd that the battle is about more than guns—"It is about freedom," *Foreign Policy* reported in January 2006.

But unfortunately for Cunningham and the NRA, the Brazilian Congress would pass the disarmament statute that set the stage for an October 23, 2005, referendum. The stakes had never been higher— a majority yes vote would have made it illegal to sell guns to civilians—and pro- and anti-gun organizations began to spend and strategize. When we spoke to Rebecca Peters in July 2005, public polls were indicating that 80 percent of Brazilians planned to vote yes. But with Brazil being home to the Americas' second-largest gun-manufacturing industry, Peters was worried. "There is a very strong gun lobby in Brazil, and obviously this will be a crucial battle for them to try to win," she said. "So we imagine they'll be trying to put in a lot of money to try to get the referendum defeated. The thing is, always with this issue, you think, 'Who stands to win off all of this?' People who are advocating prevention—i.e., us—we don't stand to profit from it. Who stands to profit from selling more guns?"

Peters's fears proved correct. The No. side launched a massive campaign that emphasized fear, crime and freedom. The message was that criminals don't obey laws, and therefore only responsible citizens would be left without guns. Further, as *Foreign Policy* pointed out in January 2006, Brazilian pro-gun activists, taking their cues from the NRA, emphasized that "loving freedom means loving guns." In a country that had suffered five hundred thousand firearm homicides between 1979 and 2003 and a long history of police and government corruption, the dual-pronged campaign proved incredibly effective. When the polls closed, 65 percent of Brazilians had voted no.

But the battle for Brazil would never be just about Brazil. The NRA's chief Washington lobbyist, Chris Cox, was quoted in *The Nation* in October 2005 as saying that Brazil is "a steppingstone for the global gun-ban lobby to inflict its will on law-abiding gun owners in the United States."

As in Brazil, the NRA was active during the UN World Conference on Small Arms in the summer of 2006. When it closed on July 7, the conference had produced no new agreements, causing the Control Arms Campaign to lament on their website, "The conference . . . collapsed after a small number of states, most prominently the United States, blocked key issues so consistently that no agreement was possible." Control Arms added that Cuba, India, Iran, Israel and Pakistan were the other culprits. The NRA released their own summary, "UN Conference on 'Small Arms' Finally Ends," stating, "No recommendations on ammunition, civilian possession or future UN meetings, or for that matter any other subjects, were adopted. The failure of this five-year program to impact the legitimate firearms industry, and the 2nd Amendment rights of U.S. citizens was total. . . . Thanks should be given to NRA Board members Bob Barr, David Keene and Jim Gilmore for their crucial participation in this significant victory."

Back in March 1997 the NRA had been involved, along with several other international firearms organizations, in the creation of the World Forum on the Future of Shooting Sports. Current WFSA president Dr. Carlo Peroni, also president of the Association of Italian Manufacturers of Firearms and Ammunition, stated the objectives of the WFSA in the June 2005 issue of *Guns & Ammo*. "If a special United Nations conference on small arms," said Dr. Peroni, "recommends against civilian ownership of semiautomatic firearms, for example, that helps gun-control advocates in your country to argue that the U.S. is out of step with the rest of the world when it comes to regulating civilian ownership of semiautomatic arms. You may defeat such proposals in your country, but isn't it better if they are never approved in the first place, anywhere in the world?"

TWISTING ARMS

U.S. manufactured missiles and M-16s
Weapons contracts, and corrupted American dreams
— Immortal Technique, "The 4th Branch," off *Revolutionary Vol. 2* (2003)

In January 1961 Dwight D. Eisenhower delivered his final speech as the U.S. president, addressing a potential threat to liberty and democracy. "In the councils of government," warned Eisenhower, "we must guard against the acquisition of unwarranted influence, whether sought or unsought, by the military-industrial complex." In the years since Eisenhower issued his sage advice, the largest weapons companies have grown into some of the most influential but least-known corporations on the planet. Rappers might influence life on the block, but the arms industry affects life in the bloc.

The expansion of NATO into former Soviet Bloc countries was partly engineered by arms corporations that saw NATO expansion into Eastern Europe as an opportunity to open up new markets and increase sales. In order to join the military alliance, new countries are required to upgrade their weapons to the standard of other NATO members.

NATO expansion isn't just about weapons sales. U.S. policy makers also see it as an opportunity to extend American political and military influence into European countries formerly aligned with the Soviet Union. "But a strong additional push for NATO expansion," William Hartung explained, "certainly came from weapons manufacturers like Lockheed Martin and Boeing and Raytheon, who realized quickly that if NATO expanded into east and central Europe, the new NATO members would need equipment that was interoperable with NATO."

During our visit to Diemaco in April 2003, Francis Bleeker mentioned a few new target markets that were becoming a focus for competition among assault rifle manufacturers: Hungary, Poland and the Czech Republic, all tentatively accepted for NATO expansion in 1998. "They will want to demonstrate a capability, with the rest of NATO," Bleeker opened up, "to show that they're part of the club. Basically, I cannot see one reason why we should not be able to provide our allies with a weapon that we use ourselves."

Speaking to us from her native Australia, anti-arms activist and Nobel laureate Dr. Helen Caldicott gave one reason. "Well, not just want to—they *have* to," she said of new NATO members buying weapons. "That's one of the rules of joining NATO. So they're between a rock and a hard place. They can't spend their money on their people." Not only will new NATO members be forced to upgrade their firearms, Bleeker himself admits that their outmoded small arms, made mostly in the former Soviet Union, will likely soon get caught up in the illegal gun mix. "If you look at, say, the Eastern European countries," Bleeker said, "they don't have a lot of money, so they will want to milk their assets, so to speak. And if they can sell their old weapons, they will do so, and not be as scrupulous as the Western European countries."

"On the other hand," he added, "I was talking to someone in Europe about this issue of the disposal of old weapons, and he just laughed. He says, 'That's very nice, it's great, but the world is awash in old weapons. You might stop it on your part, but it will come from somewhere else.'"

In February 2005 Diemaco's parent corporation, Quebec-based Héroux-Devtek, let the profitable little gun maker go. "Our acquisition of the Diemaco business was for strategic reasons," Colt vice-president Carlton Chen told us. "It solidifies our important business relationship with the Government of Canada; improves economy of scale; affords us greater R&D, manufacturing, and sales and marketing capabilities; and provides us with a 'swing plant' to help us meet the strong demand worldwide for our military and law enforcement weapon systems." Diemaco now operates as Colt Canada Corporation.

On Colt Canada's website you can find a message about another Canadian firearms manufacturer: "Colt Canada is proud to bring our customers one of the most respected and innovative pistol makers today." Para-Ordnance and Diemaco had forged a marketing and distribution agreement since our visit, and after it acquired its Canadian subsidiary, Colt kept up the connection. "Today," Colt's Chen said, "Colt Canada enjoys an excellent business relationship with Para as one of its leading distributors. Colt Canada actively promotes and sells Para products and its pistols are featured in the Colt Canada website and its 2006 product catalog."

Colt Canada and Para-Ordnance really are birds of a feather. Both have lobbied for changes to Canadian law to make their businesses more competitive. Colt Canada's predecessor, Diemaco, succeeded in convincing the Canadian federal government to amend the Criminal Code in 1991 to allow for the export of assault rifles abroad, expanding the company's access to international markets. On Para's part, Thanos Polyzos argued before a parliamentary committee in 1995 for "relaxed regulations at his plant," in the words of an April 2002 story in the *Toronto Star*. Both also focus on the military and law enforcement markets. Para once landed a contract shipping $100,000 worth of handguns to police in Thailand. But when it comes to contracts from cops, particularly elite units, that's peanuts. As *Guns & Ammo* explained in 2003, "Para-Ord's challenge was straightforward: How to get the big police buyers to beat a path to its door. The solution was simple—build a better mousetrap." And before Colt came to the rescue, Thanos Polyzos' company made just the right bait.

Norm Gardner is as big a gun nut as any rapper and a far better shot. He's had a lot of practice—some of it at the expense of Ontario taxpayers. In his late sixties, Gardner is a former chair of the Toronto Police Services Board, an unelected position through which he exercised significant influence over the law enforcement community from 2000 to 2003, and for which he was paid $90,963 a year, plus expenses. Gardner is shiftier than manual drive in L.A. traffic. In 1994 he was the first person to show up at a firearms amnesty program in North York (now part of Toronto), where he posed for pictures holding a rifle he intended to turn in. In December '98 the *Toronto Star* reported that Gardner later admitted the gun was "garbage," something he'd obtained to stunt publicly, at no cost.

At the working group in Ottawa, as Wendy Cukier spoke with us about Para-Ordnance, Gardner's name came up. "It's no secret," she said, "that idea that he got the gun for free." But Cukier was talking about another gun, and this one wasn't garbage. As the OPP's Provincial Weapons Enforcement Unit probed the matter of stolen Para-Ordnance pistols, their phone taps happened upon another concern: the people at Para-Ordnance had given a gun away.

Thanos Polyzos had cultivated a relationship with Norm Gardner for almost a decade. Gardner toured the Para-Ordnance plant a half-dozen times—an exception to the company's "long-standing policy" that kept us out—and even test-fired some of Para's new models. In the fall of 2002, Thanos Polyzos and Ted Szabo decided, in Polyzos' words, that they wanted Gardner to "have one of our pistols as a gift." According to Transparency International, a corruption-monitoring organization, million-dollar bribes are routinely added on to billion-dollar weapons deals. The $1,100 Tac-Four .45 calibre pistol that Gardner chose from the selection Para offered was just a little promotional tool. No big thing, really.

In May 2003, after intercepting communications surrounding the Tac-Four, the OPP interviewed Gardner about the gun. After the interview, Gardner scrambled to arrange payment for the pistol. But the proof is in the popping. Between June 2001 and April 2003, Gardner took 7,900 rounds of ammunition in assorted calibres from the Toronto police's arsenal—even though policy dictated that the ammo was strictly for police practice, and Gardner's job had no connection with the use of a firearm. At a January 2004 inquiry by the Ontario Civilian Commission on Police Services examining his conduct, Gardner testified that he regarded the use of police ammo as a positional "perk."

The ammunition bothered the hearing committee more than the Para-Ordnance pistol. With respect to the former scandal, the three-member committee decided that the "conduct advanced Mr. Gardner's personal interests at the expense of the service [and] discredited and compromised the integrity of the board." Of the latter affair, the inquiry judged Gardner's performance to have fallen a "'hair' below the threshold," offering a qualification on their findings. "None of this should be taken as a criticism of the actions of Mr. Polyzos," the civilian committee said. "He is a businessman. His job is to promote Para. He is free to contact whomever he can. He is not accountable to the public. He is not subject to a Code of Conduct."

WHERE THE TOOLS RULE

Never second-guess a cat who hold gats
Concealed, but easily revealed and fast
— Havoc, "G.O.D. Pt. III," off Mobb Deep's *Hell on Earth* (1999)

If you want to understand why there are fewer gun deaths in Canada than in the U.S., you don't ask teenagers outside a Taco Bell in Sarnia for an explanation. You look at the law. Concealed-carry laws are one example. At any given time only a few dozen Canadians have a licence to walk the country's streets with a hidden firearm. Concealed-carry licences are granted to a select number of Canadian law enforcement officers, prosecutors and key witnesses in organized crime cases, and civilians who can otherwise prove their lives are in serious danger—but not as a result of a criminal lifestyle. Norm Gardner had a Canadian concealed-carry permit. Gardner was given his licence because he claimed he'd received numerous death threats in his role as a police board member. In '92 he made use of his licence to shoot and wound a would-be bandit who was attempting to rob Gardner's bakery in the T-Dot's North York neighbourhood. Gardner blasted the robber in the ass with a Glock 9.

Across the border it's much easier to get a concealed-carry licence. Bonecrusher walked us through the process in his home state of Georgia. "It's easy to get a concealed weapon," he explained. "You just have no record, no felonies, and you just write down this lit-tle piece of paper and you send it off to the [state] government. They check your background, you send 'em a postcard, a picture with your passport, like a passport photo, you send that off. They send you back a licence."

"Banner got a concealed-weapons licence," Bonecrusher added of his Mississippi homie. "We got pulled over in Atlanta; he had that motherfucker on him. That cop tried to fuck with him, dog, [and] he pulled that bitch right out. Man, that cop almost lost his fuckin' mind! He couldn't believe it! He couldn't believe that this nigga had protected himself. . . . Back then Banner looked wild, wild—he kinda clean-shaven now. He looked at Banner, and he looked at that licence, and he said, 'You guys have a nice day, sir.' He said, 'Who is this nigga?' He thought that nigga was a federalee or somethin'.'"

"Why did you decide to get a concealed-carry licence?" we asked when we caught up with David Banner.

"Aw, 'cause I love guns," he answered. "And because I don't plan on doing anything but protecting myself with my gun. My thing is that I don't want anybody to be able to tell me that I can't protect myself. And if I would do it, do it the right way. To be able to pull out an AR-15 in front of a cop, and then let him try to find every reason why you a terrorist or that you this or you that, and then for you to

David Banner

pull out a licence to carry on his ass, that's true power, because when he look at me being the young black male—like, 'Damn, this nigga got a licence to carry?'—he might think twice before he harass the next black man, 'cause that man may be just like me. And they know if you went through the rigmarole to get a licence to carry, that you'll go through whatever it takes to get his ass convicted for whatever he does to you."

"So is it hard to get one?"

"Nah, it ain't hard to get one. Ain't shit hard in this world but livin'. It ain't no more than fillin' out the papers and waitin', that's it."

In many states an applicant doesn't even have to take a test to demonstrate knowledge of firearms and the law or shooting proficiency in order to acquire a concealed-carry licence. Concealed-carry laws divide most states into two categories: "may-issue" states are those that exercise discretion in granting permits, and "shall-issue" states are those in which authorities must give a licence to any applicant who meets basic qualifications—essentially, being of legal age and having no criminal record.

In 1987 the NRA began a nationwide push for shall-issue licensing, starting in Florida. Before the NRA began its drive to extend concealed-carry rights, there were fewer than a dozen states where it was legal to carry a concealed weapon. Nowadays, nearly every state grants some concealed-carry privileges. According to the January 2006 edition of *Concealed Carry Handguns* magazine, another Harris publication, there were just four states, termed "The Bad," which completely prohibited concealed gun carrying (Kansas and Nebraska have since fallen off that list; Wisconsin and Illinois remain). Nine other jurisdictions, "The (Sometimes) Ugly," have discretionary systems, among them New York and New Jersey. Thirty-five states ("The Good") have instituted shall-issue systems in concealed-carry licensing, including Georgia and Mississippi. Vermont and Alaska ("The Really Good") don't require any kind of permit in order to carry a concealed handgun.

Texas is a shall-issue state. In 1995, during his first year as state governor, George W. Bush signed his state's concealed-carry law into existence. Two years later, born-again Bush made it legal to take hidden handguns into churches.

Florida, where Bush's younger brother, Jeb, is governor, is another shall-issue state, and a gun-lover's Mecca. After Norm Gardner's Canadian licence to carry a concealed handgun expired at the end of 1996, he immediately applied for a new concealed-carry permit—this time in the Sunshine State. Just a few months into '97, Gardner, who owns a house in Pompano Beach, was granted his permit. Gardner's licence is just one of the million permits that Florida has issued in the eighteen years since its concealed-carry laws were first introduced.

To ensure self-defenders maximum flexibility in their interpretation of a potential threat, the NRA recently began another nationwide push for legal change, again initiated in Florida. As past NRA president Marion P. Hammer literally looked over Jeb Bush's shoulder, the Florida governor signed bill SB-436 into law. M. P. Hammer, a grandmother who holds the first concealed-weapon licence ever granted in Florida, nicknamed the law the "Castle Doctrine," an allusion to the old common-law notion that a king and queen have a right to protect their turf. But the bill, according to the National Rifle Association's Institute of Legislative Action (NRA-ILA), also applies beyond the walls of one's castle, in "any place you have a right to be."

Previously, Florida's self-defence law, much like most criminal law across the United States and Canada, included a "duty to retreat" when a person felt threatened by another individual. It seems like a commonsense requirement that encourages potential victims to avoid violent confrontations if at all possible. After the ink from Jeb's pen hit the paper of SB-436, the "duty to retreat" was replaced with the right to lower the boom whenever a gunman feels threatened. On the NRA-ILA website, Jeb Bush is quoted as saying of SB-436,

"It's a good, commonsense, anti-crime issue." Despite criticisms of Florida's new gun law—including the *Miami Herald*'s declaration, "Every gang-banger in the state should write a thank-you note to the NRA"—the National Rifle Association has promised to push similar legislation in other states. In the first five months of 2006, the NRA succeeded in convincing no less than ten states to pass a version of the law.

In the summer of 2004 we contacted the NRA in order to learn more about its relationship to the gun industry. A representative insisted we were barking up the wrong tree. "If you have questions about manufacturers," their public affairs manager said, "you should probably speak to the association that represents the firearm industry, as NRA only represents individual gun owners." Added the rep, "The National Shooting Sports Foundation [NSSF] represents the firearm industry."

The NRA's statements weren't technically untrue. The NSSF does represent the gun industry, and has developed what it calls, in properly Orwellian terminology, a "media education program." When we applied for the "program" ourselves, the NSSF failed to respond. Our requests for an interview with the NSSF and an opportunity to attend the annual trade conference organized by the foundation—the SHOT show—were also shot down. Really though, if you want to know who the NRA represents, just follow the trail of breadcrumbs—a trail the association lays out on its own website.

The NRA's website includes a list of its "foundation supporters," an assortment of companies, gun distributors and gun stores that have ponied up $1,000 or more. The tax-deductible deductions go towards, says the foundation's mission statement, a "wide range of firearm related public interest activities." Among the contributors to this "public" cause are private interests such as the Beretta USA Corporation, Smith & Wesson Holding Corporation, the Sturm, Ruger Corporation, ArmaLite Inc. and, perhaps more instructively, the NSSF itself. Although the NRA does indeed rep its individual members, it ain't hard to tell that's not the only thing it represents.

Pitbull, an ill Cuban emcee from Florida, named his debut album *M.I.A.M.I.*, an acronym for "Money Is a Major Issue." Evidently presidential paper bears as heavily on today's rap music, good and bad, as it does on modern politics. Just as emcees take the rap for corporations that profit from the marketing of trigger-happy music, the National Rifle Association shields the gun industry, which benefits financially from the NRA's push for trigger-happy laws. Put simply, the NRA is frontin' for the gun business.

Whit Collins was hired as an expert witness to testify in numerous lawsuits against gun manufacturers. Collins says most of the cases came about as a result of real defects in gun design. He doubts the immunity bill will survive the next cycle of Democratic presidency. In the meantime, he explained, "Some men who make very bad guns or poor guns for various reasons, or who have guns distributed in irresponsible ways into the neighbourhoods that you're concerned with, they will probably retire very lavishly. And ask yourself if that's fair."

The NRA frames its advocacy as a defence of freedom—and it is. Less central than the freedom to own, however, is the freedom to sell. In 2005 the National Rifle Association's Defender of Freedom award went to Jeff Reh, Beretta USA's general counsel and vice-general-manager. "Reh was honored," Beretta's website says, "for his efforts in support of passage of the Protection of Lawful Commerce in Arms Act."

> It sound crazy, but I pushed to L.A.
> To get away from all the murder in the streets of the Bay
> It's no betta, juveniles with Berettas
> — Will Hen, "Read," off the Product's *One Hunid* (2006)

In March 1980 *Guns* magazine ran a feature on Ruger's most famous rifle, with a cover line reading "Mini-14: Blazing Assault Rifle or Sleek Sporter." It all depends on who's holding it. On December 6, 1989, twenty-five-year-old Marc Lépine walked into the University of Montreal's École Polytechnique. He knew he would not be walking out. Lépine had arrived with a legally purchased Ruger Mini-14 and a mission—to systematically slaughter women. By the time his suicide concluded the worst massacre in Canada's history—just twenty minutes later—Lépine had murdered fourteen women between the

ages of twenty-one and thirty-one and wounded another thirteen students, including four men. Much like shooting sprees in the U.K. and
Australia, the "Montreal massacre" triggered a new era in national
gun law. At the forefront of the push for change was Wendy Cukier
and her Canadian Coalition for Gun Control, which was formed in
response to this tragedy.

Beginning in 1991, the Canadian government instituted a registry
to screen, license and register all gun owners and legally owned guns.
The long-gun registry (Canada has had a handgun registry since
1934) has cost more than a billion dollars over a decade. In addition
to the registry, Canada prohibited a range of firearms from short-
barrelled handguns up to assault rifles (ironically, the elusive Mini-14
has never been banned). "They were active in lobbying against the legislation," Cukier said of Para-Ordnance, whose short-barrelled and
high-capacity handguns were affected by the prohibition.

But in Canada we can only do so much. Living next to the United
States is like having a neighbour who blasts loud beats at all hours—
the noise pours through the walls. And with the hard-rockin'
National Rifle Association in the house, when we request that our
neighbour respect our peace and quiet, the noise only gets turned up.

The United States could learn a lot from other countries' successes and failures in regulating guns, and more so vice versa. As
Whit Collins so perfectly defined it, "Commonsense is where we
share knowledge and solve problems." But commonsense regulations might curtail sales in the gun industry's most important market. "We don't have commonsense in here," Joseph Vince said, "and
that's because we have the dollar sign. The dollar sign unfortunately
overlies, and you see that time and time again, where people are
more concerned about making a profit than they are about saving
lives, and that's sad."

Get Rich or Die Trying

THE PULL OF THE TRIGGER

GUN CULTURE STARTED hundreds of years before li'l Sammy Colt was taking shots at innocent sea creatures or Fifty got rich. In May 2005 we visited the Royal Ontario Museum in downtown T.O., where we met with curator Corey Keeble, an expert on the history of European weaponry. Tall and jovial, with white hair and a thick beard to match, Keeble moves carefully around the museum with the help of a cane that looks as if it might itself have artistic value. As the three of us sat down in his office, lined from floor to ceiling with meticulously shelved volumes, Keeble cheerfully fielded our questions on the historical connection between firearms and art. Every so often he would pull a book from his wall, showing us examples of history's most elaborate firearms, intricately engraved and adorned with an array of jewels. We wondered whether there were local collectors of such masterpieces.

"It is very difficult to collect in Canada," Keeble explained with a sarcastic chuckle, indicating the impression Canadian gun laws had made in his circle, "because we live in a culture in which firearms seem to be the most easily accessible to criminals who don't have permits."

"Do you think it's hard for people to look past the fact that it's a weapon and see the art?" Rodrigo asked.

"The fact is that the government obviously hasn't been able to do so. It's like anything else: there are some people who can't look beyond that, and they can't look beyond it because they're biased, they're bigoted, they're ignorant."

"A rose is a rose is a rose is a rose," Keeble laughed later. "And part of the appeal of the decorated firearm has been the combination of art and science, science and art. . . . What you have with the design of a [decorated] firearm is something that you might very well have involved in the design of a jet aircraft or modern luxury sports cars, maybe a Rolls-Royce, for example, or a Bentley—something that might as well be handcrafted because there's so few of them—they're very expensive, they're status symbols."

Emerging in the mid-1300s, Europe's first firearms were far too primitive to mark aristocratic status. But as the technology improved with investments of capital, the new weapons became solely the possessions of the rich and, by extension, objects of style.

> I got rubies on my Uzis and gems on my MAC-10s
> Diamonds on my 9s, and golden bullets just to match 'em
> Platinum Magnums with silver clips, real begets
> Shit, I'm gonna milk this bitch 'til I'm filthy rich
> — Cuban Link, "Terror Squadians," off Fat Joe's *Don Cartagena* (1998)

Speaking from the Royal Military Arsenal Enfield in North London, England, in the first episode of his *War* series of documentary films, *The Road to Total War*, renowned military historian Gwynne Dyer compares the classic look of the old Lee-Enfield, adopted as the standard rifle of the British military in 1895, with a more modern weapon, the Uzi, a submachine gun carried by Israel's armed forces, among others. Whereas Dyer considers the "complex curves" of the sculpted-wood Enfield a thing of beauty, he calls the black Uzi and its machined parts "very ugly." With an appreciation of the Uzi's aesthetic so often expressed in rap, we gave Dyer a shout to ask about what was for us a strange observation.

"Actually, *aesthetics* probably is the wrong word," he said over the phone from his London home. "I know what you're talking about: people who coo over them, they stroke and they cuddle and cradle them. I've seen them do it, and it's as embarrassing a sight as any you've ever seen. But I think there is something else going on here."

"There's a concentrated, immediately accessible amount of power in those weapons," Dyer clarified, "and that's where the attraction lies." When you look at an Uzi or a Tec-9 or an AR-15, the power to wreck shop is clearly visible. *Gun World* editor Jan Libourel agreed with Dyer about what makes for a handsome gun. "I would say elegance of line, good wood, good stock, leather finishing, engraving as appropriate, excellent standards of fitting," Libourel said. "Some people see it differently. A lot of people like the look of these modern assault-type firearms such as AR-15s and AK-47s. I don't."

When it comes to the aesthetic appeal of firearms, tradition dictates taste. For an old-school sport-shooter like Libourel, a "fine double-barrelled shotgun with engraving" does the trick. In like fashion, Dyer connects the aesthetic of the Lee-Enfield rifle with "romantic concepts like glory." On the other hand, he says, "the only words called to mind by this Uzi . . . are *efficient, utilitarian, ruthless.*" But when manifested aesthetically, efficiency, usefulness and ruthlessness are beautiful qualities in some eyes. For 50 Cent, as he raps on "Gun Runners," a Calico submachine gun with a hundred-round magazine gets his "dick hard."

The shotgun has a look Libourel associates with the treasured tradition of bagging wildlife—a means to eat. Fifty connects the Calico with the tradition of not being bagged by NYC's wildlife, as well as providing a means to eat. With both firearms, form follows function, and functionality can be a beautiful thing, especially when survival is at stake. "Efficient technology is often also appreciated aesthetically," University of Toronto professor Mark Kingwell said. "The purely utilitarian weapon nevertheless retains an aesthetic dimension. It's not decoration anymore. Now the aesthetic dimension is, as it were, inherent to the weapon itself. That is, just like a fast car or an airplane or a bomb, these things can be fully functional, but they have beauty which is tied up with them. So that idea that aesthetics and utility part company is actually given the lie by things like that— they're *beautiful.* They have a beauty in being sort of wickedly good at what they do. You make a more efficient weapon, and it also has this added bonus—except it's not added—of aesthetic appeal."

Gun-control advocates don't often indulge the visual allure of firearms. The 2005 *Small Arms Survey,* though, addressed the surge of guns appearing in modern art with a section titled "Shooting Gallery." Citing artist Andy Warhol's early eighties work *Gun* as critical to the introduction of firearms into pop culture, *Survey* says: "Today throughout the world, film stars, rappers, and other role models continue to actively promote that image as a symbol of power and sex appeal." The global explosion in gun imagery is no accident. The design of an Israeli Uzi quickly betrays the killer efficiency that results from over seven centuries of engineering experience. The fascination with the power of that image is what many entertainers, not to mention gun manufacturers, are using to tell stories and sell product.

Gerald Cupchik is another professor from the University of Toronto, and an expert on cultural psychology. The very forward Dr. Cupchik drew attention to an important point in analyzing the aesthetics of gun culture—it has two faces. "It's either romantic or horrific," he said.

"That's the centre of your book right there," he modestly asserted. "Finished. See, with romantic, it's beautiful and it doesn't scare me, and it can have all this symbolic shit in it. And when it's horrific, it's because I live in a community where guns are being used and you can kill me. There is no joke about it, there is no irony about it. That's not bad, huh?"

"That's a very key distinction," Chris acknowledged.

"That's good," Cupchik concluded of his own idea. "Then you've got to see what goes with romantic and what goes with horrific."

Prodigy identifies the former. On Mobb Deep's classic cut "Quiet Storm," the P raps about his pops showing him how to shoot a real gun at the tender age of seven. But that was far from his first exposure to firearms. "I guess it was just images in magazines, movies, TV," Prodigy remembered. "That's the first introduction to guns, right? Cartoons, comic books, toys. Yup, that was it."

In this Third Chamber we take a closer look at the romantic manifestations of gun culture listed by Prodigy (plus a couple more), examining the glorification of guns in society and the media, the promotion of their misuse and the obscuring of their real impact.

KILLIN' 'EM SOFTLY

"Boys and girls, get your exciting Lone Ranger rapid-fire revolver from Cheerios!" tempted an American television advertisement that aired in the 1950s. With 50 cents and proof of purchase from two Cheerios boxes, kids could mail away for a handgun that shot rubber bands. The promo picked up on the popularity of cowboy movies, which coincided with a spectacular rise in the number of toy guns sold stateside, from thirty million up to 1956 to a total of a hundred million near the start of the sixties, according to a 1999 episode of A&E's *Investigative Reports*.

When asked what motivated his old protegé Tupac Shakur's interest in firearms, Shock G—a.k.a. the one and only Humpty Hump—also pointed to the beginning: "Like all male teenagers, Pac enjoyed the sense of power, security and masculinity that a gun gives. Kids start with play guns and water guns, then BB guns, and eventually street guns and hunting rifles. All the cartoons and video games feature intense and exaggerated gunplay. Some crave it so much they become cops and soldiers later in life. Pac's interest and involvement with guns was average for this culture."

Technically classed as NPGs (non-powder guns), a category that also includes paintball guns and stun guns, gas-powered or hand-pumped air BB guns primarily fire metal ball bearings, mostly in .177 calibre. According to the U.S. Centers for Disease Control and Prevention (CDC), of the 3.2 million NPGs sold annually in the United States, 80 percent have a muzzle velocity exceeding 350 feet (105 m) per second. At that speed, the California Senate Office of Research reported in May 2005, a pellet can penetrate both skin and bone, blurring the line between these "toys" and the real thing.

The CDC found that, in 2000 alone, hospital emergency rooms treated 21,187 NPG-related injuries across the U.S. Children or teenagers sustained more than three-quarters of those, with the highest rate of injury among male children between the ages of ten and fourteen, 80 percent of whom were white. Furthermore, the Consumer Product Safety Commission (CPSC) counted sixty-three deaths due to NPG fire between 1980 and 2000. In the fall of 2001 the CPSC filed a lawsuit against the most recognized maker of BB guns, Arkansas-based Daisy Manufacturing Co.

Pumping out pellet guns since 1886, Daisy had one of its products become infamous in the 1983 film *A Christmas Story*, about a boy in 1940s middle America whose Christmas wish is "an official Red Ryder, carbine action, 200-shot Range Model air rifle." Throughout the movie every adult warns nine-year-old Ralphie Parker that he'd only "shoot his eye out" with the Daisy rifle. Despite the warnings, Ralphie's dad goes ahead and makes his son's Christmas day. Ralphie has shot himself in the face before lunch.

The CPSC's suit blamed two Daisy BB gun models for at least 15 deaths and 171 serious injuries, the bulk of which involved children. Like many real firearms involved in similar accidents, these rifles appeared empty when in fact rounds remained inside the gun. Expecting to blast themselves or friends with air, kids lodged pellets in their heads and bodies.

The National Rifle Association rushed to Daisy's defence and mailed its members a "special alert" before the CPSC could file suit. According to an April 2004 story in *The Wall Street Journal*, the NRA was largely concerned that effective action against Daisy could be used in future lawsuits against manufacturers of real firearms. Beyond such legal concerns, Daisy Outdoor Products is also an NRA "foundation sup- porter." On the same day the CPSC filed its lawsuit, George Bush Jr. nominated Harold Stratton Jr. to replace Ann Brown, a Democrat cho- sen by Bill Clinton, as the CPSC's chair. Stratton had previously been part of Lawyers for Bush in the state of New Mexico. In late 2003, under Stratton's leadership, the CPSC settled with Daisy, saving the company from the threat of a taxing recall. Instead, Daisy would have to do little more than spend $1.5 million on a five-year safety campaign involving ads in gun magazines and new merchandise labelling.

> You bitch niggas still pumpin' your guns
> Like pump pellets won't puncture your lungs
> — Beanie Sigel, "B.B. Gun," off *State Property*
> *Presents Vol. II: The Chain Gang* (2003)

NPGs aren't just for the world's Ralphie Parkers anymore. Usurping paintball as the most popular of non-lethal shooting sports, airsoft takes its name from the fact that the guns, powered primarily by either electricity or gas, fire a plastic pellet that is slightly larger, and far less dangerous, than metal BBs.

Originating in Japan in the 1980s, airsoft guns perfectly resem- ble and operate much like real firearms, complete with detachable magazines. Airsoft manufacturers are licensed to use the trademark and trade-dress of virtually any model of any brand of gun available. "Have you dreamt about shooting an AK-47," lures leading online seller Redwolf Airsoft, "a silenced MP5 SD5, or even the exotic FN P90? How about emptying a Glock 17 or a full auto Glock 18C at targets? What about the hot high speed M11?" Donning fatigues and heading out to dedicated event fields to join "skirmishes," airsofters can make all their barrel-spitting fantasies come true.

As in Japan, airsoft has helped feed a hunger for the feel of real guns left unsatisfied by the United Kingdom's strict firearms laws. An estimated ten thousand players regularly participate in airsoft events in the U.K., one of whom is Airsoft Arnie, who runs the popular website www.arniesairsoft.co.uk. Arnie measures expansion in airsoft interest by the number of retail outlets and event fields operating in his country. He claims the number of shops that exclusively sell airsoft products has surged from one to ten stores in just five years. Asked whether pellet guns could serve as "gateway" guns, triggering an interest in the real thing, Arnie couldn't see it. "As I live in a country where real guns are prohibited for all intents and purposes," he said, "it's hard to comment. From my own point of view, I see real firearms as tools, tools that deserve respect, and like any other tool I don't have an urge to buy one unless I have a use for it. I have no need to hunt or cull animals and there are no ranges for me to practise at, so ultimately I'm not interested in purchasing real firearms."

Many airsofters derive at least as much pleasure from gazing at their guns as they do from skirmishes. On most airsoft websites, enthusiasts post photos of their latest and greatest pieces, which are often equipped with functioning scopes, silencers, flashlights and laser sights. But Airsoft Arnie is above any kind of aesthetic connection with his NPGs. "I don't find guns 'cool' or attractive, I'm afraid," he said. "From an engineering and educational standpoint, I'm interested in how technology progresses through the years—that's about it."

Airsofters aren't the only people fakin' gats in the U.K. nowadays. From 2003 to 2004, the use of replica guns in British crime increased by 66 percent, while fakes were involved in as much as 30 percent of all gun crime, *The Times* reported on May 16, 2005. Making matters worse for the U.K.'s airsofters, two-year-old Andrew Morton was shot in the head with a BB gun and killed in Glasgow while looking at a fire engine in March 2005. A twenty-seven-year-old man, Mark Bonini, claimed he had intended to shoot a nearby firefighter, not Andrew, but received life in prison anyway after a jury of the Scottish high court found him guilty of murder.

In the wake of the pellet-gun tragedy, *The Times* reported on June 9, 2005: "The government is to ban the manufacture, import and sale of realistic imitation guns after a surge in crimes involving fake firearms." Up in arms over the proposed legislation, airsofters began, according to an August 16, 2005, *Guardian* article, "a campaign to pressure MPs and promote their sport, bolstered by support from enthusiasts in the US, Canada and Japan." Although advocates of the legislation argued that it was simply a matter of making airsoft guns look less like the real thing, as Frank Bothamley, who runs an airsoft event site in Cambridgeshire, explained, "People around the world want guns that look like real guns."

MO' BANG 4 DA BUCK

We gon' thug this shit out
We gon' thug this shit out
And say Bang! Bang! Bang! Bang! Bang! Bang! Bang! Bang!
Bang! Bang! Bang! Bang! Bang! Bang! Bang! Bang!
— Noreaga, "Bang Bang," off Capone-N-Noreaga's *Reunion* (2000)

In February 2001, as emcee Lil' Kim left New York radio station Hot 97 after an on-air appearance, she and her entourage came upon Capone-N-Noreaga (or CNN) and crew. Shortly thereafter, six different guns discharged thirty bullets, at least one of which entered a nearby apartment building. Just one member of Capone's click was wounded. The armed confrontation had come as the result of a musical collaboration involving CNN and Brooklyn's Foxy Brown. The song, on which Foxy responds venomously to what she perceives as a "subliminal" attack against her by Lil' Kim and P. Diddy, was called, simply,

"Bang Bang." It wasn't the first or last time rap artists had chosen that name for a track. Asked about the popularity of the song title, Capone explained: "Because you get it poppin' off that track! Everybody that made a track called 'Bang Bang' is gangsta! And you can see what 'Bang Bang' records lead up to." Fortunately, though, in twelve of thirteen cases, life didn't imitate art.

Dr. Dre	"Bang Bang," *The Chronic 2001* (1999)
Capone-N-Noreaga	"Bang Bang," *The Reunion* (2000)
King Sun	"Bang Bang," *Say No More* (2000)
Kam	"Bang Bang," *Kamnesia* (2001)
G-Unit	"Bang Bang," *Automatic Gunfire* (2002)
Big Noyd	"Bang Bang," Mobb Deep's *Free Agents* (2003)
Big Noyd	"Shoot Em Up (Bang Bang) Pt. 2," *Only the Strong* (2003)
Drag-On	"Bang Bang Boom," *Hell and Back* (2003)
Young Buck	"Bang Bang," *Straight Outta Ca$hville* (2004)
SMG	"Bang Bang," *Repossession* (2004)
Krumbsnatcha	"Bang Bang," *Let the Truth Be Told* (2004)
Shea Davis	"Bang Bang Bang," *Rush-Hour Gunfire* (2005)
Capone	"Chitty Chitty Bang Bang," *Pain, Time & Glory* (2005)

RAT-A-TAT-TAT

Got a long list and I'm a get every one of ya
Beware of The Punisher!

— Rakim, "The Punisher," off *Don't Sweat the Technique* (1992)

Rodrigo loved superheroes from the first time he slipped on his Batman pajamas. He wore the blue-and-grey until the ankle elastics met his knees and the washing machine had worn Batman in half. But by the time he was eight, his Batman pajamas had become an embarrassing memory of toddlerhood. Batman had become a saccharine superhero with a nerdy sidekick who pranced around nonsense villains in a campy TV show. The pair had become almost as loathsome as the milquetoast Superman. To be worthy of Rodrigo's weekly $3 allowance, a comic book needed a superhero with flaws, moral dilemmas, not too many powers and, preferably, a dark side.

Frank Castle, a.k.a. The Punisher, became that hero. The cover of *The Punisher* number 1–"in a four-issue limited series" that ended up being five issues–featured the new (un)caped crusader with his back against the wall, firing two-fisted at an unseen enemy. His face strained, his eyes bulged, his mouth roared, his clothes ripped, his muscles rippled, his twin barrels flared, his cartridges ejected, his bullets whizzed–he was the most intense thing little Buns had ever seen.

The Punisher, an ex-Marine, had vowed to use battle-honed skills to avenge the murder of his family by the Mafia. He also made it his mission to kill every criminal he encountered along the way. And after achieving vengeance, he just kept on killing. He was judge, jury and executioner, but mostly executioner. He had no superpowers but he had tons of guns. It's hard to find a cover of *The Punisher* that doesn't feature a firearm. As Chuck Dixon, author of many *Punisher* issues, said, "The guns are his tools. . . . His talent with weapons is his edge."

Comic book writer and editor Tony Bedard, who's worked on classic characters such as Wonder Woman and Aquaman, as well as newer, darker titles like *Kiss Kiss Bang Bang,* described the Punisher's personality. "Too often people miss the point and just think that kind of character is basically an okay guy," Bedard said. "But he's really just a glorified serial killer who happens to prey exclusively on criminals."

While Rodrigo worshipped a serial killer and disdained the schmaltzy adventures of Superman and Batman, there was a reason why the Man of Steel had gone soft and the Dark Knight had lightened up. In June 1938 Superman debuted in *Action Comics* number 1; a year later, Bob Kane's Batman was unleashed. Both characters had lost their parents, both fought corrupt cops and politicians the way they did criminals, and both were a huge success. Over the next decade, comic books experienced incredible popularity, especially during the Second World War, their heroes' exploits countering the fears of the era. The first issue of *Captain America*, for instance, pits the hero against Hitler himself. But as readers aged and the industry grew, titles became more specialized in theme and subject, and increasingly adult in subject matter.

Then, in 1953 a well-known psychologist, Dr. Fredric Wertham, published *Seduction of the Innocent: The Influence of Comic Books on Today's Youth.* Wertham fingered comic books as the culprit in the rise of youth crime. The U.S. Senate formed the Subcommittee on Juvenile Delinquency, to which Wertham proclaimed outrageously, "Hitler was a beginner compared to the comic book industry." While the Senate felt the subcommittee's findings were inconclusive, comic book manufacturers formed the Comics Magazine Association, which created the Comics Code Authority (CCA) to regulate content. Titles that did not meet the standards of the CCA were not stocked by retailers, and the CCA's restrictions bankrupted most crime and horror comic book publishers, leaving only capitulating companies to create a more "family-oriented" product.

Shredded-shorts-wearing Mississippi emcee David Banner—no relation to the shredded-shorts-wearing alter ego of the Incredible Hulk, Bruce Banner—reflected on society's tendency to blame entertainment for criminalizing youth. "If you have a weak child," Banner said, "that has an opening to be impressed or moved in a certain way, he'll be impressed to move no matter whether it's a video game, whether it's a movie, whether it's a comic book. A weak child is gonna find something to be impressed by." Chuck Dixon agrees. "I really think that kids are sophisticated enough to separate fantasy from reality," he said. "You'll always have that tiny minority that can't tell the difference between make-believe and the real thing. But those kids are heading for trouble anyway, without the help of TV or comics."

And if those kids *are* headed for trouble, comic books are one place they can learn how to handle it. John Risdall explained how he brought the Desert Eagle—which shares its name with a flip-movie comic book from the early 1940s—to a broader audience. "I would go to the San Diego ComiCon every year," he said, "for about those first five years that we had the Desert Eagle out, and give all artists the catalogue and scrap art and things like that, so they could include it. The cool thing is, the guy who really liked it is a guy named Mike Grell, who was doing *Jon Sable, Freelance.* And so we made it into—I forget which issue it was, but it was like issue 22, 23, 24, 25. And the cool part was he actually got how the gun worked, and so he showed a guy fighting some bad guys, and at the end—when the clip's empty, the gun locks open, as you know—and so he's got the gun locked open in the comic book, and so you know he's out of rounds and he needs to go to Plan B for defence."

Dixon, whose father was a gunsmith, would appreciate Mike Grell's accuracy. In researching his stories, Dixon explained, he has approached gun manufacturers and spent "lots of phone hours speaking to military personnel and policemen about guns and their uses. I've also done many, many hours of range time with all kinds of handguns, rifles and automatic weapons."

Tony Bedard feels differently about interacting with gun manufacturers. "It would probably be a bad PR move for the gun company if it got out," he remarked. "After all, comics are still seen as a kids' medium, even though the average comics reader is in his twenties and thirties these days. But the press would characterize it as Smith & Wesson marketing to ten-year-olds."

A stroll through any comic book shop will reveal that fans are closer to having kids than being them. And, like hard-core airsofters, some of these adults get obsessive over their hobby. Several comic book fansites list the Punisher's extensive arsenal with astonishing precision. Superherouniverse.com's version reads as follows: "Vietnam-era M16 automatic rifle in .223 calibre; a Sterling Mark 69mm, 34-round, clip-fed, semiautomatic rifle converted to automatic; a 14-round, 9mm Browning Llama automatic pistol; a government-issue, .45 calibre automatic frame re-chambered for 9mm ammunition with a replaceable barrel for conversion to .223 calibre; and a 4-shot derringer in .223 calibre." The result is no shortage of name-brand promotion for gun manufacturers.

UNDER PRESSURE

The first nigga to ever get the cover of *The Source*
And the cover of *Guns & Ammo*
— Royce Da 5'9", "Mr. Baller," off *Rock City* (2002)

"I started work at *Guns & Ammo* magazine on September 12, 1979," Jan Libourel offered elegantly in his languid voice from the office of his present employer, *Gun World* magazine. Libourel displays the proclivity for accuracy so commonly exhibited by gun enthusiasts.

As fellow magazine editors, we were particularly interested in discussing with Libourel the role gun magazines play in promoting firearms. Libourel (he over-enunciates his name as *Le-boo-ral* to distinguish it from the less desirable *li-ber-al*) candidly described his position as being "primarily to sell advertising," adding, "That would be the honest answer that anybody would give." Libourel's answer is an accurate assessment of the sold-out state of most print media, but his frankness still surprised us. Most editors consider themselves independent-minded disseminators of culture and knowledge. But we have also experienced what Libourel confesses to. Autonomy is a constant struggle for a magazine publisher, and concessions must be made to ensure survival. Still, in the world of gun magazines the balance swings heavily in favour of the manufacturers—a situation further confirmed by Libourel: "I certainly believe in taking care of my friends first, or if you scratch my back, I'll scratch yours. But then I'm quite willing to give editorial coverage to small up-and-coming or struggling companies. I always like to make new friends. The only

Jan Libourel

time I really take a strong position is when a company that we've given a lot of editorial coverage to doggedly refuses to advertise. Then I get angry."

While firearms appear in all media, it is in magazines that the gun enthusiast community creates its iconography. Looking over older issues of *Guns & Ammo* or *Shooting Times* clearly reveals that rifles once dominated American imaginations. Men stand proudly over slumped African oxen and elephants. Bears are felled and deer dropped. Marksmanship matters; guns are held to standards of tradition and craftsmanship. Fathers and sons cheerfully fire together at the range. Flags wave, eagles pose regally, the Wild West gleams glorious. Themes of honour, duty and liberty abound.

These images still exist in the gun press, but they're vestigial imagery, mementos of the light in which the gun enthusiasts and manufacturers would like to be seen. The world's largest firearms conference makes it immediately clear that the culture is now driven by an even stronger tradition. Every year, gun manufacturers, joined by their editorial colleagues, showcase their latest products at the SHOT show, organized by the National Shooting Sports Foundation. Jeff Cooper, *Guns & Ammo* columnist and member of the NRA board of directors, describes the event—which drew nearly forty-one thousand people to Las Vegas, Nevada, in 2006—as "a massive sales effort directed at making as many people as possible unhappy with what they have and anxious to obtain something new. Since what we already have is very fine indeed, the effort to make us feel the need for something better is considerable."

A 2004 UCLA study on firearms advertising in consumer gun magazines confirms Cooper's observation. The study surveyed the May 2002 issues of twenty-seven different publications with a total circulation of over four million copies, and featuring advertising from sixty-three manufacturers. The researchers found that 91.2 percent of firearms advertising focused on attributes of the gun. "By focusing on the technological attributes of a particular gun," the UCLA study found, "manufacturers make an effort to differentiate the performance of one gun from another, thus attempting to convince consumers that they need multiple guns."

It was at the 1988 SHOT show that Jan Libourel met the owners of Para-Ordnance, admitting that he was "at first rather skeptical" of their products. But after years of amicable association and collaboration he would proclaim in his June 1996 column: "Para-Ordnance is a dynamic, progressive force in the handgun market and builder of some of the most appealing auto-pistols around."

Libourel's father died in the Second World War before Jan was born. In the years that followed, members of the boy's extended family introduced him to guns. He explained his initiation and subsequent fascination simply: "I think there's a natural male affinity toward that sort of thing. When I was little boy I was very interested in warfare, military matters, outdoor adventures, so it formed a lot of my reading matter. So I think the transition to guns was a very natural one." Now in his sixties, Libourel has been handling and admiring guns for fifty years, his identity anchored in sport shooting and hunting, much as ours are in hip-hop. His best friends are in the gun industry: people like his "old friend" Kirby Smith, another gun writer and editor who now works as the publicist for Para-Ordnance.

As magazine publishers, we have had to make unpopular decisions that sometimes cost us friends in the music industry. But these are not generally oppositional relationships. We love many of the same things, we inhabit the same spheres and share a sense of community. It's a precarious position for a critic, because none of us wants to be an outcast. Nonetheless, when the new record sucks, when the artist is vacant or idiotic, when the industry shows its ugly underbelly, we say so. This usually isn't the case in the gun media, and Libourel admits as much. Tom Diaz's *Making a Killing* quotes him as saying, "I seldom encounter a 'bad' handgun." When we asked what happens when he does get a bad handgun Libourel answered, "If a product's no good I'll send it back. If they send me another one and it's good, then I'll mention I had some problems with the first, but not the second. But if the second one is lousy, then I just don't write about it."

Dean Speir is a former writer for *Gun Magazine, Combat Handguns, New Gun Week, Gun & Shooter* and a slew of other publications. In his time as a gun-magazine contributor he authored over six hundred articles, some under his own name, but many under assumed and assigned bylines. On his website, thegunzone.com, Speir describes one of the occasions when a moniker was thrust upon him: "The Editor at *Combat Handguns* was given an edict from the advertising department that the byline of 'Dean Speir' was not to appear anywhere Glock (and later Sig and Galco) [whose guns he'd criticized] placed advertising. But he liked my work . . . so he kept buying what I sent him, substituting bylines mostly of his own devise." As he explains in his online article "Cherry Picked," "'taint no gunzines out there no mo' who'll accept a really critical article for publication." In the end, Speir's integrity as a gun journalist would wear out his welcome.

If we thought the rest of the gun media was filled with soft coverage and hyperbole, it is in the histrionics of the NRA's 120-year-old flagship magazine, *American Rifleman*, that these qualities peak. Nowhere else are the relationships between crime, tyranny, power and liberty so complete and so confused. Typical *American Rifleman* covers read "Freedom Fighters," "Anti-Gun Frenzy," "Protect Your Freedom." Editorials like January 1994's, which produced the following extract, are filled with Orwellian imagery: "See if you can prove your innocence. After they investigate you. Fingerprint you. Snap your photograph. Check your papers. Inspect your guns. Count your ammunition. Dissect your past. Question your neighbours. Test you. Examine you. Watch you." Concludes the article of the enemy, "Their fire is fueled by their hatred of who you are and what you believe is your birthright."

American Rifleman's coverage of Second Amendment issues is unceasing. Each issue furthers the hysteria, cementing the link between personal armaments and freedom. Before every federal election subscribers receive, along with the magazine, personalized voting guides, defining politics with a pinhole view of the issues. Pro-gun? You get their votes. Nothing else matters. The NRA's close ties to manufacturers, coupled with pressure applied by the manufacturers themselves through leveraging advertising for favourable coverage, produces an environment where editorial discretion eventually collapses. Speir relates just how involved these relationships are: "How many readers of *American Handgunner* know that its Editor-in-Chief [Cameron Hopkins] had been a retained 'consultant' to Springfield Armory for more years than I

MAN KILLS GUN! DETAILS INSIDE!!!

When it comes to hysteria and paranoia, ya mama's got nothing on the gun press. Seven of the following ten headlines appeared on the covers of *Combat Handguns* and its sister publication, *Guns & Weapons for Law Enforcement.* Can you spot the fakes?

1. UNDER A LUNATIC'S GUN. You'll Have to Make a Head Shot: Front, Sight, Trigger . . . Surprise!
2. IF YOU FLINCH YOU'RE DEAD. A Maniac's Got a Gun. Your Last No-Shoot Option
3. 911 IS A JOKE. Why Personal Protection Is a Citizen's Duty
4. YOU SHOT AN UNARMED ATTACKER. Why Flight Equals Guilt!
5. 3-AGAINST-1 SHOWDOWN! Shoot the Threat, Miss the Girl!
6. WHO'S THAT PEEPING IN THE WINDOW? Pow! Nobody Now
7. MUGGER OR PANHANDLER? Do-or-Die Dilemma. Your Move: Shoot/No-Shoot
8. UNDER A MADMAN'S GUN. Your Mother's in His Line of Fire: You've Got One Last Chance
9. FRIEND OR FOE? State Your Business: Solutions for Suspicious Solicitors
10. THE MAKE MY DAY SYNDROME. It Can Kill You in Court

Answer: 3, 6 and 9 are the fakes—they're all based on rap lyrics.

can remember, and had insisted in colloquy with me that he sees absolutely no conflict there!"

'WOOD BURNERS

In October 2005 an advertisement featuring 50 Cent once again sparked controversy. This ad was for Fifty's film *Get Rich or Die Tryin'*, a movie loosely based on the life of Curtis Jackson. On the billboard advertisements a shirtless, tattooed Fifty spreads his wings à la M.J., a microphone in one hand, a Glock pistol in the other. Disturbed by the proximity of the ads to local schools, citizens in Los Angeles spoke out. L.A. County supervisor Michael Antonovich also sent a letter to Paramount president Brad Grey in which he wrote, "The billboard conveys to students a disturbing message actively promoting gun violence, criminal behavior and gang affiliation." Soon after, on October 29, 2005, *USA Today* reported that Paramount Pictures had agreed to remove the advertisements in

L.A. In the same breath the newspaper reminded readers, "*Get Rich or Die Tryin'* stars 50 Cent as a drug dealer who turns away from crime to pursue music. It is scheduled to open Nov. 9." "I do appreciate it," Fifty told ABC News, laughing off the storm.

Despite the sincere intentions of those behind it, the protest was, in view of Hollywood's historical contribution to gun culture, ludicrous. "If we go into our local Blockbuster," 50 Cent told MSN's *New Weekly*, "or any place else where we rent DVDs or movies from, we'll see a firearm and other weapons used as marketing tools on the cover of these projects consistently."

The U.K.'s Advertising Standards Authority (ASA) saw fit to ban a similar *Get Rich or Die Tryin'* movie poster, deciding that the image of 50 Cent with a gun "could give the impression that success could be achieved through violence." In that poster Fifty cradles a sleeping baby as the handle of a pistol peeks out from the back of his sagging jeans.

Agent 007 never bothered to tuck away his pistol in public. "Nearly every poster—whether of Connery or the later 007s—has him posing nonchalantly with a pistol framing his face," *Forbes* said in a February 6, 2001, story on an upcoming James Bond memorabilia auction. The tone was set in '62, with a poster from the very first Bond film reading, "The double 'o' means he has a license to kill when he chooses . . . where he chooses . . . whom he chooses!"

"Everybody's looking at rap," L.A.'s DJ Muggs, the mind behind groundbreaking musical concepts such as "A to the K" and "Hole in the Head," said backstage before a Cypress Hill show in T.O. "What are all these rappers rappin' about? *Scarface*. Who did that? The *moooooovies*. So everybody is quick to look at rap and down rap, but you got Arnold Schwarzenegger doing *Terminator*, killing forty cops in *Terminator*! And he's a hero, he's the governor. But a rapper talks about killing one cop and they ban his records. But we're learning it as children from the movies. So you need to go back to the root of it, 'cause I think a visual image is a lot more than just an audio image. I think it's a lot more stain on the brain, knowhatImean? A lot of these rappers are trying to portray what they see in these movies, and I think instead of expecting rappers to take responsibility to be fuckin' parents, maybe these actors and these directors and these movie companies that are making billions off these kids should be taking a little more responsibility than maybe we should."

> Let's peep the game from a different angle
> Matt Dillon pulled his pistol every time him and someone tangled
> So why you criticize me, for the shit that you see
> On your TV, that rates worse than PG?
>
> — Scarface, "Hand of the Dead Body," off *The Diary* (1994)

When asked what inspired his lyrics on "Hand of the Dead Body," Houston's Scarface answered modestly, "It had a lot a to do with the politicians, the powers that be, that were attacking an *art*, and something as simple as acting." As an art form, rap does share a lot with acting. But, while rappers have acquired significant cultural influence in a short time, they still can't touch the reach and influence of Hollywood. As soon as silver screens went up, the 'Wood made it cool to smoke everything from Marlboros to Magnums, showing audiences precisely which products to smoke and exactly how to smoke 'em.

"Individual weapons become bearers of social meaning and cultural meaning as they get featured in films and so on," Mark Kingwell said, citing a gun-crazy Christmas flick. "I remember going to see the first *Die Hard* movie, and there were these guys there who yelled out the make and model of every weapon that appeared in this movie. This is, I think, the first movie I can remember where—it's now quite common—cutting-edge weapons were a part of the production design of the movie. If it's an action movie, you want to have the latest version of automatic weapons in your movie, just like you want the latest sports car or fighter plane in it."

And just like the automobile industry, the gun business benefits from all sorts of free advertising, courtesy of Hollywood. That is, cultural meaning often translates into commercial appeal. "These media vignettes have real-life consequences," Tom Diaz commented. "People see them and that's what they want." Brooklyn's Big Daddy

Big Daddy Kane

Kane has observed as much in America today. "Cats have always toted guns and whatnot," Kane said, smoothly exasperated, "but I don't think as many as now, because it's like, there's those cats that want their guns to look pretty, like Nicholas Cage joints in *Face/Off* and shit like that. It's to that point."

A big-screen stuntman, writer, producer, assistant director and actor, Rick Washburn has been involved in movie production design for decades. In 1983 he founded Weapons Specialists Ltd., a consulting firm based in New York City that advises on and provides weapons to film makers. With a rental catalogue that includes everything from a Queen Anne-era flintlock to the H&K MP5K, Washburn's company has hundreds of movies and television shows to its credit. He was quick to explain that state-of-the-art weapons were being used by Hollywood long before neo-cowboy Bruce Willis was shooting assault rifles stolen from terrorists. "If you watch some of the old black-and-white gangster movies," Washburn said, "when they were using Tommy guns and Colt .45s and sawed-off shotguns in movies made in the twenties—in the *twenties*—they were even doing it then, because it's what the public wanted to see. The public really hasn't changed that much; just the equipment keeps changing."

Auto-Ordnance is the original manufacturer of the infamous Thompson submachine gun. Now owned by Kahr Arms' Justin Moon, Auto-Ordnance lists on its website over seventy years' worth of films that have featured the Tommy gun, from the original *Scarface* in 1932 to 1967's *The St. Valentine's Day Massacre* to 1998's *Saving Private Ryan.* "There's not that many directors that know that much about guns and how they're used in real life," Washburn observed. "The ones that do stand out. When you see something like *Saving Private Ryan*, there's a realism there that, no matter who you are, you pick up on. "

> I hate to brag, but damn, I'm good!
> And if mics were a gun, I'd be Clint Eastwood
> — Big Daddy Kane, "On the Bugged Tip," off *Long Live the Kane* (1988)

In 1971 actor, director and future mayor of Carmel, California, Clint Eastwood played the role of Detective "Dirty" Harry Callahan, a San Fran cop who shoots first and shoots again later. Early in *Dirty Harry*, as he stands over one of three black bank robbers—the only one still breathing—Callahan introduces his kicking co-star. As the bleeding robber's hand inches gradually closer to a nearby shotgun, Harry says with a smirk and an aggressive tone just louder than a whisper, "I know what you're thinkin'. 'Did he fire six shots or only five?' Well, to tell you the truth, in all this excitement I've kinda lost track myself. But being this is a .44 Magnum, the most powerful handgun in the world, and would blow your head *clean* off, you've got to ask yourself one question: 'Do I feel lucky?' Well, do you, punk?"

Initially written for Frank Sinatra and partially scripted by writer and NRA board member John Milius, the Dirty Harry role would make both Clint Eastwood and his .44 Magnum revolver legendary. Smith & Wesson's Roy Jinks acknowledged the boost that the film gave his company. "Certainly the Clint Eastwood *Dirty Harry* movie in 1971," he said, "had a major impact on the sale of our .44 Magnums and our products, and we continually worked to cooperate with the movies and television. We have done that for years."

Eastwood made the gun a celebrity. As Rick Washburn explained, "They just really [manufactured the .44] more to be able to say we've got the biggest, most powerful gun; they didn't think they were gonna sell a lot of them. Then *Dirty Harry* came along and every Walter Mitty in the U.S.A. wanted a *Dirty Harry* gun. All of a sudden, sales went right out the roof, which they never expected."

My 9mil, kitted wit' the infrared beam
Somethin' similar to a Roger Moore scene
That's James Bond, 007, wit' guillotine
— PMD, "For My People," off EPMD's *Business as Usual* (1994)

In 1962 the head of MI6 ordered Agent 007 to turn in his "damned" Beretta pistol after it jammed at a critical moment, costing the spy six months in hospital. MI6's chief had done some research, and he had a replacement in mind that would help Britain's top secret agent take better advantage of his licence. As he prepares 007 to face the villainous Dr. No, Major Boothroyd introduces James Bond to his new sidekick: "Walther PPK, 7.65 mil., with a delivery like a brick through a plate-glass window. Takes a Brausch silencer with very little reduction in muzzle velocity. The American CIA swear by them." It was the beginning of a beautiful friendship.

The sleek German pistol (the same handgun Adolf Hitler allegedly used to shoot himself) has in the years since become an icon permanently linked to the Bond legacy. Observed *U.S. Gun* in 1987, "It is no wonder why Hollywood decided to cast the Walther PPK as the weapon issued to Bond. Both the Walther and Bond are debonair and suave, streamlined for appearance, and have deadly success." While it was actually author and Bond creator Ian Fleming who cast the Walther PPK—an unfortunate decision for Beretta—fans of both real and replica guns have for decades been inspired by Bond's example. "We are not aware if and how many additional sales we have received through 007," Karl-Heinz Luther, vice-president of Walther, told us. "The fact is that the movies have made our products known worldwide and that we gained in additional prestige." Meanwhile, a few former Bonds have turned their backs on the icon that helped make them famous.

On April 1, 1997, *The New York Times* reported that the original James Bond, Sean Connery, who played the part at different points between 1962 and 1983, had "become a convert to the anti-gun cause." Connery had been shaken into action by the 1996 Dunblane handgun massacre in his native Scotland, and was featured in an ad shown in a thousand U.K. movie theatres urging a ban on handguns. "It is said that a total ban on handguns, including .22s," he says in the spot, "would take away innocent pleasure from thousands of people. Is that more or less pleasure than watching your child grow up?"

Sir Roger Moore, who starred as 007 from 1973 to '85, was even more active in his opposition to guns, becoming a UNICEF ambassador. "I am completely opposed to small arms and what they can do to children," declared Moore, who had a rifle blow up in his hands while serving in the British military. "I don't like guns." Moore also said he grew to despise "that awful pose" of Bond holding his signature shooter. The most recent Bond, Daniel Craig, went even further with his anti-gun statements. According to a story in the *London Telegraph* in October 2005, Craig was enlisted to "portray a tougher, grittier James Bond more akin to the cold blooded killer conceived by the spy's creator." Nonetheless, said Craig, "I hate handguns. Handguns are used to shoot people and as long as they are around people will shoot each other. That's a simple fact. I've seen a bullet wound and it was a mess. It was on a shoot and it scared me."

Other Hollywood actors have added to the words of Bonds I, III and VI in publicizing their anti-gun views, including Sharon Stone, Antonio Banderas and Sylvester Stallone. "That the star of *Rambo*," *Guns & Ammo* declared in a story titled "Six Degrees of Hypocrisy," "who made his fortune exploiting armed violence, should call on government raids to disarm millions of real veterans and the rest of his countrymen, goes beyond hypocritical. It is contemptible." But not every Hollywood star has pitched tent in the gun-control camp.

A former Marine Corps drill sergeant, R. Lee Ermey has come to define the voice of the U.S. military. Brash, sardonic and merciless, Ermey first gained notoriety with his role in Stanley Kubrick's *Full Metal Jacket*, in which he portrays the hostile drill instructor,

BANNER ACTS

The NRA has lots of enemies, and it knows every last one. The NRA-ILA's website offers visitors a number of "fact sheets," one of which has been popularly labelled "the NRA blacklist." The nineteen-page document lists hundreds of people, businesses and organizations with even a hint of anti-gun orientation, including a lengthy record of "Anti-Gun Individuals & Celebrities." Of the individuals listed, the NRA's Wayne LaPierre has said, "Our members don't want to buy their songs, don't want to go to their movies, don't want to support their careers." Here's a list of celebrities: guess which ones are gun owners/enthusiasts (G), and which ones are on the NRA's un-dreaded blacklist (B).

(a) Bill Cosby
(b) Mase
(c) Jerry Seinfeld
(d) Russell Simmons
(e) Harvey Keitel
(f) Howard Stern
(g) Richard Gere
(h) Chuck Norris
(i) Steven Spielberg

(j) Robert De Niro
(k) Shania Twain
(l) Britney Spears
(m) Tim Roth
(n) Donald Trump
(o) Mike Myers
(p) Missy Elliot
(q) Tommy Mottola
(r) Eva Longoria

(s) Tom Selleck
(t) Sean Penn
(u) Joe Mantegna
(v) Drew Barrymore
(w) Bob Barker
(x) Spike Lee
(y) Charlton Heston
(z) Oprah Winfrey

Answers: (a) G; (b) B; (c) B; (d) B; (e) G; (f) B; (g) B; (h) G; (i) G; (j) G; (k) G; (l) B; (m) B; (n) G; (o) B; (p) B; (q) B; (r) B; (s) G; (t) B; (u) G; (v) B; (w) B; (x) B; (y) G; (z) B.

Gunnery Sergeant Hartman. Some of Hartman's potent quotables have been sampled into the wide world of hip-hop long-players and, since the release of Kubrick's classic, R. Lee Ermey has appeared in productions as diverse as *The Simpsons* and *Toy Story*. Nowadays he's host of *Mail Call*, one of the History Channel's "highest rated series," according to the network's website. In mid-2004 we caught an episode.

With the same loudmouth, hard-on-the-soft image that made his character in *Full Metal Jacket* famous, Ermey gushes over Glock's special-forces pistol. "I have a handgun that fires fully automatic," he announces, "just like a big machine gun. That's right!" He also traces the history of U.S. military side arms, culminating with the Beretta M9, which, Ermey explains, is "still the handgun that you're gonna get issued if you're in the service right now. But the military and law enforcement is always sniffin' around for the next great pistol, and the agents and special operators that have picked up the Glock Model 18 say they like it just fine." After Glock's own director of training, Bryan James, demonstrates the 18's capabilities, an effusive Ermey heaps on still more praise. "Yes! Yes! Yes!" he says. "Is that sweet or what?! This is a pistol, for Pete's sake! Look at the damage you can do with a pistol!"

During our interview with Glock's lead counsel, Charles Grosse, we brought up the Glock 18's appearance on *Mail Call*. Given Glock's opposition to the mention of its name in rap music, we wondered if the company had similar concerns about its presentation on television. "Your representative was pretty, I thought, conservative in the way he talked about [the 18]," Chris said. "But were you concerned with the moderator, the host's depiction of the product?"

"The Gunny?!" exclaimed a shocked Grosse. "Well, first of all, he's our celebrity spokesperson. He goes to many different shows and speaks on our behalf. And the answer—the short answer—to your question is no, we're not concerned about that." If we'd read more gun magazines we would have known that "the Gunny," frequently front and centre in the company's ad copy, was on Glock's payroll. It was never mentioned in the segment on Glock, nor on *Mail Call*'s "About the Host" page on its website. Grosse put us in contact with R. Lee Ermey.

"What do you think the average *Mail Call* viewer is like?" Chris asked Glock's friendly and famously vocal spokesman. "You keep in touch with a lot of your fans."

"I would say a large percentage of *Mail Call* viewers are little guys between the ages of six and sixteen. They're just little kids that love to watch things blow up and love to watch weapons, and they're just military motivated. I'm with 'em all the time."

"And what about you? When did you start to play around with guns?"

"Well, I was a farm boy. I grew up on a farm. I was hunting on my own with my own 12-gauge single-shot shotgun when I was seven years old."

"Really?"

"Absoluto!"

Asked if he thought his own initiation with gats pointed to something missing today—the teaching of respect for firearms—the Gunny replied, "It's missing more now because we have too many shithead liberals that are so stupid that they actually believe that if you take all the guns away from the people in America that it would be a safer place. And you know as well as I do that just means that the bad guys would be the only ones who have guns."

"So what about the black rifles?" Chris queried, referring to a class of assault weapons defined by their black, plastic parts. "Like the AR?"

"I don't have any use for them," he answered authoritatively. "I'm a sportsman. And I feel that weapons—that if they're not for self-defence they should be for sport, and the weapons you just mentioned, those types of weapons were made for war. They're made for killing people. They're not made for sport, and I—Jesus, I couldn't imagine deer hunting with an AR. . . . I love the automatic weapons that I use on *Mail Call* that are used for war, because they're just beautiful tools for war. But I don't think they have any business being out in society."

"And what about that 18? Do you get to keep one of those?"

"A judge got in my way and it wasn't happening," the Gunny said, laughing.

Glock 18

—

In May 2005 Associated Press reported: "For Angelina Jolie and Brad Pitt, happiness is a warm gun." Jolie told *Vanity Fair* that the actors had fallen for one another during firearms training for the film *Mr. & Mrs. Smith.* "The trust," she said, "when somebody's got a loaded gun at your back . . . it made us trust each other quickly."

We picked up a copy of *Famous* magazine as we walked into the cinema to see the movie for ourselves. An article quotes Pitt: "It's a movie that the whole family can see." Then involved in matrimonial turmoil of his own, he described the characters: "They don't realize it, but they're each living a secret that they are major spies who have to try to kill each other. It's just this really funny movie about a marriage in need of a little excitement. It's good fun." In a nutshell, John and Jane Smith spend about an hour triggering weapons that make the firearms in *Die Hard* look like pre-millennial antiques. All the gunfire between the shooting stars finally reignites their flame. As the film climaxes and the reunited assassins prepare to face a final onslaught of masked hitmen, John straps one of his two Glock 18s to Jane's hip. "Watch these," he warns his wife. "They tend to jam."

"When I do a movie," Angelina Jolie is quoted by *Famous*, "not only am I expressing my creative self, but I feel like I'm saving so many people's lives." It's a strange sentiment coming from an actress whose character confesses to having murdered 312 people—"Some were two at a time," Jane Smith says—a number no rapper would dare boast. We told the Gunny we'd caught the Glock 18's performance alongside Jolie and Pitt.

"Yeah, I saw it too," he said, charmed. "I did too. I recognized it immediately."

"How much do you think appearances like that, in movies and on TV, helps Glock market its products?"

"It's like back in the early fifties and the early sixties when Western movies were really going strong, the Colt was the thing, the Colt revolver. It was because of the publicity it got from all the cowboy movies. And now if you watch any movie that basically has weapons in it, handguns in it, you're gonna see Glock, because they're a mid-priced weapon. They don't cost you an arm and a leg, and so that means that the average guy, Joe Shit the Ragman, Joe Blow, Joe Schmuckadelic can afford one."

Nineteen ninety, for example, saw Bruce Willis's rebel officer try to rally sluggish airport cops to respond to a developing terrorist threat in *Die Hard 2: Die Harder*. "That punk pulled a Glock 7 on me," John McClane said impudently. "You know what that is? It's a porcelain gun made in Germany. It doesn't show up on your airport X-ray machines, and it costs more than you make here in a month." Except, as the Gunny explained, Glocks are mid-market weapons within the price range of most Joe Schmuckadelics. And Glock's line of Austrian-made steel-and-plastic handguns began at model number 17. Hollywood is often as careless in offering details about guns as it is in showing how guns are properly used.

> Get disrespected if you front on the Birdman, you heard man
> Catch a couple shots from the Glock in my hand
> Damn! At least I'm realistic with my biscuit
> — Stretch, on 2Pac's "Pain," off the *Above the Rim* soundtrack (1994)

In August 2004 a buddy e-mailed us an advertisement for the latest handgun modification from Birdman Weapons Systems (BWS), a company with the slogan "unfriendly products for an unfriendly world." Birdman's innovation mounted sights on the side of a Glock pistol, allowing the owner to aim and shoot while holding the gun tilted on its side. According to Birdman's ad, "Rugged, sturdy installation of HoMeBoY brand Night Sights to your New Model Glock allows for a more 'modern-day' handling of your pistol as seen in today's hit movies. Contact BWS today and be the 'First in the Hood' to have your Glock modernized with side-shooting capability!" The ad further lures readers with the opportunity to fire "from car windows, over fences, bar counters, or simply while chasing someone through the hood!"

In June 2001, after being shown Birdman's violent and brazenly racist advertisement, Richmond, Virginia councilman G. Manoli Loupassi was outraged. "They're advocating destruction on our streets," he said in the June 18, 2001, *Times-Dispatch*, "and they're targeting our people." A Richmond police captain, Walter Allmon, was similarly scandalized, presenting the ad to a Public Safety Committee meeting. The ATF reported that the enterprise's website had received over a hundred thousand hits in 2000 alone. Ever the bulldog over unauthorized use of the Glock name, Glock's then lead counsel Paul Jannuzzo wrote to Birdman, the *Times-Dispatch* reported, asking that the name of his company be removed from the ad.

There was only one problem with the political outburst in Richmond—Birdman's ad was a gag. Even Jannuzzo knew that. "[Richmond] is the first we've heard of anyone taking this seriously," he said to a *Times-Dispatch* reporter. "I can't believe a police officer would look at that and not know it wasn't real. They've been watching too many movies."

We contacted BWS ourselves to get the facts. "All Birdman.org products are fakes, meant in satire only," Birdman said, explaining how his parody was designed to ruffle the feathers of conscientious reactionaries. "I actually came up with the idea after watching the John Singleton movie *Boyz n the Hood.* I noticed that not only was Mr. Singleton trying to sell our youth on improper firearms handling techniques and displaying blatant disrespect for firearms, he also glorified gang violence by making these improper firearms techniques (holding them sideways) look 'sexy and powerful.' I wonder how many role models for gang violence were created by way of that movie? How many gangbangers were out the very next day aiming their handguns sideways?"

We caught up with *Boyz 'n the Hood*'s most enduring star. "The movie was more of a mirror to what really happens to kids in South Central Los Angeles," Ice Cube said.

"But movies are part of the culture," Rodrigo responded. "So there's feedback going on."

"For sure, they're very influential, but everybody that sees that movie don't put a gun in their hand sideways," Cube maintained. "It's a compounded thing. It's not just one movie, or one incident, or one scene."

Rick Washburn has consulted on a handful of films that show handguns being shot sideways, several of which were closely connected with hip-hop. Washburn provided the weapons for 1994's *Above the Rim*, starring Tupac Shakur as "the Birdman" (no relation) and

Wood Harris as "Motaw." When the Birdman's team loses a prestigious street-ball tourney, he passes the pistol to Motaw, who promptly proceeds to shoot it sideways at the tourney hero before being shot down himself by cops. "If you shoot sideways," Washburn said slyly, "like is popularly shown in movies, you really can't hit anything. I used to tease Tupac about it. I said, 'You know, if we ever get in a gunfight, I hope you shoot like that, 'cause you're gonna be dead and I'm not.'"

Washburn marks hip-hop video director Hype Williams's first movie, *Belly*, as among the most preposterous presentations of gunplay in any movie he's been involved with. Conversely, he holds up another film starring Shakur as one of the most credible. In a breakthrough 1992 role, Pac played "Bishop," an average dude whose soul gradually becomes consumed by the power of a handgun (a poster for the movie, which pictured Shakur holding a gun, caused an outcry from intimidated citizens, and the gun was removed). There were no chic Glocks or gleaming Desert Eagles on display in *Juice*, however— just cheap revolvers and even cheaper pistols. "What we were doing," Washburn explained, "was going to the police department and finding out what guns were actually picked up when people were arrested in the course of crimes. If you listen to hip-hop mythology, you'd think every guy out there's got a Glock, and it's not true."

Last week I seen a Schwarzenegger movie
Where he's shooting all sorts of these mutherfuckers with a Uzi
I seen these three little kids up in the front row
Screamin' "Go!" with their 17-year-old uncle
I'm like, "Guidance?
Ain't they got the same moms and dads who got mad when I asked if
    they like violence?"
— Eminem, "Who Knew," off *The Marshall Mathers LP* (2000)

In 1984 California's future governor walked into a gun store in Los Angeles and asked to look more closely at several pieces, including a 12-gauge shotgun, a .45 calibre pistol with laser sighting and an Uzi. "So, which'll it be?" the store clerk said, anticipating a big sale.

"All," he answered, loading the shotgun.

"You can't do that," the employee quickly advised.

"Wrong," said the hulking man, pulling the trigger and blasting the poor, bloodied clerk against the wall.

It wasn't the last time before his career as a politician began that Arnold Schwarzenegger would rob a gun store. In November 1985 *Soldier of Fortune* magazine ran a cover story on the Austrian-American's next foray into gun theft. During a more conventional off-hours break-in, Schwarzenegger cleansed a gun shop of its most high-powered weaponry. Not long after, according to *SoF*'s count, eighty-four people lay dead: "Men died by submachine gun, assault rifle, medium machine gun, bare hands, hand grenades, HE, axe, pitchfork, anti-tank rocket, Claymore, decapitation by thrown circular-saw blade and skewering by three-inch steam-pipe." As in the above scenes from *Terminator*, in *Commando,* said *SoF*, "Superficial morality cloaks most of the carnage."

Alas, we should all be grateful Governor Schwarzenegger has altered his attitude towards guns since his acting days. "There is a sense of let-down with some of the stars," wrote *Guns & Ammo* of the prevailing anti-gun politics in the 'Wood. "Schwarzenegger, who claims Republican leanings . . . is described by the press as 'moderate on guns,' meaning your rights have been terminated." As Cali's governor, Arnold Schwarzenegger has introduced some commonsense gun initiatives such as banning .50 calibre sniper rifles, and even earned California an A- from the Brady campaign.

Guns & Ammo can't cry too much, though. Schwarzenegger has done enough in his day to prop up the gun business. Magnumfilms.com lists movies that "feature Magnum Research firearms." Among them are at least five Schwarzenegger flicks, including 1985's *Commando*, '87's *Predator*, '88's *Red Heat*, '93's *Last Action Hero* and '96's *Eraser*. But when we talked to John Risdall, he took exception with at least one appearance of the Desert Eagle in a film featuring the ex-bodybuilder. "My buddy Arnold Schwarzenegger," said the jolly CEO. "He's using it in [*Last Action Hero*] . . . he's driving down the street in his big Cadillac convertible and he's got the gun, holding it over his shoulder, shooting over his shoulder at the bad guys. Well, I don't *need* that. That's not recommended use of the product."

"So you do want the appropriate use to be depicted accurately, then?"

"Well, you'd like to see the gun used safely if you could. And yet that's not always going to work with what the people in Hollywood need or what the director needs or how the story reads. So you take the good with the bad. On the whole I can't complain about the representation we've gotten in the movies and in literature and in the video games. They've really done a pretty good job."

You could say that. Magnumfilms.com lists about a hundred movies that have cast Risdall's pistol in a prominent role. The Desert Eagle's resumé includes everybody's favourite films: *Austin Powers*, *Matrix*, *Charlie's Angels*, *Pulp Fiction*, *Menace II Society*, *La Femme Nikita*, *New Jack City*, *Desperado*, *Robocop*, *Face/Off*. A few of the films, such as *The Mask* and *Addams Family Values*, were even rated PG—essentially still kiddie flicks.

In December 2004 the *Journal of the American Medical Association* (*JAMA*) reported on recent research that found that one in four children's movies between 1998 and 2002 featured firearms. Analyzing the twenty-five highest-grossing films rated G or PG over a five-year period, AMA researchers discovered that 61 of 125 movies included at least one person with a gun. Of those sixty-one flicks, eleven had been pinned with the infantile G rating. In the nineteen scenes from the G-rated films that showed a gun being fired, just one person was killed, with no other injuries to people or animals.

JAMA was merely giving an update on a familiar trend. The number of guns in G and PG films had actually decreased since the previous study period, 1995 to '97. "Parents should continue to be aware," said the new *JAMA* study, "that many of the G- and PG-rated movies viewed by their children depict firearms and frequently omit the serious consequences of firearm use." But why would anyone want to spoil pictures with John Risdall's pretty pistol in 'em? Like Brad Pitt and Angelina Jolie, on the big screen the Desert Eagle just looks good.

Unsatisfied with its established territory in the States, the bird is expanding its migration into film culture internationally. British director Guy Ritchie's *Snatch* even gives the gun a sweet satirical shout-out. As Bullet Tooth Tony, actor Vinnie Jones confronts three

Desert Eagle

hapless black robbers, bigging up Risdall's beautiful birdie in the process. "The fact that you've got 'replica' written down the side o' your guns," Tony says, "and the fact that I've got 'Desert Eagle, *point 5-0*' written on the side of mine, should precipitate your balls into shrinking, along with your presence. Now, *fuck off.*"

"And now the same thing with the Hong Kong film factories and the Indian film factories and the Japanese film factories," Risdall observed, "where they love the gun over there. And it so fits with their movies when they're doing a contemporary piece that's not historical kung fu or something like that. I'd like to see one where like, the space guys go back in time to World War II and beat up the Nazis with them, do some time travel and off Hitler. See, I'd like that. Arnold would be good in that."

"So are you really friends with him?"

"Whenever he wants to put one of our guns in one of his movies, he calls up and asks for a couple of guns, and we're happy to give 'em to him. And those don't show up in the movies. He actually uses those and gives them to friends then. So he's a pal, yeah."

Risdall chose not to comment about Governor Schwarzenegger's politics, but did feel free to discuss Hollywood's role in driving demand for the bird. "The guys who make the [airsoft] guns at Cybergun," he said, "we're their number-one seller except for when there's a James Bond movie out, and then it'll be the Walther PPK for about six weeks. And the rest of the year we'll be their number-one seller again."

Airsoft Arnie confirmed the connection. "Movies do influence what a percentage of people buy," he said. "It's like buying replica movie props." While the subcultures are mostly distinct, lots of airsofters and hip-hoppers share an obsession with the bird, one largely instilled by Hollywood.

"The very first movie was Mickey Rourke, in *Year of the Dragon*," John Risdall remembered warmly. "Brilliant movie. And at the end, he gets a Desert Eagle out because he's gotta handle some bad craziness. That to my mind is the classic use of the Desert Eagle: you know, when everything else has failed and now you gotta—you know, the bad guys have shown their true colours, and you gotta bring out the real goods to, like, hammer these bozos.

"And then, at the same time, we were in a couple of TV shows like *The A-Team* and *Hunter* and *Miami Vice*. And *Miami Vice* was, I think, the first one where they mentioned the Desert Eagle pistol by name on a TV show."

I'm launchin' rockets and SCUDs at Crockett and Tubbs
—Ras Kass, "Miami Life," off *Soul on Ice* (2001)

Although it has since appeared on *Beverly Hills 90210*, *Saturday Night Live* and *VIP*, the Desert Eagle did indeed make its television debut on *Miami Vice*. The series, which ran between 1984 and '89, featured state-of-the-art gun handling. *Miami Vice* was also a boon for gun manufacturers, helping popularize gats like the bird and the Tec-9. "What drove that was Michael Mann," explained Rick Washburn, a consultant on the series. "Michael Mann is a gun nut, and he was the director."

While *Miami Vice* focused on guns and gunplay without much concern for reality, some film and television productions have since strived to fit guns accurately into a bigger picture. The release of Michael Mann's movie *Heat* in 1995, which seemed extreme for its gun action, preceded by two years a real-life shootout in North Hollywood between outgunned police officers and bank robbers wearing body armour and firing AK-47s and AR-15s. In order to end the armed conflict, cops were forced to retreat to a nearby gun store, where they borrowed more powerful shooters. As in rap music, authenticity sometimes requires the latest weapons.

There's also a lot of gunplay in Brazilian director Fernando Meirelles' 2002 film *City of God*—none of it gratuitous. Unlike the bloodless gun battles of *Mr. & Mrs. Smith*, *City of God* doesn't try to hide the horrors that firearms inflict. Based on a book by Paulo Lins, *Cidade de Deus* tells the story of child gangs in the slums of Rio de Janeiro after cocaine exploded there in the eighties.

The *City of God* DVD includes *News from a Personal War*, a special feature documentary filmed between 1997 and '98 that allows the viewer to, as Reginald C. Dennis put it, "see how real it is." Early in the doc, a sixteen-year-old prisoner introduces the life of "the dealer" with a freestyle rap, talking about .50 calibres and AR-15s—nicknamed "Uncle Sams" in Brazil—and about how Rio's cops can't compete with the guns carried by heroic drug dealers. "When it comes to drug dealing, we must mention gun smuggling," Rio's then police chief, Helio Luz, remarks in the doc. "The makers know that it comes to this country. Why? Because they can sell it for the highest price. Okay, then, we have to close gun factories. . . . Colt is American, and the AR-15 is made by Colt. I want to close Colt's factory."

For hip-hoppers, movies like *City of God* and *Scarface* have stood the test of time. For Rick Washburn, films like *The Cotton Club* and *Dances with Wolves* are among the few that hold water. "Guns were used in those movies in proper context," Washburn said fondly, "and I like that. I make a lot of money on stuff like *Die Hard 3*, but that's basically cartoon bullshit. Guns are not used like they use 'em in those kind of movies in real life. . . . Movies have always shown the guy getting whacked over the head with a big steel gun and it knocks him out, right? No—in real life it crushes his skull and gives him a concussion and probably kills him. If not, turns him into a vegetable."

"Kinda reminds me of that show *The Wire*," Chris said, "where they have the cop who hits the kid [in the head with a Glock] and he goes blind."

"That's a little more realistic," Washburn agreed.

I got the street smarts of Avon Barksdale
— Paul Wall, "March N Step," off *The People's Champ* (2005)

"Weapons and cars and other shit are generally just a big Hollywood jerk-off," said the usually articulate David Simon, producer and co-creator of HBO's Baltimore-centred drama *The Wire*. Baltimore, Simon's hometown, is a blue collar city of 650,000 that reported 270 homicides in 2003 alone. In the past decade and a half, "B-murder" has consistently posted some of the highest homicide rates in the United States. So Simon, having spent thirteen years as a crime reporter for the *Baltimore Sun* and an entire year following the Baltimore Police Department's homicide unit researching his 1991 book, *Homicide: A Year on the Killing Streets*, does not take guns lightly. "They're fetishized," Simon said. "I regard them in a utilitarian fashion. If they're appropriate for a story, if they're part of the story we are trying to tell, then the gun is depicted as per the story."

When Rodrigo asked Simon about a scene in which an officer accidentally discharges his Glock indoors, he explained, "There was a hole in the wall in the robbery unit where a cop was dry firing and put a bullet through it. We're just taking it from real life." Added Simon, "All drama is stylized to an extent. Yet at the same time we're feeling the need to undercut it a little by bringing it down to the human scale [so we] end up depicting some of the human cost of things like violence."

One of *The Wire*'s main story arcs tracks the drug operation of Avon Barksdale, a real-life Baltimore drug dealer. Barksdale, played by Wood Harris, is young, black and fearless. Typically, a character like Barksdale would be treated by Hollywood with an amalgam of facile stereotypes: big gold chain, big car with big rims, and super-macho "urban" dialogue crafted from hip-hop clichés. You'll find none of that in *The Wire*. Simon explained what makes his team different: "There's really a journalistic impulse on the part of the show that I don't think other American entertainment is particularly interested in. Why would they be? *The Wire* is not a show made in Hollywood by people who are from Hollywood. The creators of the show—one was a homicide detective, one was a crime reporter in

186 Baltimore. The things that Hollywood usually discards in a crime story, those are sort of the things we're interested in."

The Wire is still a violent show, but the writers' investment in the community they're depicting, their sensitivity to the consequences of violence in real life and the effects of portraying this violence guide the action. Asked how he feels about Hollywood's portrayal of violence, Simon took a deep breath and began, "I have a lot of contempt–" Unable to finish, he collected himself and started again: "I

STAND AND DELIVER

Menace II Society is all we watch
In the backseat strapped with the throwaway Glocks
— Juvenile, "Bounce Back," off *Juve the Great* (2003)

In 1993 Detroit's Hughes brothers, Allen and Albert, directed *Menace II Society*, a purportedly realistic portrayal of life in south-central Los Angeles that carried the tagline "This is the truth. This is what's real." But when it came to the movie's gunplay, *Menace* fell into the Hollywood trap of making things look—well, Hollywood. "*Menace* was a little over the top," Ice Cube said. So when *Menace's* lovable lunatic O-Dog robs the corner store and points his gun sideways at the cashier, anybody who knows anything about guns realizes that the only thing being menaced is the wall about ten feet to her left.

The Gangster Stance
Holding a machine gun is a strictly two-handed affair. The recoil from holding a rapidly firing weapon causes a gun to climb, so this stance would only endanger the local bird population.

The Thug Stance

"Look ma! I'm a gangsta!" Maybe we should be thankful that some people think this is a cool way to shoot. Its inaccuracy has probably saved some lives.

The Pistol Whip

How many movies have you seen where someone is pistol-whipped into a neat little package of unconsciousness just long enough to let the perpetrator (hero or villain) do what he needs to do? In the real world, a pistol-whipping from a four-pound metal object is enough to permanently injure someone and could even be fatal.

The Weaver Stance

Look boring? That's because it's the right way to hold a gun!

have a lot of contempt—" He stopped, pausing for a few beats, then tried one more time: "I have a lot of contempt for what the American entertainment industry has done to depict violence and poverty and race and the culture of drugs and what's at stake in the American city. I have a lot of contempt for the industry in that regard and I think American television gets all of that so hideously wrong, so offensively wrong, that it provides some real awful biofeedback for the culture. If we shoot somebody in *The Wire*, it's supposed to be disturbing and it's supposed to be emotionally alienating."

LICENCE TO FRAG

In November 2005, 50 Cent uncharacteristically allowed himself to be manipulated by a complete stranger. With all the expected hype, Universal Vivendi Games released *Bulletproof,* Fifty's pseudo-biographical third-person action shooter. Online promotions included an interview with 50 Cent as he dutifully promoted his game and the game industry: "The people who make video games ... take the things that we do in action films, the things we do in war epics, in cowboy movies, and put all of that into one video game."

In *Bulletproof,* Fifty navigates through the underworld with the two things he can trust: his heavily armed crew and his heavily armed self. Fifty's arsenal includes Mac-10s, AK-47s, Uzis and a cornucopia of other street heaters, all illustrated down to the very last scope, hammer and action. *Bulletproof* arrived at a time when rappers had become a hot commodity. From Snoop Dogg's appearances in *True Crimes* and *Fear & Respect* to D12's starring role in *Crime Life: Gang Wars,* rappers were attacking consoles across the globe. Hip-Hop and video games had crossed paths before, but the earlier wave of hip-hop-influenced games ran the gamut of the genre's aspirations: mid- to late-nineties titles included *RapJam* (basketball), *Parappa the Rapper* (rapping) and *Wu-Tang: Shaolin Style* (martial arts).

The histories of video games and hip-hop share many parallels. Both have their origins in the early seventies—Ralph Baer's *Odyssey* and Kool Herc's *Herculoids*—both experienced their first mainstream successes in the early eighties—*Pac-Man* and Kurtis Blow— and both blew up in the nineties. What's more, they involve the reinterpretation of existing technology, are staples of projects, basements and frat houses, and have been admonished by congressional hearings, protests and parents' pointed fingers. Ask hip-hop heads if they think rap and video games belong together and you'll get an emphatic "Hell, yeah." Ask a head-turned-entrepreneur like Marc Ecko the same question and you'll get an answer like the one he gave *Gamepro* magazine in August 2005: "We are in a market cycle right now where there's a tolerance for this genre."

Ecko, the man behind Ecko Unlimited clothing and several other multi-million-dollar fashion and media ventures, partnered with Atari to create *Getting Up: Contents Under Pressure*, which debuted in 2006. The game follows an aerosol artist named Trane, voiced by emcee Talib Kweli, as he tries to go all-city. "This game," Ecko tells *Gamepro*, "isn't about a character who's on the streets and he's got to make good on the streets, and he's got a gun, and he avenges something that's gone wrong or busting up a drug ring . . . it's not playing to that thread."

Ecko's clarification speaks volumes about the current consensus on being "urban" or "hip-hop" in today's video game market. With the success of Rockstar Games' *Grand Theft Auto: San Andreas*, "urban" crime games—meaning games featuring black or Latin-American characters with "hip-hop attitude"—became inextricably linked with the culture. Crime and gunplay in the video game world became part of the hip-hop experience and, more grotesquely, part of the black and Latin-American experience—and a new genre was born.

Jake Neri, the creative director for Hwy 1 Productions, the company behind the third-person cops-and-robbers game *25 to Life*, which features self-proclaimed video game addict Tech N9ne, told us about hip-hop's role in his game. "Being a B-boy has always meant being unique," Neri said, "having your own look, having the pride to rep your hood, whether that be through the way you rock your sneakers to the tag you put up every time you are at the bus stop. That is the attitude of street culture that we have tried to adapt. When you get online in *25 to Life*, you and your crew can rep yourself how you want, in the spirit of hip-hop at its core essence."

Neri and his team at Hwy 1 are well versed in hip-hop. The game's screenwriter, Frank Williams, for instance, is a former editor of *The Source*. That sets them apart from much of the competition, but the result is not much different: repping yourself in a video game still largely plays out as banging for your 'hood. "GTA + *Boyz n the Hood* = *25 to Life*," *Electronic Gaming Monthly* calculated when it reviewed the game. Neri didn't quite agree. "*Boyz n the Hood* definitely inspired certain elements of the design, but no more than classic movies like *Heat, Scarface, Way of the Gun* or *City of God*.

"We didn't set out to make a gang simulator—that wasn't that glamorous—and we had too much respect for real gangsters that are living that struggle. The goal was to build a game rooted in fantasies you may have heard in a Biggie or Tupac song or seen in the movies, and then on top of that give the player the freedom to build the character he or she wanted to—so that if they were indeed a Crip or Blood they could go that direction and look that way, but if they were more interested in looking like De Niro from *Heat*, they could go that route too."

In *25 to Life*, the player's choice to live legally (as a policeman) or illegally (as a gangbanger) determines the character's gun control (cops have better aim) and the type of weapons at his disposal. "Our weapons are balanced across both sides of the law," Neri explained, "law enforcement having more tactical weapons such as the MP-5, and criminals having more street-oriented weapons, like the Tec-9 or MAC-10. The weapon list includes a variety of handguns, shotguns and machine guns. We have the .357 and Desert Eagle, which will stop you dead in your tracks. We have a variety of shotguns from the tactical shotgun to the sawed-off, both very powerful and both different in how they affect your opponent. There are machine guns like [the] AK and my favourite, the SAW, which are extremely fun and do tremendous damage."

When it came to *25 to Life*'s ample arsenal, Neri and his team diligently tried to push the digital envelope: "From the outset the design goal was to make our weapons sound and perform as over the top as possible. In a lot of games you see handguns in the mix as throwaways; there is little to no satisfaction from using them. In *25 to Life* handguns are not only powerful but they are fun to play with, because we have turned up the juice on them. That goes for all weapons: we have kicked them up a notch because that lends itself to a fun experience." And *25 to Life* is not unique in this attempt. Much like the NRA's E-rated *Gun Club* video game for PlayStation 2, the majority of games targeted towards the hip-hop demographic—or, exploiting hip-hop—tout gunplay as their main selling point, and dedicate a great deal of research and development to making the shooting experience as visceral as possible.

Unlike in the NRA title, however, human beings are almost always the target in hip-hop games.

Scanning the covers of the popular urban-crime titles reveals that big guns and sideways gun cocks dominate. Storylines, as Ecko described, tend to follow a formula: former bad guy, faced with a dilemma, decides to do the right thing—while employing all his old tricks. The tone of the genre is summed up in the last line of the opening scene in *Bulletproof*, where 50 Cent, recovering from his bullet wounds, foreshadows the impending carnage: "The happiest thought I could think of was finding the motherfucker who bent me up."

> This game has no restarts soon as death comes to get you
> Ain't no cheat codes to life here, just the one God gives you
> — Big Neal, "Behind the Screens," off *Live from Iraq* (2005)

In 1980 Atari arcade designer Ed Rotberg created *Battlezone*, the world's first virtual reality video game. The game involved piloting a tank across a virtual battlefield rendered in green wire-frame graphics, searching for enemy tanks—and the occasional UFO—to destroy. The U.S. military asked Rotberg to create an enhanced version for training soldiers. He did, and the Bradley Trainer, a.k.a. *Military Battlezone*, was soon training Bradley Fighting Vehicle gunners.

Fast-forward to July 4, 2002—the day the U.S. Army released their $6.3-million video game, *America's Army*, an online simulator of military life from training to combat. The visionary behind the project, Lieutenant Colonel Casey Wardnyski, head of the Office of Economic and Manpower Analysis at West Point military academy, explained the game to CBS on the eve of its release: "With this game we hope to educate young Americans and present them with a realistic, engaging view of today's modern army and its opportunities." The *America's Army* website is a bit more frank regarding the game's purpose: "Elimination of the draft and reductions in the size of the Army have resulted in a marked decrease in the number of Americans who have served in the Army and from whom young adults can gain vicarious insights into the challenges and rewards of

Soldiering and national service. Therefore, the game is designed to substitute virtual experiences for vicarious insights."

Three years later, Wardnyski reflected upon the game's success at the Serious Games Summit, the gaming industry's annual conference about games with industrial or service applications. "We've had success above anticipated," he said. "Compared to the [Army-sponsored] race car, the bull riding, and so on, this is more effective than all of them, but costs less." He reported that the game brought in 60,000 daily visitors, had been downloaded 30 million times and had 6.9 million active users, making it one of the most popular online games in history. According to the website's in-depth statistics, 120,980 hours (almost fourteen years) of *America's Army* are played and 2,067,125 rounds of ammunition are fired every day, and the number keeps rising. Twenty percent of West Point's entering classes have played the game before enlisting, as have 20 to 40 percent of new army recruits.

Marksmanship is key to simulating life in the self-anointed "world's premier land force." The game's manual states that "by definition a soldier must be able to fight. Your rifle is your weapon." Players of *AA* are unable to advance to the combat stage of the game without completing the requirements of a rifleman. The game tracks detailed statistics of proficiency in marksmanship and awards titles corresponding to a player's skill. Players who subsequently enlist can reveal their online personas to help the army best place them.

The game's resounding online success prompted the U.S. Army to create a console version for PlayStation 2 and Xbox. Tony Van is the executive producer of *America's Army: Rise of a Soldier*, which was developed by Montreal's Ubisoft. He described the creation process to us: "Ubisoft and Secret Level (our developer) worked directly with the U.S. Army on all phases of the game. This included reviewing the original design, as well as 'Green-up Events' where the Army brought us to bases and taught us everything from firing weapons to coordinated movement to eating MRE field rations. In addition, we had SMEs (subject-matter experts) from the Special Forces who approved everything 'Army'—the look of the soldiers and feel of the weapons, down to the way they speak in real life."

The Entertainment Software Rating Board, which was instituted in 1994 as a self-regulating measure by the video game industry (submitting titles to the board is voluntary), has six different rating symbols. Symbols are augmented with "content descriptors" for violence, sex, humour, language and drug references. For violence there are nine descriptors, including "cartoon violence," which can be played by kids and usually earn an E (for "everyone") symbol, and "sexual violence," which can get your game stamped with the dreaded AO symbol (for "adults only"), a rating only two games have ever received.

America's Army earned a T symbol—for "teen"—which means it should be played only by those thirteen years old and up. This was by design: the makers wanted the game to be accessible to potential recruits. According to the *AA* website, "This rating provides parents guidance as to the age appropriateness of the game and is based upon the game's portrayal of the use of force and the fact that game characters show a small puff of blood when injured. We built the game to provide entertainment and information without resorting to graphic violence and gore. When a Soldier is killed, that Soldier simply falls to the ground and is no longer part of the ongoing mission."

Harlem emcee Immortal Technique takes issue with the entertainment world's depictions of death and violence. "People [don't] stumble around, and then lie on the ground, and then they say to their best friend, their hand on a fuckin' locket, 'Take care of my kids, take care of my kids,'" he said. "No. *Boom, boom.* You see them motherfuckers and they just stand there, and the next minute their whole fucking body collapses, cracked their head open, pissed their pants, leakin' all over the street. You're not Max Payne, dog [a video game character]."

Immortal Technique's observation reveals the game designer's conundrum. As Tony Van put it, "The more 'real' [games] are, the better they are." Or as Microsoft chairman Bill Gates told CBS News in August 2003, the gaming industry wants to bring the level of realism to the point where "people forget they are playing a game." But critics demand that the consequences of violence be shown. So as computer technology develops to the point where sounds, graphics and game physics approach the real thing, keeping it real gets complicated.

Jake Neri wasn't particularly concerned about the increasingly realistic violence in newer titles. "Our industry is governed by the ESRB, which ensures that games are rated appropriately and sold only to those allowed to buy them," he said. But while most video game publishers do submit their games to the ESRB for rating, once the games hit the stores there's very little control over who buys them. Parents, as a U.K. study quoted by the BBC reported, see "ratings as a guide, but not as a definite prohibition," while many youngsters see the T or M ("mature") rating as an attractive signifier of the gameplay. Late in 2005 *25 to Life* became the target of a petition by the National Law Enforcement Officers Memorial Fund, which was eventually signed by over 271,000 people, and which sought to ban the title. The associated publicity helped offset the game's poor production, pushing it to number one (for PlayStation 2) and number three (for Xbox) on Rogers Video's list of the top game rentals for February 2006.

Some governing bodies have attempted to enforce the ESRB's ratings by fining stores who sell or rent games to underage customers. The State of Washington led the way in 2003, banning sales of violent games—particularly those, like *25 to Life*, portraying violence against police—to those less than seventeen years of age; violators would be fined $500. The province of Manitoba created similar legislation in 2005, supported by a hefty $5,000 fine. Similar restrictions have been passed in Michigan, Illinois and even the Terminator's California.

The sponsor of California's bill, assemblyman and psychologist Leland Yee, explained the need for the legislation to the *Los Angeles Times* on October 5, 2005: "These games are very intense. . . . You have children scoping targets, pulling the trigger, blowing people's heads off." In response to the passing of Yee's bill, the Entertainment Software Association (ESA), the video game industry's trade organization, released a statement. "It is not up to the industry or the government to set standards for what kids can see or do," the ESA begged off. "That is the role of the parents."

Emcees like Tech N9ne are accustomed to attacks on the entertainment world, and he agrees with the ESA's assessment. "I think all that—video games and everything—that starts with the parents," Tech said. "I think if the parents were there more and make them distinguish real life from fantasy, then motherfuckers would know that. A kid should be able to play a gun game and then go outside and play kickball. It ain't like a kid is gonna go out and play his *Grand Theft Auto* and then he goes out, just shooting at cops."

We spoke to leading video game-violence researcher Dr. Craig A. Anderson, chair of Iowa State University's psychology department, about his research on how video games affect players. Dr. Anderson pinpointed a key difference between violence in gaming and in other media: "In a television show or movie you don't actually rehearse the decision processes that are involved in deciding to take aggressive action, whereas in a video game you do rehearse that decision process."

Dr. Anderson's most conclusive paper on the subject, "Effects of Violent Video Games on Aggressive Behavior, Aggressive Cognition, Aggressive Affect, Physiological Arousal, and Prosocial Behavior: Meta-analytic Review of the Scientific Literature," which he released in 2001, surveys all of the research done on video games and aggression. He told us he found that "all the studies show the same thing, and that is [that] exposure to violent video games [is] associated with increases in aggressive behaviour."

In the interview on his website to promote the launch of *Bulletproof*, 50 Cent says, "The video game definitely captures the essence of who I am." Pausing to consider the ramifications of his words—the game features Fifty murdering with impunity—he quickly corrects himself. "This is not the reality of what I would actually be doing in the street or anything," he said. "It's actually a game, but it has so much detail in it that it actually feels real." Fifty's backpedalling nicely illustrates the industry's bind.

Young bloods can't spell, but they could rock you in PlayStation
— Mos Def, "Mathematics," off *Black on Both Sides* (1999)

Grand Theft Auto: San Andreas and *Halo 2* have consistently topped video game sales in Canada and the U.S. Both games have sold in the millions, and in 2004 *Halo 2* became the first game ever to outsell the number-one movie at the box office the week of the game's release. Worldwide, the gaming industry grosses close to $30 billion annually, with North American consumers leading the way. According to the ESA's numbers, 11 percent of games sold in Canada in 2004 were classified by their publishers as "shooters" (*Halo 2* falls into this category), while another 31 percent fell into the more open-ended "action" category (e.g., *GTA*). Both of these games were, at least for a time, M-rated, and, despite their different designations, both are primarily shooting oriented.

A collector's edition of *Halo 2* includes a "making of" DVD. Game gun designer Robert McLees, unsatisfied with the reviews of his creations in the first *Halo*, explains in one feature where his game had fallen short: "It suffered from the same things that all video games weapons suffer from, and that is that they do not behave like their real-world counterparts." Seeking inspiration for the second instalment, McLees and his colleagues visited the Marines in South Carolina to see how real soldiers interacted with guns and how real guns interacted with soldiers. The result is incredibly realistic gunplay that captures every cartridge ejection, recoil action and barrel flare.

While the drive for realism in video games produces breathtaking re-creations in sports titles and racing games, such spectacular results grow troubling when achieved in shooter and action titles. As Dr. Anderson put it, "Everything you expose yourself to has some impact on you whether you realize it at the time or not. Do I believe that exposure to violent video games is going to turn everyone into a raving lunatic killer? Of course not; it doesn't work that way. But it does increase the likelihood that when faced with a conflict situation, some of the first solutions that will come to mind very quickly and automatically will be aggressive ones, and things that come to mind quickly and automatically very often are the ones that are acted upon."

Duckin' shells at the Cluckin' Bell
Jump out, bustin', gunnin', 'til they tuck they tail
— "C.J." (Young Maylay), "San Andreas Theme Song,"
off *San Andreas: The Original Mix Tape* (2005)

Well-known to millions of *Grand Theft Auto: San Andreas* fans as the voice of C.J., the game's main character, Young Maylay is also an underground rapper from Los Angeles. While we had read that Rockstar, the game's creator, shied away from interviews, Maylay had no problem talking to us about the game and his music.

When we spoke, *GTA:SA*'s "hot coffee" sex scene had just been discovered, making the game "maybe the worst of all worlds," as Craig Anderson put it. *GTA: San Andreas* was re-rated AO ("adults only"), spelling an end to its days on the shelves of Wal-Mart and Target stores. During our interview Maylay dismissed the controversy. "It's a lot more serious issues at hand," he said, "than a fuckin' video game havin' a sex scene in it."

Tom Diaz owns a copy of *GTA* and doesn't consider video games to be a major factor in gun violence. "I don't think games cause people to do bad things," he said. "It's when you take the game and you put it into a culture that you've saturated with firearms—that's where your problem is." In *San Andreas*, "Ammu-Nation" gun shops sell most guns available on the real U.S. market: silenced pistols, combat shotguns, Tec-9s, MAC-10s, AK-47s, AR-15s, Desert Eagles. "Ain't my business what ya do with it," says the clerk behind Ammu-Nation's counter.

Perhaps not surprisingly, Magnum Research's otherwise comprehensive website neglects to note the appearance of its pistol in the infamous *GTA:SA*. Nor would Ruger tell us which "violent video game it worked to have its name removed from," pending completion of litigation. But in *Grand Theft Auto: Vice City*, starring Ray Liotta as the voice of Tommy Vercetti, a "Ruger" Mini-14 is the first long gun to become available to players (in *Vice City* it functions as a blazing assault rifle). Maylay would know if the guns in *San Andreas* are really available on the streets of Cali's biggest city. "Hell, yeah! Shit, they not shootin' .22s out here, man. I mean, you out here in these streets it sounds like motherfuckin' Iraq or somethin' at nighttime. *I'm serious.* You hearin' motherfuckin' automatic artillery bein' let off in a residential neighbourhood."

As much as it offers as a video game, there's just no way to pick up a copy of *Grand Theft Auto: San Andreas* and kill someone with it. Sure, it's addictive. Watch someone's fingers control a game pad when they play something like *San Andreas*, and you'll see how fast their mind is moving. At that speed it's like a drug: your thoughts are confined to the fantasy. A game tester for Electronic Arts we spoke to calls it "hands-on escapism." If you're in the game, you're in the game—you don't have time to think about real life.

And there's no way it's a kid's game. Even before mainstreamers heard about the complicated process by which they could add an animated sex scene, players could beat a hooker into a bloody puddle with a two-headed dildo. Rockstar's designers are artists in their field, but the company can't have its cake and eat it too. Parents deserve to know what's in the games their kids are playing, especially when the video game industry excuses itself so quickly from responsibility for kids' media diets.

If any video game could lead to violent behaviour, *GTA:SA* could be it. But it would be hard to separate its impact from that of all the other violent influences creeping into the subconscious of shorties today. When U of T prof Gerald Cupchik tried to remember the name of the game his son was then absorbed in, it wasn't hard to guess. "*Grand Theft Auto*, that's what it is," the plainspoken prof said. "What kind of fuckin' horseshit have you got goin' on in there? These are rich children, and the bastion of the horseshit of their existence is pretending they're gangsters."

A former *Rap Pages* penman and Biggie's biographer, Cheo Hodari Coker, put forward another perspective: "*Grand Theft Auto: San Andreas*—which to me is incredible—it's as much a social document as it is a video game. But then you have a bunch of knockoffs. Now if you open up your average video game magazine, everyone's comin' up with their label-mature hip-hop shoot-'em-up where you can drive around, be a gangsta, shoot and kill everybody, and there's no storyline. They don't really understand what the appeal of *San*

Andreas is, but damned if they're not gonna try to cash in on it. And
I think that's kinda the same thing that happened with hip-hop in
terms of the guns—all of a sudden, you had to have a gun."

PASSED THE GAT

Keep my hand on my gun, 'cause they got me on the run
— Melle Mel, Grandmaster Flash & the Furious
Five's "The Message" 12-inch (1982)

Way back in 1982 Grandmaster Flash and the Furious Five released "The Message," one of the very first commercially successful rap tracks, and a cut on which guns play a role. In the words of the *All Music Guide to Hip-Hop*, it was "the first time hip-hop became a vehicle not merely for bragging and boasting but also for trenchant social commentary." On "The Message," Bronx-born Melle Mel does the math for would-be Pretty Boy Floyds, summing up the consequences of a stickup kid's lifestyle: an "eight-year bid" in prison being "used and abused." Mentioning a "street sweeper," Mel isn't rapping about assault rifles; he's talking about the job his son could expect if he chose to drop out of school.

When he was inking "The Message," it's doubtful that Melle Mel foresaw the global culture that his creativity was helping give rise to. And he definitely didn't see that guns themselves would one day become the message.

"I was listening to a radio interview," Mel said, "and the first guy who made the drum machine—the Lindrum—he was a drummer, and he said if he knew what the Lindrum would have done for drummers and musicians, he would've never invented the Lindrum. It's almost the same way I feel about rap."

The obsession with firearms evident in a lot of rap music today didn't develop overnight, nor did it emerge in a vacuum. Emcees are influenced by gun culture like most other males their age: they grow up reading the same comics, watching the same movies and playing the same video games. Arguably, the success of the *Punisher*, *Terminator* and *GTA*, as just a few popular examples, has impacted the content of hip-hop even more than life on any street.

By now, however, hip-hop's own social influence is undeniable. Just as video game designers look to movie directors for inspiration, and vice-versa, hip-hop inspires them both—not to mention other genres of music, and even pro sports. Hip-Hop influences how people dress, what rides they dream of driving and what gats they pack. The effect of rap music on youth especially, how shorties see issues such as gun violence, is clear.

But while other entertainment industries have found it convenient to excuse the often sour fruits of their influence, some hip-hop artists have, like Melle Mel, never had a problem acknowledging their power and accepting responsibility for how they use it.

I'm a Public Enemy but I don't rob banks
I don't shoot bullets and I don't shoot blanks
— Chuck D, "Miuzi Weighs a Ton," off Public
Enemy's *Yo! Bum Rush the Show* (1987)

Hip-Hop journalists Reggie C. Dennis and Cheo Hodari Coker both mentioned two tracks released in 1987 as critical contributions to the evolution of guns in rap: "9mm Goes Bang," from Boogie Down Productions (BDP), and Public Enemy's "Miuzi [pronounced "my Uzi"] Weighs a Ton." "When you held these records it changed your life," said Dennis, "because no one had ever thought to just make weapons of destruction a nice part of a song."

BDP recorded "9mm Goes Bang" for their first long-player, *Criminal Minded.* On the album cover Blastmaster Kris sits beside his DJ, Scott LaRock, the young artists draped in handguns, ammo belts and even a grenade. It was an image unprecedented in the culture. By the time Boogie Down Productions released its second LP, 1988's *By All Means Necessary*, Scott LaRock was gone, shot dead as he tried to make peace at a party in the Bronx. And while his partner, KRS-One, could still be found holding a Micro-Uzi on the cover of his sophomore record—adopting Malcolm X's famous pose as he peered from behind closed curtains with rifle in hand—the Teacher had emerged. KRS-One's second album featured "Stop the Violence," a song he followed a year later with "World Peace" on 1989's *Ghetto Music: The Blueprint of Hip-Hop*. When KRS did rap about guns—on "Love's Gonna Getcha (Material Love)," from 1990's *Edutainment*, for example—it was in the form of a parable, as a hot song with a chilling message.

In 1989 a young fan was killed in a fight during a BDP and Public Enemy concert. Soon after, KRS-One organized the East Coast's most popular rap artists to collaborate on "Self-Destruction," a single that addressed the violence that was victimizing hip-hoppers. We were in our early teens when the single dropped, and peace couldn't have sounded cooler than coming from our favourite rappers. KRS-One set it off, Big Daddy Kane kicked a verse, even Just-Ice, who was implicated but never charged in the murder of a drug dealer in '87, took the glory out of gangsterism with his rhymes. Public Enemy's Chuck D and Flavor Flav closed out "Self-Destruction," rhyming back and forth in classic fashion.

Chuck D's attitude towards violence in the culture hasn't changed in the years since. "The fact is, guns are our problem," Public Enemy's front man declared on PBS's *In the Mix* program. "When you happen to look on TV and see these music videos glorify guns or hear a song talking about how guns is fly, you have to begin to separate the real. As a matter of fact, in reality, guns only cause pain for everyone involved."

On the phone in 2005, Chuck explained the need to make such a statement. "I just think there's never been a time such as now that there is so much imbalance," he said. "When I was growing up, we played cowboys and Indians with little toy guns and water guns, and even my first song was looking at the gun as a revolutionary tool, but not as a leisure weapon to shoot yourself with. And that was the right to bear arms, and that was what made me come out with 'Miuzi Weighs a Ton,' using it as a metaphor for my brain in songs."

Unfortunately, while Chuck D's music and motivations have always been well-considered, his group's message wasn't so consistently understood. Many fans were taken more by the sight of S1W (Security of the First World) on stage in fatigues, swinging replica Uzis and performing militaristic dance steps, than they were with what PE were trying to communicate with the image. Some of Public Enemy's own followers believed the hype.

A share of KRS-One's fans also absorbed his messages selectively. KRS is credited with helping set the stage for both the positive-minded Native Tongues movement and gangsta rap—a testa-

Chuck D

ment to the Blastmaster's incredible artistic balance. In the movie based on the life of Curtis Jackson, as the scene shifts from the star as a boy to the star as a young man, he points a .357 revolver at the mirror. He raps along with one of his hip-hop heroes as BDP's "9mm Goes Bang" plays on his deck. A Public Enemy poster hangs on the wall behind him.

I'm the E, I don't slang or bang
I just smoke motherfuckers like it ain't no thang
— Eazy-E, "Gangsta Gangsta," off N.W.A.'s *Straight Outta Compton* (1988)

In 1989 Los Angeles' N.W.A. broke through with their second record, *Straight Outta Compton*, and revolutionized the rap game. The L.A. crack epidemic had taken hold, drug dealers were stockpiling weapons and homicide statistics were set to soar. When Ice Cube, MC Ren and Eazy-E rapped about AK-47s and Uzis, it wasn't as a metaphor for their brains. They were talking about shooting cops, "bitches" and their fans. With the controversy around the song "Fuck the Police," *Straight Outta Compton* set new standards for lyrical gunplay—and sales. It went triple platinum, selling more than three million copies, an unheard of number for a non-commercial hip-hop LP. Ironically, the album sparked another trend, one that continues to drive sales of hip-hop: its retail success was fuelled largely by suburban teens.

The album shifted some of hip-hop's focus towards the West Coast and away from the positivity of "Self-Destruction." *Straight Outta Compton* did include Dr. Dre's upliftingly unfit "Express Yourself," but the LP's dominant message was that gangsters plus guns, mixed with a scoop of misogyny, could equal commercial success. Many rappers on both coasts got the message.

In 1991, on "Same Song," a track created for Dan Aykroyd's movie *Nothin' But Trouble*, as the Digital Underground's Shock G prepared to pass the mic to a then little-known rapper and D.U. dancer, he rapped, "Just watch, 'cause my name is Shock, I like to rock, and you can't stop this / 2Pac go 'head and rock this." With the Digital Underground, Pac would clown around on the mic, keeping his lyrics lighthearted. At other times the NYC-born, Baltimore-and-Oakland-raised artist rapped about teenage pregnancy, police corruption and the frustrations of ghetto living. Sometimes Pac was straight gangsta.

"America has always celebrated bad boys and gangstas," Shock G said, "from Christopher Columbus to the wild Wild West to Scarface to Eazy-E to George Bush. This is precisely why a well-read and formally trained poet, actor, historian and activist like Tupac saw the need to incorporate some 'thug' into his style."

"Why do you think so many in hip-hop are so determined to convince everyone they're 'never scared'?" Chris asked.

"Since the fearless 'gangsta' mentality became a marketable characteristic within the entertainment industry, many artists choose to tap into that success by projecting themselves as a part of it in an attempt to capture the interest and curiosity of the average non-gangsta record buyer, as well as the camaraderie of the other fellow gangsters. Meanwhile, the young budding personalities whose minds are still supple and mouldable find themselves imitating this popular behaviour before they fully understand the repercussions of living that way. The result is often a prison term for an action of violence in response to an insignificant attack on one's pride or character. A time to kill used to be when there was no other option, but lately a mere verbal dis to one's attire or neighbourhood can lead to murder."

Shock G's belief in the significant influence of rap music on youth is nothing new. In 1990, Shock (and his alter ego, Humpty Hump) joined some of the West Coast's most respected rappers to record "We're All in the Same Gang," organized in response to an explosion of gang violence, the vast majority of which involved guns. The track featured Tone Loc, Ice-T and even N.W.A.'s Ren, Dre and the "violent hero" himself, Eazy-E. Letting listeners glimpse through their images and rapping about the real ends of a gangster lifestyle, they took a stand against the killing.

Shock G evaluated the gunplay in rap music today in a word: "BORING. It's just a popular trend right now. In some cases it's an excuse for not having anything else interesting to talk about. It's also insurance for some rappers: 'Don't criticize my style or I'll shoot you.'"

> What is hip-hop if it doesn't have violence?
> Chill for a minute, Doug E. Fresh said silence—
> What is a Glock if you don't have a clip?
> What's a lollipop without the Good Ship?"
> — Q-Tip, "What?" off A Tribe Called Quest's *Low End Theory* (1991)

While the West Coast's finest were dropping "We're All in the Same Gang," back east positivity still ruled the rap music of the day. It was, in many fans' memories, hip-hop's golden age. Groups like Main Source and A Tribe Called Quest produced timeless, and virtually gatless, classics. Brand Nubian's 1990 LP *One for All* was another masterpiece that didn't glorify pieces. When a reunited Brand Nu played Toronto in 2004, Lord Jamar talked about the influence of emcees on issues such as gun violence.

"I think they're very influential," Lord J said, as Sadat X snoozed on the side. "Life imitates art; art imitates life. Once you say something on a record, there is a segment of the population that is influenced by that. They will directly do what you tell them. People say, 'Aw, that's stupid. You can't let a record influence you.' Yeah, but people do. Not everybody does, but a lot of people do. And that's why you gotta watch what you say. Rap artists are role models. We can't raise people's kids, but at the same time, we're influencing people's kids, and you gotta be aware of that. You can't brush it off and say, 'The parents need to check the lyrics for them.' They can't always check the lyrics for them. It reaches people."

Another group who defined the vibe of early nineties hip-hop, De La Soul tackled guns on "Millie Pulled a Pistol on Santa," which tells the story of a daughter who grows sick of her father's incestuous ways and decides to pop him as he plays Santa Claus at Macy's. The group's Posdnous gave us his thoughts on all the gun talk in rap today. "It's just a part of the mentality of the youth in general," Pos said. "Yeah, rap fuels it, but it's there, in which rap is saying what's there. But then rap is also helping fuel it. It's just like this continuous circle that's just goin' around. Yeah, it's a sad way of life, but I mean, it's reality, man."

Cheo Hodari Coker sees the situation in similar terms. He compares rap music's influence to "a mirror put up to itself." As Coker explained, "When you basically write about a violent culture in your music and you hold up this mirror to society itself, it just bounces off each other for infinity. There's no solution, nothing gets better; it just feeds, and just keeps goin' over and over again."

The second person Cheo Hodari Coker ever interviewed was Chi Ali Griffith. In 1992 the fourteen-year-old rapper proved age ain't nothing but a number, releasing a quality debut by any standard, *The Fabulous Chi-Ali*. Chi-Ali was subsequently inducted into the Native Tongues coalition of emcees, which included De La Soul, A Tribe Called Quest and Queen Latifah. According to Coker, Chi Ali Griffith was also at that point "a solid member of the black middle class," with college a realistic possibility. Instead, Coker said, Griffith would become "hip-hop's version of a child actor gone bad."

In November 2000 Fox's *America's Most Wanted* featured the first of two segments on the twenty-three-year-old former rapper.

On February 14, 1999, after a disagreement with his girlfriend's brother, Sean Raymond, over a $300 debt and some CDs, Griffith murdered Raymond with five shots from a handgun. Chi-Ali spent the next two years evading police between ATL and NYC before finally being captured in a Bronx apartment in March 2001. "It just blew my mind!" Coker declared. "Like, what happened to this kid?!

"You go from being the suburban kid who then, for lack of a better phrase, sips the lemonade, begins feelin' himself, gets caught up in the real shit that's happening out there. 'Cause everyone had gone gangsta, not only in the culture but out on the street, and then next thing you know, he ends up killin' his [girlfriend's brother] over some bullshit, and then is on the run. And I think about how that culture as well as the real circumstance affects a kid like that, and if a kid like that is essentially the child of hip-hop, what's next? What does that say for the following generation?"

> Break the batter boy with my rat-tat-tatta toy
> Don't block the roadrunner boy, son enjoy
> — Chi-Ali, "Roadrunner," off *The Fabulous Chi-Ali* (1992)

Nowadays the mirror rap music holds up to society is straight out of a funhouse. When the Wu-Tang Clan initially blew up in '93, they rapped about the streets and guns, but did it wisely. On 1997's *Forever*, Ghostface Killer paints the most vivid portrait of gun violence ever put to wax with his verse on "Impossible," which fellow Clansman Raekwon then concludes with the words "Across the whole globe, the murder rates is increasin', and we decreasin'. So at the same time, when you play with guns, when you play with guns, son, that causes the conflict of you goin' against your own, ya hear me?"

Raekwon, a.k.a. Lex Diamonds, is even more frustrated with the gun focus in rap at present. "I don't respect cats that's comin' out like that," he maintained, "thinkin' it's all about guns and all that, 'cause that's not gonna win." The master criminologist explained why he said what he did on "Impossible": "I always try to give something back to the youth so they know what time it is, and know what's goin' on in the world today. A lot of rappers ain't doin' that; a lot of rappers is just about gettin' that money." When Ol' Dirty Bastard interrupted the '98 Grammy Awards show to yell, "Wu-Tang are for the children!" he meant every word.

> The Wu is too slammin' for these cold killin' labels
> Some ain't had hits since I seen Aunt Mabel
> Be doin' artists in like Cain did Abel
> Now they money's gettin' stuck to the gum under the table
> — GZA, "Protect Ya Neck," off Wu-Tang Clan's
> *Enter the Wu-Tang: 36 Chambers* (1993)

A year after Shaolin's Wu broke onto the scene, a small but powerful group once again shook up the hip-hop landscape. OutKast's *Southernplayalisticadillacmuzik* brought Southern gangsta to *Star Trek* samples, signalling the new duo's otherworldly talent. Big Boi and Dre played with pistols on their '94 debut, reflecting life amidst the heat in Atlanta, but it wouldn't take long before they'd moved as far beyond firearms as the bombs over Baghdad.

"Some people come up and ask, 'Will we ever get another *Southernplayalisticadillacmuzik* album?'" Dre said. "And I'll be like, 'I'm sorry, I don't think so,' because we were sixteen, seventeen years old. We were doin' all the things knuckleheads do in high school—you know, smokin', drinkin', carryin' guns and all that type of stuff. So all that was a reflection of what was goin' on, and I can't fake like I'm seventeen years old. . . . I think the whole term 'keep it real' killed hip-hop, because what happened was a lot of people thought keepin' it real meant keepin' it ignorant and slum."

OutKast's debut also introduced the supernatural stylings of another ATLien, with the first verse on the unforgettably inspiring "Git Up, Git Out." Cee-Lo Green provided us with some thoughts on the gat-clapping content of modern rap. "A lot of the guys talkin' tough, I think a lot of it comes from insecurity," said the vocal half of Gnarls Barkley. "I think if anything, our music is a defence mechanism. It seems like we're so passionate about being heartless—can you dig it? And how is that even possible?"

Although it would be tough to squeeze Cee-Lo into any mould, he says that setting himself apart is still a challenge in today's environment. "I'm different because I *dare* to be," he emphasized. "And I really think it's necessary, and I really empathize with today's music and with today's generation. The thought is horrifying, what their music or their lives will be like fifteen years from now, when we had a 2 Live Crew and we had a Public Enemy, understandwhatI'msayin'? To have balance, and both of them were prominent. But with today's music it's all the same and there's no alternative, and it frightens me a bit. I feel like if I condone it, man, I'm condoning a much harsher world for my son to go out into, where he has to go out there and fend for himself and survive. And so if I'm left with no choice, I have to teach him how to hold a gun as well."

So how did hip-hop lose its balance? Because SoundScan—the music industry's sales monitoring system—is the almighty redeemer. If gangsta rap is moving, gangsta rap is what gets manufactured. For GangStarr's Guru—whose references to gunplay were influenced by artists such as Scarface, Rakim and Big Daddy Kane, emcees who used guns as a metaphor or who included messages and morals—the streamlining of rap music merely reflects the influence of corporate imperatives on all media. "At this point, hip-hop is being run by people who aren't from the culture," Guru said. "It started as a culture and for fun and as an alternative to violence, because it started when the gangs were ending in New York. And now it's billion-dollar business, and what sells? Sex, drugs, violence."

Oak-Town's Paris agrees; he sees the rise of violent rap as hip-hop having gone astray in the hands of a few multinational mass media corporations such as Viacom and Vivendi Universal—labelled the "musical industrial complex" by music journalist Peter Spellman. The homogenization of the "Black CNN" parallels the homogenization of news broadcasting by CBS, NBC and the other CNN.

"Realize that 99 percent of the artists that are out there that do hip-hop are not artists in the true sense of the word," Paris said, "in that they're not true to what they believe in, in this current environment. And I say that because if the labels—if the two or three labels that are left—issue a blanket statement saying that they would no longer support music that was detrimental to the community, the majority of the artists that are out there would switch up and they would adjust to a more positive stance in order to be palatable to labels that they feel are gonna pay 'em."

> Made up gank moves and foolish fairy tales
> Said by sissies to snatch the record sales
> — Paris, "Escape from Babylon," off *The Devil Made Me Do It* (1990)

Wise Intelligent, leader of the Poor Righteous Teachers, gave us the essence of hip-hop music: "Rap is like water. If you put Kool-Aid in it, you get Kool-Aid; if you put tea in it, you get tea. One might be more healthy for you than the other one, but it doesn't change the fact that it came from that water." When most kids go for a drink, they're gonna reach for something sweet, something that'll give them a quick rush. Trigger-happy gangsta rap offers young peeps exactly that, and much like purveyors of junk food, music companies have proven willing to keep feedin' 'em and feedin' 'em and feedin' 'em.

And just as KRS-One and Chuck D's messages were often misunderstood by their fans, so too is the secret of 50 Cent's success. As Wise surmised, "When your favourite rapper's album is called *Get Rich or Die Tryin'*, he's on the front cover with a hammer, you start thinkin', 'Oh, he shot his way out the hood, he clapped his way out the hood'—when he *rapped* his way out the hood."

Fifty's gun references are both the result of his real experiences growing up in a community flooded with gats and the culmination of hip-hop's emphasis on competition—between individuals, neighbourhoods, cities and regions. As rappers have battled for supremacy, gat mentions have become gradually more detailed and deadly. Music corporations see an artist who got shot in the streets, talks a lot about guns and sold 872,000 copies of his U.S. major-label debut in its first week on store shelves. They want to duplicate those sales figures, as do a lot of aspiring emcees. But if guns and getting shot were all it took to match Fifty's commercial success, we'd see a lot more rappers going multi-platinum—and we don't.

"I think gunplay really signifies this generation becomin' suckers," X-Clan's Brother J said backstage in Van City, before opening up for

Damian Marley, whose father penned the track "Babylon System" in 1979. "And it reflects how much genocide is really bein' put into the streets, because we don't make the guns. All this high-powered shit that's touchin'—you gotta really ask the question, 'Who's puttin' it there for us to kill each other?' And they don't ask themselves the simple questions."

In 1992 a hyped-up Charlton Heston marched into a Time Warner board meeting with rhymes swirling around his aging brain. Standing before the owners of what is now the planet's biggest media conglomerate, Heston set it off. "I love my KKK bitch, she loves it when I treat her bad," he rapped with authority. "I love my KKK bitch, motherfuck her dear old dad!"

While the lyrics actually showed some promise, Heston had in fact sharked his raps from L.A.'s Ice-T. He had come to Time Warner in order to shame the company into firing the rapper, largely due to Heston's indignation over an album by Body Count, Ice's rap-rock group. Heston's campaign succeeded, a fact in which the NRA's eventual president takes great pride.

Ice-T is a gifted artist and actor, capable of playing a cop-killing gangsta rapper just as well as he plays a gangsta-killing copper with an attitude, as he did in *New Jack City*. Charlton Heston is also a gifted actor, capable of convincing people that popular music has more to do with violence than does an organization that believes in purifying society by gunfire.

Three years after Heston's office invasion, Senator Bob Dole launched his own attack on rap, targeting several hip-hop artists, including 2Pac and a group that put Texas on the hip-hop map almost a decade earlier, the Geto Boys. The GB's Bushwick Bill told us what he learned from the experience. "The fact [is] that the censors are not sensitive to makin' money," he said. "They're just sensitive to *us* makin' money."

"How so?"

"Bob Dole never stopped bein' a part of the gun and rifle association."

Back in 1995, when Bob Dole wasn't jumping on the Geto Boys' jock or falling off stages, he was hanging out with his peoples. In March '95, for example, the NRA-ILA's executive director, Tanya

Metaksa, rolled into her man's office. A soon-to-be presidential candidate, Dole appreciated Metaksa's company so much that on March 10, 1995, he wrote her a letter expressing his appreciation for her visit. "The long standing trust and support of those who value their right to keep and bear arms has been one of my strongest assets," he wrote. "It should go without saying that as long as I am Senate Majority Leader, I will continue to do everything within my power to prevent passage of anti–Second Amendment legislation in the Senate." Dole concluded, "Gun control is a completely ineffective approach to the lack of safety and security in our communities."

THINGS DONE CHANGED

I got seven MAC-11s, about eight .38s, nine 9s, ten MAC-10s
The shits never end
— Notorious B.I.G., live at Madison Square Garden (1993)

Early in the summer of 1994, as Rodrigo walked towards Toronto's landmark vinyl spot Play De Record, he was stopped by a familiar face with a tape in hand. Big C, one of Canada's first urban music industry figures and an alumnus of our high school, handed him a cassette with a hamburger box on the cover and the words "B.I.G. Mack" written across it. Side 1 of the promotional sampler featured new Bad Boy recording artist Craig Mack. On the strength of his smash single "Flava in Ya Ear," Mack was the summer's rap phenomenon, and Buns was amped to hear new music from the craggy-faced emcee. But Big C wouldn't let him overlook the real prize. Tapping the front of the cassette for emphasis, C said, "Check for the guy on the other side. His name is Biggie Smalls."

On the eve of Biggie's first release, *Ready to Die*, in September 1994, *The Source* would run its first feature on Brooklyn's most notorious. The same issue carried a reflective editorial titled "Rap Music's Identity Crisis," written by Reginald Jolley and William Upski Wimsatt, author of Tupac's favourite book while in prison, *Bomb the Suburbs*. Upski and Jolley saw a dangerous trend emerging among emcees: "Nowadays, there's no such thing as a sell-out. Rappers have established that they are not role models and therefore don't owe anyone, anything. . . . You can beat-up women. . . . You can write raps about Hollywood gangsters and label it 'reality.'"

Upski and Jolley's editorial came as a direct response to hip-hop's embrace of emerging emcees like Biggie. He smoked weed, sold crack and wrote over-the-top gangster raps like "I wouldn't give a fuck if ya' pregnant / Gimme the baby rings, and the #1 Mom pendant." He was no romantic about his art, telling *The Source*, "I would hate to be the one to be on some 'Yeah, I'm really into the hip-hop and the whole form'. . . I just know what to kick. I know what to spit to niggas." And, according to Biggie, niggas wanted him to spit gun talk. Cheo H. Coker, the last journalist to interview the "black Frank White," told us, "Big had a fascination with guns. I mean, just because of the way that he wrote about it, that was as much his genre as crime belongs to Scorsese."

Every single one of *Ready to Die*'s fifteen tracks has at least one gun reference. "Gimme the Loot" alone carries thirteen different references to guns and gunplay, and five other songs have at least five. Biggie drops Beretta, Calico, Glock, MAC-10 and Tec-9, all by name. And even the laid-back player anthem "One More Chance" contains the lyric "Fuck tae kwon do, I tote da fo'-fo'." At least sixty-nine different references to gunplay adorn the sixty-nine-minute album.

Upski and Jolley were right. Things had changed: "everything that used to be wack [was] dope now." But Biggie was right too. *Ready to Die* sold five hundred thousand copies in its first week, and within two months of its release, Biggie would be New York's first national hip-hop star in years.

It's like the game ain't the same
Got younger niggas pullin' the triggers bringin' fame to they name
And claim some corners, crews without guns are goners
— Nas, "N.Y. State of Mind," off *Illmatic* (1994)

After several years of West Coast domination of the charts, New York City was back on top. Biggie's record, alongside Nas's *Illmatic*, Black Moon's *Enta da Stage* and Wu-Tang Clan's *Enter the Wu-Tang*, signified a shift in the hip-hop nation's taste. Lyrically, the new wave of emcees emphasized the iniquity of the city, presenting a bleak portrait of urban America. They'd dropped the quick drum patterns and high-energy samples of Public Enemy, EPMD and Big Daddy Kane. Instead their producers sampled obscure down-tempo records to produce a menacing and ominous sound.

.Unlike their predecessors, who were in their late teens or early twenties when crack came to New York, much of the new wave of emcees were still kids when crack changed their neighbourhoods. David Simon, producer of *The Wire*, explained the shift that occurred and how it affected the youth: "When I first started as a police reporter, it would have been like a headline to find a fourteen-year-old selling drugs or holding a gun in the projects. It was not unusual by the early nineties to find ten- and eleven- and twelve-year-old kids as runners and scouts and be completely integrated into the drug economy. The most mature thirteen-year old in the world is going to be prone to violence, given a proximity to cocaine and guns and violent people. Cocaine changes everything."

Including rap. While some pro-black militancy remained, the new wave of hip-hop concerned itself more with documenting the effects of the crack economy—particularly the violence. The formative years of many of the emcees in New York's rap renaissance coincided with America's highest homicide rates ever. New York City's murder rate in the early nineties hovered around two thousand a year—four times its current number. Emblematic of the new hip-hop era was Nas's 1994 debut album, *Illmatic*. Written when Nasir Jones was just past his teens, *Illmatic* is considered by many to be the greatest hip-hop album ever, perfectly capturing the rugged survivalist attitude of the era.

Nas didn't agree that rap was hypocritical and manipulative in creating hard-core street images that were largely fantasy. "You can't just think about it like that," he said. "You gotta say it's entertainment. And that's like a contradictory thing to say—'Entertainers, why create images that are not real?' and shit like that. It's entertainment. The reason that hip-hop is real is 'cause it's from the streets. It's ghetto niggas talking, so we not gonna hold back no punches." Nas's statement, although made seven years after *Illmatic*'s release, still reflected the mentality that dominated hip-hop in the mid-nineties: "Keep it real."

A decade after the height of the "realness" era, we interviewed Brooklyn emcee Talib Kweli over the phone as he watched the news. Kweli broke down the corrosive effects of the mid-nineties mantra. "There was a time when the whole keeping-it-real thing happened and everybody was keeping it real. When keeping it real became a catchphrase, then everybody had to compete: 'Well, I keep it realer than you.' One person says, 'I live in a neighbourhood with drug dealers.' And then the next rapper comes out and says, 'Well, I sell drugs.' And then the next rapper says, 'Well, I sell crack and I'm the best crack dealer on my block.' And then the next guy says, 'I don't even rap. I'm just rapping on the side to hustle. I really sell drugs.' And it just gets more and more ridiculous."

Kweli then turned his focus to guns. "I think hip-hop is reckless when it comes to guns. I think there is a reality there and I think that [it] needs to be talked about. But when it becomes a way to have street cred or a way to add flavour to your rhyme—which it has become in a lot of instances—then hip-hop is being very reckless and very irresponsible in how we talk about guns and gun violence and how it really effects the community."

Unfortunately for hip-hop, Kweli's sagacity would come much too late to influence the new wave of ghetto griots. For the new school, keeping it real meant boasting about the quantity and quality of your weaponry and your willingness to use it. While songs like NWA's "Fuck tha Police" would earn headlines across North America and mentions of MACs and Tecs would raise eyebrows in the late eighties and early nineties, by the mid-nineties gun lyrics were ubiquitous in rap. At the same time, Biggie would become mired in an ill-fated rivalry with his former friend and collaborator Tupac, in the culture's defining moment.

Biggie Smalls and Junior M.A.F.I.A. some mark-ass bitches
We keep on comin' while we runnin' for yo' jewels
Steady gunnin', keep on bustin' at them fools, you know the rules
— 2Pac, "Hit 'Em Up" 12-inch (1996)

After Tupac was shot five times on November 29, 1994, outside New York City's Quad Studios, where both Biggie and Puff Daddy were recording, Pac became convinced that the two were involved. Surviving the ambush only to be convicted of a sexual assault charge a few days later, Pac had several months to ponder the situation from behind bars. Freed on $1.4-million bail by the deep pockets of Cali hip-hop magnate Suge Knight, Tupac immediately took to "ridin'" with Knight and crew. Ridin'—the West Coast version of "keep it real"—dictated that if Tupac truly believed that Biggie was involved in his shooting, then he had to retaliate. In this spirit Tupac created some of hip-hop's most venomous records, mercilessly dissing Biggie and many of his New York City contemporaries.

Hyped by the media and primed by years of competition between the two coasts' distinctive styles and sounds, the hip-hop nation quickly took sides, elevating the beef between two friends into a cultural civil war. While beefs and wars on wax had always been an important part of hip-hop, beefing and rap battles took on a much more serious tone when combined with the ethos of keeping it real. Disses grew so intense and personal that there was little room to manoeuvre an ego without taking it to a physical level.

After a series of run-ins between Biggie's and Tupac's camps and an endless war of words in the media, Tupac was shot on September 7, 1996. He died on September 13, 1996, at 4:03 p.m. Less than six months later, on March 9, 1997, Biggie Smalls, leaving a party held by *Vibe* magazine after the Soul Train Awards in Los Angeles, was also shot and killed. The hip-hop nation, shocked by the climax of a beef that they so willingly partook in, pleaded for unity again.

I got the wild style, always been a foul child
My guns go poom-poom, and yo' guns go pow-pow
— Big L, "Put It On," off *Lifestylez Ov
Da Poor & Dangerous* (1995)

Sitting with Fat Joe in a boardroom in the bowels of Canada's largest music video purveyor, MuchMusic, Rodrigo decided the time was right to begin unbuttoning his shirt. "I got some other questions for you," he told Joe. The bald, three-hundred-pound Don Cartegena didn't flinch; he just watched Rodrigo's hands. Fumbling with the shirt, Buns finally unveiled a T-shirt with an iron-on photo of a young Joe and his friend DJ Serge posing in a graffed-up stairwell. Joe's right hand is splayed upwards, and his left hand is pointing a huge gun at the camera.

"I got that shirt too!" Joe said excitedly. "Look how young a nigga look. That was a long time ago."

Encouraged by Joe's reaction, Rodrigo asked him if he thought hip-hop would be different without guns. "Hip-Hop has been really good to us," Joe said. "You know, just for the few exceptions, cats got killed. But they all got killed for different reasons. I wouldn't blame it on the gun itself. I think everyone should own a gun."

Fat Joe, known 'round the way as Joey Crack, is a hip-hop and Bronx legend, his pedigree going back to one of hip-hop's most respected crews, Diggin' In The Crates. Commonly called DITC, the crew has included Diamond D, Lord Finesse, Showbiz, Andre the Giant, O.C., Buckwild and the late Big L. Big L was one of those exceptions Fat Joe was referring to. Born Lamont Coleman on May 30, 1974, L was shot and killed on February 15, 1999, on 139th Street in Harlem, just blocks from his home.

A couple of weeks before Buns interviewed Joe, he met DITC elder statesman Lord Finesse at the annual Big L memorial show, which Finesse organizes. Proud of the turnout but saddened by the occasion, he sat in a tiny powder-blue room backstage wearing a black air-brushed T-shirt with L's face on it. A few people asked Finesse if the shirts were for sale. "Naw, not these joints," he replied. "These is special." Finesse reminisced about hearing of his friend's murder: "I never believed it, because it was like, damn, out of everybody in the crew he was like that baby out the crew, so we ain't never think that that type of tragedy could happen to him."

Gilda Coleman, Big L's mother, shared Finesse's sentiment. "We used to just call him 'TV gangster,'" she said. "That's all he was—he never *did* anything violent." L's murder, according to information Gilda received from the community, was a message for his older brother, Leroy, who was in jail when L was killed. The killers couldn't reach Leroy so they reached Lamont. A few years later the

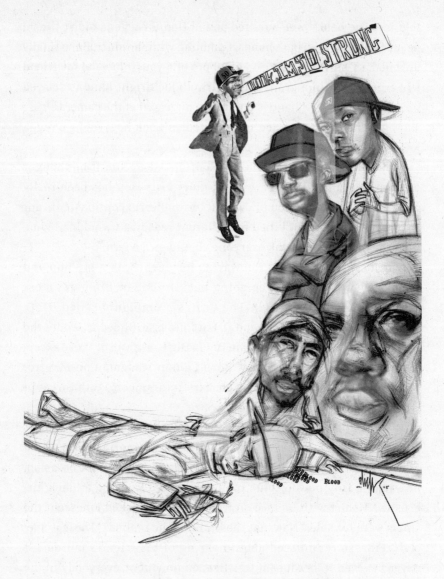

streets reached Leroy too, and Gilda was left to cope with the loss of another son to gun violence. As she explained, "I love my children, and I don't want to see nothing happen to neither one of my children, but when it happened to Leroy it was like, 'Okay, my child was out there and this was gonna happen to him.' But Lamont, when it happened to him, I was devastated because he wasn't out there, he wasn't a street kid, he wasn't selling drugs, he didn't get high. The only thing he did was rap."

To hip-hop fans, Big L was one of the most hard-core lyricists. L's music, which he explained to his mother as being "underground," included lyrics such as "I'm a devil from Hell without the tail or the red horns / Killing is fun, I'm #1 with a gun," from his song "Devil's Son." Gilda recalled hearing the track one day by accident: "When I heard that song I almost jumped out of my skin. I said, 'Lamont! They gonna put us out of Harlem because of this song you wrote.'" But Finesse explained it from an artist's perspective. "That was just his creative structure," he said. "He did these things to gain attention. The 'Devil's Son,' *Lifestylez Ov Da Poor & Dangerous* [he wrote] to let people know his skills, his potential."

Fat Joe took a position similar to Finesse's: "Rap is art. Hip-Hop is art. And we're entertainers. And when we write songs, we're writing movies, we're writing books. No one should take these lyrics as reality. They should know that we're just writing the craziest shit we wanna write, we're writing the most positive shit we wanna write, the most depressing, the most funniest things. It's art. It's like painting a picture."

Having heard that excuse several dozen times before, Rodrigo challenged Joe about hip-hop's tendency to blur the lines between fantasy and reality, which irritated him. "If the question you want to ask before I get the fuck outta here is 'Are rappers selfish and are they making music out of greed?'–yes, a hundred million percent."

"That's not what I wanted to ask."

"But that's the truth, though. That's the answer to all the questions you're asking. But at the same time, this is entertainment, my man. It's like I'm Martin Scorsese making an army film. That's the truth, unfortunately. It's not our fault that parents aren't educating their kids and letting them know right from wrong. That's not our fault."

Everything I wrote was from my heart
So it'll always be number one on my chart
I get sensitive with my shit, don't fuck with my art
Sometimes it sounds like I'm playin' but I'm sayin'
This shit is real, it ain't a game
— 50 Cent, "The Good Die Young," off *Power of the Dollar* (2000)

Over a staticky cell-phone connection from the backseat of a limo, Juelz Santana, the youngest member of Harlem's Diplomats and one of hip-hop's growing class of eighties babies, broke down hip-hop's current all-purpose excuse of choice, comparing hip-hop to filmmaking. "I think music is more effective," Santana said, "because music, especially hip-hop, has been portrayed as being so real, like this could be an autobiography of people's lives. So when you have so many people talking about guns and stuff [it has an effect], whereas acting has always been portrayed as acting, 'cause you got people playing five different roles. That's *acting*, so when you look at a movie you kinda know that. But when you listen to this music, the consumers definitely take to it a little bit more seriously, and definitely think it's more real."

If hip-hop music is autobiography, then the best-known autobiographer in hip-hop these days is 50 Cent. Fiddy, far from being the first rapper ever to be shot, was definitely the first rapper to create a cottage industry out of it. He began as just another emcee from South Jamaica, Queens. Signed to Columbia Records in 1999, he gained some profile when he released the comedic stick-up-kid anthem "How to Rob," on which he robbed (on wax) many of hip-hop's biggest names. Despite this small success, his album *Power of the Dollar*, which he completed in early 2000, would never be released, except as a mix-tape.

But things changed for Curtis Jackson in April 2000, when he was shot nine times in front of his grandmother's house—including one bullet in the cheek that would permanently change his voice. He was dropped by Columbia Records while still recovering from his wounds, and the second phase of his career began. Fifty quickly turned catastrophe into cash by recording relentlessly and releasing new music at an unprecedented rate through radio, DJs and, most effectively, mix-tapes. He had been emboldened by his near-death experience, and his music became intense and antagonistic. He dissed every rapper who had responded to "How to Rob," and a few who hadn't. The drama-setting strategy worked. Within two years of his shooting, Fifty had become hip-hop's most anticipated artist since Eminem. In the process, the story of his shooting would be repeated ad nauseum, as indisputable proof of his street-worthiness and reason for his ferocity.

Before 50 Cent's lyrical rampage, the memory and legacy of Tupac's and Biggie's deaths had buffered hip-hop beefs. Any battle that took place in the years following their murders was accompanied by pleas to "keep things lyrical." But Fifty was determined to rewrite the hip-hop playbook; his unyielding attacks on Ja Rule—and Rule's entire Murder Inc. camp, for that matter—baited his rival, pushing him to take it to the streets. By the time Fifty's debut album, *Get Rich or Die Tryin'*, was released in February 2003, Curtis Jackson had inflicted significant damage on the career of Jeffrey Atkins, a.k.a. Ja Rule, whom Fiddy had attacked for 'not being street enough.' *GRODT* would sell nearly eleven million copies in total. 50 Cent became the biggest hip-hop star on the planet, redefining the criteria for street credibility, remaking the image of the pop star and ushering in a new era of beef.

Young Chris of the Philly-based group the Young Gunz brought a different perspective to hip-hop's new world order. "Man, they got it fucked up nowadays," he said. "They analyzing the shot instead of the shooter. The game is fucked up."

Realizing our confusion, Young Chris spelled it out: "They bragging about getting hit, they bragging about getting shot. That ain't cool; you was slippin', nigga. Fucking clowns."

"But you can't really come out and say you've been shooting people . . ." Buns said.

"Nah, ain't nobody gonna say that, but give a nigga respect when respect is due. When a nigga bust when he supposed to—then he'll remember you. Now niggas talkin', 'I got shot, I got hit,' get the fuck outta here. You a target, nigga."

Young Chris's statement was an obvious attack on 50 Cent and his G-Unit camp, of which three of four members have been shot. Like Fifty, Lloyd Banks and Young Buck had played up their shootings to the media. A few weeks after we interviewed Young Chris, we spoke to Tony Yayo at the G-Unit offices in New York City. Yayo, the only member of the G-Unit who hadn't been shot, but who'd recently gone to jail on a gun charge (for carrying a Ruger P89), responded to Young Chris's statement: "For him to say that people respect the victim instead of the victor, that shit is irrelevant. If he saying that the shooter is to be respected, well, we shoot too; it's not like we only get-ting shot." Young Chris's statement and Yayo's response reveal vol-umes about the values of some of hip-hop's biggest names. It would be hard to imagine pioneers like Big Daddy Kane and Rakim engag-ing in a battle over what had more street value, getting shot or shoot-ing someone.

Kweli is one of the new school's more conscientious emcees. In con-versation our frustration with rappers' elusive attitudes boiled over. "Artists spend a lot of time trying to convince their audience that what they do is real," Rodrigo said. "So when they turn around and say, 'No, it's entertainment,' I think that's disingenuous."

Kweli paused. "I agree. But I think . . . Where are you from?"

"I'm from Toronto."

"Do you go to school?"

"No, I'm a college dropout, like Kanye."

"But you went to college. A lot of these rappers are young people, and what you just made is a very sophisticated argument." Kweli, who grew up in a middle-class family and even attended a swank boarding school, continued, "The hardest lesson I had to learn in the music industry was the idea that you were marketing yourself. I fool-ishly started thinking that I was selling music. But music has noth-ing to do with it. I don't make money because of the music I make. I have developed myself into a personality, and that's what I sell. What we're marketing is 'This is really us, this is really us, this is really us.' But this is entertainment and we're actually selling soul."

This paradoxical mixture of art and commerce taints expression of an artist's true sensibilities, especially since current hip-hop promo-tion favours a more sinister façade. As conflicted artists get pushed to the periphery, other mic wielders with no such qualms, and who are ready to deliver the market's desires, take their place.

When we talked to Fifty about hip-hop's current ethos, he said, "Kids pick the person who brings them more listening pleasure, who they like to listen to. That's what it is. You try to make music for people to enjoy themselves while they're listening to it. . . . I put 'Back Down' on my last album, on *Get Rich or Die Tryin'*, as the very last record I recorded for that album. If 'Back Down' wasn't on the album, I still would have sold eleven million records, 'cause the records that sold my album was 'In Da Club,' 'Many Men,' '21 Questions' and 'P.I.M.P.'"

While Fifty sees the song "Back Down" as proof that he makes hard-core music at a cost to himself, songs like "Back Down" give him the necessary credibility to create more radio-friendly tracks such as "21 Questions." If Fiddy only made songs like "21 Questions" he'd be Ja-Rule—and we know how that story ended.

Curtis continued, "You heard the song 'In My Hood?'"

Rodrigo nodded, and Fifty sang the hook: "'Niggas got love for me, but I don't go nowhere without my strap'—See what I'm saying? That's the mentality. It's like, I don't even got no problems but they gonna take their pistol when they walkin', when they goin' through the hood, because it might be somebody else just pull up, some bullshit. And I need to have that with me, that's real. That's the way it is."

"Do you think hip-hop would be different if there were no guns?"

"It would be totally different. Then it would be old-school. It would be back to fightin'. Back to fist fightin', back to hand-to-hand."

"You think it'd be better?"

"It'd be a lot more knife-work. A lot more stabbings."

"But think of the people we've lost to gun violence already."

"I don't think that hip-hop is the problem; I think that violence is the issue when you talkin' 'bout that. And you're not gonna escape violence. You got people that are violent, in the world. It's not actually about guns, it's about the actual mentality, the climate, of the actual area."

Fifty's success is no accident. Young Curtis Jackson knows when to indulge the fantasy and when to pull out the reality card, when to exploit a story for its marketing potential and when to flip the story into a socioeconomic criticism of America. While the line between creating art and reflecting reality is crystal-clear to Curtis, in the minds of the listeners the two easily become blurred.

The G-Unit are pimping gun fantasies, but so are Redwolf Airsoft, *The Punisher, Gun World, Mr. & Mrs. Smith, Mail Call* and *25 to Life*. They all promote demand for guns without revealing much about the pain and suffering that firearms can cause.

KILLA CROSSOVERS

"Movies and video games aren't the only places you can find the Desert Eagle Pistol," reads a section titled "Reading Eagles" on Magnum Research's website, which lists more than fifty fiction and non-fiction books that mention the bird—including, brags Magnum, at least one Oprah selection.

Another of the books is Shaquille O'Neal's biography, *Shaq Talks Back*. His life story (to date) reveals that during a hunting trip in Florida, O'Neal pulled a "huge gold-plated handgun called a Desert Eagle" from behind his coat to finish off a dying deer. Astounded, a guide said to Shaq, "That must be your homeboy special."

Despite his love of hunting, shared by the likes of Karl Malone—nominated to the NRA board of directors in 2001—Shaq wisely decided not to mention his firearms on the five rap albums he released between 1993 and 2001. But other wannabe emcee b-ball superstars did when they got on the microphone. Back in 2000, Kobe Bryant, a.k.a. K.O.B.E., rapped horribly about his black Glock 9, while Allen Iverson, who took the name Jewelz on the mic, rhymed surprisingly well about "lusting" after AKs. In November 2004 *The Washington Post* updated the public that among many of the NBA's young ballers, "the fascination with guns . . . is growing. They are accessories to some players, like a new CD collection or wardrobe." Utah Jazz all-star Andrei Kirilenko, a native of Izhevsk, Russia, even chose the number 47, earning the nickname "AK-47." Still, not every NBA hero has embraced guns.

> I said I'm sicker than the average
> Keep three shooters like the Mavericks
> Short, to the point, like Nash is
> — Beanie Sigel, "Don't Stop," off *The B.Coming* (2005)

Born in Johannesburg, South Africa, a country partly destabilized by the widespread availability of small arms, and raised in Victoria, British Columbia, Steve Nash plays ball in Phoenix, Arizona, a state with some of America's laxest gun laws. In March 2005, former Arizona State University football player Loren Wade shot and killed teammate Brandon Falkner "outside a popular hip-hop club in Scottsdale" because Falkner had tried to talk to Wade's girlfriend. The *Arizona Republic* soon ran a story titled "Suns Players Agree Guns Aren't Proof of Toughness." The *Republic* piece offered a collection of quotes about gun violence from several Phoenix Suns. As always, the Suns' two-time MVP guard was on point, holding court with one concise comment. "I've been in this country for thirteen years," Nash said. "I wish there were stiffer gun control laws. Accessibility is a killer."

BARRELS OF DESTRUCTION

FOR THOUSANDS OF YEARS the Mandari of southern Sudan have driven their cattle into greener pastures, starting daily with the rise of the sun and continuing until the fall of night. As the outside world changes at a hectic clip, the culture of the Mandari remains much the same as it was millennia ago—with one exception.

On April 6, 2006, *The Independent*'s Cahil Milmo and Kate Holt reported in a story from Kwajroji on the Mandari, titled "Global Arms Trade: Africa and the Curse of the AK-47." Mandari warriors now wear Kalashnikovs almost as consistently as the patterned scars that mark their status as herdsmen. Called *perik* by the Mandari—a reference to the assault rifle's cracking sound—aging AKs have become invaluable currency to the nomadic tribesmen, who are forced to trade cattle for rifles to protect their families and herds from enemy clans. "Mandari elders warn that their own arms race is destroying their culture," *The Independent* informs. "From child abduction by gun-toting rivals to a new and unfamiliar lack of respect for human life, the gun is seen as a necessary but corrosive evil."

As in any environment inundated with small arms, living without weapons would risk the Mandaris' security, physically and economically. The AK-47 has become both the biggest threat and best defence, terrified as they are by outsiders who would snatch their children and steal their cattle. "To the Mandari," say Milmo and Holt, "it feels like a careful balance of power built up over centuries has been replaced by savage anarchy in which guns are the sole arbiters of power." That Mandari had agreed to speak with Western reporters for the first time, they added, reflected the depth of their concern.

The solemnity with which most of the hip-hop artists answered our questions attests to a similar concern. Born in Mogadishu, Somalia, and forced to leave on the last commercial flight out of his country in 1991, K'Naan immigrated to Toronto by way of Harlem at age thirteen. "The Kalashnikov was the first thing I learned to shoot," K'Naan recalled. "Shot my first one at the age of eight. And the butt, the back of it—I was too skinny to hold it. My brother knew how to hold that thing better. But I fired it and it just jerked back at me and kinda hurt my shoulder. I also remember it taking the lives of many of my friends and my family. I lost three of my closest friends at the age of eleven. They were all shot with a Kalashnikov AK-47. And we were running along together, and they didn't make it. I made it."

> I curse the Russians who impregnated the Kalashnikov birth
> — K'Naan, "Blues for the Horn," off *The Dusty Foot Philosopher* (2005)

At the end of the Cold War, international attention began to turn from the threat of mutually assured destruction to what's been called the "human security agenda." Many now recognize that guns are causing the majority of damage to human life worldwide; that small-arms proliferation, particularly in the midst of poverty, prevents the existence of peace and stability.

On the African continent, only South Africa and, to a lesser extent, Nigeria have a significant capacity for manufacturing firearms. Nonetheless, Africa faces no shortage of small arms. The flag of Mozambique even includes an image of the Russian AK-47, a controversial symbol within the country. "The older generation of the country has kept it in their memory," General Kalashnikov told us, "that is why the picture of the Kalashnikov gun in the national flag of their country is for them a symbol of freedom and independence." But small arms have taken on new meaning for a younger generation of Africans. "The kids on the streets of Nairobi, Khartoum, Abidjan and Monrovia have guns in their pockets or up their sleeves," United Nations senior official Dennis McNamara told Reuters on February 2, 2006. "We provided the arms. We the West, we the G8." Canadian pilots, for instance, were contracted to fly guns to rebels in the war-torn Democratic Republic of Congo.

Meanwhile, Somalia, like other countries in Africa, Asia and the Middle East, has become ungovernable; vengeance killings the lone form of justice. Since civil war erupted in '91, Somalia has developed into a place where six-year-olds strapped like Rambo extort passersby and where rival warlords rule from heavily armed camps. Unregulated militias terrorize; aid agencies mostly stay away. "It's a very privileged place to speak from," K'Naan said, "when North Americans really try to share their love for posture and guns and violence, and make it out to be something linked with cool culture. It's kinda crazy, because where we come from, we know there is no way to glorify the gun."

Whatever criticisms one might level against rappers who *do* glorify guns, their lyrics nevertheless reveal tomes about the true horrors—to borrow Gerald Cupchik's distinction—that firearms perpetuate. From nightspots in the world's most sweltering cities to school hallways on remote reservations, these arrayed horrors represent the subject of this, the final chamber.

WILD HOODS

On August 14, 2005, the cover of the *Toronto Star* featured the images of thirty-three identical Browning semi-automatic pistols, "one for every shooting homicide in the city this year." The image revealed nothing of the victims, the perpetrators or the circumstances that cast these roles upon any of them. Addressing gun violence requires us to see beyond the sensational, past the guns themselves.

Canadians experience outrage at the shooting of children like Shaquan Cadougan, a four-year-old Toronto boy who survived four stray bullets in an August 2005 drive-by. But such tragedies became commonplace in New York City more than a century ago. In 1889 it was three-year-old Anna Gerner who lost her life to a stray in Manhattan; in April 2006 two-year-old David Pacheco became the latest victim of random gunfire in the Bronx to date. "So many kids are dyin' in our communities in America," hip-hop impresario Russell Simmons said during a visit to Vancouver in the summer of 2005. "It's not even newsworthy until 50 Cent get in a shootout. Kids are gettin' killed in Brooklyn *every day*. So finally 50 Cent and Game get in a shootout, it becomes the cover of the paper. Just 'cause they got a record doesn't mean that their mindset of poverty and ignorance doesn't come with them out of the place that they learn these ideas."

> Little shorties take walks to the schoolyard
> Tryin' to solve the puzzles to why is life so hard
> Then as soon as they reached the playground
> BLAOW!!! Shots ring off and now one of them lay down
> It's so hard to escape the gunfire
> I wish I could rule it out like an umpire
> But it's an everlasting game
> And it never cease to exist, only the players change
> — GZA, "I Gotcha Back," off *Liquid Swords* (1995)

"I Gotcha Back" first appeared on the soundtrack to director Boaz Yakin's 1994 film *Fresh.* Starring Sean Nelson, Giancarlo Esposito and Samuel L. Jackson, *Fresh* depicts the tale of a stoic twelve-year-old chess phenom who sets a trap for three adult drug dealers in order to free his drug-addicted sister from their clutches. Talking to the GZA, a.k.a. the Genius, you get the feeling that the head of the Wu-Tang Clan might have been like that kid in real life.

"I wrote that song for my nephew," he explained. "He's like twenty-three now, twenty-four. He was ten or eleven then. His father, who's my brother, has been locked up since 1989. I wrote that song thinkin' about him. I wrote it for him 'cause he was rhymin' at the time. It was something I wanted to give to him, but I think it was too powerful for his age. But that was about him: 'I'm from Brooklyn, a place where stars are born / Streets are shot up, apartment buildings are torn.' He lived on Amboy Street, same block [Mike] Tyson lived on in Brownsville: 'Ripped up, stripped up, shacked up'—you know, 'Kids are slingin' in my lobby.' That's what he was livin'; he was goin' through that. He'd come home everyday, kids sellin' drugs in his lobby.

"Let me tell you something that's really crazy right now," the GZA continued. "The 'I Gotcha Back' song—remember I did a video for that. There's two kids that I feature in that video. One of them is the one I'm telling you about; both of them are my nephews. One of 'em gets shot in the video and killed; the other one is hangin' out with the wrong crowd. Both of those nephews are locked up now in jail."

Movie producers, video game makers and rappers all say the gun problem starts with parents. It was certainly true throughout Dr. Deanna Wilkinson's study of 417 New York City males twenty-four-years or younger and involved in gun carrying and/or crime. Less than 17 percent of them had grown up in two-parent families. Single moms, like Shyne and Raekwon's, often working slave-like hours at low-paying jobs, raised most of the youth in Wilkinson's study. Like Trigger Tha Gambler and Lloyd Banks, 43 percent had fathers who'd been criminally active, and, like GZA's nephew's, "some fathers had been incarcerated for most of the respondents' lives." In even more tragic cases, as with B.G. and Ed O.G., the fathers of 9.7 percent of those surveyed had been killed. Broken families set the scene for gun trouble among rap artists, just as it had for the youth in Wilkinson's book.

50 Cent grew up without a father and lost his mother to a drug-related murder when he was just eight years old. Like millions of young males now facing parental neglect or loss, Fifty was brought up by the streets and by hip-hop. "They raisin' themselves," X-Clan's Brother J said of many youth today, "and [they think], 'Well, I'm in these streets, how should I survive? How should I do? Let me turn this tape on and listen to instruction.' That's they lessons, man. Game's album is a lesson for these niggas; 50 Cent's album is a lesson."

While Toronto rapper Solitair grew up poor economically, he had the benefit of a "good family base," two loving parents. He believes that the problem with gun violence can in part be traced to "a lot of kids having kids" and an increasing sense of hopelessness among youth. "Gun violence is only a symptom of a much deeper problem with the community that we have in Toronto, and in every other major city around the world for that matter," Solitair said. "I'm kind of at a loss for words, because it's so far gone. And I'm a lot older than some of these kids that are runnin' around dealin' with this kind of stuff, and it's just a mentality that's been ingrained in them."

In order to present such kids with at least "one different alternative lifestyle," Solitair—alongside Kardinal Offishall and rapper/lawyer Y-Look—volunteers his time to speak to what have been labelled "at-risk youths" in local high schools. "A lot of these kids," he explained, "were asking questions like, 'Well, what do you do if everybody that you know has a gun? Shouldn't you have a gun too, to defend yourself?'"

> If I had hustled with him, would I be dead too?
> Was a bullet through the chest worth the shit he went through?
> Fuck, I ain't a hustler, my cousin packed a gun
> And his memory's the reason I will never pack one
> — Solitair, "Easy to Slip," off *Rap Essentials 2001* (2001)

Forget movie and video game shootouts—nothing grabs a kid's attention like the real thing. In May 2005 *Science Magazine* published the results of a five-year study of 1,500 twelve- to fifteen-year-olds from seventy-eight Chicago neighbourhoods. Researchers found that kids who had been shot or shot at, or had seen someone shot or shot at, even once, were twice as likely to engage in subsequent violent behaviour of their own. As one of three authors of the study, Harvard Medical School's Dr. Felton Earls drew a helpful comparison in one press release: "The best model for violence may be that of a socially infectious disease. . . . Preventing one violent crime may prevent a downstream cascade of 'infections.'" "I'm from the Calliope projects," said New Orleans's C-Murder, charged in two separate murder cases. "I done seen nothing but murder where I'm from. That's how I grew up; that's just part of the everyday life."

Another New Orleans local, B.G. first made his mark on the hip-hop map in '93, dropping a debut album, *True Story*, on the nascent Cash Money label. Born in 1980, the Baby Gangsta was barely a teenager then, but already he was well versed in guns and the drug trade. "I was in the hood," he remembered of his early influences. "Kris Kross was talkin' about 'Jump Jump'; and I was hearin' shit go 'pump-pump,' youknowhatI'msayin', in the middle of the night."

"Respondents often characterized their neighborhoods as 'war zones,'" Wilkinson writes. Not coincidentally, rappers often characterize their neighbourhoods in the same terms. The G-Unit "soldiers" have histories that meet the diagnostic criteria for post-traumatic stress disorder (PTSD) and other trauma-related psychological illnesses, disorders that many inner-city youth suffer like ex-combatants. PTSD can affect those involved in or who have witnessed a violent event; they subsequently face difficulty with sleep and concentration, irritability and loss of temper.

Reporting for *YO! Youth Outlook*, a Bay Area–based Internet news service delivering the perspectives of young people, fourteen-year-old Young Napz expands on these symptoms in a February 27, 2006, article, "Gun Trauma–Getting Shot Has Changed My Life." "I had been having nightmares of getting shot and dying ever since one of my friends was killed recently, but I never thought I would get shot," Napz writes. "Because of all this I'm traumatized. Every time I hear a loud clap or something, I start trippin'. I'm always looking over my shoulder when I'm by myself. I don't feel safe anywhere but home, with a family member, or with a close friend."

A lost generation of kids who grew up during America's crack crisis in the eighties and nineties are now adults, and are passing on the only legacy they've ever known. If they can't give children anything else, there are always lots of guns around. Wilkinson's mid-nineties study acknowledged the ongoing trend: "According to many respondents guns were getting into the hands of youth at much younger ages."

"You got people givin' guns to kids, they want them to wreck they lives," Queens, New York's Big Noyd said a decade later. "You got a lot of people livin' like that, like, 'Yeah, here go a gun, shorty. Pick up a gun, go fuckin' shoot that nigga.' Like if niggas tell ya I just had a fight wit' a kid, somebody else, instead of goin' like, 'Yo, go back out there and whip they ass—have a one-on-one,' they like, 'Yeah, here go a gun—go shoot that nigga.'"

Wilkinson thought Noyd's comments sounded familiar. "Oh, yeah, definitely," she said. "And I think even if they don't have someone telling them that, that's the message they've already internalized from watching what happens on the street. So that's like a very powerful script that's already in their minds. The reality is if you have a conflict with someone—you've already had a physical fight—it's got to escalate to weapons next, because if you go back out there and say that you want to have a one-on-one with someone, you're putting yourself in a vulnerable position, because that person is gonna be looking for the advantage and bring in a weapon. So the way that they think about it is, have a pre-emptive strike, because that's your best chance. Whether that's real or necessary or not, that's how it's evolved in the way kids are thinking about their safety out there in the most dangerous neighbourhoods."

> Brothers are amused by other brothers' reps
> But the thing they know best is where the gun is kept
> — Guru, "Just to Get a Rep," off Gang Starr's *Step in the Arena* (1990)

In her book, Wilkinson describes the New York City neighbourhoods of those she studies as an "ecology of danger." In such a situation, reputation has often proven the best defence. Guru agreed that reps come harder for youths now, saying emphatically, "*Yeah*, because it's a younger age, and because the times we're livin' in are more severe economically."

According to Wilkinson's *Guns, Violence and Identity*, "The process of self-preservation through displays of toughness, nerve, or violent behaviour is considered a necessary part of day-to-day life for inner-city adolescents, especially young males." As the economic noose tightens and people become more desperate, the ecology of the 'hood becomes even more dangerous. Acting out violently functions as a deterrent and a means to solidify status. "Guns were used as a resource for improving violent performances," Wilkinson found.

It is from this ecology and with this mentality that many rappers enter the music industry. Emcees spend years sharpening their identities, because, as Wilkinson's book underscores, "Crafting a powerful social identity is a critical tool for survival in the inner-city context." These strong identities are part of what makes rap artists so enticing to the young public. 41.2 percent of violent events involving guns in Wilkinson's sample were caused by conflicts over "identity/status."

By the same token, a 2005 study by George Washington University assistant professor Charis Kubrin, "Gangstas, Thugs, and Hustlas: Identity and the Code of the Street in Rap Music," found that on 132 rap albums that went platinum between 1992 and 2000, 68 percent of all songs included references to respect, while 65 percent of the sampled cuts discussed violence—the two most dominant themes (the objectification of women appeared in just 22 percent of the songs)."The only way the music can make a nigga kill each other," Tech N9ne said, "is ridiculing each other over beats like we do, beefin' with each other—that's how niggas die, because people feel like their rep is on the line, and they can't let nobody *do them* like that." But while exceptions exist, as in the case of Capone and Lil' Kim, hip-hop's history hasn't shown the music to be a frequent precursor to violence. Some ferocious beefs have eventually culminated in peace between artists, the lyrical battles allowing anger to be exorcized without physical conflict.

> Gun control means using both hands in my land
> — Posdnous, "Stakes Is High," off De La Soul's *Stakes Is High* (1996)

Comparing gun violence today to the state of the streets during his youth, De La Soul's Pos said, "It's worse in the sense that [the gun is] a permanent fixture in how a lot of urban kids feel they need to come up. I have great and beautiful-minded cousins that live in really bad areas, and they can have a great upbringing and they don't want to use it, but then you have a lot of people who's caught up in feeling like, 'I have to, I have to own a gun, because even just walkin' down the street and going to school everyday someone's gonna punk me, 'cause they think that me goin' to school everyday is not the cool thing to do.'" Shorties are afraid of literally losing their shirts, cash and lives. Wilkinson's survey found that 20.3 percent of violent events involving guns were related to self-defence: "In an environment in which many individuals see themselves as having no power or control over the dangers and fears they face, guns provide a means to reduce fear and regain some defense against ever-present threats and enemies."

A rap artist from San Jose, California, Charizma saw things that way. "Charizma, when I first knew him," Stones Throw CEO Peanut

Butter Wolf said solemnly of his late hip-hop partner, "I knew he didn't have a gun or anything like that. And then later on he started carryin' his gun everywhere and saying he needed it for protection and stuff. And that was something that him and I always argued about—never saw eye-to-eye on." Left thinking he might have argued harder, PB Wolf lost Charizma in December '93. The twenty-year-old emcee was shot dead while being robbed, just as he was beginning to open for the likes of the Pharcyde and Nas. At the time of the tragedy Charizma was himself strapped.

"Got Ur Self a Gun," a track from Nas's *Stillmatic*, takes a position similar to Charizma's. Rodrigo challenged Nas on the album's content. "You mentioned the black man being peaceful," he said, "but you also have several songs about guns on the album."

"Well, the black man's a peaceful man but that doesn't mean he's dumb," Nas answered, slightly irritated and very serious. "He's smart, so if you come at me with a gun and I keep seeing everybody around me drop with guns 'cause they don't have one, what do you think I'm supposed to do? I go get myself a gun, so that's what the song is about."

Deanna Wilkinson recognized the dilemma Nas described: "One of my students sent me a wav file for 'Got Ur Self a Gun'—I'm sure you know the song. I was thinking that this could be the soundtrack of my book, because just about everything that they say in that song rings so true, and if I listen to more music I would probably find the same thing."

> Thoughts of slaughter, of leavin' my daughters
> Hours and hours of fears runnin' through my mind
> As I pick up the Zig ninnnnne
> — Des, off East Flatbush Project's "Tried by 12" 12-inch (1996)

Most young men in *Guns, Violence, and Identity* bought their guns with money earned in the illegal drug trade. Of those Dr. Wilkinson interviewed, "Eighty-four percent of the sample reported being involved in the drug business during the previous two years." While "Tried by 12" was made popular because of its slamming beat, Des's lyrics spoke volumes about life on many New York streets at the time. Indeed, Des was writing his lyrics around the same time Deanna Wilkinson was writing her book. He could've easily found himself among her sample of sixteen- to twenty-four-year-old New Yorkers. When we got in touch with Des, he'd just served a six-month stint in boot camp, a form of substitute sentencing in cases of non-violent crimes.

Des told us "Tried by 12" was inspired by a war over "hustling, drugs [and] turf" that took the life of his homeboy Phillip Phoenix. "It was street stuff," he said, in a voice sounding nothing like the adolescent emcee on "Tried by 12." "And as a matter of fact, what made it so bad, so sad, was that he got killed for something that he didn't even have nothin' to do with."

"How often do you think that happens in the street?"

"A lot of times, 'cause there's a lot of misunderstandings sometimes. That happens all the time, everyday. It's like innocent bystanders."

The murder of Freaky Tah provides another example of how mistakes and rash responses can too easily go wrong when guns enter the picture. A member of the Lost Boyz family fresh out Jamaica, Queens, twenty-eight-year-old Freaky Tah was shot once in the head outside a hotel party in his neighbourhood. A confusing mess had begun when one of the Lost Boyz was robbed earlier. A crew member associated with the LB's extended family retaliated by shooting dead Michael Saunders, who hadn't been involved in the robbery. Saunders's half-brother, Kelvin Jones, then took revenge on Freaky Tah, mistakenly believing that Tah was related to the man who shot Saunders. Jones and two other men were later charged with second-degree murder.

Continuing the cycle of misdirected anger just three days after Tah's murder, Corey Bussey, a homie of Freaky Tah, shot Roderick Padgett multiple times outside a nightclub, killing him. Bussey was sentenced in August 2005 to ten years in prison. "The victim, Roderick Padgett, was fatally wounded in an execution-style shooting in a terrible and tragic case of mistaken identity," District Attorney Richard Brown said after Bussey's sentence was handed down. "The defendant Bussey opened fire and took revenge on the wrong man in the erroneous belief that the victim had been involved in the murder three days earlier of his friend, the rapper Freaky Tah."

We'd read that Freaky Tah had been taken from the world on his best friend's birthday. "Oh, no doubt about it," the Lost Boyz' Mr. Cheeks confirmed. "March 28th, 1999. He still here. He in me."

In addition to the loss of Freaky Tah, Cheeks has also watched another member of the Lost Boyz, Spigg Nice, imprisoned for thirty-seven years without parole for his role in ten armed bank robberies. Since the murder of Freaky Tah, Cheeks has spent some of his time reaching out to youth tripping on the wrong path, arranging scholarships and other programs to help give them hope. "What would you say to kids that are running around in the streets with guns?" Chris asked Cheeks.

"What I would say is like, 'You need to put them joints down, man. Pick up some books, find out what's goin' on, 'cause there's a bigger world than what they stuck in right now. Whatever they involved in, you might grow out of it. 'Cause there's greater things in life to look forward to.' I lost a lot of friends from that—friends in jail and friends to the ground—but as you get older you learn." Youth should be able to make mistakes without destroying their lives in the process. But when they combine the impetuousness of youth with pistols, they often don't get that chance.

There are ways to rap about guns without glorifying them. Mr. Cheeks wrote "Renee" about a popular law student from Queens who was killed by stray gunfire one Christmas Eve. On wax Cheeks imagines himself as Renee's most important other, immortalizing his beloved. A gun plays the role of heartbreaker.

Deanna Wilkinson understands that the causes of gun violence on the streets extend beyond the influence of rap music. Just the same, reconsidering messages about guns could have a positive influence. "I think, in some ways, hip-hop—if they could popularize a different message," she said. "I don't know how you do that. But if people realize that their mutual self-destruction is rooted in something that they're not even consciously making a decision about, that might bother some kids."

SURVIVING THE GAME

When Harlem-born-and-bred emcee Cam'ron, a.k.a. Killa Cam, né Cameron Giles, was shot through both arms while leaving Howard University's homecoming celebrations in Washington, D.C., in October 2005, the media was thrilled to present the world with another rap-related shooting. But Cam, who took two for his blue Lamborghini in an alleged but dubiously dubbed carjacking, was not a victim of rap-related violence. "That had nothing to do with hip-hop beef," Talib Kweli said. "That had to do with him driving a Lamborghini at Howard homecoming and somebody used the opportunity to try to get at him."

Juelz Santana, a member of Cam'ron's Diplomat family, was in the car behind Cam's when the shooting went down. Happy that his man was safe, Juelz candidly commented, "We expect rappers to get shot nowadays. It ain't no thing anymore." Kweli agreed: "That's a running joke, but that's because emcees are the most visible, accessible part of the black community. Emcees are getting shot because they are young black men, and that's a point that America's not ready to face, because it's easy to accept that they're getting shot because of the lyrics that they're putting in the atmosphere. That's an easier cause to accept than it's just dangerous for young black men."

The following is a list of hip-hoppers who've survived shootings. While some have used their stories to launch their careers, most never speak of the violence that has changed their lives and scarred their bodies.

50 Cent	B-Real	Lloyd Banks
Afu-Ra (Afu shot himself in the leg when he was fourteen while trying to disarm his handgun. The shot left a small scar on his calf that serves for him as a memory of his reckless youth. He's never carried a gun since.)	Bushwick Bill	Lorenzo Gotti
	Cam'ron	LV
	Capone	MF Grimm
	Devin the Dude	M.E.D.
	Dr. Dre	Obie Trice
	Dresta	O.D.B. (When Ol' Dirty Bastard became the first
	Fat Joe	person arrested under a
AP9	FED-X	California law forbidding
Beanie Siegel	Freaky Zeeky	convicted felons from
Beelow	The Game	wearing a bulletproof vest
Big Noyd	Ghostface Killah	in '99, it was hard to blame
	Gravy	Dirt Dog for the offence.
	Lil' Flip	

He'd already been shot twice before, in '94 and '98.)
Oschino
Shyne
Slick Rick
Son Doobie
Stick-Up Kid
Suge Knight
Young Buck (The Nashville G-Uniteer was shot by armed robbers while working a crack house with a friend. True to his namesake, Buck bucked back. "We were strapped when that happened. So I got shot, but I'm still breathin'. They gone.")
Young Lay

HEAT NUTZ

So I'm outside of da club and he think I'm a puuuuunk!!!
So I go to my loaded Tec-9 that's off in the truuuuunk!!!
— Bonecrusher, "Never Scared," off *AttenCHUN!* (2003)

The National Rifle Association's blacklist includes virtually every U.S. organization concerned with the physical and mental health of Americans, including, to name a few, the American Medical Association, American Trauma Society, American Public Health Association, Black Mental Health Alliance, National Association of School Psychologists and National Association of Public Hospitals. Most doctors agree: guns are bad for people's health.

A 1994 resolution passed by the American Psychological Association (APA)—following their 1982 statement in favour of handgun control—maintained, "the psychological research on factors that contribute to human aggression indicates that exposure and access to guns can result in an increased likelihood of aggression." As if the testosterone-loaded brains of young men needed an extra charge, studies such as those cited by the APA have shown that firearms themselves can encourage aggression.

One of these is a classic 1967 study by University of Wisconsin-Madison psychologists Leonard Berkowitz and Anthony LePage, which found that the mere presence of a gun can intensify aggression. After being "angered" by exposure to electric shocks, subjects were allowed to deliver shocks to another student. The study found that when a revolver or shotgun was placed in sight, the subjects delivered more numerous and more severe electric shocks to fellow students than when the gun was replaced with a badminton racket. "It's not a gun per se, a gun in and of itself, that's important," Leonard Berkowitz, still pursuing his research in retirement, explained. "It's the meaning of the gun, what the gun means to the individual. For hunters, they don't think of guns as used to kill or shoot people; they think of guns as used for sport. So as a consequence, they're less likely to become aggressive when they see a gun. It's people who are not hunters who are more likely to be aggressively stimulated."

Commonly called the "weapons effect," Berkowitz and LePage's finding has been reproduced with mixed results by researchers in the U.S. and Europe. "There's now been quite a bit of corroboration," Dr. Berkowitz said in his slow, focused manner, "some directly repeating the study and some extending it in other ways."

Bonecrusher touched on the role of the weapons effect when we spoke. "When you got a gun on you it changes your thought process," he said. "It makes you think, 'I'm unstoppable,' and in that silliness of arrogance in your head, you'll do something stupid." Quoting Bonecrusher to Berkowitz—"*Whooooo?*" he asked—we got no further than the word *silliness* before he agreed: "Sure, sure, sure. I can believe that. I think that might well be the case for some people. That's right—to have a sense of power."

In 2002, as the weapons effect was more frequently entering discussion at the United Nations, *Guns & Ammo* ran a rebuttal of sorts entitled "The Legacy of Liars." "To instill the requisite fear of firearms needed to camouflage its agenda of power acquisition," argue Dr. Paul Gallant and Dr. Joanne Eisen, "the U.N. has forged ahead with perpetuation of the 'weapons effect' myth." In order to facilitate its campaign of "civilian disarmament" internationally, they contend, the United Nations "dismisses all damning evidence of the flawed hypothesis out of hand." Dr. Leonard Berkowitz received his PhD in psychology from the University of Michigan in 1951, while, according to *Guns & Ammo*, "Dr. Paul Gallant practices optometry in Wesley Hills, New York, [and] Dr. Joanne Eisen practices dentistry in Old Bethpage, New York." Doctors willing to toe the gun industry's line are out there, apparently; they're just tough to find.

Still, there are those outside the gun business who challenge the weapons effect hypothesis. dead prez's stic.man for one, a devoted advocate of self-defence rights. "I think that's some bullshit," stic said of Bonecrusher's observations. "A gun don't change how I act. A gun is just a normal part. Just like I got vitamins, just like I got a home, I need transportation, I need weapons. That's just a regular part [of my life]. And if you let the gun change your mentality, it's you watchin' too much of these Hollywood movies."

> Excuse me while I light my spliff, but some choose to sip
> So bullets hit brains, when bottles hit lips
> — Jeru the Damaja, "Return of the Crooklyn Dodgers" 12-inch (1995)

"When guys get shot at the clubs," Jeru said about his homerun verse with the Crooklyn Dodgers, "you know everybody's drunk. When you drink it makes you feel like you Superman." Booze and guns go together as well for the hustler with his Colt .45 pistol and Colt 45 malt liquor as for the hunter with his .22 and a two-four. On February 16, 2005, *The Washington Post* reported, "The Virginia General Assembly is considering a bill to impose strict blood alcohol limits on hunters, angering gun enthusiasts who say the legislation unjustly targets their right to bear arms." It's not clear how staying sober limits Second Amendment rights, but even U.S. vice-president Dick Cheney admitted he'd downed "a beer" in the hours before accidentally blasting his homeboy in the face with a 28-gauge Perazzi shotgun in February 2006.

The youth in Deanna Wilkinson's study similarly reported being drunk or high during more than 80 percent of their violent events involving guns. As Wilkinson says in her book, "alcohol exaggerates the sense of outrage over perceived transgressions of personal codes." And nowhere are "personal codes" more in effect than in clubs, where, as stic.man immortally rhymed, "Everybody wanna be somebody better than everybody."

When Scarface and Willie D confronted each other with hand-guns in their much younger days at a club on Houston's South Side, their beef led to numerous injuries and several deaths. Now living and working in Azerbaijan, Willie D discussed firewater's potential to spark gun violence. "A lot of dudes, they do get a little liquor in they system and what I tend to call a cup of courage," he said. "It's like they gotta have a little drink to make 'em feel strong, feel like they're invincible, and make 'em feel brave, so I'm sure alcohol factors in a lot. The thing about it, though, is that you go out there and kill some-damn-body, you can't come to court with your bottle of Hennessy. You know, Hennessy ain't gonna be standin' up there on that motherfuckin' stand, and [the] prosecu-tor ain't gonna look at the bottle of Hennessy and say, 'Okay, Hennessy, tell me, why did you allow him to consume so much of you?' That ain't gonna happen."

Attesting to the direct effect of drunkness on gun violence, a paper by *Small Arms Survey* in January 2006 reported that an 8 per-cent decrease in Bogotá, Colombia's murder rate in the nineties was attributed to closing the bars earlier, at 1:00 a.m. A city of 380,000 in the state of São Paulo, Brazil, found similar relief, according to the *Economist* on October 20, 2005. Diadema closed drinking spots between 11:00 p.m. and 6:00 a.m., helping decrease a horrifying homicide rate of 110 per 100,000 people by two-thirds. Another thing about Bogotá and São Paulo, though—they're mad hot.

> In the hood summertime is the killin' season
> It's hot out this bitch, that's a good enough reason
> — 50 Cent, "Heat," off *Get Rich or Die Tryin'* (2003)

"They say when people drink," remarked Oakland's Paris, introducing another factor in making itchy trigger fingers scratch, "and when the weather gets hot, it's on." Sure, when the weather gets hot people drink more and spend more time outside, but research has shown that hot weather can itself cause irritability, prepping the mind for aggression.

Citing the summer effect, a February 1998 article by Iowa State psychologists Craig Anderson and Brad Bushman in the *APA Monitor* reported: "Over the last 10 years, research has shown that uncomfortably hot temperatures directly cause increases in aggressive and violent behavior." According to Anderson and Bushman, "Other research has found that hotter days, months and seasons produce higher-than-normal crime rates." Hotter cities and regions also show higher rates of violent crime. "It always be crackin' in the summertime!" Mississippi's David Banner confirmed. "Man, don't nobody wanna be outside when it's cold."

Lately it's been hot in Toronto too—on the mercury scale and in the streets. "Every year people sort of go on like, 'It's gonna be a hot summer,'" Kehinde Bah said in May 2005. "Usually, I don't pay it no mind, but at the same time . . . I get that feelin' in the air, man." Whatever was in the air, Kehinde's feelings didn't betray him. In 2005, like so many other cities, the T-Dot experienced a summer season of record heat, with average temperatures in June eclipsing the annual norm by almost five degrees Celsius. It was also a summer that saw seventeen shooting deaths between June and August, compared with an average of fewer than twenty-nine gun murders annually in Toronto between 2000 and 2002.

With a population just slightly larger than Toronto's, Chicago experienced a similar increase in its murder rate between June and August 2004, a three-month stretch that averaged 48.3 homicides per month, compared with an average of 32.6 murders over the other nine months. Anderson and Bushman cite two supporting studies: with an increase of just one degree Fahrenheit above the average annual temperature in the U.S., the national assault and murder rate rose by 3.68 per 100,000 people. In a country the size of the United States, "the 3.68 figure translates into roughly 9,900 more murders and assaults per year." Add increasingly accessible burners to the mix—what poet John Milton calls the "hollow engines" of hell in 1667's *Paradise Lost*—and a few pimp cups filled up to fend off the heat, and global warming translates to a planet lit with gunfire.

STAT QUO

I'm from the murder capital where we murder for capital
— Jay-Z, "Lucifer," off *The Black Album* (2003)

Waving your neighbourhood flag is a proud hip-hop tradition—without street shout-outs, names like Queensbridge, Calliope, 5th Ward and South Central might never have entered public consciousness. Unfortunately, while those who dwell in these communities bear witness to both the joys and sorrows of life there, the outside world registers their names as synonyms for urban decay and violence.

Jay-Z, a.k.a. Jay-Hova, waves his flag for Marcy Houses in Brooklyn, a housing complex of twenty-seven six-storey buildings that's home to 4,200 people. Memphis Bleek, Hov's friend, former collaborator and employee, grew up there too. "Jay lived on the fifth, I lived on the third," Bleek said. Still true to the block, M-Bleezie named his 2005 album *534*, an homage to the address he called home for his first seventeen years. Said Bleek, "It was the best time in my life—located Brooklyn, Marcy, 534 Flushing Ave."

But things weren't always nice in young Bleek and Hov's neighbourhood. In 1990 the NYPD's 79th precinct, which serves the Marcy Houses, reported 71 murders among its 84,000 denizens—translating to a war-zone-like murder rate of 85.5 per 100,000 residents. Those were New York City's most murderous moments, playing the backdrop to 2,262 homicides in 1990 alone. Fortunately, homicide numbers would be a quarter of that by 2004, with similar drops happening nationwide. Bleek's 'hood got brighter too; no longer "murder Marcyville," the 79th reported eighteen victims in 2004, but still clocked in at four times the national murder rate and over twice that of NYC as a whole.

One thing did remain constant in all those years: about two-thirds of all U.S. homicides were committed with firearms, and in big cities like Chicago and NYC the number was usually closer to 75 percent, similar to more scandalously violent cities such as Bogotá, São Paulo and Durban. Bleek set us straight: "That's a part of the ghetto. Nobody lives in the ghetto and didn't see [people get shot]. That's impossible. If they didn't, they shoulda let me grow up where they grew up at."

City*	Population	Murders	Murder Rate/ 100,000
Atlanta, U.S.A.	430,000	112	26.0
Bogotá, Colombia[†]	6,867,000	1,607	23.4
Detroit, U.S.A.	914,000	385	42.1

Durban, S. Africa[†]	3,090,000	2,089	69.4
Johannesburg, S. Africa[†]	3,225,000	729	22.6
London, U.K.	7,200,000	182	2.5
Los Angeles, U.S.A.[†]	12,977,000	1,119	8.6
Montreal, Can. (2002)[†]	3,480,000	66	1.9
Moscow, Russia[†]	8,700,000	2,278	26.2
Newark, U.S.A.	279,000	84	30.1
New York City, U.S.A.	8,101,000	570	7.3
Richmond, U.S.A.	196,000	93	47.4
Rio de Janeiro, Brazil[†]	11,000,000	8,096	73.6
Sao Paulo, Brazil[†]	18,000,000	3,944	21.9
Toronto, Canada	2,670,000	64	2.4
Vancouver, Can. (2003)	587,000	20	3.4
Washington, D.C. (U.S.A.)	553,000	198	35.8

* Statistics are for 2004, except where noted.
† Agglomeration

Country**	Population	Murders	Murder Rate/ 100,000
Brazil (2002)	174,500,000	49,570	28.4
Canada	30,700,000	489	1.6
Colombia	42,299,000	26,539	62.7
England & Wales	52,790,000	850	1.6
Jamaica (2004)	2,700,000	1,200	44.4
Japan	127,400,000	637	0.5
Russia	145,900,000	28,904	19.8
South Africa	42,800,000	21,995	51.4
Swaziland	1,045,000	926	88.61
U.S.A. (2004)	293,400,000	16,137	5.5

** Statistics are for 2000, except where noted.

THE OTHER 'CIDE

Like so many shooting ranges across the U.S., the Los Angeles Gun Club is in the heart of the city. Chris visited in hopes of fulfilling a promise he'd made to John Risdall—that he'd fire Magnum Research's most famous pistol. Inside the club, however, the quest was frustrated. They had lots of guns under the glass, but not a single Desert Eagle.

On the other side of the display case, two middle-aged Mexican-Americans, each wearing glasses and shorts, looked as if they might be husband and wife. Smiling as they worked, each was wearing a holster with a revolver in it. Their stock would be worth a fortune on the street. The bird may be the only thing they don't offer for rent there. Chris let the male clerk know he was interested in doing some shooting.

"You need a partner," he said, pulling a release form from beneath the counter. Several months earlier we learned why such insurance requirements had come about. Chatting with a clerk at Lever Arms, a gun store back in Vancouver, and Blair Hagen, a vice-president of British Columbia's chapter of the National Firearms Association (Canada's "entirely unaffiliated" version of the NRA, president David Tomlinson insisted), Chris had asked why patrons couldn't rent guns at local ranges. The clerk explained that someone had arrived at a range five to ten years earlier, rented and loaded a gun, then immediately shot himself. "More like fifteen, twenty years ago," Hagen corrected him, subtly perturbed.

"Don't worry," Chris told the clerk at the L.A. Gun Club, "I'm not feeling suicidal today." Smiling wider, his new friend handed him a gleaming silver Para-Ordnance pistol and a hundred .40 calibre rounds, and Chris hit the range.

I swear to God I just want to slit my wrists and end this bullshit
Throw the Magnum to my head, threaten' to pull shit
And squeeze, until the bed's completely red
I'm glad I'm dead, a worthless fuckin' buddah head
— Notorious B.I.G., "Suicidal Thoughts," off *Ready to Die* (1994)

More than they're used in homicides in North America, firearms kill in suicides. In 2001, 651 Canadians used a gun to kill themselves, amounting to 77 percent of all gun deaths in our country that year. 16,869 Americans took their own lives with a firearm during the same year, totalling 56 percent of all gun deaths in the United States. The U.S. National Mental Health Association reports that there are at least ten attempts for each suicide. But according to statistics reported in the *American Journal of Public Health*, people who use firearms complete suicide in approximately 90 percent of attempts.

Unfortunately, it appears that limiting the accessibility of guns does little more than decrease the share of suicides involving firearms. In Canada the percentage of suicides in which guns were used fell during the nineties, when legal changes limited the availability of firearms, but the number of suicides remained steady. In 1991, 30.9 percent of 3,593 suicides involved guns. A decade later, guns were used in 17.7 percent of 3,688 suicides. And even with its extremely limited access to guns, Japan has one of the world's highest suicide rates.

As Bushwick Bill said, when it comes to suicide, there are lots of substitutes where guns are hard to come by. "My friend Colombo [hanged himself] when he was fifteen years old," Bill remembered of his early days in New York City. "He could've went anywhere and got a gun, 'cause we used to see guns every day just walkin' up and down the streets. The police come and somebody'll give you a gun to hold—you're a little kid, you feel me? But he never shot himself. So depression could mean pills, depression could be drownin' yourself in a tub, depression could be jumpin' as a train is comin', it could be jumpin' out of a window, it could be overdosin' on all of the drugs available, youseewhatI'msayin'?"

When Bill attempted to take his own life in Houston in June 1991, depression and the availability of "six or seven guns" in his home combined with alcohol abuse to put him in a terminal state of mind. Bill told *XXL* magazine that before he forced his baby's mother to pull the trigger of a .22 calibre handgun by threatening the child, he had consumed "a fifteen-pack of Schlitz malt liquor Bull and was drinking E&J, Guinness stouts, Heinekens and Long Island teas and Everclear." Bill lost one eye to a bullet in the attempt but survived what he told us was an "emotional war." Alcohol can be found in the bloodstreams of at least 18 per cent of suicide victims, contributing to the impulsiveness of the attempt. "People think I'm crazy, but I'm not. People think I'm suicidal, but I'm not," Bill added as he entertained one of his five children with a Chucky doll.

Tom Diaz is interested in drawing public attention to the problem of gun suicides. "Lots of people have made gestures of suicide," he said, "and they don't really want to die, and lots of these people have gone on to live fully constructive lives. But with a firearm, the chances of that—of coming out of an incident either alive or without serious damage—are very low. So yeah, it does make a difference if people use guns."

> Picture me in a casket, blasted
> Never nobody knew how long the pain lasted
> — Tech N9ne, "Suicide Letters," off *Anghellic* (2003)

When Biggie rapped about suicide, it was an act of catharsis, purging his soul of all sorts of pain. Fans worked through the hurt with him. Same goes for Tech N9ne. "Like 50 Cent say, 'Death gotta be easy, 'cause life is hard,'" Tech explained of his track "Suicide Letters." "A lot of things hurt, but I cover it up real good. And the way I can cover it up is tellin' you motherfuckers about it through rhyme," he chuckled.

Eminem is another artist who ventilates through rap. In October 2004 Todd Nelson, Marshall Mathers' uncle, shot himself as he sat in his car. He was the second uncle Em had lost to suicide. In 1991 nineteen-year-old Ronnie Nelson had killed himself with a shotgun after being dumped by his girlfriend. According to some stories, it was Ronnie who introduced Eminem to hip-hop with Ice-T's "Reckless"; on the song "Stan" Em remembers Ronnie in rap. Like so many youth who commit suicide, Ronnie took his life in what should have been a passing rush of emotion, never to see his gifted nephew shine.

Getting rid of guns won't solve the problem of suicide, but firearms aren't forgiving. With guns handy, there are very rarely gestures for loved ones to respond to. In August 2002 a team of researchers published a paper in the *New England Journal of Medicine*, "Suicide in the Home in Relation to Gun Ownership." Analyzing suicides in the home over a thirty-two-month stretch in Shelby County, Tennessee, and King County, Washington, the report laid it out: "Ready availability of firearms is associated with an increased risk of suicide in the home. Owners of firearms should weigh their reasons for keeping a gun in the home against the possibility that it might someday be used in a suicide."

"I think that that's a pretty good hypothesis," Tech N9ne said when told about the study. "Because I had a gun and I didn't have no money. And I thought about suicide with that Tec-9, and I thought about robbin' a bank with that Tec-9, I thought about jackin' niggas with that Tec-9. So havin' guns, it will give you bad ideas, I can say that. That's why I had to get it out of my hands for ninety bucks, because I was about to do somethin' stupid, homes."

GUNFIRE DRILL

I even kill myself, but don't feel sorry for me
Feel sorry for your seeds as we spread the disease
Another bloodbath coming soon to a school near you
Small-town killing-sprees that's organized by the youth
— Ill Bill, "Anatomy of a School Shooting,"
off *What's Wrong with Bill* (2003)

Eric Harris and Dylan Klebold had a Tec-9, too. And homes, they did something *really* stupid.

On a remix featuring his former G-Unit homies, "Hate It Or Love It," Compton's The Game claims that if you step out of line, he'll "creep and turn your projects into Columbine." When rappers representing some of the world's most violent neighbourhoods begin issuing "threats" with reference to carnage experienced in small-town white America, you know the game has changed.

With their carefully planned and heavily armed assault on April 20, 1999–Hitler's birthday–Harris and Klebold intended both to send a message and to motivate others to do the same. After being literally shit on (one story held that a cup of fecal matter was thrown on the inseparable chums), the Columbine killers made it clear that bullying thoroughly fucks people up, and that with guns so easily accessed stateside, the vengeance of nerds is to be feared indeed. The suicidal shooters did in fact arouse the killer instinct in copycats, from Kingston, New York, to Taber, Alberta, but doubtfully predicted they'd inspire at least one complete rap song.

"I made that track because I was really intrigued with the mind frame [of] those two kids in particular," Ill Bill said, "the way they took that teenage frustration to that horrifying level. What they did was horrific, man. That shit was fucked up, and the song by no means condones what they did, but at the same time, it doesn't condemn what they did either. It's just one point-of-view, taken from the point-of-view of one of the shooters, Eric Harris. And it's kinda hard to really get across everything that I wish I could've got across the length of the song. It's a lot deeper than even where I went with it, but I tried to really just speak on the frustrations that he had in going to school and being shitted on, by not just the students, but by teachers."

Described in an August 8, 2005, story by *Salon*'s Kimberley Sevcik as "like a ghetto in the country, camouflaged by towering evergreens and shimmering lakes," the Red Lake Indian Reservation in Minnesota is home to part of the Ojibwa tribe. In 1999, with soaring unemployment, gang activity and a homicide rate comparable to the world's most dangerous cities, Red Lake became eleven-year-old Jeff Weise's home. Two years before, Weise's father, Daryl "Baby Dash" Lussier, had killed himself with a shotgun during a standoff with tribal police, all while Weise's grandfather, Daryl "Dash" Lussier, acted as police negotiator. Meanwhile, Jeff's single mother, Joanne Weise, had suffered brain damage in a drunk-driving accident that placed her in specialized care. Following her death, Weise was forced to move from his trailer in Minneapolis to live with his grandfather in Red Lake.

It's not that Weise didn't have friends. Like many boys their age, he and his buddies would gather to play *Halo* on an Xbox and watch movies dramatizing the rampage at Columbine. Weise was especially taken with Gus Van Sant's film *Elephant*, fast-forwarding to the shooting scenes. Still, on an isolated reservation, Weise was himself isolated with generations of pain.

Without proper treatment, in Sevcik's words, Weise "retreated into cyberspace, where he found connection, distraction and identity." On the Internet, Weise chose the name "Todesengel," German for "Angel of Death," indulging a confused fascination with Nazi ideology. When he enrolled in a home schooling program to escape the ridicule of classmates and other troubles, Weise only became more alienated and angry.

It would take Weise three attempts before he completed suicide—first with a box-cutter, the second time by strangulation with a belt—his desire increasing as each plea for help went ignored. It wasn't until sixteen-year-old Weise stole a .22-calibre handgun, a police-issue shotgun and a .40-calibre Glock pistol from his grandfather that his potential for (self-)destruction reached a pinnacle. By then, Weise's sadness had mutated into anger, and on March 21, 2005, as the long cold of winter was coming to an end, the youth of Red Lake suffered that rage.

After killing his grandfather and his grandfather's girlfriend, Weise drove his grandfather's police cruiser to school and shot dead an unarmed security guard, a teacher and five students, including his cousin. Another fifteen people were wounded. The slaughter took just ten minutes, ending when Weise used his last round on himself.

As tribal leaders tried to cope with the terror, they waited for words of comfort and support from the free-world leader. One day passed without word from the president, however. Then another. Finally, five days after the massacre, George Bush Jr. took a break from another vacation at his Crawford ranch to offer condolences. As with the death toll from guns in the 'hood, the slaughter of poor coloured youth in Red Lake didn't command the same attention as a couple of rich white kids going ballistic in the suburbs. The president wasn't forced to confront gun policy in America, armies of psychologists weren't dispatched and no blockbuster documentaries are planned. But the words of one emcee did take on added resonance.

"We did a show in Baltimore this weekend," Ill Bill emailed us, "and after the latest shooting, the crowd was just buggin' the fuck out when I did 'Anatomy.' It hit a nerve."

SHOTS HAPPEN

Sitting at a friend's patio table with a recently reefered and now red-eyed Devin Copeland, a Houston emcee known to the public as Devin the Dude, Rodrigo took his recording equipment out of his bag and placed it between them. Devin is not your typical screw-facing emcee. He's usually laughing, whispering rhymes or singing bits of soul in his raspy, high-pitched voice. He smiles easily, but needlessly, since his droopy bug-eyes always beat his mouth to the punch.

"Damn," Buns thought to himself, as he pressed RECORD on his mini-disc, "I'm about to ruin the Dude's buzz." Just prior to the interview, journalist Matt Sonzala, Rodrigo's host and a long-time friend of Devin, had told him that Devin had been shot once, but that he'd never talked about it publicly before. Taking a page out of the journalist's dirty book of underhanded trickery, Buns played dumb. "Have you ever had any experiences where someone pulled out on you?" he asked. His question drained the Buddha-blessedness from Devin's big, bloodshot eyes. He paused and looked down, contemplating the memory. Then he glanced towards the heavens before settling his gaze on Buns.

"I've been in an accidental shooting," the Dude said. "I got into it with somebody. Me and my homeboy was anteing up, getting our stuff together, and he was loading a .22 up and it went off and ricocheted and hit me right here in the heart. I got stitches right there. They tried to get it out but it was too close to a nerve in my heart so it's still in there. I go through the airport [and] the metal detector in the airport goes *di-di-dit, di-dit*." Devin cracked up at the thought of the confusion he causes airport security, and in his Southern drawl imitated an even stronger Southern drawl: "What's that?!?"

Relieved that Devin, true to form, was laughing, Rodrigo asked, "How'd it feel?"

Still smiling, Devin continued: "I didn't feel it at first. Actually, it went through now my wife—at the time, my girlfriend—she was pregnant with her first child. It went through her shoulder, came out through the back side of her shoulder and went into my heart, into my chest, rather. I didn't feel it; I was worried about her and the baby and everything, trying to get her to the hospital. The ambulance came and the ambulance got her, and they saw that there was an entry wound and they saw that there was an exit wound too. And then they looked at me and they were like, 'Hey buddy, what's that there? Hey, you're shot!' And I was like, 'I am? Oh, I am!'" Devin collapsed into laughter before delivering the punchline. "And all I remember is just lying in the ambulance, lying on my back looking at these big-ass lights, digging in my pockets trying to get rid of my weed!"

Devin can laugh now, over a decade later, but he spent more than two weeks recovering in a hospital bed, and another three months at home in pain. Devin's pregnant girlfriend also recovered from the incident. In this case a mistake begat an accident. While Devin was chilling with friends on his stoop, a stranger with a beef approached. As the Dude told it, the stranger was looking for someone else and stepped to them: "He walked out towards us in the yard and when he walked out too close, then I just tap, tap [beat] on him in the yard, and then he [fought] back, and then my homeboy jumped in and we both had him for a little bit, and then he just wobbled off. 'I'll be back, motherfucker!'"

Forty minutes later the stranger returned, with a firearm. Devin and crew ran indoors for cover. The Dude recounted the story: "The people that was inside the house had an old .22 and we dashed up in there trying to regroup, and while we was in the house when we was trying to get the .22, my homeboy was trying to load it up, and there's women around and there was a lot of screaming. It was eerie. I just felt something was about to go wrong, because it was too panicky."

Devin was lucky. The same can't be said for the sixty thousand American civilians who died from accidental shootings between 1965 and 2000—more than all Americans killed in wars over that same period, which includes the Vietnam War, both Gulf wars and many lesser-known skirmishes in between. In Canada we lose about seventy lives a year to rogue bullets. Worldwide the best numbers place the loss of life due to firearm accidents at about twenty thousand per year.

It's also estimated that for each fatal firearm accident in the United States, thirteen people are accidentally injured seriously enough to be sent to the emergency room. A third of them require hospitalization. In 2004 there were 16,555 accidental firearms injuries in the U.S.; north of the forty-ninth an average of eight hundred are injured per year. Like Devin's, most of these injuries are self-inflicted during what firearms safety experts call "administrative handling"—all the stuff that doesn't include letting off shots. His story fits the profile of an average firearm accident in other ways too: like 90 percent of victims, he's male, and like 60 percent of those injured annually, he was under thirty. In fact, a third of accidental gun fatalities were people under twenty.

Apparently, word isn't getting out to everyone. In 2005 the medical journal *Pediatrics* reported that 1.7 million children in the U.S. were living in households with loaded guns. Brandon Maxfield lived in one such home. When he was seven and in the care of his family babysitter, Lawrence Morford, a disturbance outside frightened Brandon and his siblings. Morford, aware that the kids might react by seeking security in steel, retrieved the family gun first and decided to unload it.

The Maxfields owned a Bryco .380, a handgun with a receiver originally designed for smaller-calibre cartridges. This design feature necessitated the use of strong springs to withstand the larger calibre, so when Morford attempted to disarm the weapon, he pulled back on the gun and, as Whit Collins, a consultant on the case explained, "[it] snapped closed out of his hand so quickly he couldn't possibly grasp at the gun to get it back under control. In trying to grasp for it with just two fingers, his index finger touched the trigger. We think Brandon had stepped forward to see what he was doing. And then the shot was fired. And we *know* what happened after that."

Brandon Maxfield was shot in the face, leaving him, at seven years old, paralyzed from the neck down. Incredibly, like his idol and fellow quadriplegic Christopher Reeve, Brandon had more than a little Superman in him. With the help of his family, Brandon sued Bryco and its president, Bruce Jennings, and worked to make sure that guns like the Bryco .380 that paralyzed him would not continue to be manufactured.

Brandon's malefactor was made with a frame designed for .22 and .25 calibre bullets. Even at those lower calibres the Bryco had issues, and in order to address them, Jennings had created the flaw that produced Brandon's misfortune. "The pistol had had a jamming problem as a .22, .25 and .32," Whit Collins explained, "and Bruce Jennings redesigned it to the point where it wouldn't jam, but you could no longer put the safety on when you were trying to load it or unload it." That the Bryco's increase to .380 calibre had put extra strain on the gun's parts and required stronger coils further set the stage for tragedy. On May 13, 2003, the Alameda County California Superior Court, after finding Bryco's design defective, entered a judgement of roughly $24 million against Jennings and Bryco, the Ring of Fire's most successful company. But the next day, Jennings filed for bankruptcy, effectively tying up any money that Brandon and his organization, Brandon's Arms, would have received.

In 2005 Jennings, allegedly acting through his wife's Texas holding company, outbid Brandon's Arms for the remaining gun parts the factory still owned and, according to the California attorney general's office, opened as Jimenez Arms, just outside of Las Vegas. While Jennings denies any relationship with the new company, several business connections have proven that they are essentially one and the same. In fact, the new company is named after Bryco's former plant manager, Paul Jimenez, and JA is still making the same handgun models that Jennings produced. Their latest accident waiting to happen is the JA-NINE 9mm pistol, which was ruled unsafe by the California attorney general's office and banned from the state. The spokesman for the attorney general even commented to the *Las Vegas Sun* that Jimenez Arms was just the "latest incarnation" of Bryco.

So one day in your room you playin' with your MAC-10
Fully loaded automatic, just you and a friend
You're posin' in da mirror, like you a gangster clown
But the MAC-10 go off and ya friend go down!
— KRS-One, "Uh Oh," off *Return of the Boom-Bap* (1993)

Efforts to reduce firearms accidents have produced results, and the accident fatality rate has dropped considerably in the United States over the past forty years. In 1965 the rate of unintentional firearms deaths per 100,000 was 1.3, amounting to 2,344 deaths. By 2000 the rate had fallen to 0.3 and 776 deaths. But whatever guideline a user adheres to, a poorly designed or malfunctioning gun is beyond the user's control. There are so many substandard firearms on the market that Whit Collins teamed with others to compile a document listing 140 of the most common offenders, and most of the guilty guns are not cheap.

Glock gets major billing in the report that Collins helped author. It's been widely acknowledged that a three-year-old has enough strength to pull Gaston Glock's triggers. And Glock's safeties, as on the Bryco that injured Brandon Maxfield, cannot be put in the OFF position when unloading, a feature that makes the guns susceptible to unwanted firings. The result of this and other design flaws have made Glock the target of dozens of faulty product lawsuits since the early eighties.

The report also highlights guns that spontaneously fire on automatic, that fire when dropped, that fire when loading and unloading, and that suffer from a multitude of other design defects. With production numbers of many such guns in the hundreds of thousands, the results are predictable. David Hemenway, a professor of health policy at Harvard, compares the gun industry to the car industry in his book *Private Guns, Public Health.* "When airbags were shown to have been responsible for an average of six child deaths per year in the 1990s, intense media coverage, myriad studies and conferences, and manufacturer and governmental responses ensued. The deaths of these children were deemed unacceptable." By contrast, he explains, "there are no federal safety standards for firearms."

A 2006 study done by ergonomics and engineering professors from the University of Southern California and the University of Central Florida concluded that "a number of human-factors design problems are evident that prevent the firearms from fully and safely achieving their purported goals." The researchers, who didn't engage the political, social and cultural debate about firearms, insisted that the study's "sole purpose [was] the consideration of firearms from the viewpoint of their design and operation. Firearms are tools, and like any tool, they have their characteristic advantages and disadvantages." Among their criticisms, the researchers found that when it came to safeties, "almost none of the controls themselves give a clear indication of their intended purpose." For magazines "there is no standardization on different firearms as to the position of this activator; neither is it color-coded, nor on occasion is it obviously visible!" The study made similar observations regarding the lack of standardization and transferability of experience for triggers, sights and even training, finally concluding that "the aphorism that 'guns don't kill people—people do' is insufficient to the case, given that in many circumstances, it is untrained individuals who find themselves the subject of prosecution and persecution for the incorrect use of a poorly designed tool."

While all other products in the U.S. fall under some regulation since the passage of the Consumer Products Safety Act in 1972, gun manufacturers alone are responsible to no government body. With the addition of the gun manufacturers' immunity bill in 2005, the gun industry has gone from what Whit Collins describes as "operating in a grey area to operating in the dark." This is all the more lamentable when one considers that the technology to avoid many firearms accidents has existed for decades. Features like the loaded chamber indicator, which was invented in 1908, or the magazine disconnect, created in 1911, have been around for nearly a hundred years. Collins himself promotes another safety measure, though the technology is not yet market ready: personalization technology that would allow for only one user per gun. "[It's] not actually Buck Rogers," he quipped. "It's been around for an awfully long time."

Whit Collins's openness to developing safer guns is shared by those who have paid a high price for the lack of standards among firearms. As Maxfield's lawyer Richard Ruggieri told us, "Brandon isn't anti-gun, Brandon's Arms isn't anti-gun or pro-gun, but pro-safety. And our approach from the trial all the way through is that if you're going to have guns, they should be at least as safe as a toaster."

But from the industry's perspective, everything is fine as is, as NRA director of public affairs Andrew Arulanandum told the *Detroit News* in December 2003, "We believe the gun industry has taken every precaution to make sure it produces a safe product. Gun manufacturers are meticulous businessmen. They will do nothing to undermine the public's confidence in their products."

LOCKED AND CODED

The degenerate, if I get caught I'm innocent
'Cause I don't leave no sticky fingaprints
— Sticky Fingaz, "Last Dayz," off Onyx's *All We Got Iz Us* (1995)

Queens's Sticky Fingaz had been in Vancouver filming a movie when he ran into Van City's Concise. Sticky, whose group, Onyx, defined the "gangsta pop" sub-genre with their debut in '93, was walking up Commercial Drive on his way to buy a bottle of Hennessy. 'Cise convinced Stick to forsake the cognac in favour of a collaboration, inviting the rapper/actor to his nearby studio to put down a track.

Sticky Fingaz would soon realize that he wasn't in the Grand Manzana anymore. To hear Concise tell it, "We go into the studio and leave our stuff at the front. He's like, 'Where your guns at?' It was just like a regular question for him. I was like, 'It ain't like that, where we ride around wit' 'em.' That was my exact answer. He's like, '*Shiiiiit*, where I come from, I drive around with that shit right here on my lap, just like this, everywhere I go.'" Pointing emphatically to his own lap, Concise continued: "[Stick's] like, 'Nobody that I know walk around without that shit.' It wasn't on no gangsta shit. It wasn't on no 'I sell records 'cause of this.' It was just on some basic, essential life shit, like a life necessity. It was like a parachute."

Unfortunately, Sticky Fingaz sometimes forgets his 'chute before he bails. A year after Concise told us about connecting with Stick, the rapper who brags on Onyx's forgettable *Triggernometry* LP that he "was the only nigga to ever bust a gun at the mutherfuckin' Source Awards!" was arrested. Sticky Fingaz had forgotten his unlicensed and unregistered 9mm pistol in a luxury Manhattan hotel room, and an honest housekeeper had given the lost gun to police, along with the name of the room's last occupant.

Here's a list of other rappers who've had gun-ins with the law.

2Pac (Witnessing two men harassing a black motorist in Atlanta, Tupac rushed to the man's aid. When a fight ensued, Pac shot both harassers, one in the leg, the other in the ass. It turned out the men were off-duty cops. If not for the fact that the officers were drunk and in possession of stolen weapons, 2Pac would have been in serious trouble. Instead, all charges were dropped.)

50 Cent

Baby

Beanie Sigel

B.G.

Black Rob

Busta Rhymes

Cam'ron

Capone

Cassidy

C-Bo

C-Murder

Chi-Ali

Cool C

Coolio

Dizzee Rascal (He and an older friend were arrested in the rapper's native East End London after they were pulled over by police and found to be in possession of pepper spray and weed. Under the U.K.'s tough gun laws, pepper spray is classed as a "Section 5 firearm.")

DMX

Eminem

Fabolous

Flava Flav

Flesh N Bone

Gucci Mane

Guru

Jay-Z (Although he was charged with unlawful possession of a firearm in 2001, that wasn't his most dramatic encounter with the steel. When Young Hov was really young, twelve in fact, he shot his older brother Eric in the shoulder for stealing his jewellery. Charges were never pressed in that incident.)

J-Dee

Lil Cease

Lil' Eazy-E

Lloyd Banks

Master P

Megaman (So Solid)

MF Grimm

Nas

Nate Dogg

Noreaga

Notorious B.I.G.

Ol' Dirty Bastard

Peedi Peedi

Petey Pablo

Pimp C

Project Pat

Queen Latifah

Sadat X

Shyheim

Shyne

Silkk the Shocker

Slick Rick

Snoop Dogg

Spigg Nice

Steady B

Suge Knight

T.I.

Tone-Loc

Tony Yayo

Tray Dee

Trick Daddy

Youngbloodz

Young Buck

Young Jeezy

Young Turk

COUNTRY FIRE

When Peruvian-born emcee Immortal Technique and a friend were pulled over by the Texas Highway Patrol, the Harlem-dweller thought he was inhaling his last breaths as a free man. Tech's Texan host, the driver of the vehicle, had enough guns in the back seat to put them both behind bars for a long time—and to make matters worse, the weapons were in plain view. As the patrolman wrote them up for a speeding violation, Tech agonized over his fate. Handing his friend the ticket, the officer noticed the guns, and Tech could almost hear the prison doors clanging shut behind him. The patrolman leaned in, looking at the guns. "You know, son, those are supposed to be in the glove compartment, right? Next time I'm going to have to write you a ticket."

> I never leave home without the heater, I'm strapped up like a straightjacket
> — Paul Wall, "Got Plex," off *The People's Champ* (2005)

In March 2000 the Open Society Institute, an organization founded and funded by multi-billionaire liberal activist George Soros, released a report evaluating every U.S. state's gun laws. The institute rated each state based on thirty different criteria grouped into six categories: registration of firearms, safety training, regulation of firearm sales, safe storage and accessibility, owner licensing, and litigation and pre-emption. Of the twenty states that received the lowest grades, six were in the Midwest and ten were in the South.

While New York emcees keep their arsenals strictly on the downlow, reflecting the law in their neck of the woods, Houston's Paul Wall rattled off his collection of burners with pride: "I have a Glock .45; it hold seven bullets. I got a Glock .40; it's the same basic thing except it has .40 calibre, so smaller bullets. I have a .44 special snub-nose; you know, it's a revolver . . ." As Wall's stream of steel continued, it was hard not to wonder why any one person would need so many guns. But that's the wrong attitude in Texas, home to an estimated sixty million-plus firearms, nearly a tenth of all the guns in the world.

"I keep one in every car, every room in the house," Paul said, anticipating the question. "We've always been kinda paranoid."

"You got some in the car right now?" Rodrigo asked.

Paul Wall

"In the car? I just got one in the car."

"Can I see it?"

Wall gestured to follow him, and they headed outside to his candy-coloured vehicle in the driveway. He opened the car door, reached under the driver's seat and produced a Glock—the .40 cal he mentioned earlier. Host Matt Sonzala, whose house they were at, spoke up. "Be careful with that thing," he said. "I don't want no one getting shot out here." But Paul was too busy posing with his piece for Rodrigo's camera, and Buns was too caught up in the moment to feel any sense of danger. "Can I hold it?" he asked, eager to grasp his first Glock. Wall nodded and started disarming the little polymer-and-metal pistol. One by one, cartridges ejected into his hand until finally he passed it to Rodrigo.

"It's light, huh?" Wall said.

"Yeah, it doesn't weigh much at all," he replied, as he awkwardly let the Glock sit in his open hand, too inexperienced and uncomfortable to grip it.

Niggas know what to do when I'm around
Go put your pack up and pick up your fo' pound
It's 'bout to go down, Buck back on that bullshit
He even got his baby mama walkin' with a full clip
— Young Buck, "I'm a Soldier," off *Straight Outta Cashville* (2004)

As Young Buck's debut album, *Straight Outta Cashville*, was about to be released in the summer of 2004, *Vibe* magazine thought it'd be a good idea to test the young man's mettle with the metal, hooking Buck up with champion skeet-shooting pro Randy Sotowa in a head-to-head competition. In a race to hit ten skeets, Buck prevailed 10-9. As the Nashville, Tennessee, native told us, "In the South you come up huntin', you come up throwin' things like that. Outside sports. So the gun thing is kinda like breeded into you as a youngster from the get-go. It's all based upon the country lifestyle, and shootin' guns is kinda cool to a certain extent down south. It's nothin' for you to go outside in the backyard and shoot, because it's still a lot of parents that raise their kids and teach 'em how to do that."

Like Buck, Atlanta resident and gun enthusiast Killer Mike sees that guns in the South occupy a unique space in people's lives. "Being from the South," he said, "some of my family hunt; we shoot for sport and for protection. I carry a .45 on my person and in my vehicle. You gotta understand—in the South I'd be willing to bet three out of five people own guns, which is probably why everybody in the South so fuckin' nice to each other, 'cause everybody know the other motherfucker got a gun!" Killer laughed.

In the South and Midwest it's commonly held logic that guns protect people and that a community with open access to guns is safer. But the Department of Justice's 2004 stats don't bear this out. While Southern states made up 36 percent of the total U.S. population in 2004, they were also home to 43 percent of homicides and manslaughters, 44 percent of aggravated assaults and 42 percent of all violent crime in the United States. When the FBI ranked America's most dangerous cities in 2005, five of the top ten were in the South and three of those were in Texas. In addition, firearms were more likely to be used in the commission of assaults and robberies in the South and Midwest than in other regions. The differences might not be drastic, but in a hot, gun-saturated landscape where history links firearms with autonomy, safety and freedom, nobody wants to be the first to put down their piece. "If the places I went to and the people I dealt with didn't feel a need to protect themselves," another Texas emcee, Bun B, told Buns, "then why would I bring a gun to a gunless environment? But that's not the world we live in."

> David Duke's got a shotgun
> So why you get upset 'cause I got one?
> — Scarface, "Hand of the Dead Body," from *The Diary* (1994)

In October 2005 Canada's then prime minister, Paul Martin, met with U.S. Secretary of State Condoleezza Rice to discuss a number of cross-border issues. High on the PM's agenda for Dr. Rice's Ottawa visit was gun control. "I think there's an obligation on their side to work with us to prevent the smuggling of guns into Canada," CTV News, on October 25, 2005, quoted Martin as saying in anticipation of the meeting.

If the PM had known the secretary of state a bit better, he'd have realized that when it comes to that topic, Condi will always be a tough sell. Earlier the same year the Associated Press reported, "Rice says gun rights are as important as rights to free speech, religion." As a child in the Alabama of the early sixties—a state that took until 2000 to legally recognize interracial marriage—young Condoleezza had watched her father, Presbyterian minister John W. Rice, take up shotguns to help protect the black community from the White Knight Riders, a KKK offshoot. In her biography of the Secretary of State, *Condi: The Condoleezza Rice Story*, Antonia Felix writes, "the memory of her father out on patrol lies behind Rice's opposition to gun control today."

Given her devotion to said opposition, in January 2005 Rice was named Gun Rights Defender of the Month by the Citizens Committee for the Right to Keep and Bear Arms (the same honour once bestowed upon Robert Ricker). "We have to be very careful when we start abridging rights that our founding fathers thought very important," Rice told CNN's Larry King on May 11, 2005. "I think that they understood that there might be circumstances that people like my father experienced in Birmingham, Alabama, when in fact the police weren't going to protect you." Indeed, it was with murderous intent that the KKK, as President Ulysses S. Grant said in an 1872 congressional address, wanted to "deprive colored citizens of the right to bear arms." For Southern blacks, a private arsenal was very often all that stood in the way of an arbitrary lynching.

Robert Williams grasped as much. Described by University of Wisconsin-Madison professor Timothy Tyson as the "most important intellectual influence on the Black Panther Party for Self-Defense in Oakland, California," Williams was a native of Monroe, North Carolina. Trained to use firearms in the army, Williams wrote *Negroes with Guns* in the early sixties. "I have asserted the right of Negroes to meet the violence of the Ku Klux Klan by armed self-defense," he declared, "and have acted on it." Williams organized members of his community to legally purchase firearms, carefully practise target shooting and form a rifle club that adopted a charter from the NRA, all to deter attacks from the KKK. "Racists consider themselves superior beings and are not willing to exchange their superior lives for our inferior ones," Williams wrote. "They are most vicious and violent when they can practice violence with impunity."

Atlanta's Big Gipp spoke about experiences of his own that mirrored those of Robert Williams—a reminder that memories of racist violence are hardly distant for many blacks down south. "If you don't know how to protect yourself from a world that uses guns," Gipp said, "then you a fool. When I was in the country, man, my cousin got to fighting with a young kid, ya understand? I saw the Klan come try to get my cousin as a young kid—like showing up in trucks—'Yo, we about to do this and do that.' And I done seen my whole family go to the gun cage, get guns and be like, 'If they come in the driveway, kill all of 'em.'"

Such drastic actions have sometimes come at a high price. Robert Williams was labelled a communist and charged with kidnapping. He fled from the FBI to Canada, where the RCMP picked up the pursuit, then to Cuba and later China. Williams returned to the United States in 1969, the charges were dropped and he settled in Michigan.

Eh-yo, camouflage-chameleon ninjas scalin' your buildin'
No time to grab the gun, they already got your wife and children
A hit was sent, from the President, to raid your residence

Because you had secret evidence, and documents
On how they raped the continents
— RZA, "4th Chamber," off the GZA's *Liquid Swords* (1995)

Citing dictators throughout history who disarmed their populations, many Americans—particularly white Southerners, who have
never allowed memories of the Civil War to fade—see privately owned
guns as the last line of defence against government tyranny. A
freedom-loving, government-hating radio host from Austin, Texas,
Alex Jones points to the Jews who used firearms to fend off Nazis in
the Warsaw ghetto. Hitler himself foresaw such armed revolt, prohibiting Germany's Jews from owning guns and stating, "The most
foolish mistake we could possibly make would be to allow the subject
races to possess arms." For Southerners like Jones gun control is a
precursor to people control. "Look, it boils down to this: Hitler,
Stalin, Mao—they were all for gun control. The first gun laws in
America were against black people," Jones said over the phone
from his home in the Lone Star State. "It's just so ludicrous to have
the view that a lot of the left has of 'Oh yeah, we do have a corrupt,
tyrannical government. Let's turn our guns in and they'll be much
nicer to us.'"

"I particularly myself am not that into guns," Jones clarified
later, "guns themselves. Some people, to them it's a power object,
almost like a fetish. To me the gun is a canary in the coal mine. It is
a symbol of my freedom. A slave is disarmed; a free human being
has arms."

David Koresh, né Vernon Howell, saw the right to bear arms in a
similar light. As Dick Reavis, author of *The Ashes of Waco*, told a
congressional investigative committee, Koresh and his religious followers feared a final conflict with "the forces of an armed apostate
power called Babylon." Reavis believes that this prophecy, which had
persisted at the Mount Carmel compound of Koresh's Branch-
Davidians since 1934, in part explains why he started to stockpile
firearms in 1991. That and the loot.

Soon recognizing, according to Reavis, that "there is a lot of money
to be made at gun shows," Koresh bought and sold tens of thousands

of dollars worth of guns, gun parts, silencers and grenades. Gun charges brought the Bureau of Alcohol, Tobacco and Firearms to the doors of Mount Carmel, the agency citing the presence of illegally converted automatic rifles on the premises, among other violations of firearms laws. Just how much firepower was inside the compound became clear when the ATF attempted a raid on February 28, 1993.

WHAT YA GONNA DO WHEN YOU GET OUTTA JAIL?

On a track with his teenage homies in the Outlawz' "High Speed," 2Pac breaks down his post-prison protocol in order of importance: buy a gun, food, sex and house parties in the projects. Although the system can send people away for possessing guns, that doesn't eliminate the circumstances that lead many to carry in the first place. Queens's Capone, who did a three-year bid after being caught with tons of guns in his trunk, told us, "I wasn't packin' when I was shot. If I was packin' I wouldn't have been shot, ya feel me? Everybody get caught slippin' and I slipped."

"So do you stay strapped now?"

"Hey man, you asking police questions! Do I stay strapped? Oh shit, hell no—I keep about fourteen Magnums on me. Now which Magnum? Leave that for them to figure it out," Capone laughed.

We asked a few artists on lock-down whether they would pack when released.

Shyne (Brooklyn, NY)

Oh, absolutely not. Although you got the NRA [smirks], which is the number-one lobbyist on Capitol Hill, ya understand? I don't know if havin' guns is necessarily satanic, but for me it just won't be necessary, because obviously—even when my album came out and I went platinum and I had a little bit of paper, then I was able to have the right security around me. 'Cause I'm a businessman and I have business to run, and I can't be a soldier anymore.

C-Bo (Sacramento, CA)

Man, I got caught with so many guns, man, I don't have no more chances to get caught with no guns. I'm about to get me a trigger-lock, 'cause if I get caught with some guns I'll fuck around and do life without even usin' the motherfucker. And I think I'd rather just be shot, ha ha ha!

C-Murder (New Orleans, LA)

[Laughing as he sings] "Alwaaays, I keep the heater on meeee"—ya hearrrrd me? I ain't never gonna get caught slippin', man, straight up.

An ATF agent, Jim Cavanaugh, shakily told the congressional hearing, "They were throwing everything at us, and their guns sounded like cannons, and our guns sounded like popguns. We had 9-millimetres; they were hitting us with .223s, AK-47s, .50 calibres. It was more than you can imagine." The forty-five-minute shootout killed four agents of the ATF and six Branch-Davidians, and injured many more on both sides.

In the end, the guns of Mount Carmel would not be enough to match the arms of the apostate power. On April 19, 1993, Janet Reno authorized an assault with tear gas, and more than seventy people perished, including women, children and Koresh himself. As the compound at Mount Carmel burned to the ground, the notion that guns could hold back a government controlling the most advanced instruments of war went up in smoke.

ALL-POINTS BULLET-IN

> We on the grind every day of the week
> I'm from Houston, where the cops don't sleep
> — Lil' Flip, "Certified Gangstas,"
> off Jim Jones's *Diplomats Present* (2004)

After Rodrigo passed through security, Senior Officer Warren Jones of the Houston Police Department greeted him with a smile and a firm handshake. He's a tall, smooth-complexioned brother with a perfect moustache. He wears well-tailored but casual office attire and walks with the strong gait of the physically fit. For nineteen years he's worked some of Houston's toughest beats. Like many big Southern cities, Houston sees its fair share of shootings, and although it's only slightly less populous than Toronto, the Texas city has anywhere from two to seven times as many homicides every year.

These days Jones works from the HPD headquarters as a community relations specialist, which seems an appropriate placement for the soft-spoken, God-fearing, highly presentable officer. Like all HPD cops, Jones carries a .40 calibre semi-automatic with a high-capacity magazine; his is a Glock, an HPD-sanctioned brand.

"Have you ever been in any shooting incidents?" Rodrigo asked, as they took seats in his cubicle.

"No, I haven't," he answered, with a mixture of bewilderment and discomfort, giving the impression that the whole topic was foreign to him.

"Do you feel like the police are out-armed?"

"There's a lot of firepower out there for kids," Jones answered. "They have these multi-shot guns where they are able to shoot a hundred shots a minute."

"What have you seen on the street?"

"All kinds of stuff, like, um . . . I don't know the names, but they have everything out there."

"How do you prepare mentally for the possibility of being shot?"

"Just trust in God. If it's meant to happen, it'll happen."

"Is it something that you think about much?"

"No, I don't."

Officer Jones's attitude revealed a healthy perspective on the likelihood of an officer's being shot. According to the U.S. Department of Justice, in 2004 there were just under 800,000 sworn law enforcement officers in the United States. In that same year fifty-seven officers were murdered, fifty-four of them with firearms. These numbers work out to a homicide rate of 6.6 per 100,000 police officers, just above the national average of 5.5 homicides per 100,000 citizens, and well below the average of most major American cities. Of 59,373 total non-fatal assaults on officers that year, 2,109 were committed with firearms, producing just over two hundred injuries. Compare this to the number of assaults on officers with "personal weapons"—fists, feet and teeth—which produced more than fourteen thousand injuries out of 47,545 assaults, and you might think policemen would spend more time at the dojo than the range.

In fact, the deadliest decade for police was the 1970s, when over two hundred police officers were killed annually; since then there's been a steady decline. Still, in the mid-eighties, when the preferred armaments on the street went from six-shot revolvers to semi-automatic handguns, police naturally began to feel outgunned. As *The Wire*'s David Simon said, "I covered the Baltimore Police Department when they were going from .38 revolvers to 9mm, and [I remember] how intent the officers were on getting 9mm because they felt they were being outgunned, that even with speed-loaders they couldn't possibly compete with people that had sixteen, seventeen in a clip." He continued, "It's just so ingrained in the American culture—the omnipresence of firearms—that you don't get a lot of cops arguing against the availability of weapons. They want to be able to go into this weapon-saturated environment with the advantage."

Jan Libourel sees the increased demand for and reliance on greater firepower as a step backwards. "I sometimes think that we have lost something in the wholesale abandonment by police and security personnel and much of the civilian market of the revolver in favour of the automatic pistol," he said. "I still think that the revolver is a somewhat more trouble-free weapon, capable of doing most of the things a defensive handgun will be called upon to do." Libourel added, "I think that in some law enforcement circles, a spray-and-pray mentality has taken hold."

On July 18, 2005, *Newsday* reported that the NYPD's total number of shots fired had jumped from 352 in 2004 to 616 in 2005. At the same time, shooting accuracy dropped from twenty percent to eight percent. In NYC most officers carry 9mms that hold fifteen rounds—up from the ten rounds their guns held in 1993 and the six-round revolvers they last carried in 1992. A high-ranking official's words in *Newsday* mimicked Libourel, saying, "Guys are just letting loose with more and more shots."

The DoJ reports that while police pointed a gun at U.S. citizens 125,872 times in 2002, rarely do they shoot. In 1997 Boston police reported only two intentionally fired shots. The force's high mark, achieved in both 1990 and 2002, was a mere nineteen. While Boston does boast the lowest firing rate of any major U.S. police department, it does illustrate how real police work is very different from what movies—or the cops' drive for bigger guns—would have the public believe.

Still, specialized gun magazines that cater to the law enforcement community consistently peddle stories of lone cops saving the day with steel. Eight hundred thousand potential customers represents

270 big money—and the consumer vanguard. A police department's sanc-
tioning of a particular brand provides the manufacturer with a
potent selling point for the public.

It's hard to fault officers who just want to get home safely to
their families and who feel that having the latest armament will
help them survive another day on the beat. But an arms race with
the public is an unwinnable war when the public has access to all
the same weaponry with none of the accountability. It's also a step
backwards in effective policing. Emphasizing guns and gun use to
police the public creates a chasm between the cops and the community. We only need to look abroad to see the result of barrel-oriented
police work.

> Discussão, soco na cara, começa a porrada
> Mente criativa pronta para o mal
> Aqui tem gente que morre até por um real
> Equando a polícia chega, todo mundo fica com medo
> [Discussion, punch to the face, the beatings begin
> Creative minds ready for the worst
> There are people here that die for real
> And when the police show up, everyone gets scared]
> — MV Bill, "Traficando Informação," off *Traficando Informação* (2000)

As a resident of Los Angeles, producer Madlib has seen what can happen when those who serve and protect don't do their job by the book.
But as a globetrotting collaborator and deejay, he's also seen worse.
"Go to Brazil for a day," he said. "It *ain't* that bad here. Go to Brazil for
one day—it's crazy."

Between 1999 and 2004, police in Brazil's two largest cities, Rio
de Janeiro and São Paulo, killed a staggering 9,889 people, most of
whom were shot. In São Paulo alone the number of civilians killed by
police per year increased from under four hundred in 1998 to over
six hundred in 2003. When confronted by the media and concerned
citizens' groups, São Paulo police cited a rise in confrontations with
criminals. But, looking at the number of officers killed in that same
period, no corresponding rise is apparent.

Jamaican cops allude to similar reasons for the elevated rate of homicides by police officers. The country of 2.6 million has averaged over 140 citizens killed by police annually for the past twenty years, including a high of 354 killings in 1984. While Jamaican police are undoubtedly at greater risk than American police, losing 112 officers in the past ten years, their rationale for killing so many civilians fails under scrutiny. For its part, the Jamaican Constabulary Force, an organization of approximately seven thousand officers, claims in nearly every instance that its members were fired on first, hence justifying the use of deadly force. But when British police looked into the JCF's records, they concluded that—in accordance with international experience that the retaliator in a shootout always sustains more injuries—many more police injuries should have been reported by the JCF. An investigation by Amnesty International found that autopsies were performed to the lowest standards, no formal system of reporting shootings existed, and "if mechanisms currently exist in Jamaica to fairly adjudicate whether a police officer is guilty of human rights abuses, the resources those mechanisms require and the political will to enforce them appear to be lacking."

Senior Superintendent Renato Adams once led the controversial and now disbanded Crime Management Unit, which orchestrated raids in the early millennium that resulted in at least forty killings. He released his rap single "To Protect and Serve" after being acquitted by a Kingston jury on charges of murdering two men and two women and planting guns on their bodies. In the song Adams threatens criminals with the very real boast "they will feel the full extent of the law."

Rarely does an officer in Jamaica face trial, even for the well-documented extrajudicial executions that take place. With the government never acknowledging the existence of these executions and the minister of national security stating "The police must be able, if challenged [by gunmen] to respond swiftly, efficiently and effectively"—adding that a gunman's "place belongs in the morgue"—Adams's mandate is clear.

The atrocious policing environment in Brazil, Jamaica and many other parts of the world is owed in part to the officers' training. In

Brazil the police force operates as a wing of the military, and officers are trained more like infantrymen. A separate civil police force investigates crimes after the initial police response, but day-to-day police–community interactions are the purview of a deeply militarized force, and full-fledged battles in crowded areas are not uncommon. Exacerbating matters are low salaries and difficult working schedules. Most officers in Brazil must work a second job to support themselves while still adhering to the force's "twenty-four hours on/seventy-two hours off" shift system. The force, already ill equipped to deal with the civilian population, becomes prone to exhaustion and susceptible to bribes and corruption; most horrifically, it resorts to excessive force and extrajudicial killings. While Brazil and Jamaica serve as cautionary examples to North Americans of policing by the barrel, we shouldn't be too smug; some of our worst-served communities aren't far behind.

While the DoJ's annual report on the deaths and injuries of officers clocks in at over a hundred pages and is filled with every conceivable type of data, no such yearly report exists for Americans killed by police. The DoJ has released just one such report in the past thirty years. The bias of its title, *Policing and Homicide, 1976–1998: Justifiable Homicide by Police, Police Officers Murdered by Felons*, is clear. In the report's twenty-two-year survey, police killed nearly four hundred people a year in the United States. The report contains no statistics of injuries by police gunfire. This information is, not surprisingly, difficult to obtain, and would require perusing thousands, perhaps millions, of police reports.

In July 2004 the *Houston Chronicle*'s Roma Khanna and Lise Olsen did just that, and published their findings in an investigative report on police shootings in Harris County, Texas, which includes Houston. In the five years they studied, 193 Harris County Police officers had killed or wounded 189 citizens. Nearly 80 percent of these shootings involved the HPD and the sheriff's department, almost tripling the NYPD's rate of police shootings. Of the 189 citizens who were shot by Harris County officers, sixty-five were unarmed, and seventeen of these unarmed citizens were killed. Only half of those 189 carried either a knife or a gun. Only five of the 193 officers faced any disciplinary measures. Those measures were limited to three reprimands, one suspension and only one firing.

> Just business enforcers with hate in they holsters
> Shoot you in the back, won't face you like a soldier
> Kurt Loder asked me what I say to a dead cop's wife
> Cops kill my people everyday, that's life
> — Talib Kweli, "The Proud," off *Quality* (2002)

Every city has its own high-profile police shooting. In February 1999 four NYPD officers who were searching for a rape suspect shot Amadou Diallo forty-one times. When police had approached Diallo, he reached into his jacket and the police opened fire. Diallo, it turned out, had been reaching for his wallet. In 2000 his family launched an $81-million lawsuit that resulted in a $3-million settlement. None of the officers were charged.

Talib Kweli, who like so many New Yorkers was outraged by the incident, responded by organizing *Hip-Hop for Respect,* a CD whose proceeds went to combatting police brutality worldwide. Six years later Kweli reflected on the Diallo incident. "Those cops shot Amadou Diallo because they were working a community where no one looks like them and they can't relate to anyone in the community," Kweli said. "It's just a job. They don't have a respect for the people in the community. Had they been patrolling their own community, they would be less likely to shoot that quickly and that amount of times. They would have thought a bit more 'Maybe he is a good person, maybe he's not a criminal, maybe I'm making a mistake.' But because they're working in a neighbourhood where they assume everyone is a criminal, it's easy for them to make that judgement call."

Fellow New York emcee Victor Santiago, known to the public as Noreaga, doesn't need to read the papers to learn about police shooting citizens. "When I was seven or eight years old," he said, "I saw somebody get shot in the face. It was like, 'Wow.' I seen the dude run from police, and the police officer basically almost killed him for running from them. So I learned at an early age that these dudes is crazy." When citizens feel threatened rather than protected by the police, a common reaction is to take security into their own hands. "In our community, most of the time it's kill or be killed," Nore added. "You gotta protect yourself because nobody is going to protect you. Nobody trust the police, 'cause the police has done so much foul shit to you, and if not you directly, to people around you. Why would you trust them? They basically the enemy, and they basically only show you they the enemy."

Long Island native and veteran emcee Freddie Foxxx echoes many of the same feelings as Nore, as he too witnessed police brutality at a young age. "I seen a police officer beat my mother when I was a little kid," he remembered. "Like, literally beat her up. A man was beating on my mother because some lady spanked my brother and my mother said, 'Don't put your hands on my kid,' and beat the lady up. It put a bad taste in my mouth about cops."

Foxxx's view of the police surfaced when his brother was shot and killed in 2000. "The police have come at me on a few of occasions," he explained, "to try to sit down and talk with them, but I'm not interested in that, because I don't know nothing about it and I don't want to talk about it. They got a job to do and they gotta do it. I gotta deal with the everyday pain of knowing that my brother is not here." No one has ever been charged in the murder of Foxxx's brother.

Foxxx's distrust of the police is so pronounced that he wouldn't cooperate with their investigation, even if it meant the murderer going free. "I don't know a lot of the particulars of the case," he said, "but what I do know, I'd rather keep it to myself. The thing about the police is, you can't trust them, youknowhatImean? I understand why people don't want to talk to the police. I know there are people that might want to talk to them, but the police are liars. They'll sit down and they'll tell you, 'Listen, this is totally confidential and nobody will know that you were here'. They'll do anything to get the information they need."

What Freddie Foxxx sees as manipulative and deceitful, Detective Randy Carter of the Toronto Police Service, who solved Kempton Howard's case, might see as good police work. Like most officers,

Detective Carter joined the force because he wanted to help serve the community. But Carter and his colleagues, under pressure to produce results for the administration, the media, the community and often their own consciences, sometimes resort to tactics that hurt their relationship with the community in the long term. "We are always smarter than the bad guy," Carter said. "Sometimes we are hampered by a lack of witnesses, and even then we are smarter sometimes, because we have ways of giving witnesses the confidence they need to come to plead and say what they saw."

Toronto emcee Jelleestone's outlook on community cooperation reflects a common disposition among citizens who live in heavily policed neighbourhoods. "The story never gets told," he said. "The court isn't about the truth. Everything is about punishment and justification and revenge. Then you talk about why people don't talk. People understand these things on another level." It's a point that Detective Carter also concedes: "I'd like to believe that if it's your community, you should be taking an active role in making it a safe community. Now, having said that, the court system is often not kind to witnesses."

The result of the broken trust between citizens and the police produces a troublesome opportunity. "That could be a good thing for me and a bad thing for them," said Foxxx of his brother's unsolved killing, "if I decided that I wanted to deal with it—street justice." The problem with street justice is that it's usually not justice at all. It's more guns and more bodies and more grieving families—and often, more street "justice."

According to Jelleestone, the onus is on the police to become more involved in the communities that they work in, to re-form those bonds with conscientious police work, taking an interest in the communities they serve, like the officers who participated in the Kempton Howard Memorial Basketball Tournament for boys and girls in October 2005. "You gotta be part of the community so that you are going to be privy to the information that the community shares," Jelleestone said. "They talk about community policing, and that's a policeman that is in the community and works in the community, not only in an enforcement capacity. Somehow you are involved in the community and kids can come learn other things from you."

We found a policeman who agreed. Superintendent Roy Pilkington of Toronto's 31 Division, which serves the Jane-and-Finch area where Jellee grew up, told the *Globe & Mail* on November 10, 2005, that the key to good policing is for the community to "get to know police officers in the context of being people, and not just police officers." When we reached Pilkington—a 33-year veteran of the force—he had just inherited supervision of the district, in which 84 separate shooting incidents had taken place during the previous 11 months. He was affable but hesitant: "My views aren't exactly popular around here." Unable to grant his own interviews, Pilkington directed us to Toronto Police Department's media relations, "They probably won't let me talk to you," he added. Months of fruitless back and forth with the TPD proved Pilkington correct.

Much like the NYPD—who told us "Guns are illegal in this city, what good can come from talking about them?"—and the LAPD, who similarly rebuffed us, the Toronto Police Department's interactions with the community struck us as inconsistent. While policemen like Pilkington understand the positives of strong community-police relationships, we also witnessed the arrogance and hostility that alienates the public and serves to confirm perceptions police forces are trying to counter. Instead of Pilkington's progressive thinking, the public too often receives politically motivated leadership focused on budgets and media headlines instead of the public they are employed to protect. Without a community-oriented approach, the relationship between marginalized communities and the police will continue to be as dire in some areas as what David Simon describes as an occupying force: "In West Baltimore, if you're nineteen and black, twenty-two and black or fourteen and black, what it feels like is it's Gaza and these are the fucking Israeli tanks."

SHELL SHOCK

They vote for us to go to war instantly
But none of their kids serve in the infantry
The odds are stacked against us, like a casino
Think about it, most of the Army is Black and Latino
— Immortal Technique, "Harlem Streets," off *Revolutionary Vol. 2* (2003)

Throughout 2005, amidst allegations of sexual discrimination and news reports that an executive shot an up-and-coming rapper with a Glock, *The Source* magazine experienced a decline in circulation and profits. Its ad pages fell from a high of 1,648 in 2000 to just 779 through mid-November '05. Facing dire financial straits, the magazine that had once refused alcohol and tobacco advertisements included in its December 2005 edition a two-page advertorial for what today is a far more dangerous attraction. On a page designed to fit so seamlessly into the magazine that it necessitated a heading making clear that it was in fact an ADVERTISEMENT, copy from the unlikeliest of sources read: "THERE ARE BENEFITS TO BEING A SOLIDER [*sic*] IN THE U.S. ARMY. JUST ASK BRIAN: THE HIP-HOP SOLIDER [*sic*]."

In its *Source* advertorial, the U.S. Army points to one of its potential success stories, "23-year-old Sgt. Bryan [*sic*] Randall, an Army Reserve Solider [*sic*]." The exemplary warrior is an underground rapper named Jezt Bryan. "As an MC, Randall also realized practical uses for the qualities nurtured in the Army," the ad read. "He saw how his training and service translated into helping his art." Still more alluring, the army advert quotes Jezt Bryan as saying, "I put on a show while I was deployed in Cuba for the Soldiers at Guantanamo Bay and it went over well. . . . now I have the option of going on tour with Armed Forces Entertainment (AFE), which is a program that hires musical acts and goes around to all of the military bases and performs for all the troops."

Just as pictures of rotten livers and domestic abuse wouldn't sell much liquor, images of missing limbs and waning sanity won't sell a war. As dead prez's stic.man said, "Most black people that join the

Army or the military join out of a need for something—and they get sold a dream." But it isn't just black people drawn in by the dream. When Peruvian-American Immortal Technique raps that the army is "mostly black and Latino," he's perpetuating a myth unsupported by the facts.

In November 2005 the non-partisan National Priorities Project (NPP) published a report on United States military recruitment during its fiscal year 2004. According to the NPP's numbers, 64 percent of recruits in '04 came from counties with household incomes that fell below the national median, representing the poor and lower-middle-class brackets. And while the share of blacks among new recruits fell from 22.3 percent in 2001 to 14.5 percent in 2004, the proportion of Hispanic recruits increased from 10.5 percent to 13.2 percent; the share of white recruits rose from 60.2 percent to 66.9 percent. During this time the army also accepted its most poorly educated set of applicants in a decade.

Army recruiting strategically focuses on places where young people of any colour confront a shortage of jobs and educational opportunities. In the same month that the NPP reported on the Pentagon's recruiting numbers, the World Policy Institute's William Hartung wrote an article for *Common Dreams*, an online news provider, titled "Iraq: The Tunnel at the End of the Light." Commenting directly on the NPP's study, Hartung stated: "As has been the case from the outset, the burdens of the war have been unequally shared. . . . It is young people with limited opportunities who are putting their lives on the line."

It doesn't matter whether you're poor and black or poor and white—either way you're capable of adequately executing orders and, in the process, other poor people. "Whenever I meet any young man, whether he be black, white, Hispanic, whatever, I let him know that he does have options," emcee Jezt Bryan says in his *Source* army ad. "There is an expression within our world that real people do real things. WHAT ARE YOU GOING TO DO?"

Got us out here like slaves, fresh off of the ship
Where you can see us pick your cotton, and get our ass whipped
— Big Neal, "Behind the Screens," off 4th25's *Live from Iraq* (2005)

Soon after signing the police checks, sex-offender checks and other assorted enlistment papers, the reality of life in the armed forces kicks in. The military can provide soldiers with firearms and ammunition, but as Gunnery Sergeant Hartman, a.k.a. the one and only Ronald Lee Ermey, tells recruits in *Full Metal Jacket*, "Your rifle is only a tool. It is a *hard heart* that kills." The Gunny was just keepin' it real.

A wild youth in his hometown of Emporia, Kansas, Ermey was arrested several times and eventually given the choice of jail or the military. The Gunny chose the latter, and served a total of eleven years, including two as a Marine Corps drill instructor at the recruit depot in San Diego, followed by fourteen months in Vietnam starting in '68. It was this experience that Stanley Kubrick tapped into when he made Ermey technical advisor on *Full Metal Jacket*. Ermey also helped script Sergeant Hartman's part.

"If you ask anybody who has ever been in the Marine Corps," Gunny said, "if *Full Metal Jacket* was a reasonably good portrayal of boot camp the way it is, they will answer you back, 'Yes, you bet it is!' . . . And you've seen the movie, of course, and you agree with me—just full of craziness as far as the boot camp stuff goes."

"The Gunny"

"I was reading a story just recently," Chris agreed, "about a South Korean soldier who went crazy and shot a few of his fellow soldiers, and I thought immediately of that movie."

"Private Pyle, yeah," he said, remembering the "world of shit" that Vincent D'Onofrio's character found himself in. "[But] I know of at least four instances where recruits have committed suicide. So basically, what you see in *Full Metal Jacket* is the way it really works. And it was effective then, and it's effective now."

What the Gunny calls effective is a process that replaces individual dignity with collective pride and power. As recruits on Gunnery Sergeant Hartman's "island" prepare to sleep with their M-14 rifles, they recite in perfect unison an abbreviated version of the U.S. Marine Corps rifleman's creed:

> This is my rifle. There are many like it, but this one is mine.
> My rifle is my best friend. It is my life. I must master it as I
> must master my life. Without me, my rifle is useless. Without
> my rifle, I am useless. I must fire my rifle true. I must shoot
> straighter than my enemy who is trying to kill me. I must
> shoot him before he shoots me. I will. Before God I swear this
> creed. My rifle and myself are the defenders of my country.
> We are the masters of our enemy. We are the saviors of my
> life. So be it, until there is no enemy, but peace! Amen.

Before he got his big break with Kubrick, Ermey served as technical advisor on another movie set amidst the Vietnam War. It's a film the Gunny has come to hate. "There was nothing at all realistic about the film," he said of the 1979 flick. "It was just like somebody got together and said, 'Hey, let's make a movie that makes Vietnam veterans look like a bunch of fucking idiots, and we'll call it *Apocalypse Now*.'" Despite Ermey's issues with Francis Ford Coppola's acclaimed film, *Apocalypse Now* includes at least a few flashes of veracity. When Martin Sheen's Captain Willard character, for example, considers the charges of murder levelled against him by military intelligence, he exclaims, "Shit, charging a man with murder in this place was like handing out speeding tickets at the Indy 500."

Big Neal said pretty much the same thing about Iraq. Sergeant Neil Saunders believes a soldier should have the freedom to kill with impunity. "When you bring him up on some bullshit charges, like murder?" he said. "C'mon, be serious; stand behind that soldier. Be like 'We don't fuckin' care. That dude is goin' through the time of his life right now—I can't judge him, I refuse to judge him, so I don't care if he shot ten motherfuckers.'"

And if he shot and killed ten insurgents, it would have taken only about 2.5 million bullets, according to one estimate. On September 25, 2005, the *Independent* reported that for each rebel killed in Iraq and Afghanistan U.S. soldiers go through approximately 250,000 bullets. That's about 1.8 billion rounds now being used annually by U.S. forces. With manufacturers in the States unable to keep pace, the U.S. military has taken to importing bullets from Israeli and Canadian sources.

"Contagious fire" helps explain the surging demand—one member of a group pulls his or her trigger and the rest recklessly follow suit. It usually starts when armed units are already on edge, and normally doesn't end until every magazine is emptied. Contagious fire accurately describes how four police officers fired forty-one bullets into Amadou Diallo in New York, and the 120 rounds that a dozen or so deputies poured on an unarmed Winston Hayes in Los Angeles in May 2005.

For most Westerners, war exists as a distant reality. We often forget that soldiers can bring war home with them. Sociologists Dane Archer and Rosemary Gartner studied crime patterns among 110 nations between 1900 and 1974, finding that countries that fought wars experienced significant postwar surges in homicide rates. One explanation might be that, as psychologist Craig Anderson speculated when we interviewed him, "In times of war, a sizable portion of the high-violence age group is gone; they're in another country." When the young males come back, however, many are both traumatized and trained to kill.

As a twenty-seven-year-old member of the 1st Cavalry Division 1-12 Taskforce, Sergeant Saunders survived Iraq and managed to come back with his sanity intact. He does, though, carry his share of anger after the experience. On *Live from Iraq* Big Neal expresses frustration at everything from the superior equipment provided to private military contractors to rap artists who attempt to live in his image without having lived his reality. "Did you have to kill over there?" Chris asked him.

"Man, we had to handle our business, man."

"How do you think that affects most soldiers?"

"Well, it could shut 'em down or it could blow 'em up. The degree is variable, anywhere from you just become the quietest person when you get back, to you can't control yourself anymore—you think this is how you have to handle every situation."

"Did you ever see any soldiers who lost it over there on themselves or on other soldiers?"

"When we were over there, you'd see people all the time that can't handle it. But that just happens, it's gonna happen."

> To all my universal soldiers, stand at attention
> While I strategize an invasion, the mission be assassination
> Snipers hittin' Caucasians, with semi-automatic shots heard around
>   the world
> My plot is to control the globe and hold the Earth hostage
> — ShoGun Assason, "Blood for Blood," off Killarmy's
> *Silent Weapons for Quiet Wars* (1997)

Addressing his recruits in *Full Metal Jacket*, Gunnery Sergeant Hartman asks the budding killers whether they know who Lee Harvey Oswald and Charles Whitman were. After the recruits return a satisfactory answer (Oswald famously shot President Kennedy; Whitman was the Texas Tower Sniper who killed fifteen people before being shot dead himself), Hartman proceeds to elaborate on their significance to Marine training. "Do any of you people know where these individuals learned how to shoot?" Gunny enquires. Following a quick and correct answer from Matthew Modine's character, Gunnery Sergeant Hartman continues, "In the Marines! Outstanding! Those individuals showed what one motivated Marine and his rifle can do. And before you ladies leave my island, you will all be able to do the same thing!"

John Muhammad learned to do the same thing in the Marines. He enlisted in the U.S. Army in 1985 and was honourably discharged in '94, having served in Desert Storm. Trained as a truck driver, mechanic and specialist metal worker, Muhammad also scored at the highest of three levels of shooting skill assigned by the army. He applied this expertise during a string of murders in the fall of 2002, in which thirteen innocent victims were hit with single bullets; ten of them died. It was the second time a Gulf War veteran had orchestrated a devastating terrorist attack against American citizens. In 1995 a paranoid firearms fanatic and former army gunnery sergeant, Timothy McVeigh, enraged by events near Waco, Texas, bombed an FBI building in Oklahoma City, killing 168 people, including nineteen children he classified as "collateral damage."

When *Time* named Muhammad and his teenage sidekick, Lee Malvo, their "People of the Week" on October 24, 2002, the magazine added, "The men were said to be sympathetic to the terrorists responsible for the 9/11 attacks." No shit. In addition to allusions to Socrates' philosophies, *The Matrix* and Bob Marley lyrics found in Malvo's notebook, he calls Osama bin-Laden "the prophet" and Saddam Hussein "the protector." When law enforcement officers finally slapped the cuffs on the Beltway snipers in October '02, they allegedly found two items of note in their car: a semi-automatic rifle and a rap CD. Neither man was legally permitted to have the gun, unlike the rap disc. Muhammad's second wife, with whom he'd gone through a bitter divorce, had taken out a restraining order; Malvo was a minor. But, as most terrorists stateside know, there are ways to get around such inconveniences.

The U.S. Army had trained Muhammad with an assault rifle much like the .223 calibre Bushmaster AR-15 used in all but two of the shootings, and for young firearms enthusiast Malvo the gun was a relative snap to master. His new-found father figure, who carried the laser-scoped weapon in a silver briefcase, beamed with pride at his "son's" gift with the black rifle. Soon after the snipers were apprehended, Maine's Bushmaster broke the news to its seventy-plus staff members that Muhammad and Malvo had used one of the company's products in their killing spree. "We just talked it through with our employees," Bushmaster vice-president Allen Faraday said in the October 25, 2002, *Washington Post*. "It's too bad a crazy person like this can use our rifle and create a black eye for the whole firearms industry." Bushmaster staff were told, "You have nothing to be ashamed of."

Disagreed. Bushmaster supplied the AR-15 used by the snipers to Tacoma's Bull's Eye Shooter Supply in July 2002, a gun store that defined what it means to be a bad-apple dealer. The store had been the subject of ATF inspections, a relatively rare measure by the Bureau, four times between 1998 and 2002. Malvo told investigators that at seventeen years of age he had walked into Bull's Eye, where the Bushmaster rifle with scope was on display for any customer to handle, picked it up and walked out without paying a penny. The AR-15, valued at $1,600, was just one of at least 238 guns that "disappeared" from Bull's Eye in the three years before the snipers took aim at so many innocents. Muhammad had obtained a .308 calibre Remington rifle from Bull's Eye in a straw purchase, and also frequented the store's large shooting range.

Started by two old army buddies, including a former army ranger, Brian Borgelt, Bull's Eye raised every one of the ATF's red flags, selling numerous guns that quickly appeared at crime scenes. But as a retired ATF supervisor, William Vizzard, said in the April 20, 2003, *Seattle Times*, the Bureau was reluctant to take serious action "because they're afraid. They have no backing in Congress or this administration." Following the arrest of Muhammad and Malvo and the discovery of the AR-15, neither Bull's Eye nor Bushmaster admitted wrongdoing. Nevertheless, facing a lawsuit launched by the families of eight victims, Bull's Eye agreed to pay out $2 million, and Bushmaster another $500,000.

For the first time a gun manufacturer settled a suit claiming negligence leading to a crime, the Brady Center to Prevent Gun Violence said in the September 10, 2004, *Washington Times*. Despite the settlement, the *Times* reported, Bushmaster had no intention of changing its "corporate practices." With immunity from liability since signed into law by President Bush, Bushmaster no longer needs to.

And who really cares about technicalities like liability anyway, when there's rap music to blame? Not NBC. When the snipers were captured and facts started to surface, MSNBC didn't talk about trained killers who occasionally turn on their creators. Nor did the network address the issue of bad-apple gun dealers. MSNBC talked about rappers.

Alongside the AR-15 found in Muhammad and Malvo's Chevrolet Caprice, officers discovered an album by a group of budding emcees affiliated with the Wu-Tang Clan. On the October 23, 2002, episode of *Meet the Press*, host Tim Russert brought it all together. "This is a CD from a group called Killarmy," Russert explained. "It's named *Silent Weapons for Quiet Wars*. There's a song called 'Wake Up'—'Word is bond this is as real as it's going to get.' Then here is the letter which [the snipers] left behind at the shooting in Ashland, Virginia: 'Word is bond.'"

Sure *Silent Weapons for Quiet Wars* is a spine-tingling listen—especially when you imagine serial killers getting hype to it. But in the booth, rappers can adopt any persona they want, and Killarmy chose camouflage-wearing end-times terrorists obsessed with guns and ammo. "When we did our first album," explained Steubenville, Ohio's Beretta 9, a.k.a. Kinetic, who was sixteen when *Silent Weapons* was recorded, "our thing was just go in the studio, do it, hand it in. We was young when we did that." And if the album was violent, it only reflected Killarmy's environment. Soon after *Silent Weapons* was released, the group's manager, twenty-seven-year-old Wisegod Allah, was shot dead by Crips in Steubenville. The .357 Magnum he was packing didn't save him.

The rap record might have had an influence on the snipers, but so could have the unidentified gun magazine with Malvo's fingerprints on it, which was left at the scene of a liquor store robbery in Montgomery, Alabama (the two men were also allegedly responsible for earlier shootings as far away as California, Florida, Texas and Louisiana). For that matter, *Silent Weapons for Quiet Wars* heavily samples *Full Metal Jacket*. One track, "Under Siege," features the voice of Gunnery Sergeant Hartman ordering the recruits to recite the rifleman's creed. Another song, "War Face," samples Hartman teaching Private Joker—appropriately—how to put on his "war face." One could argue that the power of the Gunny's acting and script contributions were a major influence on Muhammad and Malvo's murderous rampage. One would only be as off the mark as the people over at *Meet the Press.*

> They got money for wars, but can't feed the poor
> — 2Pac, "Keep Ya Head Up," off *Strictly 4 My N.I.G.G.A.Z.* (1993)

On April 4, 1967, the Reverend Martin Luther King Jr. stood before a congregation at Riverside Church, sharing his wisdom on the state of American society and international affairs. "A few years ago there was a shining moment in the struggle," Dr. King said. "Then came the buildup in Vietnam." Speaking for "the poor of America who are paying the double price of smashed hopes at home and dealt death and corruption in Vietnam," King acknowledged, "Something is wrong with capitalism."

Four decades after Reverend King delivered his Riverside address, as soldiers are cut down in the anarchic streets of Iraq while social programs are cut at home, it once again appears that something is askew within the system. "There have been few places for investors to hide in what's been a lackluster market lately," *CNN Money* said in April 2005, the story's headline offering just one exception: "Defense! De-fense!" As *Money* reported, so-called "sin stocks"—shares in military contractors such as Lockheed Martin, Boeing, Raytheon and L-3 Communications—are all off the chain. "The war is a business," 50 Cent told *The Guardian* on January 20, 2006. "You have to think about how much money is being made by companies who manufacture weapons." And most of that money is being made off the backs of American taxpayers.

In November 2005, Fifty got a few of his dollars back when he and Tony Yayo played a wonderland bat mitzvah for the daughter of David H. Brooks, CEO of bulletproof-vest maker DHB Industries. Performing at New York City's Rainbow Room alongside the likes of Aerosmith, Stevie Nicks and Kenny G, the G-Unit proved that street cred takes a backseat if the cheque's big enough. Brooks dropped a reported

$10 million celebrating his seed's passage into womanhood. After the CEO's success in '04, it was chump change.

An August 2005 report by the American non-profit research group United for a Fair Economy (UFE), titled "Executive Excess," reported that Brooks had made $70 million from his company in 2004, a 3,349 percent leap from the $525,000 he earned in 2001. At the same time, Brooks banked another $186 million selling off stock and options in late 2004. DHB shares, which had risen from below a dollar per share in the late nineties to $22.53 in December '04, soon plummeted to less than $7 in value. Not long after, in May 2005, the Marines recalled more than five thousand "Interceptor" armoured vests produced by Point Blank, a DHB subsidiary, based on concerns that they were incapable of sufficiently protecting soldiers against even 9mm pistol rounds.

And while gun manufacturers haven't seen cream on par with that pocketed by David Brooks, much less the high-tech research firms, war apparently suits the gun business. "If we receive government contracts," Richard Grantham, operations manager with Heckler & Koch, told the *Ledger-Enquirer*, "we're in the position where we can grow and expand in a very fast fashion." Along those same lines, "Smith & Wesson is coming back to life," *The New York Times* announced on April 11, 2006, "thanks to an expanding Pentagon budget." Having already earned a contract to supply Afghan security officers with pistols, S&W has its sights on the ten-year, half-billion-dollar-plus contract to replace the Beretta M9 as the U.S. armed forces designated sidearm, a matter to be decided in 2007.

But for now at least, Beretta remains the brand to beat. In 2005 Beretta received contracts from the U.S. military for 18,744 pistols in May and an additional 70,000 M9s in July. What's more, 20,318 Beretta 92S semi-automatics were shipped to the Coalition Provisional Authority in Iraq for distribution to local police in February 2005. A March 19, 2006, report by *The Observer*, however, found that many of the 92Ss had ended up in the hands of the "friends of [Abu Musab] al-Zarqawi," al-Qaeda's now deceased leader in Iraq—mostly because of police corruption. Glock, which can't compete for U.S. military contracts because its products don't meet minimum safety standards, still scored a Pentagon contract supplying 100,000 pistols to Iraqi police. A May 2006 report by Amnesty International further revealed that another 200,000 AK-47s that the U.S. Department of Defense arranged to have shipped from Bosnia to security forces in Iraq couldn't be accounted for.

And with some estimates of the Iraq war's total cost now surpassing the quarter-trillion-dollar range, "This cannot afford to be a guns-and-butter term," U.S. senator Judd Gregg, the Republican head of the Senate Budget Committee, said in the *Wall Street Journal* on December 21, 2004. "You've got to cut the butter." For American citizens, that means gutting federal spending on education, job training, Amtrak and Medicaid for the poor. It also means slashing federal funding to programs focused on gun trafficking and criminal intelligence gathering. As New Haven police chief Francisco Ortiz said in Hartford, Connecticut's *New Britain Herald* said on February 22, 2006, "Bush has dismantled most of the task forces that helped make this country safe."

PICKING UP THE PIECES

In 2005 Amnesty International published *The Impact of Guns on Women's Lives*. Its aim? Nothing less than summarizing the effect of the world's six hundred million–plus small arms on the world's three billion–plus female population. Duska Andric-Ruzicic, director of Medica Infoteka, an antiviolence women's centre in Bosnia-Herzegovina, told Oxfam after reading the report, "I've learned that there's really little difference between violence in war and violence in peace—for women it's just the same."

If men's gamble in war is death, it is often rape for women. Rape can be politically motivated—intended to destroy the fabric of families and communities—or opportunistic—when men, emboldened by their authority and debased by the horrors of combat, defile women and girls. Testimonies of armed abductions and forced servitude at gunpoint are not hard to come by, though they rarely make headlines. In Sierra Leone between 1999 and 2000, roughly two thousand

CRUCIAL CONFLICT

While the threat of chemical weapons and nuclear bombs torments the protected masses, the reality is that 60 to 90 percent of direct conflict deaths involve the use of small arms. Many more die as a result of the devastation left behind. In the Democratic Republic of Congo (formerly Zaire), for every person killed in armed combat, eleven die from disease and starvation. A total of four million Congolese have died since 1990—at the rate of a thousand people a day. Below is a list of the top ten ongoing conflicts and their combat casualties.

Conflict	Year of First Casualties	Estimated Casualties from Direct Conflict
Afghanistan	1979	1,500,000
Somalia	1988	400,000
India (Kashmir)	1989	38,000–100,000
DR Congo	1990	350,000
Algeria	1992	100,000–150,000
Burundi	1993	300,000
Uganda	1998	500,000
Russia (Chechnya)	1999	25,000–55,000
Iraq	2003	40,000
Sudan (Darfur)	2003	50,000–70,000

women were freed after being abducted by armed men; 1,900 had been raped, most had sexually transmitted diseases and many were pregnant.

The Red Cross estimates that 35 percent of all war casualties are civilian, and more than 80 percent of these are women. Yet, as Duska points out, when the fighting is over for the men, violence against women continues post-conflict with much the same frequency. As most conflicts today take place in communities rather than on isolated battlefields, women, who are still the primary caregivers in most cultures, must contend with food shortages, lingering insecurity and caring for the injured, traumatized or brutalized men who have returned home—all problems that are exacerbated by the presence of firearms.

—

In North America there has been a movement to change the status of weapons from destabilizer to equalizer. The NRA is leading the charge to promote firearms to women; its "Women on Target" program holds several hundred female-only clinics every year where women shoot together, and its "Refuse to Be a Victim" seminar teaches women self-defence strategies.

With some variations in technique, marketing firearms to women generally employs themes of self-protection. The same year that *American Rifleman* published an article recommending that manufacturers seek out the female market, Smith & Wesson released its LadySmith line of handguns. Its advertising evoked scenes of urban terror with copy such as "You thought no one could fit in your backseat." Old-line giant Colt chose a different strategy, suggesting that women need handguns to protect their children. Colt's strategy proved effective; a study by the *Willamette Law Review* found that 85 percent of women had a strong emotional response to their advertisement— higher than to any gun advertisement directed towards women.

In April 2005 NRA member Charles Jones held a clinic at Penn State University; the event echoed industry scare tactics. Holding a fake gun and real knives, Jones asked the mostly female students, "What value do you place on your life?" before proceeding to answer his own question: "It's alright to be a little paranoid, because they are out to get you." Jones also emphasized the strength imbalance between men and women, telling the students that a "105-pound woman doesn't stand a chance against a large man." It's a powerful image in a country that reports roughly a hundred thousand rapes a year, and where the Department of Justice estimates that a third of all American women will be raped, assaulted or robbed in their lifetime. And it's an image that has some women sold. The DoJ's 1997 study, *Guns in America: National Survey on Private Ownership and Use*, found that 67 percent of female gun owners have a gun primarily for self-protection, compared to 41 percent of men.

In her 2004 book, *Blown Away*, an "unbiased exploration on the right to bear arms," Canadian-born, New York-residing journalist Caitlin Kelly reasons that "while carrying guns won't solve the larger and more complex issues of living within a violent society, it is one of the few ways a woman can level the field." Although Kelly admits that she wouldn't bring a gun into her own home, she brushes off the magnitude of the damage for which firearms are responsible: "gun deaths, each hideous, each unnecessary and perhaps preventable, do not represent the typical demise of Americans. In 2001, 17,424 Americans were killed by guns—while 43,051 died in motor vehicle [accidents] and 16,274 in falls."

Kelly's statement understates the industry's complicity in the death toll. It's hard to imagine legislating behaviour or creating conditions that would significantly reduce deaths by falls, and the auto industry spends millions making safer cars. But the same can't be said for guns and gun manufacturers. Effectively, Kelly is allowing that gun deaths may be a necessary price to pay for women to have the ability to defend themselves. In Wendy Rowland's 1996 documentary about women and guns, *Packing Heat,* one of Rowland's interview subjects, Judith Ross, a University of Toronto psychology professor, puts a finer point on the rhetoric: "When the government says that you can't use a firearm to defend yourself I think they should realize that they are discriminating against women, who generally have less strength than men and less ability to defend themselves."

Although *Packing Heat* includes testimony from a cross-section of women who use guns for various reasons, it does not suggest that weapons make women's lives safer. *Blown Away,* however, implies through anecdotes of women fighting criminals with "defensive gun uses" (DGUs) that guns *can* be a solution. DGU stats lie at the centre of the debate about whether guns create a better or worse society for women. Supporters of handguns as self-defence tools, like the NRA, tend to cite Florida State criminologist Gary Kleck's study, which found that Americans use guns for self-defence 2.5 million times a year.

In contrast, the National Institute of Justice, a U.S. government body, estimated that the annual total of DGUs was probably closer to 108,000, almost twenty-five times less than Kleck's result. While DGU numbers continue to be disputed, other, incontrovertible statistics are having an impact on the debate. According to the 2005 Control Arms report, despite the fact that men outnumber women as homicide victims by a factor of ten, women continue to outnumber men as victims in family killings. While some women buy the line that a firearm will reduce their vulnerability to strangers, most murdered women are killed by someone they know—usually their partner—with a gun they know.

The same guns that women purchase for protection greatly increase their risk of being murdered, with American studies showing that women who live in homes with handguns are nearly three times more likely to be murdered. Countries with greater concentrations of firearms typically showed higher female homicide rates. Data collected from twenty-five high-income countries found that although the U.S. accounted for 32 percent of the female population of those countries, it was home to 70 percent of the group's female homicides, and 84 percent of its women killed with firearms.

> I was mad at this news and so was my brothers
> And I wanted to get violent but I'm a lover of black mothers
> And black mothers need sons
> Not children that's been killed by guns
> — Derek X, "Concerto in X Minor," off *One For All* (1990)

Elaine Lumley sat at a small desk with three other women. She looked nervously around the room filled with reporters. Her gaze alternated between cameras, not exactly sure which lens to direct her blue eyes towards. She fidgeted with her curly blonde hair, needlessly rearranging a lock. She placed her crossed hands on the desk, paused and dropped her hands back in her lap. Her eyes welled up. The edges of her mouth began to pull down. She breathed deeply. She listened. She exhaled. She waited.

On November 27, 2005, Lumley's son, Aidan Lumley, a twenty-year-old swimmer and university student, was shot in the back after leaving his friend's birthday party in Montreal. The murderer was never found, but the handgun was. Less than two months later, his mother sat in a pressroom in Queen's Park in downtown Toronto, to talk about her son and his killer. Finally, it was her turn. "We need

to enforce a complete ban on handguns and implement serious mandatory minimum sentences for illegal possession and gun crime," she said. "I see no legitimate purpose for a handgun in an urban environment. They are designed to kill."

Elaine Lumley's co-panellists, all women who had lost sons, nodded in agreement. But Elaine's loss was more recent, and the pain was too much. She cried. In front of the cameras. In front of the country. When she regained her composure she explained the mothers' ultimate goal—beyond the legislation, the politics, the rhetoric—"We're here so we don't have another group of mothers up here in a year."

While female self-defence proponents like Caitlin Kelly will point to the NRA's 170,000-strong female membership and to a rally for the Second Amendment Sisters that attracted five thousand women to Washington, these numbers are dwarfed by female participation in anti-gun and gun-control movements. The Million Mom March rally, which the Second Amendment Sisters had rallied to counter, brought 750,000 women together.

The mother of slain emcee Big L, Gilda Coleman has lost two sons to guns and shares the prevalent view among moms. "I hate 'em," she told Rodrigo, "because it's not just my children. Other parents are losing their children, and now with the guns and stuff they're getting younger and younger." Gilda has spent much of her time since the death of her Lamont speaking to the media and to children to raise awareness of the issue. Other mothers of hip-hoppers have been active in fighting gun violence. The Notorious B.I.G.'s mother, Voletta Wallace, started Books Instead of Guns (B.I.G.), a program that promotes literacy in the late Biggie's Brooklyn. Snoop Dogg's mother, Beverly Broadus Green, launched Mothers of Entertainers, a group of rap-related moms who talk to youth across the U.S. about the dangers of guns. Giving hope to grieving women, Gilda Coleman explained, "It's hard for mothers that lost their children. When I lost Lamont I really didn't think I was going to make it for a long time. You just have to pray. Even after losing my children there's always a rainbow."

> Everyday I wake I feel like crying
> Every second I feel like praying
> Everywhere I turn my people dying
> Brothers and sisters now listen what I'm saying
> — Ms. Dynamite, "Watch Over Them," off *A Little Deeper* (2002)

The murders of teenagers Letisha Shakespeare and Charlene Ellis in January 2003 outraged Britain, and many in the black community took the incident as a rallying call to fight the gun violence that had increased despite the ban on handguns and assault rifles and the overall decline in shootings. When the verdict was handed down, Charlene's mother, Bev Thomas, told the BBC that no one should be complacent about the presence of firearms. "Today for me can be tomorrow for you," Thomas said. "Don't wait for it to reach your doorstep."

U.K. emcee Ms. Dynamite, known for her politically motivated rhymes, became one of the strongest voices for the cause, stating, "in terms of gun violence and gun crime [women] definitely have a responsibility to the people," and more famously announcing at a memorial concert for Letisha and Charlene, in front of eight thousand, that black people need to "start loving instead of killing each other." Ms. Dynamite, as part of the English generation most affected by gun violence, feels that women can play an active role in creating responsible, peaceful men: "A lot of women, especially nowadays, [get caught up in] 'I need a car, this and that, the clothes,' and at the end of the day men want to be whatever we want them to be." Ms. Dynamite's analysis may strike some as simplistic. Men undoubtedly carry the onus of reducing gun violence. But women, as co-definers of attitudes and norms, can expedite the process by discouraging retaliation and retribution, and by not succumbing to the fearmongering that would see them join men in a dead-end arms race.

"I think women can set the standards and stick to them. If we do that, I promise you, you'll see an instant change. They can't live without us, trust me."

GUNS, GANGS AND GOD

I wish my pops didn't die when I was seven years old
If there's life after death, is heaven this cold?
I wish I could wipe the tears of all the cryin' mothers
Wish New York niggas didn't start flyin' colors
— Ed O.G., "Wishing," off *My Own Worst Enemy* (2005)

In December of 2005 *Time* magazine contacted us for our take on a Boxing Day shootout among more than a dozen youth in Toronto's downtown core. The reckless showdown left an innocent fifteen-year-old woman lifeless and another six passersby injured. The reporter told us the publication's angle: "The police said it was gang related." Yeah, but the police always say it was gang related—letting stereotypes fill in where their account leaves off.

Most people hear the word *gang* and imagine the sensational: white-rock-slangin', black-hearted youth draped in red or blue, toting MACs and AKs. But the reality of gang life ain't quite as cool as the film *Colors* made it seem. A professor at the University of Southern California, Malcolm Klein has been researching gangs in the Los

Angeles area since the early sixties. Klein made it clear that not only are most gang members not violent, neither are the majority of gangs stateside involved in drug dealing. In fact, the best estimates suggest that less than 10 percent of L.A. gang members are responsible for most of the gang violence in that county, while only a third of all U.S. gangs play a significant role in the drug trade. And though many gang members may regularly carry guns, few will ever shoot someone. The media tend to package gangs, gun violence and drugs. But it's a package that largely falls apart upon closer inspection.

Instead, Klein said, a street gang is defined simply as a "durable, street-oriented youth group for whom illegal behaviour is part of their identity." A result of extensive research by the Eurogang working group, the definition relayed by Klein helps separate street gangs from other types of gangs such as terrorist gangs, motorcycle gangs or the better-organized and hierarchical drug gangs. When Klein began as a researcher in southern Cali, gangs were using "zip guns and tire irons and big chunks of asphalt," he laughed. But "gradual" change came in the eighties with the "greater availability of semi-automatic or automatic firearms—not so much the rifles, not the Uzis and things like that—but the Glocks, the handguns also that became automatic."

The Canadian media would have people believe that T.O.'s problem with "hardcore gun-crazed gangsters" is now on par with that of many American cities, but it's a myth built on hype. In order to justify expanding budgets and scare votes out of people, police and politicians everywhere are exploiting gun violence as eagerly as has any Hollywood movie. Australian MP Michael Gallacher, Opposition police spokesman, declared absurdly in March 2006, "The Labour Government has allowed crime to spiral to the point where it is now easy to confuse Sydney with downtown L.A."

Professor Klein commented during what the *Toronto Star* and *Toronto Sun* both called the T-Dot's "Year of the Gun" (the respective *Sun* cover depicts a Glock held sideways by a blurry hand), "You have gangs in Toronto, and then in Vancouver and in Edmonton and other places, but there is not much gun action associated with them, I

would assume, given the fact that you guys are so nasty about guns."
As in Australia, because Canada has been so "nasty" about guns, our
situation pales in comparison with the places Malcolm Klein has
studied—even during T.O.'s "gang-gun" crisis. Compton, California,
for example, saw an increase in homicides of 85 percent in 2005.
The seventy-two deaths, which the L.A. County sheriff's department
said mostly "appeared to be gang related," compare with the total of
seventy-eight homicides in Toronto in 2005. But Compton has a population of fewer than 100,000 people, catapulting these seventy-two
killings into a murder rate more than twenty times higher than that
in Toronto, a city of 2.5 million.

If Canadians want to act pragmatically on the problem of street-
gang violence, we really need to get it all in perspective. While T-Dot
cops and media point to the influence of Mafia movies such as *The
Godfather* and *Scarface* on Toronto gangs, most gang members are
small-time lawbreakers, poor minority youth trying to hustle up loot
through what *Foreign Policy* magazine quoted a criminologist as
calling "cafeteria-style" crime. Most of the 750,000 members in
America's 28,000 gangs—compared with roughly 340 gangs in
Canada—come from society's lower strata and are struggling just to
get by, to feed themselves and their families. Reporting on the connection between globalization and a dramatic surge in street gangs
and gang violence around the globe, *Foreign Policy* concluded, "As
the global economy creates a growing number of disenfranchised
groups, some will inevitably meet their needs in a gang."

A "Gang Education and Outreach" workshop during the first
National Hip-Hop Political Convention (NHHPC) in Newark, New
Jersey, drove home the economics of street-gang development.
Facing innumerable obstacles in that summer of 2004, local gang
members had forged a truce in their city. Face, a Newark Crip and
founder of the organization SOS (Saving Our Selves), took the stage
to discuss one reason he had decided to work towards peace. "What
motivated me is that two years ago," he began sombrely, "I lost one of
my homeboys—died in my arms. I seen a lot of deaths, I seen a lot of
things happen, but to actually have a brother shakin' in your arms is
a real traumatic experience. I used to always say I ain't scared to die,

I'm not scared of this, afraid of that—that was one of the most scari-
est moments of my life. So that's what really made me say, 'You know
what, I'm'a try to save my brothers, 'cause I don't want to go through
this no more.' And I don't want young brothers comin' up under me
experiencin' this."

Face explained that he was also motivated by fear for the safety of
his children. "I'm willin' to put my life on the line for this," he told the
audience in Rutgers University Theater. "I want them to be able to
play in that playground and not take a stray bullet." Despite all their
tough talk about addressing gang violence, few politicians offer to
make the same sacrifice.

"You want to know what can keep the peace?" Face asked the rapt
assembly from across the U.S. "In my neighbourhood, 'keep the
peace' means give us somethin' else to do: recreation, jobs. We need
jobs. A lot of us are fathers and we're strugglin'. And all we was
taught is just to survive, that's it. Any means necessary to do that, you
feed your family, you make sure your kids have food on the table."
Face explained that many gang members are raised in fatherless
homes, sharing clothes and beds. "Comin' up like that, it's *hard*," he
said. "So we know we got to work for whatever we want." For working-
age gang members like Face, finding a job means, as Malcolm Klein
explained, less "street time. And if you reduce their street time, they
are less likely to be getting into trouble."

Chaired by Newark's deputy mayor Ras Baraka, one of a growing
number of American political leaders raised on hip-hop, the gang
workshop nearly fell apart when a Newark teenager burst in and
told the audience that she had just witnessed "gang violence" while
playing tour guide for visitors to her city. "It was just a stabbin'
between Crips and Bloods, just right now, and I just came from
it," she stormed at the panel, shaking. "You representin' a colour,
for what?" she shouted angrily at Face. "You're not gettin' nothin'
out of it."

Maintaining his calm while refusing to make excuses, Face
explained that from the outset it was clear that not every Crip and
Blood would be down with the treaty. Local media helped feed the
perception that gang members were incapable of change. "We had to

fight so much in this city," he said, "'cause every time a murder happened, they said it was 'gang related.'"

A panellist from Watts, California, Aqeela Sherrills, jumped to Face's defence as other members of the audience knocked the gang truce. Calling the term *gang* a "societal scapegoat," Sherrills showed rare compassion, saying, "A lot of pressure is being put on these brothers because of the peace treaty that they've organized in this city. And I want to say this to you guys: give these individuals the benefit of the doubt. Hold space for the possibility of greatness to show up in what they've done, as opposed to continuously judging them."

"If you give us some other alternative to live or to apply in our life," Face reiterated, "then we'll have the alternative to go another way. But a lot of us, like I said, grew up in broken homes, so we're forced to be men at ten years old. And with that it's hard out here, man. It's hard for me to sit there and tell twenty young brothers who just lost a good friend of years to put they gun down, it's peace. Peace is very hard." Emphasizing the fragility of the truce, Face said that while he and others would try to make it work, they wouldn't try alone for long. "We gonna put our gun down," he added, before qualifying, "We gonna save a few bullets."

> Behold the burnin' malice of a treacherous soul
> First time I shot a gun, duke, I was twelve years old
> But since then, I never put it down my friend
> She go to war when I tell her, fuck a who? why? when?
> 'Til the end
> — JuJu, "Do You Believe," off the Beatnuts' *Stone Crazy* (1997)

At the small arms working group in Ottawa, six months after his experience at the NHHPC, Chris listened to a presentation by Alhaji Bah, a researcher originally from Nigeria. His words were a flashback to Newark.

Bah has studied the effect of United Nations Disarmament, Demobilization, Reintegration and Rehabilitation (DDRR) programs in Liberia, a country of 3.5 million on the African coast of the Atlantic. Following fourteen years of Liberian civil war, a U.N. mission was mandated to solidify a peace agreement by disarming combatants and integrating them into civil society. Unfortunately, according to Bah, the U.N. focused more on disarmament and demobilization than it did on reintegration and rehabilitation. "We realized that a good number of the ex-combatants have gone through the DD phase," Bah told the group of his recent trip to Liberia, "but then they are hanging around with nothing to do. And these are a significant percent of the country's population. And with a country where you have an unemployment rate of 85 percent, and you have youths hanging around with nothing to do, chances are high for those people, for that country, to relapse into conflict."

Chris mentioned to Dr. Bah the gang workshop at the NHHPC, and his concern that society so often calls for youth to put down guns without addressing the reasons they picked up those guns to begin with. "Which is why I brought up the issue of the disconnect between the DD and the RR phases in post-conflict processes," Bah said. "Because, let's say a child who was adopted into a fighting force when he was twelve or so, now he's eighteen—for the past six years he depended on his weapon for his survival. So if I convinced him to [participate in] a voluntary scheme to [hand] in that weapon, now the next challenge is, what next? How is he going to be able to at least make sure that he survives in society, and he's able to have an interesting, profitable life, where life does not become meaningless? Because to him the gun adds meaning to his life, because through the gun he was able to rob people. You have to be able to empower that person using other means."

> God help me, 'cause I'm starvin', can't get a job
> So I resort to violent robberies, my life is hard
> Can't sleep, 'cause all the dirt make my heart hurt
> —2Pac, "My Block," off The Show soundtrack (1995)

Driving a rental around Los Angeles five months after meeting Alhaji Bah, Chris was lost. An overcast afternoon sky accentuated the greys of East L.A. As he did his best to navigate neighbourhoods we've been conditioned to fear, he tried to match the surrounding streets with the overwhelming map on the seat beside him. Then, like the beacon of hope it is, a brightly coloured graffiti mural beamed a signal from the home of Homeboy.

Homeboy Industries provides intervention services to gang members, and its slogan, "Nothing stops a bullet like a job," suggests that they remember to do in L.A. what the U.N. sometimes forgets. Founded in '92 by Father Gregory Boyle, a Jesuit priest working in the poorest parish in East Los Angeles, Homeboy Industries began out of an effort to find employment for gang members facing the huge obstacle of a criminal past. In addition to assisting disadvantaged youth with job training and placement, Homeboy has since added tattoo removal, a profitable silkscreening business and a myriad of other services. While Malcolm Klein is quick to point out that no gang intervention program has been independently evaluated to determine its effectiveness, Homeboy's success speaks for itself.

Take Chino, Homeboy's official office tour guide. After Chris parked his ride and walked into the bright one-storey building bursting with young Latinos, Chino escorted him around Homeboy's impressive headquarters. The shiner healing beneath his left eye attested to the inescapable severity of this neighbourhood. Barely into his twenties, Chino treated his responsibilities at Homeboy with the highest level of professionalism, walking Chris thoroughly through each aspect of the Homeboy enterprise, from the critical role of the job developers and counsellors to the non-profit's newest initiative, the Homegirl organic café.

Lining the walls of Homeboy are photos of hundreds of youth who have come in seeking Father Greg's unconditional support. Representatives of about five hundred of L.A. County's 1,200-plus gangs have visited Homeboy since 1998. Chino, who's known Father Greg since the age of thirteen, readily admitted that not "everybody that comes in through here is a success story." Nevertheless, offering himself up as an example, he said, "The type of influence that he has had on me is like, I'm still here, so you could tell. Like, I grew up in this neighbourhood and not a lot of other people that Father Greg knows has been lucky enough not to go to a state penitentiary or end up in a cemetery, and stuff like that, because of the gang violence."

When Kanye West says "Jesus Walks," it ain't just talk. Affectionately called G-Dog by the young homies he's helped, Father Greg walks that walk on the daily. And just as Jesus showed the greatest love to those most often targeted for judgement, G-Dog stands by youth who got a horrible start in life but who sincerely want to stop destroying their communities and themselves, young people willing to work to change their lives. Even Malcolm Klein, a man swayed solely by empiricism, a man who contended, "Nobody can let you down harder than gang members," said of Boyle, "I think he is a damn saint."

Chris had arrived on one of the busiest days in Homeboy's history. Guided to Father Greg's office by Chino, he sat down to witness multitasking of a divine order. Father Greg called in and assigned tasks to Homeboy employees, approved spending requests and fielded calls from the young cats he's given his life to, ending each conversation with a firm "I love you, son." In his first free moment, the fifty-something Irish-American priest looked his visitor in the eye with a smile and said, "So, fire away, dog."

Chris asked about the philosophy represented by Homeboy's slogan. "This whole thing was born of trying to find employment," Father Greg said, "because we felt this was what everybody asked for, this is what all the homies wanted. It's evolved since then into lots of things." He explained further that, with gang members' literacy issues, tattoos and frequently lengthy felony records, the most difficult aspect of the Homeboy operation is finding "employers willing to hire these guys." When asked how much those who find employment and don't work out hurt the organization's reputation, Father Greg admitted that Homeboy does sometimes "get burned," but reminded us, "We're not called to be successful; we're called to be faithful. You want to be faithful to an approach."

Evidently the approach is working. A staff member entered Father Greg's office and suggested hiring a publicist to advertise a visit taking place the following day. "Laura Bush is coming tomorrow," Boyle explained. Less than enthused, he told his employee, "I don't want to do it. It'll be what it'll be—a brief little photo op. It's just too slick, and I'm not interested." The staffer smiled, begrudgingly accepting Boyle's decision, and stepped out.

"How effective has the present government been in dealing with gangs?" Chris asked.

"Oh gosh, not at all, not in any way. But, you know, nobody hopes for *that*. You proceed without them," G-Dog answered. "They don't get it, and that's okay."

Of the most important lesson that other communities and countries can take from Homeboy, Father Greg said, "It announces kind of a truth to the world: 'What if we were to invest in these folks rather than trying to incarcerate our way out of this problem?' That's what this is about."

"How does the accessibility of guns exacerbate the problem?"

"It complicates things enormously," he responded. "That's the thing that kinda set these last two decades off from all the previous ones—the emergence of crack, which brought you guns. So they're heavily armed and that makes an absolute difference. Even ten years ago, fifteen years ago, I used to spend a lot of time going to hospitals to visit the wounded. Well, you don't really do that anymore. Now if somebody gets hit with a gun, chances are they're not going to make it. So you just see the kinda weaponry changing."

As Father Greg explained from first-hand experience, not only has evolving firepower increased the level of lethality, guns have also changed the very nature of armed conflict among gangs. Malcolm Klein observed, "You get a lot more retaliation and a lot more serious retaliation now than you used to several decades ago, and that's clearly, in my view, a function of the firearm. It requires, in and of itself, a greater response than did the spiked board or the chain."

Returning to Homeboy's main interaction area, Chris found Chino again, and gave him a copy of *Pound* with 50 Cent on the cover. Chino thanked him, apparently making no connection between Fiddy's music and the gang problem in his neighbourhood. He did, however, connect the presence of firearms to the problems where he lives. "That's a big part," Chino acknowledged, "when it's really easy to get a gun around here—for anybody. For a fifteen-year-old, it's really easy to get a gun." He led Chris to a corner where news clippings had been framed. During the summer of 2004, two employees of Homeboy's graffiti removal service were gunned down on the job. Likely victimized by a gunman angered by the removal of his gang's graffiti, thirty-four-year-old Miguel Gomez had completed a ten-year prison sentence just three months before he was murdered. "It was just down the street in broad daylight," Chino said. "Not everything is peachy, dog."

Chris wanted Chino to know the struggle wasn't in vain, giving props to Homeboy and telling him how the organization deals with a need that Face talked about all the way across their country. "You say you from Canada," Chino said, "come from New Jersey—your mind is able to expand more, because you travel and stuff like that, and you see all the people that give you wisdom. But all I know is right here.

"Anybody who's involved with gangs and stuff like that, pretty much, you're nothing. Ain't nobody give a fuck about you, not the police, not the government, not even the people around you in your neighbourhood, 'cause they scared of you, they don't respect you. They scared of you now, 'cause they think you gonna fuckin' shoot and kill their little babies."

> These days it's hard to tell who really cares for me
> So when you hear this song, you should say a prayer for me
> I put a message in my music, hope it brightens your day
> If times are hard, when you hear it, know you'll be okay
> A O.G. told me "God's favorites have a hard time
> You out the hood, that's good, now stay on the grind"
> — 50 Cent, "God Gave Me Style," off *The Massacre* (2005)

There was another person we wanted to see while we were in Los Angeles. We'd listened to Aqeela Sherrills address the audience back in Newark; his empathy for the struggle faced by gang members had made a big impact. But while we were in his hometown, Aqeela was travelling to "sacred places" in countries such as Serbia and Cambodia and "recharging" after years of service to others.

As Chino said, society prefers to dehumanize gang members. They're portrayed as animalistic killers beyond all hope. So long as gangbangers aren't catching innocents with their crossfire, we couldn't care less about their deaths. Over a twenty-year period beginning in 1981, there were more than ten thousand gang-related deaths in L.A. County alone. Among those ten thousand, Aqeela Sherrills lost thirteen of his friends. As with Face in Newark, the wave of bloodshed brought to the surface Sherrills's need to seek peace in his neighbourhood.

In 1992, teaming up with his elder brother Daude, Aqeela helped negotiate a peace treaty between gang leaders from four housing projects in Watts, modelling the truce on a ceasefire agreement reached between Egypt and Israel in 1949. Even the police were compelled to credit the effect of the treaty as homicides fell dramatically in the following years, from twenty-five killings in Watts's three main projects in 1989 to just four homicides in the same reporting districts in '97. It wasn't long after he returned to the States that we called Aqeela back into service, phoning him for an interview.

A survivor of child molestation, thirty-six-year-old Aqeela maintains that most violence in the streets has its origins in the home, that when young people join gangs they're often fleeing painful situations. In Aqeela's view, gangs constitute surrogate families for poor youth. "One of the things we don't recognize today," he explained, "[is that] it's the same physical and psychological abuse in many cases that we experience in our households that give birth to this psychosis. We see it manifest itself in Watts as homicide, and in Beverly Hills it's suicide."

Discussing how the accessibility of guns changed the situation in Los Angeles, Aqeela said, "It's like, all of a sudden there was thousands of guns on the streets, right after the early eighties. . . . Someone says something to you and it triggers those wounds from your childhood, and the next thing you know, you're doing something that you never imagined that you'd do, out of anger and frustration." That same anger and frustration again hit home for Sherrills in January 2004, when his eighteen-year-old son Terrell, a freshman at Humboldt State University home for the holidays, was shot in the back at a house party. "A group of uninvited visitors with possible gang ties barged in and became violent," *LA Weekly* reported on January 22, 2004, of the police investigation.

Since Terrell, who looked so much like his father, was wearing a red Mickey Mouse sweater to the party, the police and media guessed his murderer was connected to the Crips (Aqeela later wrote in a letter to *Utne Reader* that his son simply liked Mickey Mouse because the pair shared big ears). The killer remains at large. Despite Terrell's tragic death, his father refused to give in to vengeful feelings, sitting beside and standing up for Face at the NHHPC just five months later. Sherrills shared how he maintained his resolve after such a profound loss.

"I mean, I'm totally broken-hearted," he said after a pause. "Two days ago I was crying like a baby, just thinking about how much I miss seein' my son. I'm not consumed by anger being that my son died, because I have a different type of belief system as it relates to death. I don't see death as the end. It's not over, youknowhatI'msayin'? I feel like I gained an elder on the other side, and although I can't see his physical face, I feel Terrell every day in my heart. And I know that if it was me, my hope is that he wouldn't go out looking to retaliate and take someone else's life, as if that's going to solve anything."

Aqeela Sherrills believes that peace is not so much an objective as a journey with "valleys and peaks along the way." At present his city is descending into another valley of death. In July 2005 *LA Weekly*'s Michael Krikorian wrote, "President Bush keeps saying America is safer now that Saddam Hussein is out of power. Prez hasn't been to Watts lately." In the same article Sherrills calls L.A. gang violence the worst it's been since '92. Los Angeles' five-year average for gang-related homicides has risen from 164 per year between 1995 and '99 to an average of 308 annually between 2000 and 2004. The increase is hardly random, and goes beyond a shifting preference from drive-bys to walk-ups among gangs in southern Cali.

In recent years, funding for the social programs that keep kids out of gangs has been cut dramatically in California, just as the

Rockstars of the world are glorifying gang life. Sherrills has little appreciation for games like *Grand Theft Auto* when it's obvious that the bloody shootouts on Grove Street in San Andreas are intended to satirize the realities on Grape Street in Aqeela's Watts. Poverty is the biggest factor in gang violence, but when they promote violence and desensitize people to real suffering, video games, movies and rap music change how society perceives and responds to the problem. But just as rap can make the problem worse, hip-hop has as much potential to point youth back towards a peak on the journey of peace. "I think that hip-hop can play a critical role in really shifting popular imagination about peace and violence," Sherrills said. "Like 50 Cent, he says a lot of crazy stuff in his music. However, people love his voice tone and the track. He can say anything and they would buy it."

It makes perfect sense that the response to gangs has been much the same as the response to hip-hop: authorities pointing fingers and pounding fists, serving only to strengthen solidarity amongst the targets of their attacks. Hip-Hop and gangs both emerged in opposition to mainstream culture. The more that politicians, police and the media come down on either, the more that identities and bonds within both countercultures are sealed, the clearer the "us" that's against "them" becomes.

What's more, rappers and gang members like to brag about their brutality, but in a vast majority of both cases the "violence is more rhetoric than it is fact," as Malcolm Klein said of gangbangers. All the gun-slinging tough talk is part of a protective, terror-inducing image. But while there are similarities between the two cultures, there are at least as many differences. For one thing, a career in rap is a legal job, one of those things Homeboy Industries believes "can stop a bullet"—though, as hip-hoppers know too well, not always.

ABOVE THE CLOUDS

When Bronx veteran Lord Finesse reflected on the loss of his friend and fellow emcee Big L, who was shot on his block in Harlem, he spoke of a sad reality that can be applied to all young black men, mic-wielders or not. "They ain't find the killers of B.I.G. and Pac—the leaders, the coastal leaders. They ain't find them dudes. Now magnify it a couple of levels down and look at L," the Funky Man said. "There's a greater significance to them than when L got killed in his hood. He just got killed."

On October 27, 2005, the Oval Office set the scene for a major peace initiative. The office was a stage arrangement for a concert by Jay-Z in New Jersey. Putting four years of beef, which produced some of rap's best records, behind them, Jay-Z and Nas did what hip-hoppers never got the chance to see 2Pac and the Notorious B.I.G. do: the two artists hugged before performing together for a packed and goose-bumping crowd. "It takes blood for people to want to stop and go in another direction," said Canibus, formerly a soldier in the U.S. army. "And hip-hop has shed its fair share of blood."

The following is a list of hip-hop artists whose lives were ended by gunfire. It's a small gesture towards acknowledging that no one just got killed. R.I.P.

2Pac (Asked what he thinks happened to his father's other son, Mopreme Shakur looks quietly away. "Pac was too much for this world," Preme answers after a long silence. "People loved him too much, hated him too much, he was too talented, he had too much money, he was too *hard*. He was too much!")
Bankie (American Cream Team)
B-Doggs (Wreckx-N-Effect)
Big Hawk
Big L
Big T (Almighty RSO)
Blade Icewood
Bugz (D12) (Following a water-gun fight that developed into a fistfight, someone at a Detroit picnic went to his truck for a shotgun, returning to shoot twenty-one-year-old Bugz three times and run over his body while fleeing the scene. Remembered on D12's track "Good Die Young," Bugz had selected Swifty to join the group just before he was killed. As Swifty says of the song, "All I do is think about him being in that better place." After Bugz was murdered, Eminem would become the Dirty Dozen's sixth member.)
Bulletproof
Camoflauge
Cartoon
Charizma
Cornelius "Katt" Davis
DJ Cee
D.O. CannonEclipse (Cydal)
E-Money Bags
Fat Pat
Fat Tone (Kansas City, Missouri's Fat Tone was in hospital recovering from gunshot wounds when Tech N9ne saw him for the last time. Months later, in 2005, the former stick-up kid was lured to Las Vegas by someone pretending to have a connection to Snoop and a music industry opportunity for Tone. In Vegas, the twenty-three-year-old would be slain while waiting in his car for a meeting with the pretender. Despite Fat Tone's criminal past, says Tech

N9ne, "We was one of the few people who loved him." With the assistance of *America's Most Wanted*, Bay Area rapper Mac Minister was arrested for Fat Tone's murder in March 2006.)

Forty (Still Risin')

Freako

Freaky Tah (Lost Boyz)

Half-a-Mil

Hate Eye

Hawk

Hitman (R.B.L. Posse)

DJ Irv

Jam Master Jay (Run D.M.C.)

JoJo White (Bored Stiff)

Kenfolk da-Mac (West Coast Headbustaz)

Kilo-G

Lil Slim

The Mac

Mac Dre (Debuting in '89, Mac Dre would have his music career suspended when he refused to become a patsy for the FBI and snitch on neighbourhood friends involved in bank robberies. After four years in prison, Dre returned home to Vallejo, California, to again focus on music. In 2004 his career was once again cresting when he was killed in a freeway shooting in Kansas City that was falsely blamed on Fat Tone. "They got him like that, and that's fucked up," says Sacramento's C-Bo,

who was also shot at in K.C. months before. "Mac Dre is my partner.")

Makhendlas

Mausberg

MC Ant

Mr. Cee (R.B.L. Posse)

Mr. Livewire

Mooseman

Noncents

Nonpareil C

Notorious B.I.G.

Paul C (Irish-American New York–based producer Paul McKasty is the only Caucasian on the list. The largely unknown but hugely influential producer perfected many early hip-hop sampling techniques, and his production protégés still run circles around most beat-makers. Tragically, Paul C's life was ended in 1989 at the age of twenty-four, when he was shot three times in the head and neck inside his Queens home in a still unsolved murder.)

Pimp Daddy

Plan Bee (Hobo Junction)

Proof (D12)

Q-Don

Rappin' Ron (Bad Influenz)

Rockafella

Sabotage

Sazon Diamante

Scientifik

Scott La Rock (BDP)

Seagram

Soulja Slim (Raised in New Orleans's Magnolia projects, Slim's criminal lyricism was based on the reality of his criminal life, a life he found hard to leave behind once he became a rapper. Gunned down on the porch of a house he purchased for his mom, Slim had bought five guns in the week before his death in 2003. "Where we come from," says B.G., a close friend of Slim, "you never got too many." Asked about his homeboy's murder, B.G. answered, "It hurt me in an amazing way.")

Stretch (Live Squad)

Tarus (The Coup)

Tone Capone

Yaki Kadafi (Outlawz) (Killed in 1996, just two months after the murder of his cousin Tupac, Yaki died in what the Outlawz believe was an accidental shooting. The cousin of ex-Outlaw Napolean reportedly shot Yaki unintentionally while intoxicated. "Pac passed away, and then right after that, Kadafi passed away," says the Outlawz' Young Noble, who was then just a teen. "It was real fucked-up, like really just kinda out of our mind.")

Yella Boi (UNLV)

CONCLUSION
UNLOADING

"THERE'S NO GOING back to what we once were," the *Toronto Star*'s Rosie DiManno eulogized on December 28, 2005, as the year came to a close. "A culture of nihilism and reckless wrongdoing has caught up with us." The T-Dot's petrifying thugs, thrilled with the fame an active trigger-finger can bring, had found an unlikely ally in the media. With Torontonians terrified daily by cover stories of precipitate malice, polls in early 2006 revealed that three-quarters of the city believed "those charged with gun crimes should face a 10-year mandatory sentence without parole," the *National Post* reported. His knees jerking as he ran the prime ministerial campaign trail, Conservative leader Stephen Harper threw out similar numbers for gun crimes, promising to put thousands more cops on the beat. Responses like Harper's are all too familiar below the border.

"When there's a breakout of this kind of violence in some place like Toronto, people act as if nobody has ever done anything effective," said a "deeply frustrated" David Kennedy, a member of the team that put together the "Boston Miracle" in the mid-1990s. "They simply go back to their original, essentially uninformed preconceptions and play out the same old tired, ineffective scripts."

> We all make mistakes, and these are the breaks
> But I'm sick and tired of goin' to wakes
> And seein' an end, to my friend
> — Ed O.G., "Love Comes and Goes," off *Roxbury 02119* (1994)

Beginning in the late eighties and continuing into the mid-nineties, Ed O.G.'s hometown of Boston, like many U.S. cities at the time, experienced a soaring murder rate, largely a product of the crack epidemic and the increase in handguns that came with it. Most of the victims were, like Ed

O.'s friends, young black males. "It's actually like therapy, man," he said of "Love Comes and Goes," "when you can release stuff like that."

David Kennedy, then a researcher at Harvard University's School of Government, helped head up a community-driven initiative to deal with the violence in Boston. Commonly hailed as the "Boston Miracle," the extraordinary resuscitation of Boston's most dangerous neighbourhoods began in January 1995 with the planning of "Operation Ceasefire." The ambitious project integrated a range of community representatives with law enforcement agencies to end the violence. Organizers—who identified Ed O.G.'s Roxbury as the "highest-risk district"—determined that "any workable intervention would have to address both the supply and demand sides of the equation."

Understanding which firearms represented the greatest threat was a critical first step. Operation Ceasefire gathered intelligence and concentrated enforcement measures on the illicit trafficking of the calibres and brands of firearms most often found in the hands of youth. In Boston, gang members were buying "new in the box" handguns, those without "bodies" on them, mostly 9mms and .380s. At the time sales of Saturday night specials were booming.

"I don't participate in any firearms business as a human being," Bruce Jennings, king of the junk-gun world, quipped in a June 18, 2002, deposition during Brandon Maxfield's lawsuit. There's a little truth in every joke, though. And while Bruce Jennings is no longer an industry leader, his moral sensibilities still are. Colt, Ruger, Glock—no matter how clouded the debate becomes with cries for freedom, these names are about one thing. The gun business, like any industry, fiercely protects and pursues its economic interests. But when the gun business is in the black, society is often in the red.

Easin' my pain, from where He came I don't know
But He's tellin' me, 'It's not the right time to go'
Back of my throat, tubes suckin' the ooze from my mouth
As nurses run about, tryin' to send me down south
'Who shot ya?' That's words from the detect' and the doctor
Before I got flown to Beantown in a helicopter
— Krumb Snatcha, "Closer to God" 12-inch (1997)

"Basically I felt I was given a second chance," Lawrence, Massachu-setts's Krumb Snatcha said of his debut single. "It was at a time where Biggie had just passed and I just felt a lot of [artists] glorify the shootouts and all that stuff, but they don't tell both sides of the story." For youth caught up in the street life, public health workers insist that getting shot can serve as a "teachable moment." Krumb Snatcha learned his lesson at twenty-two, given another opportunity at life and a career in rap.

Krumb didn't hold back on wax about the agony he experienced as a gunshot victim, unlike many rappers who portray bullet wounds as badges of honour. "I would say that's moronic," he remarked. "I got shot five times—I'm lucky to survive. There's some people that get shot just once and bleed to death." On Krumb Snatcha's 2004 LP *Let the Truth Be Told*, he argues that the war in Iraq has taken atten-tion away from the ongoing violence in American cities. "There's ter-rorists runnin' around in every ghetto and every hood," he said. "They may not run up with bombs, but there's shootouts."

Operation Ceasefire specifically targeted those people Krumb called terrorists and the team in Boston referred to as a relatively small number of chronic offenders—approximately 1,300 in sixty-four Boston gangs—who were mostly shooting each other in gang rivalries. "They burn out fast, but they burn real bright," David Kennedy said. "These are people who very often create around them something like a subculture, and they're high-profile, they're often leading kind of dramatic lives, they're people who are having a lot of contact with criminal justice and other authorities, and usually, effectively, they're winning those encounters. If they get away with it and get props, then they influence a whole lot of other people."

Operation Ceasefire held meetings directly with these hard-core offenders, communicating in no uncertain terms that violence would no longer be tolerated and that they were attempting to protect gang members from themselves. For those that didn't take the message to heart, the team enforced every law on the books, which included fed-eral prison time (no parole) in the most intractable cases. At the same time acknowledging the lack of opportunity that gang members faced, organizers didn't ignore the issues of demand, and extended much-needed assistance to those who turned away from the bloodletting. Operation Ceasefire was subsequently credited with helping reduce the number of homicides on Beantown streets from a high of 152 murders in 1990 to just 31 homicides by 1999.

Although the approach worked, Kennedy, now a faculty member at John Jay College of Criminal Justice, is quick to point out that what happened was no miracle. It took a lot of work and a profound commitment from the community that was itself most affected by the violence. It took mothers and grandmothers and ministers and community workers and ex-offenders getting together to take a stand. "And to that we can add the artists," Kennedy said, "who have, many of them, actually had a piece in driving this stuff."

"Everybody says to [the offenders], 'This has got to stop; the community can't have this. We're not the cops; we're not the white folks. We're you; you're us. And we're not sleeping in the bathtubs because of the CIA. We're sleeping in bathtubs because you guys are shooting each other out on the streets in front of the house. And we want you to live, we want you to stay out of prison, we want you to succeed. We're gonna help you. But you are doing what you're doing because you choose to, and we need you to stop it today.' And what we're seeing is that they do."

It took the determination of an entire community to set Boston's gun problem straight. Krumb Snatcha thinks the same thing is needed to fix the gun problem in rap music. "A lot of people who consider theyself the voice of the people," Krumb concluded, "need to step up, take a stand."

Rappers have long positioned themselves as the voices of the community. But closer inspection of much of today's music reveals discrepancies between life in the community and the realities related on wax. Today, with the world in rapt attention, many rappers use their fame to promote product instead of progress, trumpeting their influence when it fattens their pockets but denying responsibility for any trouble they inspire. Apologists point to social inequalities that force young black and brown men into a survivalist frame of mind, but they forget that rap's politically minded pioneers developed their art in an even more violent era, and that hip-hop's ascendance was forged by the undeniable urgency and sincerity of their messages. When artists trade authenticity for marketability, they forfeit the music's greatest asset. When rappers so thoughtlessly employ lyrics and images of guns and gun violence to sell their music, weapons become decontextualized and their effects trivialized, creating dangerously false impressions in more impressionable listeners. As Krumb Snatcha alluded, hip-hop's direction is determined by its most popular creators and the power to strip guns of their glamour lies largely with them.

> Say 'There ain't no hope for the youth'
> Then the truth is, it ain't no hope for the future
> — 2Pac, "Keep Ya Head Up," off *Strictly 4 My N.I.G.G.A.Z.* (1993)

Youth need hope. Operation Ceasefire, while numerous in its imperfections, succeeded because it delivered a clear message. The message wasn't "Drop the guns, or else"; it was "Put down the guns, and we'll be there to protect you and help you onto a better path."

As gun violence in Canada generates talk about cuffs and cages, the nation's growing economic divide goes mostly ignored, as if it wasn't a factor. In May 2006 a U.N. panel on economic, social and cultural rights expressed of Canada a "particular concern that poverty rates remained very high among disadvantaged and marginalized individuals and groups such as Aboriginal peoples, African-Canadians, immigrants, persons with disabilities, youth, low-income women and single mothers." At the same time, "Vital Signs 2005," a report by the charitable organization Toronto Community Foundation (TCF), exposed a level of youth unemployment in T.O. that was more than double that of the Greater Toronto Area—the highest rate of unemployed youth in a decade. "Many youth are shut out of the workforce," TCF president Anne Swarbrick explained in the report, pointing further to "the challenges faced by students in our school system [that] risk the creation of an underclass unable to participate in an information economy."

"You know what pulled me out of school," Hu$tlemann's Mayhem Morearty explained when asked about the role of education in the problem of gun violence, "is bein' in school and feelin' those hunger pains, man. Everyone else is eatin' lunch, and sometimes all you got is like, gum and you drinkin' a pop. You better stay in the 'hood and hustle, and get you some lunch." In Toronto it's young people like Mayhem, youth confronting what academic circles call "cumulative disadvantage," who are killing and being killed.

A native of Toronto's "Jungle," Mayhem brought Jet Black and C-4 to our May 2005 interview because he believed they had special insights to offer on the gun issue. Introduced to guns at around nine years old, C-4, who's rapped that he has "links on AKs like bin-Laden's troops," never smiled while we hung out. His demeanour wasn't a thug front—he really doesn't have much to smile about. His community is suspicious of individuals like him, and the cops just harass him. The best parts of C-4's life, maybe the only things that make him feel good about himself, are his homeboys and hip-hop. Nihilism comes naturally to a cat like that.

"Since I was probably like nine," C-4 said when the conversation turned to solutions, "I've been hearin' people tellin' me, 'What do you think should be done to change around where you're from?' And every year more and more fucked-up shit's happenin'. It's like, we came to a point where it was just like, 'Fuck it!'" The next we heard of C-4, he'd been arrested in a shooting incident.

In December 2005, after fifteen-year-old Jane Creba was killed in a downtown shootout between two gangs of Toronto youth with a "fuck-it" attitude, the *Star* speculated on December 31, 2005, "It may be that young people . . . will be listened to at last." Indeed, in Boston the role of the "frontline practitioners"—youth activists from the communities in question, young people like Kehinde and Taiwo Bah—was critical. "It comes down to the fact that these people in the streets are poor," Kehinde said, "don't have education, don't have that upward mobility, don't have the same power as other people, [so] they'll do things that gain you respect in the street, because that's the last place you can go in terms of being seen as worthy at all."

"The most startling thing about Kempton's death—or murder," Tai added, "was that youth did it. And they're the same youth that are doin' arts and crafts and goin' on trips and goin' swimmin'. They came up in

318

the community, and for them to take that turn down some other path altogether to take a life, that's crazy." Kempton Howard was killed because he took it to a local bully and a couple of his ego-inflating friends for smoking weed around the Torch Club kids. As with any act of extreme violence from Red Lake to the Beltway, Kempton's murder was the result of a complex composite of risk factors. Taiwo simplifies it: he blames what happened on anger and the accessibility of guns.

"For some reason," Tai said, "Kempton wasn't scared." The encounter thus became what Tai called an "oh my god" moment for the bullies, their cowardice and powerlessness exposed by Kempton's courage and desire to protect the children under his care. Enraged, and urging one another on, they came to the building the Howards called home the next day, their sense of self-worth momentarily restored by a 9mm pistol.

We may never know the origins of the handgun that was used to take Kempton's life. Maybe it was bought from a bad-apple dealer in a straw purchase and moved illegally over borders. Or perhaps it was stolen from a collector's home or a factory floor. Regardless, those who put narrow and obvious self-interests above common-sense and human safety—whether for fun, pride or money—bear responsibility for contributing to the continuation of a situation that sees individuals like Kempton killed.

Kempton Howard's murder was hardly without precedent. In 1995 the South Bronx's Geoffrey Canada wrote about the threat to community workers in his account of the urban arms race, *Fist, Stick, Knife, Gun.* "They are seen as the alternative role models to the dealers," Canada observed of leaders like Kempton, "so they feel they can't let the drug dealers make them take a low profile on the block. They feel that if children and others who look up to them see them intimidated, ridiculed, or pushed around by the gangsters, it makes it look like there are no forces of good that can withstand the twin evils of drugs and guns."

We've gained too much experience with the gun problem—understanding that's come with a lot of suffering—for us to simply give in to our own "culture of nihilism." With seventy-eight murders, Toronto had a violent year in 2005, as did Boston, its homicide total rising to a ten-year high of seventy-five. But Boston has about a fifth of T.O.'s population. Exaggerating Toronto's gun problem undermines graver issues with gun violence in the rest of Canada, and abroad. Furthermore, both Toronto and Boston knew still more violent years in the early nineties. If these cities were able to rein in violence before, we have every reason to believe they can do it again.

When we interviewed Toronto's San Francisco–born, Harvard-educated mayor, David Miller, in 2005, we had no idea where he'd just come from, nor why he seemed so shaken. Miller had been visiting a work-placement program in Toronto's Jane-Finch area, C-4's community, when somebody told him that a few kilometres due west, eighteen-year-old Amon Beckles had been shot and killed outside a church while attending the funeral of his friend Jamal Hemmings, whose shooting Amon had witnessed nine days earlier. Miller filled us in. Exhausted and agitated, he pleaded for perspective. "Guns don't protect people," he said. "They make it worse. We don't want to get to the type of violent society like they have in the United States, where the murder rate is ten times ours because people have that philosophy." Miller acknowledged that the number of shooting homicides was increasing in Toronto, but that was the only violent offence doing so. Nonetheless, he would not concede that this trend was a cue for personal armament. "Safety isn't about the absence of crime only," he declared. "It's about everybody knowing that they have a real role in society and they have a place and they're going to have the opportunity to be able to express themselves and have their needs fulfilled."

Hip-Hop has created an untold number of opportunities for young people to express themselves and fulfill their needs. The culture gives voice to the voiceless, building influence and power from scratch. Fans of 50 Cent love everything he does because it comes to him naturally, from his skill to his style to the way he stays strapped. His life is an embodiment of the culture's own rags-to-riches story. As Buckshot, another among Kempton's favourite rappers, sees it, that kind of innate influence can't be tamed: "You can't compete with 50 Cent goin' 'I got a semi-automatic,' 'Ruger and Lugers and M1s, and they all for sale.' You can't stop the power of what a person feels when a melody goes into their head like that and the words is about guns and they like it. You can't stop it at this point."

But rappers are making billions of dollars off of hip-hop, and control of this culture's values lies primarily in their hands. If they contribute to stereotypes, we can't complain about how our culture is perceived by mainstream society. On the other hand, if grand-standing cultural gatekeepers continue to attack hip-hop based on cursory knowledge of a single artist, it's gonna be tough for young people to see any sense in the system. "I don't think people in Toronto or any urban centre need or want to hear Mr. Jackson's mes-sage right now," Liberal MP Dan McTeague said in November 2005, echoing Julian Fantino.

"Rappers reach inside and bring out more truth," Russell Simmons told us while in Van City, "and even anger and frustration, that is buried in the consciousness of Americans, and in Canadians, when they rap. It's something that they bring up that makes people uncomfortable that makes them special." And while McTeague's campaign to keep 50 Cent out of our country met with little success—proving Buckshot right—his letters to Immigration did increase Fifty's fame. That helped earn the Queens-born artist C$91 million in 2005 and put the G-Unit's general at number eight on *Forbes*'s list of music's top money-makers that year, just behind Céline Dion. So what happens if you get rich and don't die trying, what then?

"Don't expect me to evolve into a new person in eight months," Fifty told *Playboy*. "People shot *me*. Where I grew up, you were sell-ing drugs or you were starving." Everyone is quick to judge 50 Cent, but they couldn't walk the block in his G-Unit-brand sneakers. Curtis Jackson came up like the young New Yorkers in Deanna Wilkinson's study: a victim of poverty, a broken home, drugs and guns. But he survived, and found a way to make millions legitimately (which is more than we can say for the company McTeague's Liberals have been keeping). And there's no reason that Fifty can't now follow in Bono's footsteps. "I feel like I should be doing positive things," Fiddy mused. "I want to build a community centre for kids."

Curtis Jackson knows the needs of his neighbourhood, and of oth-ers like it. As Professor Wilkinson found from her 417 interviewees,

"Many respondents felt that community centers were important for preventing violence in their neighborhood. Frequently in neighborhoods without community centers youth would lament about how the centers could help make the neighborhood a better place for children." Ask Kehinde Bah about areas around Toronto without community centres, and he'll snap off the names of "neighbourhoods that don't have shit"—Regent Park, Eglinton West, South Etobicoke. If we're really listening, people like Kehinde will tell us where we need to start investing if we want to address our gun problem. Four walls, a roof, a couple of basketball nets, a few computers with access to the 'Net, and maybe a little recording studio, and we'll have a lot of what we need to attract youth away from the streets.

"I wouldn't be the person that I am today if it wasn't for that community centre," Taiwo said. "Same with Kemp'n, he wouldn't have ever been the person that he was if it wasn't for him interacting with all the kids and doin' what he does, and them *employing* him."

Arguably more important than community centres, programs like the Blake Boultbee Youth Outreach Service (BBYOS) are needed to address the deeper psychological stresses some young people struggle with. Started eighteen years ago by psychotherapist Rod Cohen, who spent time with one of the youth charged in Kempton Howard's murder before his death and with Taiwo after it, BBYOS offers free counselling to traumatized youth. Handguns and assault weapons may kill, but broken people often pull the triggers.

A fifty-seven-year-old mother and grandmother, Elizabeth Bishop-Goldsmith founded Mothers Against Guns in March 1994, after her godson was shot in New York City while working as a bouncer. Six years later her nephew died in a random shooting in Washington, D.C. Today she advocates uniform gun laws across all states. Mrs. Bishop-Goldsmith told us that she's often forced to listen to NYC's Hot 97—now famous for the frequency of shootouts outside its doors—by her four-year-old grandson, who updates Nana on all the hottest artists. She hates to hear music fan the flames of gun violence, saying of rappers, "They just need to clean up their act when it comes to reaching out to the public, especially the young people, because they are the ones that it's affecting most, and they're the ones who we're burying every day because of this copy-cat reaction."

"I wish 50 Cent would get in touch with us," she stressed later. "He is actually from the neighbourhood, here in Jamaica, Queens, and we were trying to reach out to him because he has a story to tell also. And we would love to have him on a positive note come and speak with some of the youth, because they idolize him, and I'm quite sure he could tune it down to them and let them know that what he's doing and what he's saying are things that he saw in his lifetime, but it's not for them to go out there and imitate."

But many young people have that much figured out. "A lot of people think that rappers like Fifty or Jay-Z or those guys are a bad influence," one fifteen-year-old girl explained during a talk about *Pound* we gave at Eastern Commerce, a high school in the T-Dot attended by "less advantaged" teens. "These people experienced what we're experiencin' right now. When you think about what they've been through and how they made it and stuff, those kind of things should influence us to reach our goals."

When some of the world's most powerful people are so absolutely corrupt, so ready to go wild with their guns in order to fatten their pockets, it's really hard to convince intelligent youth that hip-hop is a serious threat to our collective safety. The effect of drive-by shootings is worrisome, but what about the effect of drive-by headlines: CORRUPTION, MILITARIZATION, DECEPTION, INVASION? When we speak of Babylon, we are not referring to skin colour, nor are we pointing to any place on a map; we speak instead of a blinding and destructive greed as visible in the grimiest street as it is in the squeakiest-clean office.

Canadian media and politicians are quick to demonize young black men, even as our armed forces' "diversity cells" scour the country looking to fill out the army's ranks with visible minorities. And we don't complain when the military uses weapons by Colt Canada to lure high-school students into its co-op program. "You will learn how to safely operate and maintain your C-7 service rifle, and the C-9 light machine gun," its information page promises. "You will fire all these weapons." And as Canadian soldiers carry their guns into

Afghanistan, Canada's involvement allows for redeployment of U.S. troops—increasingly in short supply—to Iraq.

"That's why I say hip-hop music is just a factor," Mayhem Morearty commented of the latest war in a place long ago called Babylon. "*That* was the most blatant form of gangsterism I seen in my whole entire life!"

ACKNOWLEDGMENTS

WE MUST FIRST THANK our patient and gifted editor, Craig Pyette, for his inexhaustible faith in this project and for guiding us so steadily through our first book. We also thank our publisher, Anne Collins, for seeing what could be achieved out of what was then little more than a seed of an idea. We thank especially Taiwo Bah for sharing the life of his friend with us, and Joan Howard for allowing us into her home for the interview. Daphne Hart and Jon Festinger are also due special thanks for helping us with our contracts at the best imaginable price. And Ron Eckel, for taking the *System* to the rest of the world. Michael Evans is also due a special shout-out for hustling *Pound* behind the scenes for all these years. We wish there were more space to acknowledge the unique contribution from each of the people we can only list below. In mentioning their names, we hope instead that they'll understand how much we appreciate their significance.

The following people have loved and supported us throughout our lives and careers. They are always in our hearts and minds: The Bascuñán family (Patricio, Luz, Daniela and Cristobal, Carlos and Millaray), the Pearce family (Ron, Mia, Steven, Ronald, Richard, Emily and Gerianne R.I.P.), Elena Ikonomou and the Ikonomou family (Louis, Nana, Alythia, Joell and Mael), Majid Mozaffari, Luke Fox, Celine Wong, Edward Schall, Toby Scott, Andrew Cappell, Patricia Pliner, Kostas Pagiamtzis and family, Paul Holden, Ricardo Carvalho and family, Matthew Carter, Kevin Charbonneau, Nicolas Burtnyk, Lori-Ann Christie, Steven Marco, Sarah Hellman, Owen Elliot, Yaiza Fernandez, Luvdeep Randhawa, Maneesh Sehdev, Silvano Todesco, Mark Dewairy, Asad Kiyani, Ryan Danziger, Kevin Brereton (aka k-os,) all the contributors of *Pound,* Ignacio Morales, Roberto Cortez, Paulo Clavero, Rodrigo Clavero, Ricardo Bravo, Joven Narwal and La Pobla.

This book represents a cooperative work, for without the time and/or wisdom of the following individuals we could never have realized our vision. We owe them our sincerest thanks: Betsy Bolte, Jay Swing, Kehinde Bah, Aqeela Sherrills, Deanna Wilkinson, Matthew Mei, Travis Bader and the Bader family, Gillian Watts, Pam Robertson, Nicole Kozicki, Jacquie Newman, Wendy Cukier, Elizabeth Bishop-Goldsmith, Gilda Coleman, Denise Burnett, Richard Ruggieri, William Hartung, Whit Collins, Craig Anderson, Tom Diaz, Ras Baraka, Joel Reodica, Noam Chomsky, Todd Boyd, Russell Simmons, Melle Mel, Pos, Gyasi Ferdinand, Ian Robertson, Capone, Noreaga, Trigger Tha Gambler, Mr. Cheeks, 50 Cent, Lloyd Banks, Young Buck, Tony Yayo, Prodigy and Havoc, Tony Touch, Joel Bakan, Josh Sugarmann, Murray Smith, Tony Bedard, Steven Clegg, Robert Ricker, Joseph Vince, Lynne Griffiths-Fulton, Ken Epps, Matthew Behrens, Blair Hagen, Rebecca Peters, Tracy London, Alhaji Bah, Mighty Casey, Guru, Ed O.G., Krumbsnatcha, Madlib, M.E.D., Peanut Butter Wolf, Rick Washburn, Reginald C. Dennis, Jeff Chang, Cheo Hodari Coker, Face, Chino, Father Greg Boyle, Malcolm Klein, Gerald Cupchik, Corey Keeble, Big Neal, Tragedy Khadafi, Littles, Canibus, Airsoft Arnie, Gwynne Dyer, Helen Caldicott, Mark Kingwell, Leonard Berkowitz, stic.man and M1, Pharoahe Monch, Devin the Dude, Dre 3000, Klashnekoff, Mopreme Shakur, Common, David Banner, Killer Mike, Bonecrusher, Cee-lo Green, Joe Budden, Big Gipp, Paul Wall, Bun B, Alex Jones, David Hardy, Big Daddy Kane, Nas, PMD, Ice Cube, Chuck D, Brother J, Dru Ha, Ghostface, Matthew Conaway, Buckshot and Evil Dee, Rebel INS, Raekwon, the Genius, Smif-n-Wessun, Jeru the Damaja, Tech N9ne, Swifty, Ill Bill, Necro, Clive Edwards, Jeton Ademaj, Chuck Dickson, Jake Neri, David Simon, Randy Carter, Robert Caunt, Sean Trowski, Mary Ainslie, Mark Levitz, Fat Joe, Paris, Immortal Technique, Cormega, Lord Jamar, Rasco, Wise Intelligent, Kool G. Rap, Scarface, Willie D, Bushwick Bill, Kinetic 9, Lord Finesse, Shyne, K'Naan, Sol Guy, Sara Milne, Mary Mills, Ken Witt-Yates, Daphne Gray, Tyson Parker, Chris Tripodi, Charles Grosse, Ronald Lee Ermey, John Florey, Mark Westrom, Francis Bleeker, Mikhail Kalashnikov, Jan Libourel, Ken Jorgensen, Roy Jinks, John Risdall and the people at the Risdall Advertising Agency, C-Bo, C-Murder, Shock G, DJ Muggs, Concise,

326   Rex Smallboy, B.G., RA the Rugged Man, Young Maylay, Flame, Young Chris, Young Noble, Kastro, E.D.I., Des, Y-Look, Kardinal Offishall, Solitaire, Mayhem Morearty, Jet Black, C-4, Shaun Richards, Matt Sonzala, Antonio Evora, K-Rino, Icey Hot, Umi, Jelleestone, Royce Da 5'9", Duke Da God, Freddie Foxxx, Juelz Santana, David Miller, Ethan Brown, Tara Chase, Ms. Dynamite, Warren Foster, Theology 3, Gavin Sheppard, Warren Jones, John Singleton, Memphis Bleek, Dr. Rose, Dr. Schwab, Juvenile, Case, Shingo Shimizu, Steve Jenkinson, EGR, Jacqui Oakley, Roxanne Musterer, Mirak Jamal, Elicser, Berzerker, Patrick Martinez, Damian Marley, Sean Paul and anyone we may have forgotten.

SOURCE NOTES

SYSTEM KEYS

Except where we've said so, all interviews quoted in *Enter the Babylon System* form part of our original research. In the case of Melle Mel, Lord Jamar and Big Gipp, *Pound* magazine's Luke Fox conducted interviews on our behalf, while Elena Ikonomou interviewed Ms. Dynamite for us in the U.K. Additional excerpts from our 200-odd other interviews will become available on www.enterthebabylonsystem.com. While we checked books out of libraries, bought boxes full of old magazines at gun shows and ordered dozens of docs for background, most of our key sources can be found for free on the Internet. One such source, the Official Hip-Hop Lyrics Archive (www.ohhla.com), deserves a big shout-out, although we independently verified the transcription of all lyrics quoted in this book. We tried to include the name and date of our sources as we introduced information, but in the few spots where it wouldn't have served flow you will find our source below.

INTRODUCTION: WALK THROUGH THE VALLEY
OF THE BABYLON SYSTEM

A fabulous February 8, 2004, collection of pieces on gun violence in the *Toronto Sun* included the quoted story by Ian Robertson. Linda Diebel's article, "Who Killed Kempton Howard? Youth leader's murder unsolved: Fear, violence and a 'wall of silence,'" ran in the *Toronto Star* on February 28, 2004. The August 14, 2003, edition of Toronto's *Now* magazine referred to the *Toronto Sun*'s description of the T-Dot's "gang time bomb." On June 15, 2006, *Bloomberg* reported the gifts received by President Bush in 2004. Julian Fantino's and Denise Burnett's town-hall comments are taken from an April 14, 2004, story in the *Toronto Star*, "Fantino labels rap star 'criminal.'" Denise Burnett confirmed the sequence of events and remarks for us. Fantino refused to comment.

328

FIRST CHAMBER: THE TRADE OF THE TOOLS

The Canadian Firearms Centre (CAFC) sent us updated "Firearms Statistics" based on Statistics Canada data, prepared by Dr. Kwing Hung of Canada's Department of Justice for release in January 2005.

Para-noid: The brief history of Attila "Ted" Szabo's life is derived from "The Para-Ordnance Saga," a June 1996 article in *Guns & Ammo,* researched compellingly by Jan Libourel, available on Para's website, www.paraord.com. Noam Chomksy's 1994 comments on gun control appear on the *Z Magazine* website, www.zmag.org, and first appeared in David Barsamian's 2004 collection of interviews with Chomsky, *Secrets, Lies and Democracy.* Robert A. Slayton's quote on John Browning is taken from the historian's 2004 book, *Arms of Destruction.* Other information on Browning came from the History's Channel's four-part *Story of the Gun.* "Canada and Small Arms Exports," Ken Epps's March 2006 report for Project Ploughshares, relayed the Industry Canada information on Para exports.

Blowing Smoke: The "D.C. Jail Gun Identification Survey" by John May, Khalid Pitts, Earnest Williams and Roger Oen is the source of knowledge on young inmates' familiarity with gun brands. American Brandstand's full reports are available at www.agendainc.com/brand.html.

Gun Slangin': Jack Kelly's 2005 book, *Gunpowder,* speculates on the origin of the word *gun,* while Anthony Smith's *Machine Gun: The Story of the Men and the Weapon That Changed the Face of War,* first published in 2002, mentions Bogart's contribution to the coining of the term *gat.* The *Small Arms Survey 2006* includes a list of hip-hop gun slang, some taken from Deanna Wilkinson's research, which supplemented our own knowledge on the subject.

Original Blast Masters: Information on the history of Beretta and Smith & Wesson appears on the companies' websites, www.smith-wesson.com and www.beretta.com. ATF statistics throughout the first chamber are taken both from the Bureau's December 2002 "FFL Newsletter" and Tom Diaz's *Making a Killing,* published in 2000.

Stock Up: *Making a Killing* also cites the November 9, 1992, *Forbes* article, "Steady Finger on the Trigger," quoting Ruger on his "money-making machine." Ruger's history comes from *Shooting Times* in November 1992. Anthony Smith's *Machine Gun* relates young Samuel Colt's porpoise popping exploits.

Plastic Hammers: Glock's website, www.glock.com and the *Forbes* article provided the history of the company. A January 2006 story in *Mother Jones,* "Light Triggers,

Hefty profits," and Austrian journalist Bettina Lurz's 2005 story on Glock, "Finger on the Trigger," in the Hamline University student newspaper added further details (the latter was also useful in the fourth chamber's "Shell Shock"). The video of the DEA agent accidentally shooting himself can be viewed on the *Smoking Gun*'s website, www.thesmokinggun.com—Agent Lee Paige is suing the DEA for the release of the clip, information also reported by *Smoking Gun.*

The Glock 17: A study released in 1999, "Gangsta' Rap and A Murder In Bakersfield," supports C-Murder's claim that his status as a "gangsta rapper" impacted his processing through the legal system. A professor from California State University Los Angeles, Dr. Stuart Fischoff, found that respondents judged an individual who had written gangsta rap lyrics more harshly than a person who had been "charged with murder." MTV reported on March 21, 2006, that C-Murder had been released pending retrial.

Big Bird: Facts on Magnum Research came from its website, www.magnumresearch.com, and Wikipedia, www.wikipedia.org (judged as accurate a source as Britannica by a study published in *Nature* in December 2005).

Top Guns: The ATF stats on crime guns in New York were prepared for a January 2006 report titled "Yearly statistics for crime guns recovered within New York State and submitted to ATF—January 1, 2005 to December 31, 2005." The report was drawn to public attention by a May 20, 2006, story in the *New York Daily News.*

Junk In The Trunk: Background on the Pinto and Ford's inner-workings comes from a *Mother Jones* article in the September/October 1977 issue, "Pinto Madness." Crime gun statistics come from the Bureau of Alcohol, Tobacco and Firearm's (ATF) *Crime Gun Trace Reports (2000): National Report,* released in July 2002. Quotes from Ring of Fire companies come from "Hot Guns," which aired on PBS *Frontline,* June 3, 1997. Statistics of guns manufactured come from various years of the ATF's *Annual Firearms Manufacturers And Export Report.* Raven Arms's and George Jennings's histories are covered in the March 1979 issue of *Guns & Ammo.* Tom Diaz refers to the "old line" in his *Making A Killing.* Charlie Brown of Hi-Point was featured in the October 2005 edition of *Shooting Times.* Brown referred us to Doug Painter at the National Shooting Sports Foundation (NSSF) for an interview, but calls to Painter were never returned.

The Freaks Come Out at Night: Information on the Apache and Kolibri were found on a multimedia CD, *100 Guns,* ordered from the J.M. Davis firearms museum in Claremore, Oklahoma (which has reportedly lost as many as 6,000 firearms and firearm-related items since the death of John Malone Davis in 1973,

330 including a few cannons). Various media have reported on cell-phone guns, including *Time* magazine, January 25, 2004.

Crime Sprays: Background on the Tommy gun comes from *Machine Gun* by Anthony Smith, and modern-day Tommy gun manufacturer Auto-Ordnance's website, www.auto-ordnance.com. Background on the MAC line of guns come from *Lethal Passage: The Story of a Gun* by Erik Larson, 1994, and *A MAC History Lesson* by William D. Ehringer, January, 2001, www.firearmsid.com. TEC-9 background also comes from Larson's book and from the Modern Firearms & Ammunition website, http://world.guns.ru. Intratec production statistics come from information compiled by the Violence Policy Center, which can be found on its website, www.vpc.org.

From Russia With Slugs: Kalashnikov quotes were taken from *The Guardian,* October 10, 2003, "I Sleep Soundly"; *The Arizona Republic* on November 23, 2003, "Assault weapon inventor never received royalties"; and the *Moscow Times* on August 4, 2005, "Russia Defends Rights to Arms." Additional quotes come from the German documentary *Automat Kalaschnikow,* directed by Axel Engsfeld and Herbert Habersack, and released in 2000. Background on the creation and many iterations of the AK comes from *Legends and Reality of the AK: A Behind-the-Scenes Look at the History, Design, and Impact of the Kalashnikov Family of Weapons,* by Charlie Cutshaw and Valery Shilin, 2000, and *Machine Gun* by Anthony Smith. The AK's status at the world's most common firearm was established in *Small Arms Survey 2002.*

Black Rifles: Websites for ArmaLite, www.armalite.com, and Colt, www.colt.com, informed our account of the AR-15's evolution. Details of Buford Furrow's shooting spree are taken from an August 11, 1999, *Salon* story, "Guns and money." (After the manufacturer was sold to Cerberus Capital Management—which keeps Bush Senior's Vice President, Dan Quayle, in its employ—in April 2006 executives at Bushmaster expressed hopes of tripling the company's output.)

How the Pyramid was Built: Information on Metal Storm is taken both from the *Guinness Book of Records* and the corporation's own newsletters. Reuters reported on the Active Denial System on July 20, 2005, while the Federation of American Scientists (FAS) website includes a history of the Project Babylon Supergun, supplemented for us by a story on Gerald Bull on www.damninteresting.com.

Ready to Diemaco: If not from the Canadian government's online information, www.gc.ca, or Project Ploughshares, www.ploughshares.ca, then facts on Colt Canada came from Francis Bleeker and company documents.

SECOND CHAMBER: LOOSE CANNONS

The numbers on household ownership of guns in Canada and Japan come from the Canadian Coalition for Gun Control and the CAFC's report, "Focus on Firearms." Figures on U.S. gun ownership come from *Small Arms Survey* and the Violence Policy Center (VPC). A December 7, 1999, story in the *Globe and Mail* reported extensively on the "Just Desserts" case and convicted shooter Lawrence Brown, a part-time rapper inspired by "the prototype," Eazy-E.

Hit Factories: O.P.P. officer Stephen Clegg provided background documents on the Provincial Weapons Enforcement Unit. Information on the theft of gun parts from the Para-Ordnance plant came from November 2001 stories in the *National Post* (11/27) and *Hamilton Spectator* (11/30), and a 2004 *Toronto Star* article, now available on www.christianaction.org.za. The Brady Center's Legal Action Project, which served as co-counsel in the lawsuit filed against Kahr Arms by Danny Guzman's family, provides case information on its website, www.bradycenter.org, and in its 2003 report, "Smoking Guns: Exposing the Gun Industry's Complicity in the Illegal Gun Market."

Robbin' Steel: The Vaughan gun store robbery and John Fullerton's murder were detailed in the *Toronto Sun,* January 22, 2006. The Bay Area gun shop robberies and subsequent arrests were covered in the *San Mateo County Times*, February 18, 2005, and the *San Francisco Chronicle*, February 17, 2005. Satistics on the average number of guns stolen annually from homes in Canada between 1997 and 2001 come from the *Small Arms Survey 2003.* Information on the NRA's Visa card was first brought to our attention by a cunning February 7, 2006, piece in the *SF Gate,* "The loving arms of arms lovers," written by newly inducted NRA member David Lazarus. The story on the theft of guns from the Hummer in Texas ran in the *Courier* on April 22, 2005. Figures from the FBI's NCIC were published in a July 1995 report by the U.S. Department of Justice, "Guns Used In Crime: Firearms, Crime and Criminal Justice."

Shop 'Til They Drop: Susan Sorensen and Katherine Vittes conducted the UCLA study "Buying a handgun for someone else: firearm dealer willingness to sell," published in the journal *Injury Prevention* in September 2003. Wal-Mart opted to stop selling firearms at a third of its stores in April 2006, reported by Binghamton's *Press & Sun-Bulletin.* The VPC did the research on the decrease in the number of licensed firearms dealers in the U.S., information released in the March 2006 report, "An Analysis of the Decline in Gun Dealers: 1994 to 2005." A June 11, 2006, article in the *Pittsburgh Post-Gazette* did the most significant

reporting on the "Tiarht amendments." Tiarht's allegiance to the NRA is well documented, with the NRA-ILA website (www.nraila.org) having defended the Kansas
congressman: "Representative Tiarht Under Attack For Protecting Our Rights!"
The information Tiarht has kept private, said the NRA-ILA on June 26, 2004, "is
being sought in various reckless civil lawsuits against the firearms industry."
Two of the most fascinating documents on the illegal gun market—especially
when read together—are the ATF's February 2000 report, *Commerce in Firearms in
the United States,* and Robert Ricker's affidavit. Both are available online: the former at http://permanent.access.gpo.gov/lps4006/020400report.pdf, the latter at
www.csgv.org/docUploads/ca4095%5Fproceeding%5F3703%2Epdf. The June 4,
2006, *Milwaukee Journal Sentinel* reported the latest crime gun numbers on
Badger Outdoors. In addition to PBS's coverage of Robert Ricker's testimony on
April 11, 2003, Ricker's story has been covered numerous times by the likes of
the CBC and the *New York Times,* the latter referring to Ricker as a "whistle-
blower" in a February 3, 2003, article by Fox Butterfield, "Gun Industry Ex-
Official Describes Bond of Silence." Larry Keane's quote appeared in the NRA's
American Rifleman magazine, July 2003. Also available online, the decision in
NAACP v. Acusport, et al. is lengthy, but the section titled "Structure of the
Firearms Market" (119) includes some of Judge Jack Weinstein's key findings.

Gun for the Border: Robert Ricker's affidavit discusses multiple sales to gun
traffickers, while the Brady Campaign on July 16, 2003, published the ATF numbers on Badger Outdoors's record for selling handguns in multiples. Other ATF
figures on gun trafficking come from the Bureau's *Crime Gun Trace Reports
(2000),* published in July 2002. Brady state report cards are available at:
www.bradycampaign.org/facts/reportcards. The number of gun shows held
annually across the U.S. was reported by the *Kansas City Star* in a March 26,
2006, article, "Gun shows caught amid heated crossfire." A June 2, 2003, story
in the *New York Daily News,* "Gun traffic is murder on N.Y.," refers to the "iron
pipeline." As one of several sources, the Canada Border Services Agency's website, www.cbsa-asfc.gc.ca, posted notice of stun-gun smuggling in September
2005. The I-95 nickname "firearms freeway" became the title of an 1998
episode of A&E's *Investigative Reports.* The CBC report on Robert Farnsworth
was complimented, and in places corrected, by a May 27, 2006, story in the
Montreal Gazette. The *Washington Post* on March 7, 2006, was one source on
the assassination of Alejandro Dominguez, while the *San Diego Union-Tribune*
reported on Nuevo Laredo, Mexico, on July 2, 2005. The *Small Arms Survey 2002*

refers to the "ant trade." Boniface Mutakha of the Kenya Broadcasting Corporation reported on the recommendations of an intergovernmental meeting of experts in the African Great Lakes region on May 21, 2005, "Arms meeting wants laws harmonized."

Beware of Buyer: We averaged AK-47 prices from several sources: *Small Arms Survey 2002, 2003, 2004;* Associated Press, "Large Amount of Weapons Smuggled in Gaza," September 15, 2005; the *Guardian,* "Beirut on the brink of an abyss," March 13, 2005; the *Guardian,* "Misery of children enslaved by the gun," July 10, 2001; the *Guardian* "Small arms under fire," September 24, 1999.

Critical Mass: Background on Michael Ryan came from the BBC's *Case Closed: Hungerford and Michael Ryan,* available at www.bbc.co.uk. The United Kingdom's Firearms Amendment Act was implemented in 1997, it can be read at www.opsi.gov.uk/ACTS/acts1997/1997005.htm. The March 14, 1992, *Guardian* provided details on the Dunblane Massacre. An in-depth story of the Port Arthur Massacre is available on CourtTV's *Crime Library,* titled "Suddenly One Sunday," published in 2005. Background and statistics regarding the effect of the British and Australian bans is from the *Small Arms Survey* 2004. The Columbine Massacre is extensively documented and several sources were used, including a "Chronology of Events," available on the *Boulder Daily Camera*'s website, www.dailycamera.com, BBC News from November 13, 1999, "America's Columbine gun supplier jailed," and the *Denver Rocky Mountain News* on June 24, 2000, "Duran Gets Prison Term." George Bush's quotes on Columbine and the politics of the 2000 election come from the *New York Times* on May 5, 2000, "Gore Accuses Bush of Allowing Gun Lobby to Influence Policy Plans"; *Salon*'s May 17, 2000, article, "Gunning For The Center"; the Coalition to Stop Gun Violence's website, www.cgsv.org, "George W. Bush's Public Statements"; www.ontheissues.org, "George W. Bush and Gun Control"; and http://issues2000.org. Campaign donations are archived by Opensecrets.org. The NRA's position is detailed in its "Fact Sheets" and online article "Myths and Fables," both available at nraila.org, where their description of IANSA's Rebecca Peters is included in "Rebecca Peters, The U.N., Your Guns." Comments from Todd Vandermyde come from the May 22, 2005, *Chicago Tribune,* "Gun lobbyist hits bull's-eye this season in Springfield." *Slate* documented Wayne Lapierre's comments about Andrew McKelvey on May 2, 2002, in "The NRA's Moral Equivalence." Wayne LaPierre's speech at the NRA's annual meeting is archived on the NRA's website, and George Bush's address to members can be found at www.nranews.com.

Bandied About: LaPierre's comment regarding the Assault Weapons Ban was reported in *The Toronto Star* on May 24, 2003, "Return of assault weapons feared in U.S." Intratec statistics come from the Violence Policy Center's website, www.vpc.org. The National Institute of Justice's *Impacts of the 1994 Assault Weapons Ban: 1994-96,* was released in March 1999 and is available on their website, www.ncjrs.gov. George Bush's quote comes from the August 12, 1999, *Houston Chronicle,* "Bush says White House lax in enforcing gun laws."

Terror Risks: The exchange between Chris Van Hollen and Alberto Gonzales was captured by *Congressional Quarterly, Inc.,* FDCH Political Transcripts, House Committee on the Judiciary, Hearing on PATRIOT Act Reauthorization, April 6, 2006. CBS's report, "Buying Big Guns? No Big Deal: Gunrunner Buys Rifles In U.S. To Equip Guerrilla Army," aired on January 9, 2005; the transcript is available on www.cbsnews.com. The subsequent backlash to Bradley's *60 Minutes* report is best represented by the NSSF's press release on January 10, 2005, "Major Errors In 60 Minutes Reporting," which is available on the organization's website, www.nssf.org. Bush's speech to the UN was made on November 11, 2001, and can be found on the White House's website, www.whitehouse.gov. The GAO's report *Gun Control and Terrorism* was released in January 2005.

If The Suit Fits: Mayor Morial's quotes come from "New Orleans First City To Sue Gun Manufacturers; Center To Prevent Handgun Violence Co-Counsel In Landmark Lawsuit," October 30, 1998, and can still be found on www.commondreams.org. New Orleans' crime statistics come from the New Orleans Police Department, www.nopdonline.com, and the Associated Press as published by MSNBC on August 18, 2005, "New Orleans murder rate on the rise again." Further background on the lawsuits comes from *Reason* magazine in October, 1999, "Big guns plaintiffs' lawyers declare themselves the 'fourth branch of government' and go after firearms," and *Salon*'s July 13, 1999 piece, "City Slickers." Dave Kopel's commentary comes from *National Review Online,* "Unintended Consequences," run on www.nationalreview.com on March 6, 2002. NSSF chief Doug Painter's editorial "Gun Liability is all about tort reform" appeared in the *San Francisco Gate,* August 7, 2005. The Clinton–Smith & Wesson deal was documented on PBS's *Newshour* in a segment titled "Targeting Guns," which aired March 20, 2000. The Gun Owners of America's March 21, 2000, press release, "GOA Announces Boycott of Clinton & Wesson," can be read at www.gunowners.com. The April 11, 2006, *New York Times* piece "Smith & Wesson Is Fighting Its Way Back" documents Smith & Wesson's reemergence. Larry Craig's press release was published on July 29, 2005; his membership on the NRA board of directors is confirmed at www.nrawinningteam.com/bod/index.html. Background and documentation on s.397 comes from *USA TODAY* on July 28, 2005, "Senate Republicans move up vote on gun lawsuits," and the *Washington Post* on July 29, 2005, "Liability Shield for Gunmakers near passage." Smith & Wesson's revenues come from their 2005 Securities and Exchange Commission filings. *Business Week* reported on the manufacturers stock surges on July 29, 2005, in "Smith & Wesson, Ruger up on gun bill."

Arms Around the World: The figures come from *Small Arms Survey* and Project Ploughshares. In countries such as Afghanistan, however, it is impossible to assess accurately the number of small arms in circulation. "I suspect there is not a person on the planet," Ken Epps told us, "who knows many guns there are there." But in the 2000 documentary *Automat Kalaschnikow,* Ahmad Shah Masood, the former leader of the Northern Alliance (assassinated September 9, 2001), declares, "Everyone in Afghanistan owns a gun."

UNRA: Background on the PoA and other UN initiatives comes from *Small Arms Survey 2004,* "From Chaos to Coherence." The NRA's attitude towards the United Nations was covered in part by the *Washington Times* in "NRA bashes UN on small-arms reduction," which ran February 18, 2005. Background on the Brazilian referendum comes from http://iansa.org, "Historic Decision: Disarmament Statute passed in congress," published September 30, 2005, and *The Nation* on October 21, 2005, "As Brazil Votes to Ban Guns, NRA Joins the Fight." The UN 2006 Small Arms Review Conference commentary comes from Control Arms, "UN world conference on small arms collapses without agreement," and www.nraila.org, "U.N. conference on small arms finally ends," both of which were published on July 7, 2006.

Twisting Arms: President Eisenhower's quote comes from Helen Caldicott's *New Nuclear Danger,* though the use of his words has become popular as their pre-science is evidenced. Caldicott's aforementioned book, the World Policy Institute's William Hartung and Colt Canada's Bleeker each explained aspects of NATO expansion. Colt sent us company press releases on the acquisition of its Canadian subsidiary. The spring 2006 volume of *The Ploughshares Monitor* referred to Diemaco's efforts to amend the Criminal Code of Canada. The *Toronto Star* on April 29, 2002, "Most Illegal Guns Come From U.S.: Firearms Crossing the Border Sold at Double or Triple the Cost," pointed to Thanos Polyzos lobbying for gun law changes. Norm Gardner's troubles have been covered in a December 3, 1998, story in the *Toronto Star,* "Gardner cleared in secret gun probe," a September 27, 2001, piece in *Eye* magazine, "Gardner reappointment jumps the gun," and in the January 14, 2004, *Globe and Mail,* "Don't call him a gun fetishist." The report of the Ontario Civilian Commission on Police Services, "In the Matter of an inquiry into the conduct and performance of duties of Norman Gardner of the Toronto Police Services Board," was another key source, and was heard between January 12 and 15, 2004. A January 20, 2000, report on Transparency International's website, www.transparency.org, discussed corruption in the weapons business, "Construction and Arms Industries Seen as Leading International Bribe-Payers."

Where the Tools Rule: Reports dispute whether Gardner shot the robber in the ass or in the thigh. We confirmed for many states Bonecrusher's analysis of the application process for a concealed carry license. Larry Arnold of the Texas Concealed Handgun Association writes in his 1998 article, "The History of Concealed Carry," that while the modern history of concealed carry weapons (CCW) goes back to Bonecrusher's Georgia in 1976, Florida really "opened the way." A May 3, 2000, *Salon* story, "Gunning for the center," reported on George W. Bush removing churches from the list of places that CCWs were forbidden, because, Bush told *Today,* "preachers wanted to carry a concealed weapon in their own home on church grounds." Facts on Gardner's Florida CCW license came from the above-mentioned sources. *Fox News* drew attention to the "castle doctrine" in a May 3, 2005, story, and subsequent October 2005 stories by the Associated Press, October 4, 2005, and the *Independent,* October 2, 2005, covered the new risk to tourists in Florida. Interviews with Tracy London, J.D., M.S.W., and her December 2004 paper for Project Ploughshares, "Small Arms and Corporate Social Responsibility," helped us understand the role of associations like the NRA and the WFFSSA. Court TV's *Crime Library* offers vast amounts of information and analysis of Marc Lépine's case, as does Gendercide Watch. Information on the history of Canadian gun laws come from the Coalition for Gun Control and the Canadian government, www.guncontrol.ca and www.gc.ca.

THIRD CHAMBER: THE PULL OF THE TRIGGER

Our research for this introduction was original, except for the Gwynne Dyer documentary, *The Road to Total War,* the first installment in his *War* series, and the *Small Arms Survey 2005.* Clive Edwards of the B.C. chapter of the Pink Pistols also provided some helpful insights on the relative appeal of firearms.

Killin' 'Em Softly: The quote from the Cheerios ad was drawn from a 1999 edition of A&E's *Investigative Reports,* "The Gun Makers." The California Senate Office of Research report, prepared by Max Vanzi and revised for May 2005, was titled "Pellet Guns and BB Guns: Dangerous Playthings in the Open Market," and included the facts on NPGs. Information on Daisy and the CPSC suit comes from a November 28, 2003, editorial, "A Red Ryder Christmas," and an April 29, 2004, article, "Triggering Liability," both from the *Wall Street Journal,* as well a December 22, 2004, Associated Press story, "BB-Gun Maker shuns Christmas publicity." A huge phenomenon largely unexplored by the media, we learned about airsoft culture by visiting airsofter websites, and from Airsoft Arnie, www.arnie-sairsoft.co.uk. The quote comes from www.redwolfairsoft.com/redwolf/airsoft/Beginners. The hysteria in the U.K. surrounding replica firearms was covered by an April 22, 2005, *Guardian* story, "Tough gun laws help to drive boom in fakes," and May 16 and June 9, 2005, *Times* pieces, "Trigger-happy teenagers boost crime figures with toy guns" and "Is this a real gun? You've got two seconds to decide." The *Guardian* covered Mark Bonini's pitiful fate on August 31, 2005.

Mo' Bang 4 da Buck: Stories on the shootout involving Lil' Kim and Capone-N-Noreaga were published on March 18, 2005, in the *Guardian*, Allhiphop.com on March 4, 2005, which had picked up on a *New York Newsday* report, and also by the *Chicago Sun-Times* on April 15, 2004.

Rat-A-Tat-Tat: Wertham's "Nazi" quote was cited in a *Time* magazine story on April 18, 2004, "The Glory and Horror of EC Comics."

Under Pressure: *Guns & Ammo* columnist Jeff Cooper, regarded as the "Father of modern combat pistol shooting," has his thoughts posted online, http://dvc.org.uk/jeff/. His SHOT show comment comes from *Jeff Cooper's Commentaries Vol. 13, No.2* February 2005. The cited research regarding firearm advertising was contained in a 2004 study, "Firearm Advertising: Product Depiction in Consumer Gun Magazines" by Elizabeth A. Saylor, Katherine A. Vittes and Susan B. Sorensen, published in *Evaluation Review.* Dean Spier declined an interview request saying, "I imagine your editorial position holds the same concerns as most of us in the firearms culture do, though from a different perspective . . . but just as *Pound* magazine undoubtedly cannot bear the responsibility of young people of color resorting to violence and then composing lyrics about how 'bad' they are, the 'gun press' should not shoulder the blame for abetting that violence." Speir's "Cherry Picked" article can be found at www.thegunzone.com/gunwriter.html.

'Wood Burners: In addition to watching the films themselves, the Internet Movie Database (IMDb; www.imdb.com) was a useful resource throughout this section. The 50 Cent movie poster controversy, which played out from Philadelphia to L.A., was well covered by the Associated Press, October 26, 2005, ABC News, November 8, 2005, and BBC, October 27 and 28, 2005, and January 4, 2006, the last of which discussed the ASA's response to the *Get Rich or Die Tryin'* movie ad. Besides IMDb, information on Rick Washburn and Weapons Specialists Ltd. is available on his company's website, www.weaponspecialists.com. The Dirty Harry role being offered to both Frank Sinatra and Paul Newman has been documented by cinema studies expert Rick Thompson, while a May 2006 story by *Guns & Ammo,* "Shooting Scripts," mentions Milius's contribution to *Dirty Harry.* The *New York Times* article from April 1, 1997, "National Rifle Association is Turning to World Stage to Fight Gun Control," is an excellent read and reports on Sean Connery's gun-control campaigning after the Dunblane Massacre. An October 25, 2005, piece by the *Evening Standard* quoted Roger Moore on guns, while *Starpulse* discussed his military rifle accident in a July 17, 2006, article. And Daniel Craig's comments, originally made in *OK!* magazine, were subsequently published in the *Telegraph* on October 25, 2005. David Codrea's stirring *Guns & Ammo* article, "Six Degrees of Hypocrisy," quoted both Sean Connery's anti-gun ad and Sylvester Stallone (www.gunsandammomag.com, *G&A* online articles are not dated). Sharon Stone's and Antonio Banderas's love-hate relationships with firearms were covered in a May 21, 1999, story by *E! News* and an October 24, 2005, piece in *Contact Music,* respectively. The Associated Press quoted from *Vanity Fair*'s May 2005 story on Angelina Jolie. While we understand that Jolie meant to say she can sponsor many impoverished children with her million-dollar movie cheques, this doesn't change the fact that her work benefits an industry that devastates the lives of poor kids worldwide. Birdman's HoMeBoY NyTe SyTeS creation and the *Times-Dispatch* article can be viewed at www.the-gunzone.com/glock/glock-gag.html. Leigh Ramsey and Andrew Pelletier produced the 2004 report for the Journal of the American Medical Association (JAMA), "Update on Firearm Use in G- and PG-RATED Movies." The Magnum Films website, www.magnumfilms.com, was our source for most of the information on the Desert Eagle's big- and small-screen history. Whit Collins discussed the use of Southwest Pistol League shooting in *Miami Vice.* The North Hollywood shootout, which anecdotes suggest may have been partly inspired by *Heat* and in which AKs and a fully automatic Bushmaster AR-15 were used, has been widely documented, on film and in print, including in a February 28, 1997, story by CNN, as well as on the Gun Zone website, www.thegunzone.com. Baltimore homicide statistics are available in the FBI's *Uniform Crime Reports*, which compiles information from American cities yearly at www.fbi.gov.

Banner Acts: The NRA Blacklist can be found at www.nraila.org/Issues/FactSheets/Read.aspx?ID=15. Celebrities who own or who have an interest in guns were identified by stories in the *New York Post, New York Metro,* Hollywood.com and Court TV. Wayne LaPierre commented on the anti-gun celebrities on the *Today Show.*

License to Frag: 50 Cent's *Bulletproof,* which Buns completed, received mediocre reviews but sold well. Fiddy's interviews about the game can be watched at www.50centbulletproof.com. Background on *Battlezone* is available on Wikipedia, www.wikipedia.org. America's Army information is available on their website and interviews with Col. Wardynski are available online at cbsnews.com in "Join The Interactive Army" from July 2, 2002, and from *Wired,* "Army Sets Up Video-Game Studio," dated June 21, 2004. Statistics on the incredible success of *America's Army* were reported by the *Army News Service* on October 22, 2004, in "Online Army recruiting game reaches top 5 list," and in "America's Army game gets new firepower," a November 3, 2005, piece on gamespot.com. Bill Gates's quotes come from CBS *60 Minutes II,* "Sex, Lies & Video Games," produced on August 6, 2003, by Bob Simon. The U.K. study which showed that ratings provide few barriers comes from BBC News on June 24, 2005, "Parents 'ignore game age ratings.'" California's video-game control initiatives were documented by the *Los Angeles Times* on October 5, 2005, in "Video Game Violence Debate Grows." Canada's own efforts were reported online by CTV in "Manitoba set to restrict video game rentals" and by the *Globe and Mail* in "No Grand Theft Auto for Manitoba Kids," both of which ran on May 9, 2005. Video game industry statistics come from the Entertainment Software Association, "Essential Facts about the Canadian computer and video game industry," a pamplet published in 2005, and "Halo 2 outsells Spider-Man 2," published January 28, 2005. The U.S. National Law Enforcement Officers Memorial Fund's petition against *25 to Life* is available at www.nleomf.com/25tolife. The Canadian Press reported on Roger's video-game rental rankings on February 18, 2006. On July 20, 2005, CNN *Money* reported on the *Grand Theft Auto: San Andreas* controversy. A November 16, 2005, article in the *New Scientist,* "Gaming fanatics show hallmarks of drug addiction," pointed to new research on excessive video game play.

Passed the Gat: The *All Music Guide to Hip-Hop,* published in 2003, and edited by Vladmir Bogdanov, Chris Woodstra, Stephen Thomas Erlewine and John Bush, was helpful throughout this section. SOHH (Support Online Hip-Hop) posted updates on the Chi-Ali saga, including a March 13, 2001, piece on Griffith's capture. The National Organization for Women includes on its website, www.now.org, information concerning the consolidation of media ownership. "Charlton Heston's speech to Time Warner shareholders" is number 69 on *NME* magazine's list of 100 Rock Moments. In a December 1997 speech Heston boasted about the success of his actions at the Time Warner offices (available at www.vpc.org/nrainfo/speech.html). Bob Dole's letter to Tanya Metaksa can be found at www.rkba.org/nra/dole.10mar95.

Things Done Changed: New York City homicide statistics are from the NYPD's *Compstat* reports available on their website www.nyc.gov/html/nypd/ and from www.disastercenter.com/crime/nycrime.htm. *Get Rich or Die Tryin'* CD sales figures have been variously quoted at 11, 12 and 18 million worldwide and are available on Wikipedia, www.wikipedia.org. First week sales of *GRODT* were reported by Yahoo News "Rich Without Tryin'," on February 13, 2003. According to 50 Cent's manager, Sha Money XL, *Pound* was the world's first magazine to feature 50 Cent on the cover (*Pound #15,* December 2002).

Killa Crossovers: Information on Karl Malone can be found on the NRA Winning Team website. The November 2004 story in the *Washington Post* was titled "NBA Meltdown Provides Blame Aplenty." The *Arizona Republic* quoted Steve Nash on March 31, 2005.

FOURTH CHAMBER: BARRELS OF DESTRUCTION

On February 2, 2006, Reuters quoted the United Nations's Dennis McNamara in "Forget charity, stop Africa arms sales—UN official." Peggy Mason, chair of the Group of 78, an arms research institute, shared information about the Canadian connection to arms shipments into the Congo during the working group we attended in Ottawa, Ontario, in December of 2004. Stories on Somalia included the BBC's "Somalia—where the gun rules," February 9, 2005, and Deutsche Presse Agentur's "No end in sight for Somalia's rule of the gun," February 17, 2005.

Wild Hoods: Reference to the deaths of Anna Gerner and David Pacheco was included in an April 26, 2006, article by the *New York Daily News,* "What might have been. . . ." The Chicago study of adolescents, "Firearm Violence Exposure and Serious Violent Behavior," released in May 2005, was to the credit of Jeffrey Bingenheimer, Robert Brennan and Felton Earls. The press release with Earls's quote was published in the *Psychiatric News* on July 1, 2005. Facts on Post-Traumatic Stress Disorder are available on the National Center for PTSD's web-site, www.ncptsd.va.gov. Freaky Tah's murder was covered by Davey D on April 12, 1999, and SOHH on April 22, 2004, with other information gleaned from AllHipHop.com, the Rap News Network and *Chronic* magazine. Raptism.com mentioned Mr. Cheeks appearance on Judge Hatchett in a February 25, 2002, piece. AllHipHop also ran an update on Spigg Nice's case on January 26, 2004. 2003's *All Music Guide to Hip-Hop* also informed this section.

Surviving the Game: *MTV News* reported on Ol Dirty Bastard's arrest under the California bulletproof vest law.

Heat Nutz: The American Psychological Association statement on Firearms Safety and Youth can be found at www.apa.org/pi/cyf/res_fire.html. *Social Psychology* (third edition) by Eliot Aronson, Timothy Wilson and Robin Akert contains a section on the Leonard Berkowitz and Anthony LePage study, "Weapons as Aggression-Eliciting Stimuli," originally published in 1967 in the *Journal of Personality and Social Psychology. Time*'s February 27, 2006, story, "Inside the shooting at the ranch," pointed to Cheney's consumption of alco-hol prior to the well-publicized accident. Cheo Hodari Coker's classic article on the Geto Boys for *Rap Pages* magazine, "Boyz To Men," included a history of the brief beef between Scarface and Willie D and can be found on the Virgin records website. A July 20, 2005, story by *No Minimo,* picked up on the World Press web-site, www.worldpress.org, included information on Diadema, guns and alcohol in a section, "Beer and Booze Against Life." CBC News's June 30, 2005, piece, "Heat Waves," covered the record temperatures in Toronto that month. Figures on mur-der in Toronto and Chicago come from the respective cities's police departments.

Stat Quo: Homicide statistics for Memphis Bleek and Jay-Z's neighbourhood are available on the New York City Police Department's website. Murder stats for all U.S. cities comes from the FBI's *Uniform Crime Reports 2004.* Canadian statistics come from Toronto Police Services, *Statistics Report 2004* and *2005*; Vancouver Police Department, *Annual Report 2004;* and Statistics Canada's *Canadian Homicide Rates.* Homicide rates for Colombia and Brazil were cited by World Press in "Crime Rate Decreases in São Paulo and Bogotá," on July 20, 2005. Worldwide Statistics come from the World Health Organization's *World Report on Health and Violence* 2002. City Populations are from www.geohive.com.

The Other 'Cide: Figures on suicide in Canada were provided by the Canadian Firearms Centre. U.S. statistics are available on the Center for Disease Control and Prevention (CDC) website. A July 28, 2004, article in *Asia Times* reported on the rising incidence of suicide in Japan. Other facts on firearms and suicide were found on the Illinois Council Against Handgun Violence website. Information on firearms, alcohol and suicide was taken from the Suicide Reference Library online. Eminem's experiences with suicide were covered by the *Mirror* on October 20, 2004, and by SOHH on October 21, 2004. Arthur Kellermann et al. conducted the cited study published in the *New England Journal of Medicine.*

Gunfire Drill: The *Salon* story, "Reservation for death," ran on August 8, 2005. *The Independent* also ran articles on the Redlake shooting spree on March 22 and 23, 2005. Other information was gleaned from the *Minneapolis Star Tribune* on March 25, 2005, "Friend says Weise enjoyed school shooting movie," and from pieces in the *Times,* March 30, 2005, and CBC News and the *Winnipeg Sun,* both March 22, 2005.

Shots Happen: American accident statistics come from David Hemenway's *Private Guns, Public Health,* 2004, and from the Center for Disease Control www.cdc.gov/ncipc/wisqars. Statistics of American children living in homes with guns come from the Associated Press on September 6, 2005, "Study: 1.7M Kids Live With Guns." Jennings's and Jimenez Arms's operations were documented by the *Las Vegas Sun* on February 16, 2005, "Gun maker expands to Nevada after ruling by California AG." The report that Whit Collins was involved in, "Buyer Beware: Defective Firearms and America's Unregulated Gun Industry," was published by the Consumer Federation of America in February 2005. The study on ergonomics, "Human Factors Issues in Firearms Design and Training" was published in *Ergonomics in Design,* winter 2006, and was undertaken by Peter Hancock, Hal Hendrick, Richard Hornick and Paul Paradis. Andrew Arulanandum was quoted in the *Detroit News* on December 14, 2003, "Defective Firearms go unchecked."

Locked & Coded: Sticky Fingaz's forgetfulness was reported by AllHipHop (www.allhiphop.com) on October 18, 2005, and by the *SF Gate*'s "Daily Dish." Information on Tupac's shooting encounter with cops can be found on *Blender*'s website, www.blender.com, while Dizzee Rascal's arrest was covered by *NME* on March 3, 2005.

Country Fire: Estimates of the number of guns in Texas were published in 1997 by the *Houston Chronicle,* "Guns In America," www.chron.com/content/chronicle/

nation/guns/part3/pro.html. Young Buck's skeet shooting success was reported in *Vibe* in August 2004, "They Shootin.'" Regional crime statistics come from the FBI's *Uniform Crime Reports 2005.* The list of the top ten most dangerous cities comes from a New York City press release from June 6, 2005, "Mayor Bloomberg and Police Commissioner Kelly Announce FBI Report Shows Safest Big City Got Even Safer in 2004." U.S. Newswire published word of Condoleezza Rice's award from the Citizens Committee for the Right to Keep and Bear Arms in January 2005. The relevant part of the Ulysses Grant speech can be found at www.secondamendmentdocumentary.com. Information on Robert Williams comes from his book, *Negroes With Guns,* and the PBS documentary of the same name. The history of gun policy in Nazi Germany is the subject of a 2000 paper by Stephen Halbrook, "Nazi Firearms Laws and the Disarming of the German Jews." Congressional testimony by author Dick Reavis and ATF agent Jim Cavanaugh is drawn from the revealing documentary produced in 1997, *Waco: The Rules of Engagement.* General background on the events at Mount Carmel also come from this doc, in addition to a June 28, 2000, article "Waco on trial" by *Salon,* and "What happened at Waco?" on the Court TV website, www.courttv.com. A July 13, 1995, press release from the ATF with the subject "Weapons Possessed by the Branch Davidians," verified the stockpile held by those at the compound.

All-Points Bullet-In: Houston homicide statistics come from the Houston Police Department from 1984 to 2004 and from various years of the FBI *Uniform Crime Reports.* Police Statistics come from the National Law Enforcement Officers Memorial Fund, "153 Law Enforcement Officers Die in the Line of Duty in 2005," published December 27, 2005, and from the FBI's report *Law Enforcement Officers Killed & Assaulted 2004.* Shooting statistics were printed by the *Boston Globe* on March 20, 2005, in "Straight Shooter," as well as in the DOJ Bureau of Justice Statistics *Contacts Between Police and the Public,* 2002. Background on Brazil comes from an Amnesty International report of December 2, 2005, "Brazil: They Come in Shooting." Background on Jamaica comes from Amnesty International's "Jamaica: Killings and violence by police: How many more victims?" published April 10, 2001. The Renato Adams story was reported by the CBC on December 29, 2005, "Controversial cop turns rapper in Jamaica." The in-depth investigation by the *Houston Chronicle,* "Police gun sanctions infrequent," was published July 26, 2004. Police homicide statistics come from the DOJ Bureau of Justice Statistics of March 2001, "Policing and

Homicide, 1976-1998." The Kempton Memorial Basketball Round-Robin was mentioned in a November 2005 Holy Name Catholic School newsletter.

Shell Shock: The *Village Voice*'s November 22, 2005, article, "*The Source* Under Fire," detailed the demise of the once established publication, including the figures on its ad sales. On July 25, 2005, SOHH covered the story of Orlando Orenga, an unknown rapper who was shot in the head after reportedly refusing to play his music for *Source* executives Leroy Peeples and Alvin Childs. The National Priorities Project (NPP) numbers were reported on November 4, 2005, in the *Washington Post,* "Youths in Rural U.S. Are Drawn to Military." The original NPP recruiting data is available at http://nationalpriorities.org. The June 2005 killing spree in the demilitarized zone between South and North Korea was covered by the *Korea Times,* which reported that the soldier had "committed the shooting in a burst of anger due to habitual harassment by his superior." IMDb also helped in this section. A May 12, 2005, *Los Angeles Times* story, "Another Case of 'Contagious Fire,'" covered the incident involving Winston Hayes. The aforementioned edition of *Social Psychology* also discusses the study by Dane Archer and Rosemary Gartner. General information on the Beltway Sniper case was widely reported in the international press. Sources for more specific information included the *Washington Post*'s October 25, 2002, piece, "The Bushmaster XM15: A Rifle Known for Its Accuracy," *Slate*'s October 30, 2002, article, "What Kind of Rifle Training Did John Muhammad Get in the Army?" and the *Seattle Times*'s April 29, 2003, in-depth investigation of Bull's Eye, "Errant Gun Dealer, Wary Agents Paved Way for Beltway Sniper Tragedy." A June 17, 2006, piece by ABC News, "Report: Malvo, Mentor May Have Shot Others," updated information on other shootings now believed to have been at the hands of the snipers. A September 10, 2005, article by *The Washington Times* covered the settlement between Bushmaster, Bull's Eye and the victims' families. Michelle Malkin's December 10, 2003, syndicated column, "Lee Malvo, Muslim Hatemonger," discussed Malvo's drawings that were submitted as evidence. We also used court documents from Muhammad's trials. The *Meet the Press* episode in which Killarmy became the target of blame for the Beltway spree was the subject of a story by BlackElectorate.com on November 1, 2002, "Rap COPINTELPRO [sic] XI: Meet The Press and Tim Russert Connect The Sniper Shootings with Hip-Hop and the 5 Percent Nation of Islam," written by Cedric Muhammad, and of an *In These Times* article by Salim Muwakkil, "Hip Hop Hysteria," published December 20, 2002. The

Steubenville Herald Star briefly covered the death of Killarmy's manager and the short pieces, including obituaries, are now available on an angelfire.com fansite, http://www.angelfire.com/oh/wutang360/articlez.html. One of Martin Luther King's lesser-known speeches, "Beyond Vietnam: A Time to Break Silence" is nevertheless among his most important, and can be read in its entirety at www.hartfordhwp.com/archives/45a/058.html. Anthony Lappé of the Guerrilla News Network covered "Mitzvahpalooza" in a December 1, 2005, story titled "50 Cent, the War Profiteer and the $10 million Bat Mitzvah." "Executive Excess 2005," published August 30, 2005, can be found atwww.faireconomy.org/press/2005/EE2005.pdf. News of the Beretta army contracts was released in two press notices on the company's website, www.beretta.com, posted May 13, 2005, and July 27, 2005. The Amnesty International investigation into the missing AK-47s bound for Iraq was covered in the *Guardian* on May 12, 2006, and in the *Mirror* on May 10, 2006. The December 21, 2004, *Wall Street Journal* article, which included the quote from Judd Gregg, was headlined "Sharpening the Knife: As Bush Vows to Halve Deficit, Targets Already Feel Squeezed."

Crucial Conflict: Statistics for the sidebar were taken from *Small Arms Survey 2001, 2005* and Project Ploughshares *Armed Conflicts Report 2006*, available at www.ploughshares.ca.

Picking Up The Pieces: Many of the statistics come from the Amnesty International/Oxfam/IANSA paper, "The impact of guns on women's lives," 2005. Oxfam published reaction to the study in "The impact of guns on women's lives: Testimonies," March 2005. The Bonn International Center for Conversion provided additional background and statistics in "Gendered Perspectives on Small Arms Proliferation and Misuse: Effects and Policies," July 2002, as well as the Norwegian Church Aid's March 2005 report, "Who Takes The Bullet: The impact of small arms violence." Handgun marketing was reported by the Brady Center's August 2004 editorial by Sarah Brady, "Marketing Handguns to women: Fair advertising or exploitation?" Charles Jones's visit to Penn State was reported by the *Collegian* "NRA member tells women to tote guns," April 22, 2005. DGU statistics are discussed and provided in the National Institute of Justice's "Guns In America: National Survey on Ownership and use of firearms," published May 1997, and in the NRA-ILA's "Armed Citizens and Crime Control," posted July 16, 1999. Additional statistics come from a fact sheet by Women Against Gun Violence, "Women and Guns: The Facts," and IANSA's "Case Study:

Gun Violence against women drops in Canada," written by Wendy Cukier for publication in 2005. Ms. Dynamite's initial quote was printed by the BBC News in "Ms Dynamite's plea over gun crime," published January 13, 2003.

Guns, Gangs and God: A September 26, 2004, article in the *Los Angeles Daily News*, "Homegrown terror," and a follow-up October 3, 2004, piece in the same publication, "Finding solutions," were both critical resources, as was a package by L.A.'s Department of Gang Violence and Youth Development, originally released in December 2004. Statistics on homicides in Compton were taken from a January 2, 2006, story in the *L.A. Times*, "Compton's killings highest in years." Census data provided facts on Compton's population. Murder numbers published by the Los Angeles Police Department were also cited. We alluded to "Mafia movies influence gangs," a May 13, 2004, story in the *Toronto Star*. "Gang World," ran in *Foreign Policy*'s March/April 2005 edition, featuring Condoleezza Rice, Dick Cheney, Donald Rumsfeld and George Bush on the cover. Statistics on the number of gangs in the United States and Canada come from the *Los Angeles Daily News* (above) and the May 17, 2006, *Toronto Star*, respectively. Background on Homeboy Industries was found on its website, www.-homeboy-industries.org, in *USA Today* on July 11, 2005, and in CNN's "Homicide in Hollenbeck," by Anderson Cooper, which first aired April 10, 2005. *La Prensa San Diego* reported on Father's Greg religious philosophy, January 17, 2003. *Tidings* posted a piece on the murder of Miguel Gomez on July 9, 2004. Other useful pieces were "The Streets Are Hollerin' Peace" by AllHipHop on April 30, 2004, the "Satya Interview with Aqeela Sherrills" in the November 2002 issue, and Michael Krikorian's two-part story "War and Peace in Watts," which ran in *LA Weekly* on July 14 and 21, 2005. Another article that ran in *LA Weekly*, "Murdered Dreams," covered the death of Terrell Sherrills on January 22, 2004.

Above the Clouds: The Jay-Z concert was covered by the *Village Voice* on October 28, 2005, in "Status Ain't Hood," and *Newsday*'s October 31, 2005, piece, "A small step for peace in hip-hop world." On July 28, 2005, Kansas City's *The Pitch* reported at length on the murder of Fat Tone in the two-part "Tone Death," while *Baller Status* followed the subsequent arrest of Mac Minister. The *San Francisco Bay Guardian*'s Garrett Caples admirably remembered Mac Dre in "Don't hate the playa . . ." in November 2005. Information on Soulja Slim was found in the January/February 2005 issue of *XXL*. Yaki Kadafi's mother has made a place online to remember her son, www.yakikadafi.com.

Conclusion: Unloading

On January 5, 2006, the *National Post* story "73% advocate mandatory 10-year terms for gun crimes" cited a survey by Ipsos Reid. The same day, CTV covered the campaign promises of Canada's current Prime Minister in "Harper promises tougher sentences for gun crime." The most important resource for information on the "Boston miracle" was a September 2001 report, "Reducing Gun Violence: The Boston Gun Project's Operation Ceasefire," prepared for the U.S. Department of Justice by Anthony Braga, David Kennedy, Anne Piehl and Elin Waring (www.ncjrs.gov/pdffiles1/nij/188741.pdf). Additional history and statistics on the Boston experience were pulled from numerous stories published by the *Boston Globe*. A 2006 story by Kike Roach in the May/June issue of *New Socialist Magazine*, "Racism and gun violence in Toronto's Black community," pointed us to the Toronto Community Foundation's paper, "Vital Signs 2005." Deanna Wilkinson's *Guns, Violence and Identity among African-American and Latino Youth*, 2003, discussed the significance of "teachable moments." The findings of the United Nations Committee on Economic, Social and Cultural Rights were posted in a press release on the website of the UN Office at Geneva. *Fist, Stick, Knife, Gun* by Geoffrey Canada was published by Beacon Press in 1995. Statistics on homicide in Toronto come from the Toronto Police Service. Dan McTeague was quoted by the BBC, November 24, 2005, and CTV, November 25, 2005. *Playboy*'s interview with 50 Cent appeared in April 2004. Rod Cohen's program was discussed in the March 2, 2006, edition of Toronto's *Now* magazine in an article titled "In for the Long Haul." Information on Elizabeth Bishop-Goldsmith came from *New York Newsday*, "Rosedale woman turns her anguish to activism," January 7, 2006. Ryerson journalism student Stephanie San Miguel's article on the faculty website, www.journalism.ryerson.ca/online/mosaic, "A call to arms" (undated), references the recruiting role played by "diversity cells." The quote on "Army coop" can be found on the Cayuga Secondary School website, http://schools.gedsb.net/css/coop.htm, and was first brought to our attention by a piece by Homes Not Bombs's Matthew Behrens in April 2006.

INDEX

INDEX

360